Walt Disney World with Kids 2016

with Universal Orlando®

Kim Wright Wiley and
Leigh C. W. Jenkins

Twenty-sixth Edition

Fodor's WALT DISNEY WORLD WITH KIDS 2016

Publisher: Amanda D'Acierno, *Senior Vice President*

Editorial: Arabella Bowen, *Editor in Chief;* Linda Cabasin, *Editorial Director*

Design: Tina Malaney, *Associate Art Director;* Chie Ushio, *Senior Designer*

Photography: Jennifer Arnow, *Senior Photo Editor;* Mary Robnett, *Photo Researcher*

Maps: Rebecca Baer, *Senior Map Editor;* Henry Colomb and Mark Stroud, Moon Street Cartography; David Lindroth, Inc. *Cartographers*

Production: Linda Schmidt, *Managing Editor;* Evangelos Vasilakis, *Associate Managing Editor;* Angela L. McLean, *Senior Production Manager*

Sales: Jacqueline Lebow, *Sales Director*

Marketing & Publicity: Heather Dalton, *Marketing Director;* Katherine Punia, *Publicity Director*

Business & Operations: Susan Livingston, *Vice President, Strategic Business Planning;* Sue Daulton, *Vice President, Operations*

Fodors.com: Megan Bell, *Executive Director, Revenue & Business Development;* Yasmin Marinaro, *Senior Director, Marketing & Partnerships*

Authors: Kim Wright Wiley and Leigh C. W. Jenkins

Editor: Douglas Stallings

Design/Illustrations: Chie Ushio

Editorial Production: Carrie Parker

Cover: Jonathan Pozniak; *photographer*, Joy Fennell; *hair/makeup*

Published by Fodor's Travel, a division of Penguin Random House LLC

Fodor's is a registered trademark of Penguin Random House LLC

www.fodors.com

Every effort has been made to make this book complete and accurate as of the date of publication. In a time of rapid change, however, it is difficult to ensure that all information is entirely up-to-date. Although the publisher and authors cannot be liable for any inaccuracies or omissions in this book, they are always grateful for corrections and suggestions for improvement.

All products mentioned in this book are trademarks of their respective companies.

This book is available for special discounts for bulk purchases for sales promotions or premiums. Special editions, including personalized covers, excerpts of existing books, and corporate imprints, can be created in large quantities for special needs. For more information, write to Special Markets/Premium Sales, 1745 Broadway, MD 3-1, New York, New York 10019, or e-mail specialmarkets@randomhouse.com.

Twenty-sixth Edition

ISBN: 978-1-101-87833-0

ISSN: 1945-9238

Printed in The United States of America

10 9 8 7 6 5 4 3 2 1

To all the families who have shared
their Disney stories with
us throughout the years.

Kim & Leigh

Contents

Abbreviations, Terms, and Icons

ABBREVIATIONS AND TERMS

Downtown Disney A shopping, dining, and entertainment complex

Hollywood The Disney's Hollywood Studios Theme Park

Water parks Typhoon Lagoon and Blizzard Beach

Major parks The Magic Kingdom, Epcot, Disney's Hollywood Studios, and Disney's Animal Kingdom

Off-season The less crowded times of the year—specifically those weeks between September and May that do not flank major holidays

On-season The most crowded times of the year—specifically summers, holidays, and spring break

Off-site Any resort or hotel not owned by Disney

On-site A Disney-owned resort

TTC Ticket and Transportation Center: The monorail version of a train station, where you can transfer to monorails bound for Epcot, the Magic Kingdom, or monorail-line hotels. You can also catch buses at the TTC bound for the parks and Downtown Disney.

ICONS

Helpful Hint

Insider's Secret

Hidden Mickey

Helpful Phone Numbers

All Orlando numbers have a 407 area code. Be sure to make all Disney hotel reservations by calling ☎ *934–7639 (W–DISNEY)*, and use the resorts' direct lines only to report a delayed check-in, to call Guest Relations (a.k.a. Guest Services), or to reach a registered guest.

GENERAL WALT DISNEY WORLD INFORMATION PHONE NUMBERS

General Information 824–4321

WDW Resort Information .... 934–7639 (W–DISNEY)

WDW Dining Information and Advance Reservations ..... 939–3463 (WDW–DINE)

WDW Recreational Information .... 939–7529 (WDW–PLAY)

WDW Golf Information................................ 939–4653 (WDW–GOLF)

WDW Tour Information ....939–8687 (WDW–TOUR)

Disney Cruise Line... 800/951–3532

Disney Travel Company 828–8101

WALT DISNEY WORLD RESORT PHONE NUMBERS

All–Star Movies 939–7000

All–Star Music 939–6000

All–Star Sports..939–5000

Animal Kingdom Lodge 938–3000

Art of Animation Resort 938–7000

Beach Club Resort 934–8000

Best Friends Pet Care 877/493–9738 (877/4–WDW–PETS)

BoardWalk Inn and Villas 939–5100

Caribbean Beach Resort..934–3400

Contemporary Resort 824–1000

Coronado Springs Resort 939–1000

Dolphin Resort..934–4000

Fort Wilderness Campground...................................... 824–2900

Grand Floridian Resort 824–3000

Old Key West Resort 827–7700

Polynesian Resort..824–2000

Pop Century Resort..938–4000

Port Orleans Resort 934–5000
Saratoga Springs Resort and Spa 827–1100
Swan Resort 934–3000
Wilderness Lodge and Villas 824–3200
Yacht Club Resort 934–7000

UNIVERSAL ORLANDO PHONE NUMBERS
General Information 363–8000
Universal Orlando Resort Information 888/273–1311

OTHER HELPFUL PHONE NUMBERS
Alamo Car Rental 800/462–5266
American Airlines 800/433–7300
Avis Car Rental... 800/331–1212
Budget Car Rental..800/527–0700
Delta Airlines 800/221–1212
Dollar Car Rental 800/800–4000
Hertz Car Rental.. 800/654–3131
Mears Shuttle Service...423–5566
National Car Rental..800/227–7368
Orlando Visitors Bureau 800/255–5786
US Airways 800/428–4322

Helpful Websites

Walt Disney World ....www.disneyworld.com
The Disney Corporation .... www.disney.com
The Disney Cruise Line................................... www.disneycruise.com
Universal Orlando .... www.universalorlando.com

Preface

HOW HAS WALT DISNEY WORLD CHANGED?

The simple answer is, it's gotten bigger. And they're still building.

In the 26 years since we first began researching this guide, Disney has added one major park, three minor ones, eight hotels, a cruise line, and more attractions and restaurants than we can count. It was once possible for a fleet-footed and well-prepared family to see most of Walt Disney World during a four-day stay. But that's no longer true. As the Disney complex expands, it's more vital than ever that you target what you want to see, work these priorities into your schedule, and then relax. Anything beyond that is pure gravy.

Sometimes we're asked if the prevalence of travel guides makes them less useful to their readers. After all, if everyone knows about a "secret tip," is it still a secret?

Good question. But even with all those books on the market, a relatively small number of WDW visitors actually make advance preparations. Most people still show up late and wander around aimlessly, so anyone with any sort of touring plan at all is automatically a step ahead of the crowd.

It's tempting to treat Orlando as if it were a kiddie version of Las Vegas—you go there to play the numbers, and a family that hits 24 attractions in a day must, by definition, be having twice as much fun as a family that sees 12. Not so. You'll find a lot of crying kids and exasperated parents by mid-afternoon, largely because everyone is frantic with the idea that this trip is so expensive they darn well better squeeze the most out of every minute. Actually, the most successful touring plans boil down to a few simple guidelines:

1. Plan your trip for those times of year when the parks are less crowded. When people write to us about having had bad experiences at Disney World, it seems that about 90% of the disasters happen either over spring break or in July.

2. Buy tickets and arrange a hotel and dining reservations and FastPass+ well in advance. Think of it this way: Every phone call you make from home is a line you won't have to stand in later.

3. Read up on attractions and let each family member choose three or four must-see attractions per park. An amazing number of parents plan this trip for their kids without really consulting them about what they'd most like to do.

4. Accept your differences and be willing to split up occasionally. Forcing a sullen 13-year-old onto "it's a small world" or strapping a terrified 5-year-old into Rock 'n' Roller Coaster in the interest of family togetherness will guarantee at least one tantrum per hour.

5. Arrive at the parks early, rest in the afternoon, and return to the parks at night. Walt Disney World can be very tiring and regular rest stops are key.

Those five tips are always relevant, but since 2012 there have been five other changes worth noting:

1. The popularity of the Disney Dining Plan has changed the face of Disney restaurants—even for families who don't opt to purchase the plan. The reason? Families who once would never have considered herding the kids into top on-site restaurants are now deciding it's cost-effective to give fine dining a try. So suddenly you're seeing even toddlers in restaurants like the Brown Derby, Cítricos, Flying Fish, or California Grill. Although they're still great places to eat, the dining plan is indirectly taking a little of the adult feel and glamour out of these top restaurants. And the fact that so

many more visitors are vying for seats inside the restaurants means that making reservations before you leave home is more important than ever. I've gotten tons of mail from families who waited until they got to Orlando to make dining reservations and found themselves closed out of the restaurants they most wanted to visit.

2. Similarly, the introduction of more preplanning tools, such as the app called "My Disney Experience," means that families willing to arrange not just dining reservations but even to reserve FastPass+ in advance will get a bigger-than-ever jump on families who just show up and wing it. In some ways it's regrettable that you can no longer approach a vacation in a spontaneous fashion, but in other ways it means that guests who are willing to plan—including you, we presume, since you're reading this book—will have a wider array of options for customizing and streamlining their Disney visit.

3. Spring and fall are becoming slightly more crowded, especially during the two weeks flanking Easter and the fall weekends in which the Mickey's Halloween parties are offered. Disney has figured out that festivals and parties scattered throughout the year are a great way to tempt people to vacation at times when they would normally stay home and has been adding these special events at a steady clip. Bottom line? The off-season is still a better choice than visiting in summer or at Christmas, but be aware that it's not quite as "off" as it used to be.

4. Princess power continues to reign supreme. The character breakfasts have always been popular, but those featuring the princess characters are so hot that they require more planning than a NASA launch. Little girls can also get styled like their favorite princess at the Bibbidi Bobbidi Boutique, and you see more little girls than ever walking around the parks in full princess regalia. "Frozen" doesn't seem to be cooling off any time soon; the line to meet Elsa and Anna is the longest in all of Disney World. There's some effort to counterbalance this girl-power invasion with activities that boys will enjoy, such as the Jedi Training Academy at Hollywood, the Pirates and Pals Fireworks Cruise that leaves from

the Contemporary Resort, the Pirates League, and Captain Jack's Pirate Tutorial at Adventureland in the Magic Kingdom. But for now, at least, the prevalence of the princesses is undeniable and most little girls come under its spell. Bring costumes from home if you have them. If not, prepare to purchase.

5. The big trend in attractions is toward more interactive experiences. In existing attractions, more and more queues have games and entertainment to help you pass the time. And, based on the popularity of shows such as the Jedi Training Academy at Hollywood Studios and Agent P's World Showcase Adventure at Epcot, Disney is introducing participation-oriented activities geared to kids in every park. New offerings include the Wilderness Explorer in the Animal Kingdom and A Pirate's Adventure in the Magic Kingdom. Rather than merely riding a ride or sitting passively in a show, these activities get kids up and moving, thinking, solving a puzzle, or mastering a skill.

What hasn't changed in 26 years is our belief that Walt Disney World is the best family travel destination on the planet. There's truly something for everyone within these gates, and the spectacular, awe-inspiring rides are juxtaposed with sweet, small moments of joy. As one father shared: "My best-of-all moment was my 23-month-old daughter standing on the seat of Disney's Magical Express as we entered the gates of Walt Disney World yelling 'Mickey … don't worry … I coming!' That made it worth all the trouble and expense before we'd even arrived."

Throughout this book we've included such comments as the one above from Disney visitors who've written to share their best tales, tips, and "never again" stories. We'd love to hear how your trip went and any feedback you have about this book. If you'd like to share your travel experiences with us, please take a few minutes to respond to our survey online at ⊕ *www.fodors.com/ disneysurvey,* email us at ✉ *kwwiley@fodors.com,* or write to us at Fodor's, 1745 Broadway, New York, NY 10019. Thanks for your time, and have a great trip!

—Kim and Leigh

CHAPTER 1

BEFORE YOU LEAVE HOME

When it comes to visiting Walt Disney World, there are plenty of decisions you need to make in advance: when you'll go, how long you'll stay, which hotel you'll choose, and how much you plan to spend. But there are also some less obvious things to consider, such as where you'll put your focus and what attitude you'll bring to the trip. Our checklist will help you plan the perfect vacation for your particular family.

At Disney, timing is everything, and savvy travelers must understand the difference between the on-season and off-season. You also need to consider which money- and time-saving tips are worth it, and which ones are just too much hassle for the payoff. Finally, we will learn how to best use that bewildering bevy of high-tech planning tools that Disney now offers visitors.

It may sound like a lot of preplanning. And it's true that the advent of programs such as the Disney Dining Plan, FastPass+, and MyMagic+ means that more and more decisions need to be made before you leave home. You may even feel that all spontaneity is going out the window and your so-called vacation is feeling more like a part-time job. But look at it this way: By making these decisions now, you're saving yourself a lot of lines, hassles, and headaches down the road. Once you get into the parks, you will be able to relax and focus on family fun.

What Time of Year Should We Visit?

Crowd levels at Walt Disney World vary seasonally, so one of the most important decisions you'll make is deciding when to go.

To check projected hours of operation during the weeks you're considering, visit ⊕ www.disneyworld.com. Park hours generally remain as projected but can change; to be safe, revisit the site a couple of weeks before you leave home to reconfirm.

Spring

Spring can be a great time to visit. Except for the two weeks flanking Easter, when many schools have their spring break, crowds are manageable—not as sparse as in fall, but smaller than in summer. Although park hours don't run as late as they do in summer, they're generally longer than in either fall or winter. The weather is sublime, with highs in the 70s, lows in the 60s, and less rainfall than in any other season.

Summer

The good news about summer is that everything is open and operational and the parks run very long hours. The bad news is that it's hot and crowded—so crowded that the wait for many rides can be as long as 90 minutes.

If you have preschoolers, babies, or seniors in your party, avoid summers like the plague. But if the schedules of school-aged kids dictate that you must visit in the summer, the first two weeks of June and the last two weeks of August are your best bets.

Fall

Fall has lighter crowds than summer, and the weather is often great, but the season does have some disadvantages, too. You have to work around the fact that older children are in school, and the parks run on shorter hours. The Magic Kingdom, Animal Kingdom, and Hollywood may close as early as 5 pm, although Epcot always remains open later. Earlier closings mean that

INSIDER'S SECRET

Throughout the last few years, Halloween has grown in importance as a holiday within Disney World, making the entire month of October more crowded than it used to be. If you want to go to Mickey's Halloween Party, great. The fun is worth the extra effort. But even if you don't, be aware of the dates. The Magic Kingdom closes early on evenings the parties are scheduled to run, so you can't go there without a ticket to the event, but with so much of the crowd clustered in the Magic Kingdom, it's the perfect time to visit the other parks. Tickets to the party will often let guests in at 4 pm even if the party doesn't start until 7, making this a good choice for your first day of vacation.

some of the special evening presentations, such as the evening parade in the Magic Kingdom, are scheduled only on weekends.

Fall is the season for two of Walt Disney World's most popular events: Mickey's Halloween Party at the Magic Kingdom (with selected dates throughout September and October) and the Epcot International Food & Wine Festival. These events are doing exactly what Disney designed them to do—drawing people in during slower times. The Food & Wine Festival is open to all guests, but the Halloween Party requires a separate ticket. Consult ⊕ *www. disneyworld.com* for dates and prices and be aware that October 31 always sells out first.

Late summer and early fall make up hurricane season in Florida, so there is some risk that you'll schedule your trip for the exact week that a hurricane pounds the coast. Fortunately, Orlando is an hour inland, meaning that coastal storms usually yield only rain. And, should worse come to worst, Disney has "ride out" plans to ensure your safety. Furthermore, there are more rainy days in summer than in the fall, so, in general, the advantages of autumn touring far outweigh the disadvantages.

■TIP→ **The size of the crowds corresponds with the school schedule. Any time kids are out of school (i.e., summers, spring** break, and major holidays) is the "on-season." Any time children are traditionally in school is the "off-season."

Winter

Winter is a mixed bag. The absolute worst times to visit are holidays. Christmas and New Year's can pull in as many as 90,000 visitors per day, and even extended hours can't compensate for crowds of this size. But if you avoid the holiday weeks, winter can be ideal. With the exception of the weekends around the main winter holidays (Martin Luther King Jr. Day and Presidents' Day), January and February aren't crowded—and they're pleasantly cool. The first two weeks of December, when the Christmas decorations are already up but the crowds have not yet arrived, are a wonderful option. The parks run the same shortened hours in winter as in fall, but because the crowds are so much lighter, you'll still have time to see everything you want.

Mickey's Very Merry Christmas Party, held each year on several evenings throughout December, is wildly popular. If you want to attend the party, get tickets early—they sell out months in advance. Dates for each year's parties are listed on ⊕ *www. disneyworld.com*.

Visiting in the Off-Season

Some parents have written to say that they'd like to take the kids to Orlando during the off-season, but they've heard that this time of year is when Disney is most apt to close attractions for refurbishing. It's a valid point, but we still believe it's better to tour during the off-season. Here's why: In January, wait times for the most popular attractions are about a third of what they are in the summer, so even taking closings into account, you'll still ride more and wait less during the off-season. If your kids have their hearts set on a certain attraction, you can avoid last-minute disappointments by checking ⊕ *www.disneyworld.com* to see what's scheduled to be closed during your trip.

However, water babies should take note: Pools may be closed for refurbishing in January and February. Generally, only one water park is open at a time in winter, and both may shut down if the temperature dips below 55°F.

How Long Should We Stay?

It will take at least four days for a family to tour the major parks. If you also want to visit the water parks and Downtown Disney, make that five days. Six days are best for families who'd like to work in sporting options like boating or golf or those who would like to tour at a more leisurely pace.

If you plan on visiting other area attractions, such as Universal Orlando, allow a week.

INSIDER'S SECRET

Certain annual events—most notably the marathon in January, College Week in April, Gay Day in June, and various press events throughout the year—bring large groups into the parks. Check the Disney World website to see what events might be taking place or what large groups may be visiting before you book so you'll know what to expect.

Should We Take the Kids out of School?

Even if you're sold on the advantages of off-season touring, you may be reluctant to take your children out of school. But there are ways to highlight the educational aspects of a trip to Disney World. Work together with your child's teacher to create a plan that keeps him from falling behind. Ideally, half of the makeup work should be done before you leave: The post-trip blues are bad enough without facing three hours of homework each night. Also, timing is everything. Don't plan your trip for the week the school is administering exams or standardized testing.

Happily, visiting the parks can also be a learning experience of sorts, and Disney offers several programs for parents who want to enhance the learning value of their vacation.

In addition to the suggestions below, help your child create a project that's related to the trip—perhaps something like a scrapbook. The mother of one first grader helped him design an "ABC" book before he left home, and he spent his week at Disney World collecting souvenirs for each page—Goofy's autograph on the "G" page, a postcard of a Japanese pagoda on the "P" page, and so on. An older child might gather leaves from the various trees and

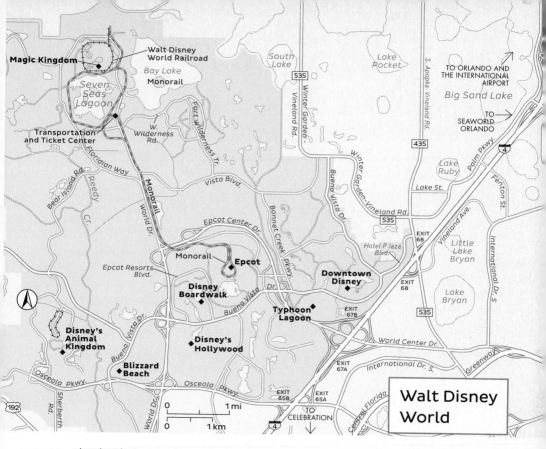

shrubs that were imported to landscape the countries in the World Showcase. A young photographer could demonstrate her proficiency with various lighting techniques by photographing Cinderella Castle at early morning, high noon, sunset, and after dark.

You can also work on math. If a car containing six people departs from the Test Track loading area every 20 seconds, how many riders go through in an hour? A day? If the monorail averages 32 mph, how long does it take it to travel the 7 miles from the Magic Kingdom to Epcot? Once you get going on these sorts of questions, they're addictive. Or give your kids a set amount of mythical money to spend, such as $1,000. Then let them keep track of expenses, deducting purchases from their starting total and making decisions about what they can and cannot afford on their budget.

Epcot Projects

✦ The Behind the Seeds greenhouse tour in the Land is full of information on futuristic farming.

✦ Marine biology is the theme of the Seas pavilion.

✦ The World Showcase demonstrates the culture—including music, architecture, food, and history—of several foreign countries.

Animal Kingdom Projects

✦ Rafiki's Planet Watch is the park's research-and-education hub, where kids can observe veterinary labs and watch interactive videos about endangered animals.

✦ The Wilderness Explorer interactive experience—based on the movie *Up*—is tailor-made for kids 5 to 10. By showing their knowledge of facts about animals and their habitats, participants earn "badges" (actually stickers) from "troop leaders" (actually cast members) stationed at marked kiosks throughout the park. With 33 available badges, it's unlikely you'll get through them all in a single day, but the challenges are well designed and perfect for getting kids to both slow down and notice the animals. The sticker book is also a good souvenir to bring back to your child's teacher.

✦ It's always fun to do a report on one of the animals you see on Kilimanjaro Safaris or along one of the exploration trails. Animal-crazy kids who are eight or older will get a lot out of the Wild Africa Trek, a three-hour tour that takes you behind the scenes.

Other Orlando Educational Programs

Disney World isn't the only place in Orlando that can be educational. Consider the following:

✦ **Orlando Science Center:** This impressive facility has hands-on exhibits and programs for kids of all ages. Something is happening all the time—especially in spring and summer when most of the camps are held—and the prices are reasonable. Admission to the center is $19 for adults, $17 for students and seniors, and $13 for kids ages 3 to 11. Classes are individually priced. To see what's happening during your visit, call

☎ 888/672-4386 (☎ 888/OSC-4FUN) or ☎ 407/514-2000 or visit ⊕ www.osc.org.

✦ **Kennedy Space Center:** Orlando is only about an hour's drive from the Kennedy Space Center, which can make for an easy day trip. Kids will enjoy seeing the rockets and the IMAX films about space exploration. The Shuttle Launch Experience takes place in a looming, six-story structure that looks like the real thing. It requires that riders be 44 inches tall and is included in your general admission ticket.

> ### INSIDER'S SECRET
>
> The Kennedy Space Center's Astronaut Training Experience (ATX) is ideal for kids seven and up. The full-immersion experience includes riding in flight simulators, building and launching rockets, and playing crew in a mock-up of a shuttle mission. The half-day experience is $175 per person ($165 for ages 7–11).

The two most recent additions to the Space Center are an interactive attraction called the Angry Birds Space Encounter, based on the popular video game, and the $100 million home of the space shuttle *Atlantis*. Needless to say, the Angry Birds game, which is included with general admission, is especially popular with kids. Crew passes, which include a bus tour of the space center as well as the IMAX film, are $50 for adults and $40 for kids ages 3 to 11. A second day at the Astronaut Hall of Fame is also included.

✦ If your kids are really into space exploration, weeklong summer day camps begin at $295. Make reservations for programs or get details on classes, camps, and tours at ⊕ www.kennedyspacecenter.com.

Vacation Packages

Should you buy a package? This is a toughie. There are advantages to package trips, most notably that if you play your cards right, you can save money. It's also helpful to know up front exactly what your vacation will cost. Packages often require hefty prepayments, which are painful at the time, but at least you don't return home with your credit card utterly maxed out. And with the mega-popular Disney Dining Plan package, there's the convenience of having one card (or MagicBand) serve as your room key, theme-park ticket, and dining ticket. It eliminates the hassles of carrying cash and tracking how much you're spending.

But package trips can have drawbacks. Like buying a fully loaded car off a dealer's lot, you may find yourself paying for options you don't want and don't need. Unless you're certain you'll use most of the features contained in the package, you'll probably end up losing money on the deal.

Disney Vacation Packages

By far the most popular packages are those offered by Disney. The basic Magic Your Way package includes a hotel room on Disney property and theme-park tickets. You can choose any resort in any price range as well as the ticket options that suit your family's needs. Magic Your Way allows you to customize your package to the nth degree, fine-tuning the time of year, length of stay, resort, type of ticket, and type of dining (more on that below). The good news is, it gives you lots of options. The bad news is—it gives you lots of options.

Park Ticket Options

So how do you know what to choose? Let's start with tickets. The rule of thumb is, if your kids are young or this is your first trip to Disney World, you'll probably be spending most of your time in the four major theme parks, so choose a package with base tickets. If your kids are eight and up, consider upgrading to the Park Hopper Pass, which gives you the flexibility to move from one park to another in the course of the day. The more expensive premium and platinum options are really only helpful for families who've been to Disney World before and want to explore beyond the basic parks and those whose kids are old enough to enjoy the water parks, sporting options, tours, and Cirque du Soleil. For most families, either the base ticket or the base ticket with the Park Hopper Pass works fine.

How does the ticket type affect the cost of the trip?

Let's look at a typical family of four and walk them through the process. If they're traveling during the off-season—let's say in September—a five-night package at a value resort with base tick-

Theme-Park Ticket-Price Chart

TICKET OPTIONS

TICKET	10-DAY	7-DAY	6-DAY	5-DAY	4-DAY	3-DAY	2-DAY	1-DAY
BASE TICKET Ages 10–up	$365	$335	$325	$315	$305	$275	$192	$97–105
Ages 3–9	$345	$315	$305	$295	$285	$256	$179	$91–99

Base Ticket admits guest to one of the four major theme parks per day's use (the Magic Kingdom costs $105). Park choices are: Magic Kingdom, Epcot, Disney's Hollywood Studios, Disney's Animal Kingdom. **8-day** and **9-day** tickets are also available.

ADD: Park Hopper	$64	$64	$64	$64	$64	$50	$50	$50

Park Hopper option entitles guest to visit more than one theme park per day's use. Park choices are any combination of: Magic Kingdom, Epcot, Disney's Hollywood Studios, Disney's Animal Kingdom.

ADD: Water Park Fun	$64	$64	$64	$64	$64	$64	$64	$64

Water Park Fun option entitles guest to visits to a choice of entertainment and recreation venues. Choices are: Blizzard Beach, Typhoon Lagoon, DisneyQuest, Wide World of Sports, Disney's Oak Trail Golf course, or either mini-golf course.

ADD: Both	$90	$90	$90	$90	$90	$90	$90	$90

Adding both the *Park Hopper* and *Water Park* option entitles guest to all the privileges under both specific options above.

MINOR PARKS AND ATTRACTIONS

TICKET	AGES 10–UP	AGES 3–9
Typhoon Lagoon or Blizzard Beach 1-Day 1-Park	$58	$50
DisneyQuest 1-Day	$47	$40
Cirque du Soleil's La Nouba	$63–150	$52–123

*All prices are subject to Florida sales tax.

ets will cost them approximately $1,600. Pretty reasonable, huh? If they add the Park Hopper option to their tickets, the price will rise to $1,800.

How does the type of lodging affect the cost of the trip?

The resort category—from value to moderate to deluxe to deluxe villa—and the season also affect the price of a package. (Chapter 2 outlines the pluses and minuses of each on-site resort; for now, you just need to consider how much this choice affects costs.) For our family of four, that same package will cost them approximately $1,900 during peak season because the cost of accommodations (even at a value resort) is higher. Still pretty reasonable. But what if they upgrade their hotel? A stay at a deluxe hotel for five nights during the off-season will cost them approximately $3,300 (closer to $4,200 during peak season). So by making two changes—the type of resort and the time of year— our family has almost tripled its vacation price.

How do I make a final decision?

Going through the exercise above has probably done two things: given you sticker shock and overwhelmed you. Still, it's a good introduction to the Disney vacation experience, which involves an almost staggering number of choices.

Your best bet is to go to ⊕ *www.disneyworld.com,* click on the pricing bar, then start tweaking, eliminating, or downgrading options, changing the dates of your visit, and so on, until you arrive at a price you can afford—or at least live with.

Before you finalize your plans, however, you also need to decide whether to add a dining plan, which ups the package price by from $120 to $160 a day for a family of four.

■TIP➔ **Disney runs specials during the off-season, sometimes dropping the price of an on-site hotel room or including a free dining plan. The pricing examples in this chapter assume no specials are in play, but if you are lucky enough to snag one, the savings average 20%.**

Non-Disney Packages

Travel-booking websites can offer genuine bargains, especially if you don't plan to stay on Disney property. For deals online, check out the following:

- *www.aaa.com* (discount vacation packages)

- *www.expedia.com* (for general vacation packages)

- *www.hotels.com* (discount hotels and rental cars)

- *www.mousesavers.com* (tips and tricks for saving money at the parks)

- *www.smallworldvacations.com* (Disney vacation packages)

- *www.vacationoutlet.com* (discount vacation packages)

■**TIP→ If you're calling to book your room, whether on-site or off-site, always ask, "Are there any discounts or special offers available?" Sometimes you'll learn about deals over the phone that aren't listed on a website.**

Cruise Packages

Some of the most popular Disney packages are those that combine a cruise with a vacation in the parks. Check out ⊕ *www.disneycruise. com*, call ☎ *800/951–3532,* or contact a travel agent, who may also be able to offer discounts on cruises and vacation packages that include a cruise. See Chapter 12 for more information.

Disney Dining Plans

The standard dining plan includes, for each day of your trip, one full-service meal, one counter-service meal, and a snack from a list of the 100-plus participating Disney restaurants scattered throughout the four theme parks and on-site hotels. Dining plans are only available for guests who stay on property, that is, at a Disney-owned hotel, and they raise the price of your package by about $160 a day.

Is the standard plan worth it? If you have big eaters in the party, then yes, as the standard plan can save you about 30% over the cost of individual meals. But if six-year-old Katie eats nothing but cereal and three-year-old Danny grows so restless that sit-down dinners are a nightmare, it's unlikely they'll eat enough food to justify the cost of the standard dining plan.

A couple from Georgia with three children under age 10 said that the standard meal plan wasn't for them: "In our opinion," said the father, "adding meals to your package only makes sense if you're prepared to eat 6,000 calories a day and spend three hours a day in restaurants." A mom from New York added, "We considered it a hassle to have to plan all our full-service meals in advance and make reservations. Normally we're pretty flexible on vacations—but not this time."

Quick-Service Meal Plans

If your kids are too young to sit still for table service—and you're not planning to splurge on a character meal—then consider the quick-service plan. It covers two quick-service meals and a snack—perfect for kids who get hungry frequently but don't eat a lot at one sitting—and increases the package price for a family of four by roughly $120 a day.

If that sounds like a lot for fast food and snacks, welcome to Disney. Most of the families who've written to me report they believe the quick-service plan is still a good deal. One mom did the math and reported a 30% savings over ordering the same meals à la carte. If you're worried about facing a whole vacation eating nothing but burgers and fries, relax. Disney has done a good job of expanding quick-service options, especially at Epcot. With a little preplanning, you should be able to find a wide variety of food options.

Character Meals and Premium Restaurants

Certain experiences, like dinner shows, some character meals, and the "signature" (i.e., most upscale) restaurants, cost more than your daily full-service meal allowance. If you have a standard dining plan, you must swap out two of your regular full-service meals for one of these exceptional dining experiences. But the swap can still save you a bundle on what would otherwise be a very expensive dinner. One mother wrote, "By eating at counter-service places for a couple of days beforehand we saved enough credits for dinner at California Grill and it was superb."

Another mom wrote that "the standard dining plan makes a lot of sense if you want to take in multiple character meals. We were able to attend three: at Crystal Palace, Chef Mickey's, and 1900 Park Fare, and we could not have afforded all this without the plan."

A father from Texas added, "I'm a little compulsive, at least according to my wife, and I ran a tally of what we would have paid if we'd ordered menu items on our own versus going with the dining plan. Trust me, the dining plan is a great value."

One family of foodies from New York opted to upgrade to the deluxe dining plan, which allows sit-down dining at every meal, and further added the "wine-and-dine" option. "For us, it was worth it," said the mother. "We had some terrific meals which were, thanks to the plan, reasonably priced. And our kids are old enough to enjoy the ambience of the restaurants, which are actually as full of Disney atmosphere as the resorts and parks."

Getting Your Money's Worth

To make sure you get your money's worth from the dining plan, follow these steps, which are explained in more detail on the Disney website, ⊕ *www.disneyworld.com/dining.*

Choose a Price-Level Option

There are five price options, but most people traveling with kids can safely eliminate the deluxe, premium, and platinum plans, which include so much food you'll spend your entire vacation in restaurants. The vast majority of families go with the quick-service dining plan (two quick-service meals and one snack per person each day) or standard plan (one table-service meal, one quick-service meal, and one snack per person each day).

Study Your Options

To get the most use out of your dining plan, study up in advance. The menus at ⊕ *www.disneyworld.com/dining* will help you decide which, if any, signature restaurants are worth a multicredit splurge. Remember that a dining credit works the same if you order a burger and fries or a steak. Knowing the restaurants beforehand can make sure you get the most bang for your buck. You can also find out which character meals require two credits and which don't. And—perhaps most important with kids—you can find restaurants that serve foods your whole family will enjoy.

Choose Your Upgrades

If you want to try one of Disney's swank signature restaurants or if your kids have their hearts set on a certain character breakfast, combine two table-service credits for these special experiences and book them well in advance.

Make Your Dining Reservations

Lock in your dining reservations at table-service restaurants at least 90 days in advance, either by booking them online or calling ☎ 407/939-3463 (☎ 407/WDW-DINE). This is especially key if you're traveling during the on-season.

Pick Up Your MagicBand

If you have planned far enough in advance (and live in the United States), then you will get your MagicBand in the mail before you leave. Otherwise, when you arrive at your Disney hotel, your dining plan information will be preprogrammed into your MagicBand, which is also your theme-park ticket and room key. Handy, huh? The band automatically monitors your allotted meals, and your receipt from each meal will show your balance so you can easily keep track of how many meals are left on the plan.

Plan Your Meals

For families on the standard plan, meal choices usually shake out like this: an in-hotel muffin or bagel breakfast as the "snack," a quick-service lunch, and a full-service dinner. But you certainly don't have to have your big meal at night; some families sit down at lunch to rest up, regroup, and escape from the parks during the hottest and most crowded times of the day.

Another thing to consider: The number and categories of meals you've purchased are loaded into your ticket or MagicBand, but you can redeem them in any order. So if you want to use two of your full-service credits on your day at Epcot, which has lots of good restaurants, and use two quick-service credits on your day at the Magic Kingdom, which isn't exactly a dining mecca, that's fine.

■TIP➔ **Deals and packages that include the dining plan are most commonly offered to guests at Disney resorts during the off-season, so make sure to ask about them when booking your room. If your dates are flexible, you may be able to save some** money by traveling during a week when the dining plan is included.

Disney Park Tickets

Under Disney's flexible Magic Your Way ticketing system, you can customize your tickets to reflect your family's priorities and length of stay.

How Pricing Works

Let's say you have a long weekend to visit and want a three-day ticket. The base price is $275 for ages 10 and up, which comes to about $92 a day, a savings over the one-day ticket price of $97 (10 and up) for all but the Magic Kingdom ($105 adults, $99 kids 3–9). This base price lets you into only one park per day. The more days you buy, the less your per-day cost. An adult buying a five-day basic ticket ends up paying around $63 per day, a significant savings over the one-day ticket price.

The more options you add, the more the price increases. If you add the Park Hopper Pass, which increases the price of your three-day 10-and-up ticket (regardless of length of stay) to $325, you can move from park to park within a day. If you add on Blizzard Beach, Typhoon Lagoon, and DisneyQuest—the Water Park Fun & More option—you add $64 to the price of each ticket (regardless of length of stay), raising the price to $339. If you want *both* the Park Hopper Pass and the Water Park Fun option, you pay an additional $90 per ticket, increasing the price of a three-day pass to $365.

Disney "adjusts"—that is, raises—prices regularly, so you should always confirm these numbers by visiting ⊕ *www.disneyworld.com*. Also note that children under age three are admitted free.

Ticket Expiration

Most tickets expire within 14 days of first use. The only way to prevent this is to add the No Expiration Option onto the tickets. Some guests will buy the maximum ticket possible and then add this option, intending to use their ticket over multiple trips. Just be aware: This option is only available if you order your tickets by phone (☎ *407/939-7679*) or purchase them at the gate, and it isn't worth the extra cost unless you are already planning your next vacation to Disney World. If you are planning repeat visits, call or visit Guest Relations (a.k.a. Guest Services) and have them run the numbers for you.

Sticking to the Basics

So, how do you know which ticket to buy? If this is your first trip to Disney World, keep it simple. If you have young kids, you'll likely spend most of your time in the four major parks, so a base ticket is fine. As a mom with three preschoolers said, "We bought the Park Hopper option but the logistics of moving around with that many strollers and backpacks was just overwhelming. After one day of trying to park hop we decided it would be less stressful to stay in a single park every day. So we basically paid extra for nothing."

■**TIP→ Not sure about upgrades? Buy the basic. If you get down to Orlando and decide that you'd like to park hop or go to the water parks, you can always upgrade your ticket there, which is much better than paying for options that you don't end up using. "We paid for the water-parks option," said one mom from Massachusetts, "only to arrive on a week full of thunderstorms, when the water parks were closed at least half the time."**

Considering Your Upgrade Options

If your kids are older and able to withstand a long day, the Park Hopper Pass is worthwhile. It also comes in handy if you're traveling during the off-season, when the Magic Kingdom and Hollywood Studios close early; without it you may find yourself with little to do after 6 pm (Epcot is the only park that's always open late). It's good for people who've been to Disney World before and know exactly what attractions they want to see or who know they like to move around swiftly, revisiting these favorites. (Many of the touring tips in this book assume that you have the ability to move from one park to another in the course of a day.) If any of these conditions applies to you, the vote on the Park Hopper Pass should be "yes."

The Water Park Fun & More option makes sense if you have older kids who would enjoy the water parks and DisneyQuest, or if you've been to Disney World before and are looking to venture outside the four major parks. On the other hand, if this is your first trip to Disney World, you'll have all you can handle just visiting the four major parks. If your kids are very young, you may find that your hotel pool is a far more practical way to cool off. So, it's a "yes" on Water Park Fun & More only for families with kids over eight or who are visiting Disney World for the second time. For first-time visitors or families with kids under eight, the answer is usually "no."

Bottom line: If in doubt, go with the base (and thus cheapest) ticket. If you get to Orlando and change your mind, you can add these options at any time during your vacation.

MagicBand

MagicBands have reinvented Disney vacation planning and can drastically streamline your experience while in the parks. You can use MagicBands whether staying on-site or off-site. If you are staying on-site, you will get one automatically, either in the mail before your trip (assuming you have planned far enough ahead) or at the hotel once you arrive; if you are staying off-site, you can buy a MagicBand on arrival for $12.95. No matter where you stay, your MagicBand links to all personal information regarding your type of theme-park ticket, reserved FastPass+ reservations, and PhotoPass pictures. If you are staying on-site, it also serves as your room key, grants you charging privileges throughout Disney property, and stores information on your dining plan.

In other words, that one little wristband is pretty much your everything. It drastically cuts down on how much you have to take with you and keep track of as you tour the parks.

Because so much information is encoded into a typical MagicBand, Disney has taken extraordinary security measures. No personal information is stored in the MagicBand, which contains a code that links to an encrypted database. A band that has been lost can be immediately disabled. If the technology makes you nervous, you can certainly opt out of using MagicBand in lieu of a standard ticket, but most guests are thrilled with the convenience.

In addition, Disney uses a biometric identification system to keep track of exactly who is using the band. The first time you enter a Disney park, you'll be asked to do a finger scan, which records minute measurements (not fingerprints). You'll be res-

Advance Planning Is Your Friend

If used strategically, Disney's new technologies can help guests streamline their vacations, making a trip to Disney as simple as life on a cruise ship or a stay at an all-inclusive resort. The bad news is that not everyone understands quite how they work yet, which means that in the short run there can be massive confusion, especially at check-in. We recently stood in line for over an hour at The Art of Animation resort, noting to our frustration that the line wasn't moving at all. The reason? Cast members spent an average of 35 minutes per guest explaining the MagicBand system. In contrast, the line for preregistered guests, who presumably had done their homework and handled most of the details online, was zipping along.

The moral? Do as much as you can in advance, and learn about the MagicBand and My Disney Experience systems (which are collectively called My Magic+) before you ever set foot in the parks.

- ❏ Download the free My Disney Experience app as soon as possible. Explore it to get a sense of all the types of information it can provide.

- ❏ If you plan to stay on-site, include your theme-park tickets in your package when you make your hotel reservation. Then go immediately to ⊕ *www.disneyworld.com* and create a MyMagic+ account.

- ❏ Enter your hotel and ticket reservation number so that the app and your reservations are linked before you leave home.

- ❏ Off-site guests will have to work a little harder. Buy your tickets as soon as possible after you begin planning your trip and also create a MyMagic+ account. Once you have tickets in hand, enter the ticket numbers (or scan the bar code) to link them to My Disney Experience. (Note that to do this you will have to have your actual ticket in hand, not a voucher.)

❑ Once the system "knows" you have tickets and how many days you will be in the parks, you can use FastPass+ to make three attraction reservations for each day of your trip (60 days in advance for on-site guests and season-pass holders, 30 days in advance for off-site guests). Remember that each person will need his or her own FastPass+ for each attraction.

❑ On-site guests should now personalize their MagicBands. Each member of the family can pick their own color. This keeps you from getting them mixed up when four MagicBands are lying around the hotel room, and also adds a bit of fun. (Disney, always quick to recognize a marketing opportunity, has even come up with charms to allow you to decorate your MagicBands, in effect turning them into jewelry.) Once you've picked out the colors, the personalized bands will be sent to your house—and boy, is it an exciting day when they arrive. If you've cut it too close on time to have them shipped, the bands will be waiting for you when you check into your resort.

❑ Use online advance check-in (detailed instructions will arrive by email a few days before departure). This will make your on-site check-in experience go much faster, and you can start having fun while everyone else is still standing at the front desk asking "What are these MagicBands, anyway?"

❑ Keep in mind that the MyMagic+ tools, including MagicBands, the My Disney Experience app, and all the things you can do with this technology—especially reserving FastPass+ attractions—is still relatively new and in flux. Disney promises that new perks could be added at any moment. Carefully read the information you receive when you book your trip, and vow to exploit each tool to the max.

canned each time you enter a Disney park to make sure that the finger measurements match.

MagicBands make everything easier—including spending money. Rather than the old method of swiping a room key like a credit or debit card, which did at least signal to your subconscious that you were making a financial transaction, the bands require you to merely tap your wrist against an electronic plate to charge a purchase. You tap, the Mickey turns green, and boom, you can have whatever you want.

> **INSIDER'S SECRET**
>
> The free in-park Wi-Fi is certainly convenient, but drains your phone battery very quickly. If you plan to use the service frequently during your visits, it's a good idea to bring your charger with you. Or you can simply limit your phone use.

■TIP➔ **Paying with your MagicBand is a little intoxicating—at least until the cold-water slap of the bill arrives—so consider carefully whether you want to give charging privileges to kids and teens. Or maybe even your spouse.**

My Disney Experience

Another new user-friendly guest technology is the My Disney Experience app, which allows guests to preplan their vacations to an unprecedented degree and then access that information once they're in Orlando. The app, which works on iPhones, iPads, and Android smartphones, is free and easy to navigate. Moreover, Disney now offers free Wi-Fi throughout the theme parks, so you don't have to use your own mobile phone minutes or data-plan bandwidth to access the useful features of the app while you're enjoying the parks.

Just as MagicBands can be used by guests staying at Disney resorts or by those staying off-site, the My Disney Experience app is also available to anyone, including people sitting at home on their couch just wanting to learn more about Disney. Download and install it to start poking around.

My Disney Experience gives you general info about the parks and resorts, and helps you to make dining reservations in advance. But the best perk of all? It allows you to make FastPass+ reservations in advance. FastPass+ will be explained in detail in Chapter 4, but for now the main point is that you can reserve times to visit the most popular attractions at Disney World, thus vastly cutting down on the amount of time you spend waiting in line once you get to Orlando.

On-site guests with their hotel reservation and tickets in hand can reserve their FastPass+ options 60 days in advance. Off-site guests with tickets in hand can reserve their FastPass+ options 30 days in advance. You get three FastPass+ choices per day to begin with, through the app. These reservations can be used in only one park, and they have to be for different attractions (i.e., you can't make a reservation for Space Mountain three times). Each family member needs his or her own FastPass+ reservation to enter the FastPass line.

Let's say you know you'll be at Hollywood Studios on Wednesday of your vacation. As soon as possible, you can reserve a time to ride the most popular attractions there. Just be aware: At Hollywood Studios and Epcot, the FastPass+ rides are divided into tiers, and you can choose only one ride from tier one. For example, at Hollywood Studios you can get one FastPass+ reservation for either Toy Story Mania or Rock 'n' Rollercoaster—but not both, since they are in the same tier. Then you can use your other Fast-Pass+ reservations for attractions such as Tower of Terror and Star Tours, which are in a different tier.

Clever readers will have deduced two things by now. The first is that you should use your precious FastPass+ choices for the most popular attractions. Don't burn them on minor rides or theater-style attractions where the wait would only be 20 minutes. Save them for either big-deal rides or for interactive attractions like Enchanted Tales With Belle, which is so popular that 90-minute waits are the norm, and Princesses Anna and Elsa at Princess Fairytale Hall, which can have waits of more than two hours (the single-longest wait in all of Walt Disney World). But if you have made a FastPass+ reservation and arrive to find only a five-minute wait, you can change the ride or time through the app or at a FastPass+ kiosk before the time expires. ■**TIP→ One of the really cool things about FastPass+ is that the reservations can be changed on the fly.**

INSIDER'S SECRET

While FastPass+ only allows you to reserve three attractions per day in advance, it is possible to make additional FastPass+ reservations once you're within the park. You can visit one of the FastPass+ kiosks, the locations of which are marked on your theme-park map, and see what additional FastPass+ times are available. Be aware that these aren't going to be "cream of the crop" FastPass+ options for major attractions at the most desirable times; those were all taken up weeks ago. But you can save some time on middle-tier attractions. If you want to change a Fastpass+ reservation, you can do that at a kiosk as well. There are always cast members nearby who can help.

How does this work? Let's say you've reserved a time to ride Space Mountain, but when you get to the Magic Kingdom you see that the wait is only 20 minutes. There's no need to burn one of your three FastPass+ reservations on such a short line. So you can cancel that FastPass+ either by using your phone or at one of the FastPass+ kiosks located throughout each theme park. Just be sure to make the change before your original FastPass+ expires. Or say you have a FastPass+ reservation to ride Tower of Terror at Hollywood Studios at 1:20 but lunch is taking longer than you anticipated. Don't let the FastPass+ simply expire. Use your phone or the nearest kiosk to either change your reservation time or choose another attraction.

Transportation

Since Disney provides free bus transportation from the airport to your on-site hotel, it's important to consider whether it's worth it to rent a car. For most families staying on-site and focusing primarily on Disney attractions, the answer is probably "no." Quite a few families have reported that they used their rental car less than they anticipated. "We paid $350 for the privilege of driving from the airport to our hotel and back," wrote one father.

But for families staying off-site or anyone planning to visit both Disney and non-Disney attractions, renting a car can make sense. "We got a great hotel rate, but it was about 15 miles from Disney World," one mother reported. "We also spent a day at Universal and a day at SeaWorld, so we would have been sunk if we hadn't had our own transportation."

Renting a Car for Walt Disney World

While a rental car isn't a necessity in Orlando, especially for guests staying on Disney property with access to the Disney transportation system, some families simply prefer driving themselves. They argue that having a car makes it easier to visit non-Disney destinations, such as Universal Studios or SeaWorld, and that a car allows them to eat off-site more easily, since eating all meals at Disney parks and hotels can indeed get expensive. "After our first $50 breakfast in the food court of our Disney hotel," wrote one father of three, "we decided to drive to the parks, stopping for a fast-food breakfast along the way. This saved us at least $30 a day." It's also worth noting that some people are irked by waiting even 20 minutes for a bus and like to come and go entirely on their own schedule.

An average weekly rental fee for a midsize car is around $350. Don't be fooled by the quoted rate of $30 a day; by the time you add on taxes and insurance it's closer to $50. Gas may add another $50 or $60, depending on how much you drive.

Disney Without a Rental Car

If you're not staying at a Disney resort and not renting a car, you have two options for airport transfers. The fastest and easiest is a cab; prices average about $50 to the Universal–International Drive area and $60 to the Disney area, plus tip. Alternatively, you can take the Mears Shuttle Service, which costs $30 round-trip for adults and $24 for kids. You can reserve your shuttle before leaving home by calling ☎ 407/423–5566. Shuttles may seem like a money-saving option, but if there are more than two people in your party, it's cheaper to take a cab. The other option is the Magical Express Service.

Magical Express Service

If you're staying at a Disney resort, the Magical Express Service makes transport from the airport to your hotel room less costly, and potentially more convenient.

You simply check your bags at your hometown airport. This is the last time you'll see them until you're in your Orlando hotel room, so be sure to put anything you may need in the meantime, such as medication or summer-weather clothing, in your carry-on. When your plane arrives, you don't have to go to baggage claim; instead, follow the directions of the Disney representative waiting on the baggage-claim level. You'll board a bus and head for your resort, and—if all goes smoothly—your bags will arrive in your room about three hours after you do. You don't have to be on-site to sign for your luggage; if you want to go straight to the pool or theme parks, the bags will be waiting for you when you get back.

The Magical Express Service not only saves you the hassle of tracking and dragging your bags every step of the way, but it also means free airport-to-resort transport for all Disney hotel guests. This single perk saves a family of four between $120 and $350 when you consider that they would otherwise be taking a shuttle or a cab or renting a car.

The biggest downside of the Magical Express airport buses is that buses usually stop at several hotels, which can mean a long commute time. If you're really eager to get your vacation going fast, take a cab. Some families have also reported significant wait times for their luggage, so pack essentials in a carry-on. "It took seven hours for our luggage to be delivered to our room," said one mother from Wisconsin. "We couldn't take the kids swimming, and we ended up spending the whole first day walking around in 90-degree weather in long sleeves and jeans."

■TIP→ You just got to Orlando, so, of course, you're not thinking about going home yet. But, as a sadder-but-wiser mother from Ohio advised, "If you use the Magical Express for your return service to the airport, don't book your return flight before noon. They require you to be on the bus three hours before your flight time, which for us basically involved getting up and checking out in the middle of the night."

Walt Disney World Transportation System

The Disney Transportation System, which is composed of buses, monorails, and boats, is designed to transport guests from one side of Walt Disney World to another. But is it good enough? The ease of your transportation options depends on two things.

The first is the popularity of the destination. It's relatively simple to get to Epcot, for example, from anywhere on Disney property. If you're trying to get to the less popular Wide World of Sports, you'll have a more complicated journey. The second factor is the price point of your resort. One of the things guests staying at the luxury resorts are paying for is faster and more direct transportation around Disney property, and they often have a fleet of options at their disposal, ranging from boat launches to monorails. Guests at the budget resorts (and all the resorts at Animal Kingdom) must rely on buses alone. But the key thing to remember is that with a little planning and patience, on-site guests can use the Disney transportation system to not only get back and forth to the airport, but to everywhere within Walt Disney World as well.

Whether or not you decide to use the Disney transportation system, the time difference between driving yourself and the bus ride is unlikely to be more than 15 minutes, so it pretty much boils down to your preference. Do you want to be in complete control of your destiny, able to change plans on a whim? Take your car. Do you want to zone out and forget all about maps, traffic, parking-row numbers, and dead batteries? Leave the driving to Disney.

Using Taxis

At times it may make more sense to use taxis than to rent a car or even take Disney's transportation. Taxi rides within Disney property average $15, and parking (at least for guests not staying at a Disney resort) is $17—virtually equal. If you plan to drive a lot, it makes sense to have your own car, but if you need direct transportation only occasionally, a cab is a perfectly fine option. Consider taking a cab if:

✦ You'd like quick direct transportation from the airport to your hotel.

✦ You'd like quick direct transportation from one resort to another. If you're all dressed up for your special parents'-night-

INSIDER'S SECRET

Here's a time-honored question. You're staying on-site, and you have a car—either a rental or your own. Is it faster to drive to the theme parks or to take Disney transportation? The answer varies. If your resort offers monorail or boat access to a certain park, take it. It will always be your fastest way there. If your resort offers only bus service, the decision is a little trickier. The buses can be slow, especially if you're staying at a big, sprawling resort like Port Orleans/Riverside or Caribbean Beach, where it can take 15 minutes for the buses simply to circle the property.

If you're planning to park hop, having your own car will save you some time, and, as long as your hotel car pass is visible on your dash, theme-park parking is free to on-site guests.

out dinner at Victoria & Albert's, you probably won't feel like taking the bus.

✦ You're headed to a minor park like Downtown Disney or the water parks and don't want a lengthy shuttle commute.

✦ You're staying at a Disney hotel but heading to Universal Orlando for the day.

✦ Everyone's absolutely exhausted. If you've pushed too far and the kids are having a meltdown, cabs are the fastest way to get back to your room.

Taxis are always waiting near the theme-park exits and, at times, this $15 is well worth spending. As one mother wrote, "Our kids get so excited at Disney that they go full-out the whole time, running around in a frenzy. But when they collapse, they really collapse. There were a couple of times when even having to wait 15 minutes for a bus would have been a disaster. Every time we left a theme park, they'd be asleep in the car before we were even out of the parking lot."

Countdown to Disney World

Okay, let's summarize. Here's everything that needs to be done—and when.

As Soon as Possible

❏ **Choose your resort.** To help find the best on-site hotel for you, consult Chapter 2, and once you've narrowed your options, make reservations at ⊕ *www.disneyworld.com* or by calling ☎ *407/934-7639* (☎ *407/W-DISNEY*).

❏ **Book your room.** Even if you're staying off-site, booking early is smart. A great way to get discounts on off-site lodging is to go to the Orlando Travel Bureau website at ⊕ *www.orlandoinfo.com* for instructions on how to get a free Orlando Magicard discount card.

❏ **Buy your theme-park tickets.** You can either buy online at ⊕ *www.disneyworld.com* or by calling ☎ *407/934-7639* (☎ *407/W-DISNEY*).

❏ **Download the My Disney Experience app.** Then link your tickets to your personal MyMagic+ page on ⊕ *www.disneyworld.com*. Select how you will use your three FastPass+ options for each day of your trip.

Six Months in Advance

❏ **Airline tickets.** Flying? Book now.

❏ **Car rentals.** If you need a rental car, reserve it now.

❏ **Make dinner plans.** You can arrange for dining reservations, including character meals and dinner shows, 180 days in advance (90 days in advance during special promotions) by calling ☎ *407/934-7639* (☎ *407/W-DISNEY*) or booking online at ⊕ *www.disneyworld.com*. Making your reservations online is faster if you know exactly what you want; if you need advice, make the telephone call and talk to a real Disney cast member.

❏ **Book a stylist.** Does your little princess want to be styled at the Bibbidi Bobbidi Boutique? Sign her up 180 days in advance by dialing ☎ *407/939–7895* (☎ *407/WDW–STYLE*).

❏ **Plan Tours.** Families who would like to take a behind-the-scenes tour or enroll their kids in one of the Grand Floridian programs—such as the pirate-theme scavenger hunt or tea with Alice and the other Wonderland characters—should book at this stage. Call ☎ *407/939–8687* (☎ *407/WDW–TOUR*) for the tours and ☎ *407/939–3463* (☎ *407/WDW–DINE*) for the Grand Floridian programs. Kid-friendly tours and programs are explained in Chapter 10.

Four Months in Advance

❏ To book a fireworks cruise, call ☎ *407/939–7529* (☎ *407/WDW–PLAY*). See Chapter 10 for more information.

❏ Interested in golf, parasailing, surfing, or some other sport? Book your time by calling ☎ *407/939–7529* (☎ *407/WDW–PLAY*). See Chapter 10 for details.

❏ For Cirque du Soleil tickets, call ☎ *407/939–7600* or visit ⊕ *www.cirquedusoleil.com*.

Two Months in Advance

❏ On-site guests should make their FastPass+ reservations.

One Month in Advance

❏ Off-site guests should make their FastPass+ reservations.

Just Before You Leave Home

❏ If you're staying on-site, utilize advance online check-in for your resort. Then you should be good to go. Just reconfirm theme-park hours at ⊕ *www.disneyworld.com* or on the My Disney Experience app, and review your reservations, so when you get to Orlando all you'll have to focus on is having fun.

Useful Websites

Numerous websites provide information and advice on Walt Disney World. Disney's official site, ⊕ *www.disneyworld.com*, is definitely the place to start, but the Disney site will present every ride and restaurant as equally wonderful. For no-holds-barred reviews, check out the following: ⊕ *www.mousesavers.com*, ⊕ *www.disboards.com*, and ⊕ *www.fodors.com/community*.

■**TIP➡ The Magicard, offered through the Orlando Travel Bureau, is a great source of savings for families staying at off-site hotels. You can download the card, as well as get lots of general Orlando information, by visiting ⊕ www.orlandoinfo.com.**

What to Discuss with Your Kids Before You Leave

It's important to include the kids in the vacation planning, so discuss the following topics before you leave home.

The Trip Itself

There are two schools of thought on just how far in advance you should tell the kids you're headed to Disney World. Because many families make reservations as much as a year in advance, it's easy to fall into a "waiting for Christmas" syndrome, with the kids nearly in a lather of anticipation for weeks before you leave. To avoid the agony of a long countdown, one couple packed in secret, then woke the kids up at 5 am and announced, "Get in the car, we're going to Disney World." The best method is probably somewhere in between. Tell your kids at the time you make the reservations and solicit their opinions about what activities to book in advance, but don't begin poring over the brochures in earnest until about a month before the trip.

The Layout of the Parks

Testimonies from the more than 1,500 families surveyed or interviewed for this book have shown that the amount of advance research and planning you do directly correlates with how much you enjoy your trip. There are still some visitors who wing it, showing up with no advance preparations at all, but their comment sheets are peppered with "Next time I'll know . . ." and "If only we had . . ."

If you're letting preteens and teens roam around on their own, brief them on the locations of major attractions, but the pleasures of being prepared can extend even to preschoolers. If you purchase a few Disney World coloring books or a kids' touring guide, even the youngest child will arrive able to identify Spaceship Earth and Splash Mountain. A little knowledge before entering the gates is essential to helping you spend your time in the parks wisely.

> **HELPFUL HINT**
>
> One thing you shouldn't bring with you is the family pet. If you do, board it at the kennel on Disney property, Best Friends Pet Care (☎ 877/493–9738 ⊕ www. bestfriendspetcare.com/ waltdisneyworldresort). They take excellent care of the animals there, and our readers have been impressed with the cleanliness of the facility and professionalism of the staff.

The Classic Stories of Disney

If your kids are under eight, another good pretrip purchase is a set of Disney books with CDs. Even though parental eyes may glaze over when Dumbo starts for the 34th time, these recordings and books help familiarize kids with the characters and rides they'll be seeing once they arrive. "I made sure my 1-year-old was familiar with the Disney characters, but what really helped was buying the Disney Classics CD before the trip," wrote one mom. "We listened to it in the car every day and when we were at Disney, we would get so excited when he heard a song; we knew that he would jump around and try to sing along."

Some families rent Disney movies before the trip. Watching an old favorite like *The Little Mermaid* or *Aladdin* can refresh your child's memory and make it doubly exciting when, a few weeks later, he or she comes face-to-face with the characters in the park.

Special Academic Projects

See the section "Should We Take the Kids Out of School?" earlier in this chapter for ideas. Whatever project you decide on, it's essential you get the kids on board before you arrive in Orlando.

Once there, they'll be too distracted for your lectures on academic responsibility.

Souvenirs and Money

Will you save all souvenir purchases for the last day? Buy one small souvenir every day? Are the children expected to spend their own money, or will you spring for the T-shirts? Whatever you decide, set the rules before you're in the park. Otherwise the selection of goodies will lure you into spending far more than you anticipated. One excellent technique for limiting impulse buys is to give kids a gift card preloaded with a certain amount of spending money.

The Scare Factor

Finally, give some thought to the scare factor. A disappointing meal or boring show can ruin an hour, but misjudging a ride can leave you with a terrified or nauseated child and ruin the whole day.

How frightening a ride is can be tough to gauge because Disney World scariness comes in two forms: the atmospheric or creepy kind (as in the cobwebbed old hotel in the Tower of Terror), or the motion-related kind. And note that while Space Mountain and Expedition Everest are obviously risky, some guests can lose their lunch on sweet little charmers like the Mad Tea Party.

Disney's guidance comes in the form of height requirements, but saying that a 40-inch-tall five-year-old can ride Big Thunder Mountain is no indication that she should. As we all know, some 6-year-olds are fearless and some 11-year-olds easily unnerved. Read the ride descriptions and scare-factor ratings in this book to find out what you're dealing with.

Strategies for Dealing with Fearful Children

✦ If you're still unsure about what you kids can handle, employ these strategies:

✦ **Do a Baby Swap.** (No, this does not mean you can trade your shrieking toddler for that angelic napping infant behind you!)

Height Requirements

Not all rides at Walt Disney World have height requirements. Here are the ones that do.

THE MAGIC KINGDOM

Barnstormer	35 inches
Big Thunder Mountain	40 inches
Seven Dwarfs Mine Train	38 inches
Space Mountain	44 inches
Splash Mountain	40 inches
Stitch's Great Escape	40 inches
Tomorrowland Speedway	32 inches

EPCOT

Mission: SPACE	44 inches
Soarin'	40 inches
Test Track	40 inches

HOLLYWOOD STUDIOS

Rock 'n' Roller Coaster	48 inches
Star Tours	40 inches
Tower of Terror	40 inches

ANIMAL KINGDOM

Dinosaur	40 inches
Expedition Everest	44 inches
Kali River Rapids	38 inches
Primeval Whirl	48 inches

If you have doubts about whether a ride is appropriate for your child, inform the ride attendant that you may need to do a Baby Swap. One parent rides and returns with the verdict while the other parent, who was given a FastPass+ by the attendant, waits with the child. If the first parent thinks the child will do okay, the second parent uses the FastPass+ to immediately board and ride with the child. Otherwise, the second (yet-to-ride) parent uses the FastPass+ to simply ride by him- or herself. It sounds confusing, but the attendants help you, and it actually works smoothly. An added bonus: Older kids in the family often get to ride twice, once with Mom and once with Dad.

✦ **Slowly increase ride intensity throughout the day.** This advice runs counter to the touring tips you'll find later in this book that recommend you ride the big-deal attractions first thing in the morning. But if you're not sure whether your seven-year-old is up for a roller coaster, start her off slowly. Kids who begin with something relatively mild like Pirates of the Caribbean often build up their nerve throughout the day and close out the night on Space Mountain.

✦ **Avoid motion sickness.** Obviously, steer clear of bumpy rides after eating. If you feel queasy on a motion-simulation ride like Star Tours, stare at something inside the cabin, like the seat in front of you, instead of the screen.

The Frantic Factor

Although we rate rides throughout this book according to their "scare factor," we've often thought that we should include ratings on the "frantic factor" as well, measuring how hysterical the average parent is apt to become in any given situation.

We're often asked to speak to parent groups on the topic of family travel. Almost inevitably, someone wants tips on how to make a Disney vacation relaxing. These people are very earnest, but they might as well be asking us to recommend a nice ski lodge for their upcoming trip to Hawaii. The only honest response is, "If you want to relax, you're going to the wrong place."

Don't Leave Home Without...

❑ **Comfortable shoes.** Forget about wearing sandals or slides in the parks—stick to sneakers. This is no time to be breaking in new shoes.

❑ **Minimal clothing.** Many hotels have laundry facilities, and you can always wash clothes in the sink. Most families overpack, not figuring on all the souvenirs they'll bring back. Disney T-shirts are great for touring and can also serve as swimsuit cover-ups and pajamas. Unless you're planning a special evening out at Victoria & Albert's, casual clothing is acceptable everywhere.

❑ **Sunscreen.** Keep a tube with you and reapply it often. Sunburn is the number one complaint at the first-aid clinic in the Magic Kingdom. You need sun protection all through the year in Orlando, not just in summer.

❑ **A waist pack.** Unlike a purse, a waist pack frees up your hands for boarding rides, pushing strollers, and holding on to your kids. A backpack is another option and good for carrying snacks and water, but even a light one can start to hurt your shoulders after a while. Plus, some rides don't allow backpacks, so you may have to keep putting yours in a locker.

❑ **Resealable plastic bags.** Disney serves such large dining portions, even for kiddie meals, that some parents report they save some of the fruit or chips for a snack later.

❑ **Sunglasses.** The Florida sun is so blinding that more than once I've reached into my bag for my sunglasses only to realize I already had them on. Kids too young for sunglasses need wide-billed caps to cut down on the glare.

❑ **Strollers.** Most Orlando hotels are huge, so if you have an infant or toddler, you'll need your own stroller just to get around your lodgings.

Disney World is a high-stimulation environment, a total assault on all five senses mixed in with a constant and mind-boggling array of choices. This is not the week to take your kids off Ritalin or discuss marital issues with your spouse. It helps to keep a sense of humor and to go in with a full understanding that, vacation or not, this is unlikely to be the most relaxing week of your life. As one French mother of three sagely pointed out, "You can sleep later, when Mickey is done with you."

Actually, high stimulation and a lively pace may be the reason most people go to Disney World in the first place. Families who slip over the line from happily stimulated to unhappily frantic often do so because:

✦ They forget to build in adequate rest breaks.

✦ They've planned their trip for the busiest time of the year.

✦ They failed to preplan and showed up with no dining reservations or FastPass+ reservations.

✦ They're confused about the logistics of touring.

✦ They're hell-bent on taking it all in because "We're paying through the nose for this!" and "Who knows when we'll get back?"

This book is full of tips to help you avoid the first four mistakes, but your attitude is pretty much up to you. Just remember that doing it all is not synonymous with having the most fun, and if time is tight, limit your touring to those attractions that have the most appeal for your group. As for when you'll get back, who knows? But using this as a rationale for pushing everyone in the family past his or her exhaustion limit only guarantees that you'll never want to return. The way for parents to relax at Disney (besides spending time in hotel hot tubs with adjacent bars) is to do a little less and enjoy it a little more.

CHAPTER 2

CHOOSING
A HOTEL

To stay on Disney property or to stay off-site? The answer depends entirely on your family and how much you're willing to pay for certain conveniences, such as proximity to the parks.

There are thousands upon thousands of hotel rooms to choose from in the greater Orlando area, with the properties ranging from fabulous to frightening. In this chapter, we'll sort through the decisions you need to make in terms of location, price, amenities, and ambience. There's a lot to consider, but it's worth studying the options because your hotel sets the stage for the rest of your vacation.

In the ratings for the hotels discussed in this chapter are based on three factors: the responses of families surveyed; the percentage of repeat business at resort experiences, which is a reliable indicator of guest satisfaction; and the quality of the resort in relation to the price. Obviously, you'd expect more amenities and a higher employee-to-guest ratio at a $300-a-night resort than at a $100-a-night resort, so it's unfair to hold them to the same standard.

With that in mind, we've rated the hotels on the basis of value for cost. Simply, are you getting what you paid for? Do the advantages of this resort make it worth the price? And would you recommend this resort to families with the same amount of money to spend?

On-Site Disney Hotels

Disney offers advance check-in, which works much like advance check-in for airline flights. By checking in just before you leave home, you can expedite your experience once you arrive at your resort.

Is It Worth the Expense to Stay On-Site?

Staying at one of the Disney-owned hotels is very convenient, and with rates as low as $96 a night at the All-Star resorts and Pop Century Resort, it may be more affordable than you think.

Off-site hotels fight back with special promotions and perks of their own, arguing that the Disney hotels still cost more and bring you only slightly closer to the action. On-site or off-site? Ask yourself the following questions to help you decide:

What time of year are you going?

If you're visiting Disney World in summer or during a major holiday, you'll need every extra minute, so it's worth the cost to stay on-site.

How old are your kids?

In the Florida heat and humidity, it's nearly a medical necessity to keep young kids out of the sun in the middle of the afternoon, and an on-site hotel makes it easier to return for a nap. If your kids are preteens or teens who can handle a whole day in the parks, the commute is less of a factor.

Are you flying or driving?

If you're flying and doing only Disney World, it may make more economic sense to stay on-site and use Disney World's transportation system in lieu of a rental car. If you're driving to Orlando, it may be as easy to stay off-site. You'll be able to drive into the parks at hours that suit you without having to rely on shuttles.

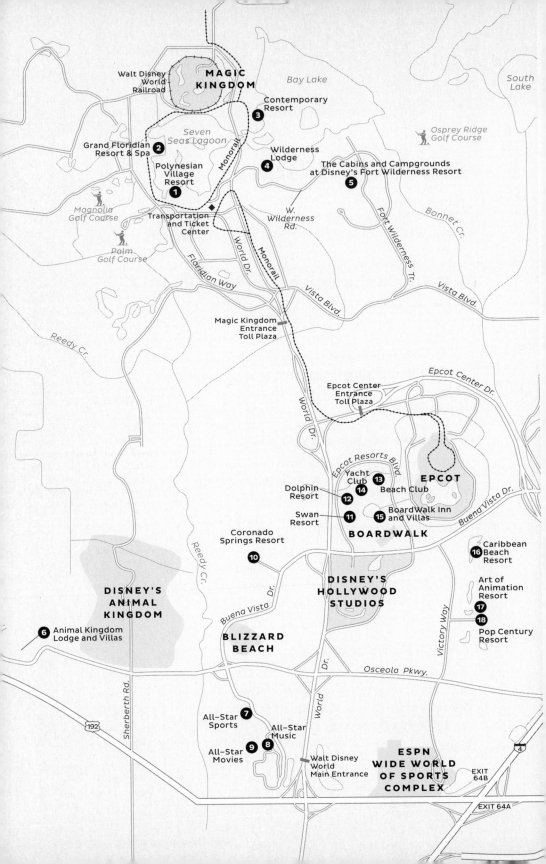

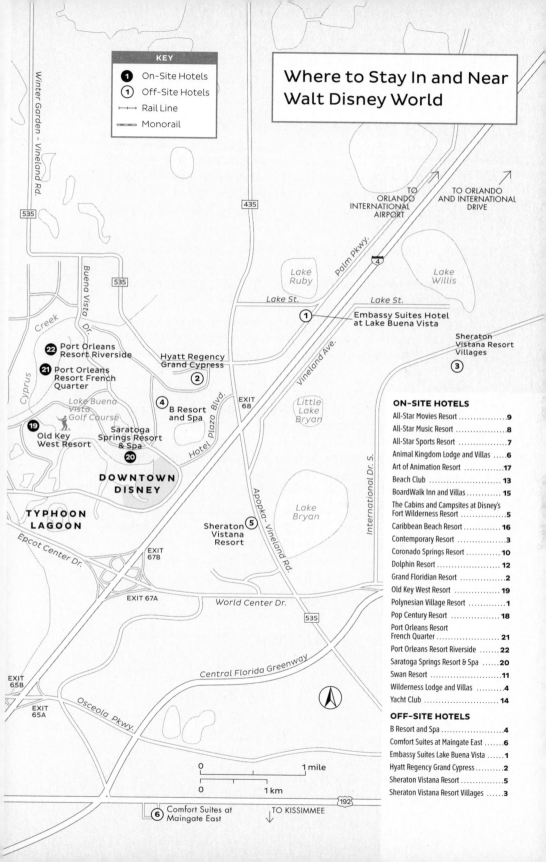

Where to Stay In and Near Walt Disney World

KEY

- **1** On-Site Hotels
- (1) Off-Site Hotels
- ⊢—⊣ Rail Line
- Monorail

22 Port Orleans Resort Riverside

21 Port Orleans Resort French Quarter

Hyatt Regency Grand Cypress **(2)**

(4) B Resort and Spa

19 Old Key West Resort

Saratoga Springs Resort & Spa **20**

DOWNTOWN DISNEY

TYPHOON LAGOON

Lake Buena Vista Golf Course

(1) Embassy Suites Hotel at Lake Buena Vista

Sheraton Vistana Resort Villages **(3)**

Sheraton Vistana Resort **(5)**

(6) Comfort Suites at Maingate East

Lake Ruby

Lake Willis

Little Lake Bryan

Lake Bryan

TO ORLANDO INTERNATIONAL AIRPORT

TO ORLANDO AND INTERNATIONAL DRIVE

ON-SITE HOTELS

All-Star Movies Resort	**9**
All-Star Music Resort	**8**
All-Star Sports Resort	**7**
Animal Kingdom Lodge and Villas	**6**
Art of Animation Resort	**17**
Beach Club	**13**
BoardWalk Inn and Villas	**15**
The Cabins and Campsites at Disney's Fort Wilderness Resort	**5**
Caribbean Beach Resort	**16**
Contemporary Resort	**3**
Coronado Springs Resort	**10**
Dolphin Resort	**12**
Grand Floridian Resort	**2**
Old Key West Resort	**19**
Polynesian Village Resort	**1**
Pop Century Resort	**18**
Port Orleans Resort French Quarter	**21**
Port Orleans Resort Riverside	**22**
Saratoga Springs Resort & Spa	**20**
Swan Resort	**11**
Wilderness Lodge and Villas	**4**
Yacht Club	**14**

OFF-SITE HOTELS

B Resort and Spa	**4**
Comfort Suites at Maingate East	**6**
Embassy Suites Lake Buena Vista	**1**
Hyatt Regency Grand Cypress	**2**
Sheraton Vistana Resort	**5**
Sheraton Vistana Resort Villages	**3**

0 — 1 mile

0 — 1 km

TO KISSIMMEE

Things to Know about On-Site Hotels

Disney's on-site hotels vary about as much as hotels can, and they appeal to different budgets and interests, but there are seven things all of them have in common:

✦ Disney hotels operate under the family plan, meaning that kids under 18 stay free with parents.

✦ Check-in time is 3 pm at most Disney hotels. If you arrive before your room is ready, you can check in, store your bags, pick up your MagicBands (if you haven't already received them by mail), and go straight to the parks.

✦ Checkout time is 11 am, but, once again, you need not let this interfere with your touring. Check out early in the morning, store your bags, then go enjoy your last day in the parks.

✦ When you check in, you'll be issued a room key/resort ID—usually in the form of a MagicBand that allows you to charge meals, drinks, tickets, and souvenirs to your room and gives you access to all Disney World transportation. You can also add theme-park admission. If you've chosen the dining plan, your resort ID serves as your meal pass. In short, one card or MagicBand does it all.

✦ If you pay with a credit card, you can arrange for automatic checkout—a definite time-saver. An itemized statement is emailed to you on the day of your departure. If it's correct, you can keep it as your receipt and leave immediately.

✦ All on-site hotels have a food court and a bar. In-room pizza delivery is another option for families on the run.

✦ On-site guests get free parking, both at their hotel and at the theme parks.

What's your budget?

If money isn't a major issue, stay on-site. If money is a primary consideration, you'll find your best deals at the budget hotels along Interstate 4. Exits 62 and 68, which flank Disney World, are chock-full of chain hotels and restaurants.

How much do your kids eat?

Food is expensive at Disney World, both in the parks and at the on-site hotels. If you're staying off-site, you can always eat in the numerous fast-food and family-style restaurants along Interstate 4, Route 192, and International Drive. Many off-site hotels have complimentary breakfast buffets, while the all-suites properties have in-room kitchenettes where you can fix your own meals.

■TIP➜ **Disney doesn't discount often, but when times are slow they're as eager to fill their rooms as any other hotel chain. The trouble is that they don't always announce these discounts. When you call to make your reservations, always ask, "Are there any special offers available during the times I'll be visiting?"**

Do you plan to visit other attractions?

If you'll be spending half your time at Universal Orlando or the other non–Disney World attractions, stay off-site—at least during those days. There's no need to pay top dollar for proximity to Disney if you're headed for Islands of Adventure.

Will your party be splitting up at times?

Does Dad want to golf one afternoon? Do you have teenagers who can spend a day at Blizzard Beach on their own? Will there be times when it would make sense for Dad to take the younger kids back to the hotel while Mom stays in the park with the older ones? Is your 5-year-old raring to go at dawn, but your 15-year-old sleeps until noon? If so, stay on-site, where the use of the Disney World transportation system makes it easy for each of you to go your own way.

What's your tolerance level for hassles?

If you don't want to deal with interstate traffic, big parking lots, toting luggage, and carrying cash or credit cards, stay on-site.

The Advantages of Staying On-Site

Disney offers its guests certain extra services that are not available to anyone else. In short, they entice you to spend more time with them, and many of these extras are worth considering.

Extra Magic Hours

Extra Magic Hours work like this: Each day, year-round, one of the four major theme parks opens for Disney resort guests an hour early or stays open an extra hour or two after the regular closing time. Mondo perk! This gives resort guests the chance to ride some featured attractions and greet the characters in a relatively uncrowded park. (Note the word "relatively." There are so many Disney resort guests that there are still plenty of people around, just not as many as usual.)

When you check into your hotel you'll receive a brochure printed with the Extra Magic Hours schedule for the week; if you'd like this information in advance to help with your planning, visit 🌐 *www.disneyworld.com,* where you'll find "Park Hours" under "Parks & Tickets."

Generally, only a few attractions per park are open for the Extra Magic Hour, but this is your chance to ride them easily. Just as important is that in the morning you'll be deep inside the theme park when it officially opens so you can dash to other big-deal attractions before the rest of the crowd gets there.

For morning Extra Magic Hours your resort ID or MagicBand gets you into the park to ride anything that's up and running. For evening Extra Magic Hours you'll need to show your resort ID or MagicBand to board the rides.

FastPass+

On-site guests can make their FastPass+ reservations 60 days in advance. This is a huge boon during the busiest times. It allows you to get a jump on off-site guests (as well as other on-site guests who don't understand the value of this perk) in terms of reserving prime times for the most popular attractions. Read the

> **INSIDER'S SECRET**
>
> The on-site resorts often have fun little activities for kids such as scavenger hunts, pool races, trivia contests, or dance parties. Activity schedules are posted in the pool areas and child-care centers.

theme-park chapters and decide how you want to spend your three FastPass+ choices per day, and then reserve them ASAP.

Magical Express Service

The Magical Express Service allows you to check your bags at your hometown airport and not see them again until you walk into your hotel room in Walt Disney World. You also get free shuttle service from the Orlando airport to your resort.

When it's time to go home, the system works in reverse. You check your bags and receive your boarding passes before departing from your Disney resort. Take another complimentary shuttle back to the airport and go directly to your flight. Your luggage will be waiting for you at baggage claim in your hometown. This also saves you the inconvenience of having to store your bags on the last day of your trip.

The service is supposed to save you time and money, but in reality it doesn't always work seamlessly. Quite a few readers have complained of long delays, and one dad dubbed the system "Magical Distress." Comments range from "We stopped at three hotels, and it took over an hour to get to ours from the airport" to "Thanks to this so-called benefit we began the whole trip with confusion and irritation."

But families have also praised the perk, agreeing with the Chicago mom who wrote, "It's like Disney starts taking care of you the minute your plane wheels touch down in Orlando." The consensus seems to be that the system works well at times when it's not too crowded, but during peak travel times slow service is common. If you're traveling at such a time, consider handling your own bags and arranging for your own transportation between the airport and your hotel.

Transportation

On-site guests have unlimited use of the monorails, buses, and boats of the WDW transportation system. Between this and the Magical Express Service, many on-site guests find they are able to forgo the cost of a rental car.

Free Parking at the Theme Parks

You don't have to pay the $17 daily fee to park. The attendant will wave you through when she sees the resort parking ID on your dashboard.

Package Delivery

Don't lug your souvenirs around while touring. When you make a purchase, you can fill out a form, and Disney will deliver the package to your hotel gift shop for free. Your purchases generally don't show up until the next day, however, so don't use the service on the last day of your visit.

> **HELPFUL HINT**
>
> If you lose a MagicBand or room card with charging privileges, report it to the front desk immediately to avoid unauthorized charges. They can cancel it and issue you a new one.

MagicBand and Charging Privileges

Talk about hassle-free. This all-in-one wristband (or plastic card, if you prefer) that you receive upon check-in is your room key, theme-park ticket, FastPass+ reservation system, and dining-plan credit card. It also allows adults (and kids, if you opt to give them privileges) to charge tickets, food, and souvenirs to their hotel room. It's certainly easier not to have to carry around huge amounts of cash, especially at the pool, water parks, and marinas.

It's up to you whether older kids have charging privileges. Giving them the card makes it easier to send Johnny to the snack bar for a round of Cokes, but be sure to impress upon kids that these IDs work like credit cards. They're not an open invitation to order pizza for all their new friends at the arcade, purchase all seven dwarfs from the hotel gift shop, or, heaven forbid, obtain cash advances.

Dining Plans

Many families swear by the Disney Dining Plan, which can be added to any on-site package. The plan saves you from having to carry around cash and—at least on the surface—masks the sting of coughing up 12 bucks for a cheeseburger.

Family Atmosphere

All the on-site hotels are designed with families in mind. The ambience is casual, security is tight, and there are always other children around to play with. The on-site hotels have laundry facilities, generally near the pools and arcades, so that you can run a quick load while the youngsters play; there's late-night pizza delivery to your room; and if there's not a child-care facility at your particular hotel, Guest Relations (a.k.a. Guest Services) can help you arrange for an in-room sitter. The emphasis at the Disney hotels is on making life more convenient for parents.

Cool Themes

All the on-site hotels have themes that are carried out in mega-detail. At the Polynesian the staff greets you with "Aloha"; at the Port Orleans, jazz music plays all day; and at the All-Star Sports the dressers in the rooms look like gym lockers. This makes staying at an on-site hotel almost as exciting for kids as being inside the parks.

In fact, because the on-site hotels are all so different from each other, it's fun to visit other hotels. Many families surveyed told us they enjoyed eating dinner at a different resort from their own.

Location, Location, Location

Proximity to the theme parks makes it easier to return to your room after lunch for a nap, a dip in the pool, or a change of clothes.

Evaluating the On-Site Disney Hotels

The Orlando area has more than 140,000 hotel rooms, and a fair percentage of these are owned by Disney. In other words, a family who has already decided to stay on-site still faces a bewildering number of choices. Does the convenience of being on the monorail line justify the increase in price? Do you want to stay amid Victorian splendor, or is a fort more your style? At which park do you plan to spend most of your time? As with all of WDW, making the best choice hinges on your awareness of what your family really needs.

Available Accommodations

On-Site Luxury Hotels

Luxury hotels are full-scale resorts with fine dining, health clubs and spas, valet parking, on-site child-care facilities, full room service, and lots of sporting options. There's a price attached—the Disney luxury hotels cost, on average, twice as much a night as the mid-price hotels. Luxury hotels include the BoardWalk, Yacht and Beach clubs, Contemporary, Grand Floridian, Polynesian, Swan, Dolphin, Wilderness Lodge, and Animal Kingdom Lodge. (Note: The Wilderness Lodge and Animal Kingdom Lodge are at the lowest price point in the luxury category.)

On-Site Mid-Price Hotels

"Mid-price" is something of a misnomer, because both the price and the quality are higher than what you'd find in an off-site chain hotel in Orlando. You may pay a little more than you might at a typical Hilton Garden Inn, but the hotels are beautifully maintained and landscaped, with their themes carried out to the nth degree. Resorts that fall into this category include the Caribbean Beach, Port Orleans, and Coronado Springs.

On-Site Value Hotels

The on-site value hotels include the All-Star resorts, the Pop Century Resort, and the Art of Animation Resort.

Again, the resorts are well maintained and have eye-popping, catchy graphics that dazzle the kids. You can find a food court but no sit-down dining; a swimming pool but no other sporting options; a lengthier check-in line and smaller staff, but rates that more than compensate for the minor inconveniences. The most important on-site benefits—transportation to the parks, help with tickets and priority-seating reservations, MagicBands, Extra Magic Hours, and charging privileges—are just as available to those paying $96 a night at All-Star Sports as to those paying $396 a night at the BoardWalk. And, hey, the housekeepers still leave your kids' stuffed animals in the window to greet them in the evening, so who can complain?

Villa-Style Accommodations

Larger families or those who like to prepare their own meals may want to rent a villa. Resorts included in this category are Bay Lake Tower at the Contemporary Resort, Wilderness Lodge Villas, Saratoga Springs Resort, BoardWalk Villas, Grand Floridian Villas, Beach Club Villas, Animal Kingdom Lodge Villas, the Art of Animation Resort, and Old Key West Resort. The new Polynesian villas are under construction at this writing and promise to be especially glamorous and evocative.

On-Site Camping

The Fort Wilderness Campground is a great choice for families who love to camp and is by far the least expensive way to get on-site privileges.

Recommended Disney On-Site Hotels

We've rated each hotel with a score of one to three stars to represent our opinions about the quality of the hotel and the accommodations it offers.

★ ★ ★ This resort was a favorite among families surveyed and offers solid value for the money.

★ ★ Surveyed families were satisfied with this resort and felt they got what they paid for.

★ This resort is either more adult-oriented, with fewer amenities designed to appeal to families, or is more expensive than you'd expect considering the location or level of service.

Magic Kingdom Hotels

If the Magic Kingdom is your focus and you're willing to pay up, consider these resorts.

$$
★★   **THE CABINS AND CAMPSITES AT DISNEY'S FORT WILDERNESS RESORT**

Fort Wilderness has campsites for tents and oversize, concrete parking pads for RVs as well as air-conditioned cabins. The cabins, which sleep six, rent for approximately the same nightly rate as a luxury hotel. The wide-open spaces of the campground are perfect for volleyball, biking, and exploring, making the resort a

Quick Guide to

On-Site Hotels

Hotel	Description
Bay Lake Tower at Disney's Contemporary Resort	Sophisticated, high-tech villas adjacent to Contemporary Resort
The Cabins and Campsites at Disney's Fort Wilderness Resort	Great for families who like to camp
Disney's All-Star Resorts	Very popular, great price
Disney's Animal Kingdom Lodge	An exotic African theme
Disney's Animal Kingdom Lodge Villas	Beautifully themed details, great views of animals
Disney's Art of Animation Resort	Elaborate theming and value-priced suites
Disney's Beach Club Resort	Homey, lovely, and fantastic pool area
Disney's Beach Club Villas	Big suites in a great location
Disney's BoardWalk Inn	Rooms are spacious, modern, and attractive
Disney's BoardWalk Villas	Great location for both Epcot and Hollywood Studios
Disney's Caribbean Beach Resort	Tropical theme and the price is right
Disney's Contemporary Resort	Convenient and lively
Disney's Coronado Springs Resort	Elaborate pool with pyramid slide
Disney's Grand Floridian Resort	Expensive and luxurious
Disney's Old Key West Resort	Lots of room, quiet
Disney's Polynesian Resort	Relaxed and casual with a loyal, repeat clientele
Disney's Pop Century Resort	5,760 budget rooms, lively theme
Disney's Port Orleans Resort	With French Quarter or Riverside options

Note: The central reservations number for on-site hotels is 407/W-DISNEY.

On-Site Hotels

Location or Nearest Theme Park	Rating	Price Range
Magic Kingdom	★★★	$533–$1,653
Magic Kingdom	★★	$56–$148 (sites), $330–$541 (cabins)
Animal Kingdom	★★	$96–$216 (standard room), $240–$450 (suite)
Animal Kingdom	★★★	$320–$2,300
Animal Kingdom	★★★	$420–$1,573
ESPN Wide World of Sports Complex	★★	$118–$249 (standard room), $299–$487 (suite)
Epcot	★★★	$394–$2,404
Epcot	★★★	$400–$1,444
Epcot	★★★	$411–$1,182
Epcot	★★★	$405–$1,444
Epcot	★★	$182–$367
Magic Kingdom	★★	$378–$3,129
Animal Kingdom	★★	$205–$1,534
Magic Kingdom	★★	$549–$3,007
Downtown Disney	★★	$368–$1,119
Magic Kingdom	★★★	$483–$1,554
ESPN Wide World of Sports Complex	★	$106–$231
Downtown Disney	★★★	$182–$369

Quick Guide to On-Site

On-Site Hotels

Hotel	Description
Disney's Saratoga Springs Resort & Spa	Amazing grotto pool, spacious
Disney's Wilderness Lodge	Rustic-looking, with an intimate feel
Disney's Wilderness Lodge Villas	Great setting, a bit more space
Disney's Yacht Club Resort	At the door of the World Showcase
Walt Disney World Dolphin Hotel	Adult atmosphere, great restaurant selection
Walt Disney World Swan Hotel	Adult-oriented, great water areas

Off-Site Hotels

Hotel	Description
B Resort and Spa	Funky decor and great location, good choice for teens and older kids
Cabana Bar Beach Resort	Family friendly, with tons of amenties, and a true resort feel
Comfort Suites at Maingate East	Inexpensive but close to Disney, free breakfast, best value for suites
Embassy Suites Lake Buena Vista	Good location, free breakfast buffet, lots of sporting activities
Hyatt Regency Grand Cypress	Luxury hotel, magnificent pool, camplike activities for kids
La Quinta International Drive North	Convenient location for all three parks, free breakfast and shuttles
Magical Memories Villas	Private homes and condos, for rent, good choice for large families
Residence Inn Orlando at SeaWorld	Quiet and homelike suites, SeaWorld packages, free breakfasts
Sheraton Vistana Resort	Popular with our readers— well maintained and quiet
Sheraton Vistana Village	Popular with our readers— well-maintained and plenty to do
Universal Resorts: Cabana Bay, Hard Rock, Portofino Bay, Royal Pacific	Three great options on Universal Orlando property

Note: The central reservations number for on-site hotels is 407/W-DISNEY.

and Off-Site Hotels

Location or Nearest Theme Park	Rating	Price Range
Downtown Disney	★★	$368–$1,287
Magic Kingdom	★★★	$325–$1,024
Magic Kingdom	★★★	$420–$1,438
Epcot	★★★	$400–$2,437
Epcot	★	$299–$517
Epcot	★	$299–$517
Downtown Disney	★★★	$149 and up
Universal Orlando	★★★	$139 and up
Walt Disney World	★★	$89 and up
Walt Disney World	★★	$113 and up
Walt Disney World	★★★	$195 and up
Universal Studios, SeaWorld	★★	$74 and up
Depends on location	n/a	$109 and up, most $144 and up
SeaWorld	★★	$94 and up
Walt Disney World	★★	$140 and up
Equidistant from all	★★	$140 and up
Universal Orlando	★★	$219 and up

good choice for families with kids old enough to enjoy all the outdoor options. "Fort Wilderness lights two campfires every night for marshmallow roastings and sing-alongs," reported one mom from Maine. "The s'mores packages, which are $7 and include toasting sticks, are a real bargain, and after the singing a Disney movie is shown in the amphitheater under the stars. Perfect!" ■**TIP→ Fort Wilderness Campground is so sprawling that many families rent a golf cart to make it easier to get around.**

HELPFUL HINT

Disneyworld.com is a great planning tool, allowing you to compare the prices of different on-site hotels during the week you'll be visiting. You can comparison shop at leisure without a travel agent or phone reservation agent nudging you into a quick decision.

Proximity to the Magic Kingdom:	Good, via bus or launch
Proximity to Epcot:	Fair, via bus
Proximity to Hollywood:	Fair, via bus
Proximity to the Animal Kingdom:	Fair, via bus

Pluses

+ Fort Wilderness offers tons of activities for kids: wagon rides, horseback and pony riding, and a petting zoo.

+ Hookups and tent sites, starting at $56, are your cheapest lodging options. The upgraded campsites start at $75 a night. Fort Wilderness Cabins start at $330 a night.

+ Groceries are available at the on-site trading post. And the bountiful buffets at the Trail's End restaurant are one of the best food bargains on Disney property.

+ Fort Wilderness is pet-friendly; dogs have a playground at the Waggin' Trails, an off-leash play area.

Minuses

− A large number of people share relatively few facilities here.

– This place is so spread out that it requires its own in-resort bus system to get you from one area to another. You can rent golf carts or bikes, but make no mistake: Fort Wilderness is huge and hard to navigate.

Overall Grade: If you like to camp and can put up with a little inconvenience for great savings, this is a good option. ✉ *4510 N. Fort Wilderness Trail* ☎ *407/824-2900* ↗ *799 campsites, 421 cabins.*

$$$$
★★
DISNEY'S CONTEMPORARY RESORT

You'll either love or hate Disney's original, always-hopping resort, which has nearly 1,050 rooms surrounding a mammoth, high-tech lobby full of shops and restaurants. The glamorous Bay Lake Tower Villas are sleek and user-friendly, and the location of the more expensive rooms is among the best on property. Where else can you sit in your own bathtub and watch the Magic Kingdom fireworks?

Proximity to the Magic Kingdom:	Excellent, via monorail
Proximity to Epcot:	Good, via monorail with a change at the Transportation and Ticket Center (TTC)
Proximity to Hollywood:	Fair, via bus
Proximity to the Animal Kingdom:	Fair, via bus

Pluses

+ On the monorail line.

+ The easiest Magic Kingdom resort to book; discounts are sometimes available.

+ Exceptional sporting options, including WDW's largest tennis center and a full marina with parasailing and waterskiing options.

+ Outstanding dining choices, including the California Grill, one of Disney's premier restaurants; The Wave, which is excellent for breakfast; and Chef Mickey's, a great place to meet the characters for breakfast and dinner.

Minuses

— It's loud, with a big-city feel, which is exactly what some families come to Florida to escape. "Like sleeping in the middle of Space Mountain," wrote one mother. However, rooms in the Garden Wings are quieter, cheaper, and more spacious than those in the main building.

— The futuristic ambience strikes some guests as sterile and ugly. "The pool area reminded me of a scene from a 1970s B-movie that would depict future decay," wrote one disgruntled Canadian dad. "I expected Charlton Heston to come around the corner any minute, being chased by apes."

— Like all the other hotels on the monorail line, the Contemporary is expensive, with prices starting at $378 a night. Bay Lake Tower starts at $533, but can quickly climb higher.

Overall Grade: Convenient and lively. Perhaps a little too lively. ✉ 4600 N. World Dr. ☎ 407/824–1000 🛏 1,013 rooms, 25 suites.

$$$ ★★ DISNEY'S GRAND FLORIDIAN RESORT

Modeled after the famed Florida beach resorts of the Victorian era, the Grand Floridian is possibly the prettiest of all Disney hotels, with more than 900 rooms ensconced beneath its gabled roofs and soaring ceilings, and off its broad white verandas. This elegant and stately lady is also the hub of many activities, including a variety of programs for children. The Grand Floridian Disney Vacation Club villas offer a charming Alice in Wonderland–theme water-play area.

Proximity to the Magic Kingdom:	Excellent, via monorail or launch
Proximity to Epcot:	Good, via monorail with a change at the TTC
Proximity to Hollywood:	Fair, via bus
Proximity to the Animal Kingdom:	Fair, via bus

Best On-Site Hotels at a Glance

Many of the on-site Disney hotels are great, but here are our favorites:

BEST MAGIC KINGDOM RESORT: POLYNESIAN

Always a favorite with readers, the lovely Polynesian combines a casual, family-friendly feel with great amenities and unbeatable access to the Magic Kingdom.

BEST EPCOT RESORT: THE YACHT AND BEACH CLUBS

You like Epcot and Hollywood Studios? They're both easy to get to from this prime location—and the pool is to die for.

BEST MID-PRICE RESORT: PORT ORLEANS

Relaxed and homey, the Port Orleans resorts have the charm of the luxury resorts for less. The French Quarter, smaller and quieter than its sister, Riverside, is easier for families with young kids, and the pool area is adorable.

BEST VALUE RESORT: POP CENTURY

Pop Century has recently overtaken the All-Star resorts in this category, largely due to more efficient bus service.

BEST FAMILY SUITES: THE ART OF ANIMATION RESORT

These value-priced suites come with a great water area and compact but visually exciting spaces for families. One of the greatest perks is that each suite has two bathrooms, which are very useful in the morning when you're all rushing to get ready.

BEST VILLAS: BAY LAKE TOWER AT THE CONTEMPORARY

The trendy Bay Lake Tower has a major wow factor, and the location is unparalleled.

Pluses

+ Convenient location on monorail line.

+ A private beach and marina on the Seven Seas Lagoon and numerous boating options.

+ On-site child-care center and programs for children.

+ On-site health club and full-service spa.

+ Exceptional array of restaurant choices. Cítricos and Victoria & Albert's are among the finest restaurants in all of WDW. For more casual and kid-friendly dining, check out 1900 Park Fare, which hosts breakfast and dinner character buffets.

+ Lots of special little touches, such as afternoon tea and live music in the lobby each night.

> **HELPFUL HINT**
>
> The Disney Vacation Club, or DVC, is Disney's answer to vacation time-shares. Members receive an allotted number of days per year to use at a Disney resort, but you do not have to be a member of the DVC to rent a villa. Call ☎407/934–7639 (☎407/W–DISNEY) for information on available villas during your stay.

Minuses

– Starting at $549, these are the most expensive rooms on Disney property.

– The elegance puts off some families, who feel funny trooping past a grand piano with squalling babies in their arms.

Overall Grade: Luxurious and expensive. ✉ *4401 Floridian Way* ☎*407/824-3000* ⤴*867 rooms, 90 suites.*

$$$
★★★
DISNEY'S POLYNESIAN VILLAGE RESORT

Designed to emulate an island village, the Polynesian is relaxed and casual. Activities take place at the Great Ceremonial House, where all the shops and restaurants encircle a beautiful garden with orchids, parrots, and fountains. Guests stay in one of the sprawling "long houses" along the lagoon. "The Polynesian was worth every penny," wrote one satisfied mom from Connecticut:

"The rooms were gorgeous, and we sat on the beach two magical nights in a row to catch the Magic Kingdom fireworks."

Proximity to the Magic Kingdom:	Excellent, via direct monorail, boat launch, or ferry
Proximity to Epcot:	Good, via monorail with one change at the TTC
Proximity to Hollywood:	Fair, via bus
Proximity to the Animal Kingdom:	Fair, via bus

Pluses

+ There's a private beach with an attractive pool, a hot tub, plus numerous boating options. Canvas shells shade napping babies and toddlers digging in the sand, and a new water play area for older kids is a blast.

+ The Kona Café is one of the best places for desserts in all of Disney World.

+ Excellent on-site child-care center (Lilo's Clubhouse) with five distinct sections for kids to enjoy; contact them well in advance for reservations.

+ The recently refurbished rooms are some of the prettiest on Disney property.

+ Technically there's no spa here, but the Grand Floridian's excellent spa is on a walkway between the two hotels—close enough that it's easily accessible.

+ The new Disney Vacation Club villas are among the most beautiful and exotic rooms in all of Disney World. Each as its own hot tub.

Minuses

− Without a discount, expect to pay $483 a night and up.

Overall Grade: The Polynesian enjoys a loyal repeat clientele, and that says it all. ✉ *1600 Seven Seas Dr.* ☎ *407/824–2000* ↪ *847 rooms, 5 suites.*

$$$
★★★

DISNEY'S WILDERNESS LODGE AND VILLAS

Starting at $325 a night, the Western-spirited Wilderness Lodge is aimed at filling the gap between the mid-price and luxury resorts. The theme of the Wilderness Lodge extends into every aspect of the hotel's design. The pool begins indoors as a hot spring and flows through the lobby into a waterfall that tumbles over rocky caverns and culminates in the outdoor pool. The awe-inspiring lobby, which looks like a Lincoln Log project run amok, centers on an 82-foot fireplace that blazes all year. The Native American–theme wallpaper, the staff dressed like park rangers, and even the hobby horses children ride to their tables in the Whispering Canyon Café all combine to evoke the feel of a National Park Service lodge built in the early 1900s.

Proximity to the Magic Kingdom:	Good, via launch
Proximity to Epcot:	Fair, via launch followed by a transfer to monorail. You can also take the bus, but expect longer-than-average commute times.
Proximity to Hollywood:	Fair, via bus, but expect longer-than-average commutes.
Proximity to the Animal Kingdom:	Fair, via bus, but expect longer-than-average commutes.

Pluses

+ The lodge is heavily themed, and the pool area, with its erupting geyser and stone hot tubs, is especially dramatic.

+ On-site child-care facilities.

+ Tons of happy quasi-campers here. Families return to the Wilderness Lodge again and again.

+ The Wilderness Lodge Villas, starting at $420 a night, provide all the great amenities and a little more space.

Minuses

- Although it's one of the least expensive luxury options, it still isn't cheap.

- This is the only Magic Kingdom resort hotel without direct monorail service. The boat takes slightly longer than the bus. And bus service is frequently shared with Fort Wilderness, which means an extra stop on the way to the theme parks.

- The rooms are small and sleep only four people; the other luxury resorts sleep five. "It's a great resort once you get outside of your room," said a mom from Indiana. "But while inside the room we were practically on top of each other."

Overall Grade: A great family-pleasing setting and a favorite with many of our readers. ✉ *901 Timberline Dr.* ☎ *407/824-3200* ↘ *727 rooms, 31 suites.*

Epcot Hotels

Most of the Epcot resorts—the Yacht and Beach clubs, Board-Walk, Swan, and Dolphin—share their own "back-door" entrance into Epcot's World Showcase, accessed by water taxis and walkways. Unfortunately—and somewhat ironically, considering that these properties are marketed as "Epcot resorts"—it can be tricky to get to Epcot's front gates. The Future World section of Epcot usually opens at 9 am, but Epcot resort guests enter through the World Showcase, where the rides, shops, and restaurants don't open until 11 am. That means guests have to walk through the World Showcase and enter Future World at a special rope-drop area. (Many people assume that the Epcot hotels offer bus service to the main entrance of Epcot. They don't.) The bad news is that this stroll through the World Showcase adds 10 minutes to your commute. The good news is that there are fewer people at this entrance point, so you can still get a jump on the crowds, a key factor if you're heading to a popular attraction like Soarin'.

By contrast, getting to Hollywood is a breeze. Water taxis leaving from the Epcot resort marinas will have you at the Hollywood gates within minutes. In addition, there are plenty of restaurants, clubs, and entertainment options around the lagoon.

"We never left the Epcot resort area," wrote one mom from Texas. "Everything we wanted to do was right there."

The one Epcot hotel that doesn't follow this plan is the Caribbean Beach Resort, which is a mid-price property located a bit apart from the others. It runs buses to both Hollywood Studios and Epcot; the Epcot bus lets you off at the Future World entrance.

$$$
★★★

DISNEY'S BOARDWALK INN AND VILLAS

The BoardWalk Inn and Villas form the hub of a large complex with convention space, several restaurants and shops, the ESPN sports club, and a dance club and piano bar. The mood is turn-of-the-20th-century Atlantic City. Bright, attractive rooms are clustered above an old-fashioned boardwalk, and the action on the waterfront goes on until late at night.

"Once you stay at the BoardWalk, nothing else is good enough," wrote one enthusiastic grandmother of two in Ohio. "The location is perfect for both Epcot and Hollywood, and there's always free entertainment, like jugglers or comedians, to keep the kids happy."

Proximity to the Magic Kingdom:	Fair, via bus
Proximity to Epcot:	Excellent, via a short stroll or water taxi
Proximity to Hollywood:	Excellent, via water taxi
Proximity to the Animal Kingdom:	Fair, via bus

Pluses

+ Lots of entertainment: surrey (two-person, four-wheel) bikes for rent, midway games, and a wider variety of restaurants and bars than you'd find at most resorts.

+ On-site health club.

+ On-site child-care facilities.

+ Great location for both Epcot and Hollywood.

+ Great restaurant choices, including the excellent Flying Fish Café.

Minuses

- Expensive, at $411 and up per night.

- Maybe too lively and hopping for families with very young kids. The boardwalk can get loud at night.

Overall Grade: You'll feel like you're right in the middle of the action—because you are. ✉ *2101 Epcot Resorts Blvd.* ☎ *407/939-5100* ↗ *372 rooms.*

$$
★★
$$

DISNEY'S CARIBBEAN BEACH RESORT

This family-priced, 2,112-room resort is on 200 acres with a private lake surrounded by beaches. Each section of this mammoth hotel is painted a different tropical color and named for a different Caribbean island, and each "island" has its own shuttle-bus stop, beach, and pool with waterslide. The rooms, although small, are attractively decorated—some have a *Pirates of the Caribbean* or *Finding Nemo* theme. There's a nightly surcharge of $25–$50 (depending on the season) for these special rooms.

Proximity to the Magic Kingdom:	Fair, via bus
Proximity to Epcot:	Fair, via bus
Proximity to Hollywood:	Fair, via bus
Proximity to the Animal Kingdom:	Fair, via bus

Pluses

+ The price is right, starting at $182 a night.

+ The Pirate and Nemo rooms are absolutely adorable and themed to the max—for example, some of the furniture looks like cargo chests. "A little cheesy, but our boys flipped out with joy," said a mom from Texas. "The excitement was well worth the extra $25 a night!"

+ Caribbean Cay, an artificial island with a playground, climbing fort, and small aviary, is fun for young kids.

+ The pirate-themed water-play area, which offers small slides and fountains, is a hit with young kids.

+ A marina with watercraft is available.

Minuses

– Although the buses are regular, they stop at all of the resort's many "islands." Expect a considerably longer commute time to the parks.

– The place is huge. It may be a major hike from your hotel room to the food plaza or marina. If you have young kids, bring your own stroller.

Overall Grade: All the moderate-price resorts offer solid value for the money, but due to its size, Caribbean Beach is overwhelming. Try the others first. ⊠ *900 Cayman Way* ☎ *407/934-3400* ↝ *2,112 rooms.*

$$$
★★★
DISNEY YACHT AND BEACH CLUBS

Designed to resemble a turn-of-the-20th-century Nantucket seaside resort, the Yacht Club and Beach Club are side-by-side resorts that share many facilities. Both hotels are charming yet casual, with sunny, airy rooms overlooking a freshwater lake and a wide variety of restaurants and sporting options.

Proximity to the Magic Kingdom:	Fair, via bus
Proximity to Epcot:	Excellent, via a short stroll or water taxi
Proximity to Hollywood:	Excellent, via water taxi
Proximity to the Animal Kingdom:	Fair, via bus

Pluses

+ Stormalong Bay, the water recreation area the two resorts share, is like a private water park. The sand-bottom "bay" contains pools of varying depths, whirlpools, waterslides, and a wrecked ship for atmosphere.

+ On-site child-care facilities.

+ Disney characters are on hand for breakfast at the Cape May Café in the Beach Club.

+ The two resorts share an on-site health club.

Minuses

− Price is the only real drawback. Rates begin at $400 per night.

Overall Grade: These hotels enjoy a lot of repeat business from satisfied families. ✉ *1700 Epcot Resorts Blvd.* ☎ *407/934–8000 Beach Club, 407/934–7000 Yacht Club* ⇄ *1,213 rooms, 112 suites.*

$$ ★ WALT DISNEY WORLD DOLPHIN AND SWAN RESORTS

This convention-resort complex made up of two side-by-side hotels is connected to Epcot and Hollywood by water taxis and bridges. The Swan and Dolphin are the only hotels not owned by Disney that are on Disney property and whose guests qualify for on-site perks. Sometimes called "twin" hotels (like the nearby Yacht and Beach clubs), the Swan and Dolphin have separate check-ins but are alike in architecture and mood.

Proximity to the Magic Kingdom:	Fair, via bus
Proximity to Epcot:	Excellent, via water taxi
Proximity to Hollywood:	Excellent, via water taxi
Proximity to the Animal Kingdom:	Fair, via bus

Pluses

+ On-site child-care facilities.

+ The beach area has a playground, kiddie pools, waterslides, and a small marina with paddleboats.

+ Bike rentals, tennis courts, and a health club.

Minuses

− Somewhat expensive, with rates beginning at $299 per night, but if you can live without the full-throttle Disney ambience, this is the closest you'll get to Epcot and Hollywood Studios for the price.

- Conventioneers can erode the family feel.

- Since these resorts aren't owned by Disney, they don't qualify for the Magical Express Service and they don't have their
own airport shuttles. In other words, you'll have to arrange for
transportation from the airport to your hotel.

Overall Grade: A great place to go if you're visiting Orlando as
part of a convention or business trip and the company is picking
up the tab. Otherwise, try the Yacht and Beach clubs first. ✉ *1500
Epcot Resorts Blvd. (Dolphin), 1200 Epcot Resorts Blvd. (Swan)*
☎ *407/934–4000 or 800/227–1500 (Dolphin), 407/934–3000 or
800/325–3535 (Swan)* ⊕ *www.swandolphin.com* ⤴ *1,509 rooms,
112 suites (Dolphin), 756 rooms, 55 suites (Swan).*

Downtown Disney Hotels

These hotels are the first ones you encounter when you enter
Disney property and are a good choice for families who'll also be
visiting Universal Studios or other Orlando attractions. Proximity
to the action of Downtown Disney vastly increases your restaurant options.

$$
★★

DISNEY'S OLD KEY WEST RESORT

At the villas of Old Key West you'll get all the standard amenities
of a Disney resort, plus a lot more room. The setting is pleasant,
casual, and very Floridian in spirit. "We love the quieter atmo-
sphere of Old Key West," wrote a mother of three from Maryland.
"Our kids are young (ages 2, 5, and 7), so even with naps they're
often too exhausted at night for us to take them to a restaurant
and expect them to behave. We like being able to go 'home' to a
villa and order pizza or make sandwiches. The villas are more like
an apartment than a hotel room."

Proximity to the Magic Kingdom:	Fair, via bus
Proximity to Epcot:	Fair, via bus
Proximity to Hollywood:	Fair, via bus
Proximity to the Animal Kingdom:	Fair, via bus

Pluses

+ If you have more than two children and need to spread out, or you'd like a kitchen to prepare your own meals, Old Key West is a good on-site option.

+ A water taxi provides swift transit to Downtown Disney.

+ Tennis courts, pools, bike rentals, shuffleboard, basketball, a marina, a sand play area, an arcade, and a fitness room are all on-site.

+ Prices run from $368 for a studio with kitchenette to $1,370 for a Grand Villa that can accommodate up to 12 people. If you're willing to swap proximity to the parks for more space, Old Key West may be just what you need.

Minuses

- Still pricier than off-site villas such as the Sheraton Vistana or Embassy Suites.

- Quieter, with less going on than at other resorts.

- No on-site child-care facilities, which is unusual in a resort at this price point.

- A longer-than-average commute to the theme parks. "We were impressed with the accommodations at Old Key West," reported a mom from Toronto, "but transport to the parks involved surprisingly lengthy trips."

Overall Grade: Very homey, with nice touches, and a great option for families seeking peace and quiet at the end of the day. If you want lots of amenities and food choices, look elsewhere. ✉ *1510 N. Cove Rd.* ☎ *407/827–7700* 🔖 *761 units.*

$$$
★★★

DISNEY'S PORT ORLEANS RESORT

This mid-price resort has two sections. The French Quarter has manicured gardens, wrought-iron railings, and streets with cute names like Rue d'Baga. The Mardi Gras mood extends to the pool area, where alligators play jazz while King Triton sits atop a funky-looking waterslide, regally surveying his domain.

The Riverside section is a bit more down-home, with a steamboat-shape lobby, general stores run by gingham-clad girls, and a swimming area themed on *Song of the South*. Schizophrenic in architecture, with white-column buildings encircling fishing holes and cotton mills, Riverside manages to mix in a variety of Southern clichés without losing its ditzy charm. If Huck Finn married Scarlett O'Hara, this is where they'd come on their honeymoon.

As the French Quarter is only half the size of Riverside, it's a shorter walk to the lobby, pool, food court, and shuttle-bus station; at Riverside, getting around is a bit more of a headache. Both resorts have a fast-food court and a bar that offers live entertainment; Riverside also has a full-service restaurant called Boatwright's, which serves a mix of Cajun food and American classics and has a few nice extras such as a selection of New Orleans microbrews.

> **INSIDER'S SECRET**
>
> If you want to go all princess all the time, check out the over-the-top 512 castle-themed Royal Guest Rooms in the Magnolia Bend section of Port Orleans Riverside, which are inspired by *The Princess and the Frog*. The fiber-optic art hanging over ornate gold-and-crystal beds is great. Although they cost $25 to $50 a night extra, families rave about them, and they sell out quickly.

Proximity to the Magic Kingdom:	Fair, via bus
Proximity to Epcot:	Fair, via bus
Proximity to Hollywood:	Fair, via bus
Proximity to the Animal Kingdom:	Fair, via bus

Pluses

+ Affordable, starting at $182 a night, and well designed.

+ Great pool areas (especially at the French Quarter).

+ Both hotels have marinas with a selection of watercraft as well as bike rentals. The Sassagoula Steamboat offers easy water transport from both resorts to Downtown Disney.

+ Refurbished rooms now have flat-screen TVs, queen-size beds, and upgraded amenities. Riverside-section upgrade includes 512 princess-themed Royal Guest Rooms.

+ Riverside hosts Disney's Bayou Pirate Adventure, a two-hour outing (young buccaneers seize a boat and follow clues to find treasure) three mornings a week for ages 4–12 ($37). Call ☎ *407/939-7529* (☎ *WDW–PLAY*) to book.

Minuses

− In the off-season these two resorts share a bus to all major parks, which means a slightly longer commute.

Overall Grade: You get a good deal here in more ways than one. ✉ *1251 Riverside Dr.* ☎ *407/934–5000* ⌂ *1,008 rooms (French Quarter), 2,048 rooms (Riverside).*

$$ ★★ DISNEY'S SARATOGA SPRINGS RESORT & SPA

Saratoga Springs recalls the posh upstate New York retreats of the 1890s, complete with a horse-racing theme. Villas here are numerous and roomy. The recently updated and very attractive Treehouse Villas, for instance, have raised decks and enough space to accommodate large families. They're truly a home away from home.

Proximity to the Magic Kingdom:	Fair, via bus
Proximity to Epcot:	Fair, via bus
Proximity to Hollywood:	Fair, via bus
Proximity to the Animal Kingdom:	Fair, via bus

Pluses

+ Proximity to the restaurants and entertainment of Downtown Disney via water taxi.

+ Access to the biggest and best health club in WDW and a full-service spa.

+ The location is great for golfers—Saratoga Springs is adjacent to the Lake Buena Vista course.

✦ A good choice for family-reunion groups seeking larger accommodations and a relaxed atmosphere with plenty of space for the kids to play.

✦ The grotto pool, complete with man-made hot springs, is one of the most dramatic hotel pools in WDW. Even the auxiliary pools are beautifully themed, with great play areas for the kids.

Minuses

– With villas starting at $368, Saratoga Springs is more expensive than off-site villa accommodations. The larger, home-style villas can run as high as $1,370.

– Saratoga Springs is often used by corporations for retreats and conferences, so you may find yourself in the middle of a group of businesspeople.

– It's pretty far out of the Disney loop, so expect a longer commute time via bus to any of the major parks.

– At 65 acres, Saratoga Springs is so spread out that you might find yourself in a room far from the food court and main pool. Request to be as close as possible to the main building when you make your reservation.

Overall Grade: Roomy and close to Downtown Disney. The trouble is it's not particularly close to anything else. ✉ *1960 Broadway* ☎ *407/827-1100* 🛏 *924 units.*

Animal Kingdom Hotels

These hotels are in a surprisingly central location vis-à-vis the four theme parks and Downtown Disney.

$$
★★
DISNEY'S ALL-STAR SPORTS, ALL-STAR MUSIC, AND ALL-STAR MOVIES RESORTS

The All-Star resorts have built such a loyal following that, despite having about 6,000 rooms, they fill up quickly. There are three reasons for this success: price, price, and price.

All-Star Sports has five sections, each decorated with a tennis, football, surfing, basketball, or baseball theme. At All-Star Music, you can choose among jazz, rock and roll, country, calypso, and

Broadway tunes. All-Star Movies offers The Love Bug, Toy Story, Fantasia, 101 Dalmatians, and The Mighty Ducks.

> **HELPFUL HINT**
>
> If you don't care which All-Star resort section you're in, request a room near the lobby when you book. It's a little more expensive, but can save you lots of walking each time you leave your room to catch a bus or eat a meal.

The in-your-face graphics of the brightly colored buildings and the resort's general zaniness appeal to kids. There are giant tennis-ball cans and cowboy boots, a walk-through jukebox, and footballs the size of houses. At the diamond-shape baseball pool at All-Star Sports, you'll find Goofy as pitcher; Mickey conducts sprays of water in the Fantasia pool of All-Star Movies; and show tunes play all day under the marquee in the Broadway district of All-Star Music. It may be budget, but it ain't boring. ■**TIP→ The All-Star resorts are enormous, and check-in time can be a madhouse. Online check-in is a must. If your room isn't available when you arrive, you can store your bags and return later, when you'll only have to wait in the shorter, swifter-moving "key-pickup" line.**

Proximity to the Magic Kingdom:	Fair, via bus
Proximity to Epcot:	Fair, via bus
Proximity to Hollywood:	Fair, via bus
Proximity to the Animal Kingdom:	Good, via a short bus ride

Pluses

+ In a word, cost. Rooms start at $96.

+ The 215 suites at All-Star Music are, along with those at the Art of Animation Resort, among the most affordable on-site suite options. Units that sleep six start at $240 a night. "We used to get two rooms side by side," reported a mom of three from North Carolina, "which meant a girls' room with me and our daughters and a guys' room with my husband and son. All staying together in a suite is endlessly easier and better, and the kitchen, while small, was an added bonus."

+ All the All-Stars have special rooms for people with disabilities. For $109 a night, you can have a slightly larger ground-floor suite with a roll-in shower.

+ The free shuttle buses are a good transportation option, considering the price. When you get into this price range at off-site hotels, you often have to pay for a shuttle.

> **INSIDER'S SECRET**
>
> If your child adores *101 Dalmatians* or is a big football buff, you can indeed ask to be lodged in that section of the All-Star resorts when you make your reservation. Disney won't guarantee you'll get your request, but they'll try.

Minuses

- Food options are limited to fast-food courts and pool bars only, with no restaurants or indoor bars.

- Sports options are limited; swimming is it.

- The rooms are very small. They sleep four, but you'll be bunched.

- Long check-in lines.

- By breaking each resort into five separate sections, Disney is striving to eliminate that sleeping-in-the-middle-of-Penn-Station feel, but the bottom line is: It takes more effort to get around a huge hotel than a small one.

Overall Grade: Lots of bang for the buck here. Just don't expect too many amenities. ✉ *1701 W. Buena Vista Dr. (Sports), 1801 W. Buena Vista Dr. (Music), 1901 W. Buena Vista Dr. (Movies)* ☎ *407/939–5000 Sports, 407/939–6000 Music, 407/939–7000 Movies* ⮑ *1,700 rooms, 215 family suites at Music; 1,920 rooms at Movies and Sports.*

$$$
★★★
DISNEY'S ANIMAL KINGDOM LODGE AND VILLAS

Step inside the massive lobby of the Animal Kingdom Lodge and you'll be transported—outdoors. From the thatched roof to the enormous mud fireplace and from the rope bridges to the tribal art to the lighting that's designed to simulate sunrise to sunset, the resort creates the feel of a game lodge in the middle of a wildlife preserve.

The Animal Kingdom Lodge is in the middle of a 33-acre savanna where more than 200 animals freely roam. Thirty-six species of mammals, including giraffes, zebras, and gazelles, and 26 species of birds, such as the sacred ibis and African spoonbill, live within the working wildlife preserve. The kopje, a series of rock outcroppings, serves as a natural barrier but is also an elevated walkway that offers panoramas of the landscape and the chance for you to come within 15 feet of the animals. If you'd rather engage in animal viewing from the comfort of your own balcony, many of the guest rooms have a savanna view. The villas have their own animal reserve, check-in, and a cool Indian restaurant, and the rooms are lovely.

Proximity to the Magic Kingdom:	Fair, via bus
Proximity to Epcot:	Fair, via bus
Proximity to Hollywood:	Fair, via bus
Proximity to the Animal Kingdom:	Excellent, via a short bus ride

Pluses

+ A dramatic and exotic setting.

+ The Animal Kingdom Lodge has truly fantastic restaurants, including Boma, a buffet restaurant with especially good breakfasts, and Jiko, which serves excellent and authentic African food and an exclusively South African wine list.

+ Lots of extras for the kids, including tours that tell about the animals and "bush camp activities" such as African crafts, games, and folktales. You can even track the animals with night-vision goggles!

+ On-site child-care facilities, spa, and health club.

+ Some Animal Kingdom Lodge rooms have bunk beds, a good choice if your kids are older, different sexes, or for some other reason balk at sleeping together.

+ The Animal Kingdom Lodge Villas are relatively new and very attractive.

Minuses

− Although not as expensive as many of the other luxury hotels, the Lodge can be pricey, with rates beginning at $320 a night. Villas begin at $420.

− The out-of-the-way location means a longer-than-average bus ride to the Magic Kingdom, Epcot, and Hollywood. Buses stop at both the resort and the villas, which adds five minutes to every commute.

− Architectural drama is saved for public spaces. Rooms are small and basic.

Overall Grade: The most unusual resort on Disney property. ✉ *2901 Osceola Pkwy.* ☎ *407/938-3000* ✈ *972 rooms, 499 suites and villas.*

$$ ★★ DISNEY'S CORONADO SPRINGS RESORT

Disney's only moderately priced convention hotel—rooms begin at $188—has a Mexican theme, with Spanish-tile roofs, adobe walls, and a pool area dominated by an imposing Mayan temple. The rooms are scattered around a 15-acre lake. There's a full-service restaurant called Maya Grill, a food court, and a club called RIX with a bar and small dance floor.

Proximity to the Magic Kingdom:	Fair, via bus
Proximity to Epcot:	Fair, via bus
Proximity to Hollywood:	Fair, via bus
Proximity to the Animal Kingdom:	Good, via a short bus ride

Pluses

+ Dramatic pool area with waterslide, arcade, bar, fast-food stand, and theme playground.

+ Marina with standard boat and bike rentals.

+ Coronado Springs offers plenty of choices when it comes to food. In addition to the full-service restaurant, the food court provides far more options than the typical moderate resort, and RIX has a tasty bar menu.

Minuses

− Coronado Springs is a convention hotel, meaning it has more busi-nesspeople and fewer families than is typical for a Disney resort.

− The resort is quite spread out, even by Disney standards. If you're in one of the more far-flung rooms, you face a 15-minute walk to the food court and shuttle-bus stop.

Overall Grade: Coronado Springs has more amenities than are typ-ical in this price range. But the conventioneer vibe can also be a turnoff. ✉ *1000 W. Buena Vista Dr.* ☎ *407/939–1000* ✈ *1,917 rooms.*

ESPN Wide World of Sports Resorts

In Disney-speak, saying you're near the Wide World of Sports is another way of saying you're not near anything. The two value resorts here are less expensive partly because their out-of-the-way location means a longer commute to the parks. But if you have your own car or don't mind an extra 10 minutes on a bus, there are bargains to be found.

$$
★★
DISNEY'S ART OF ANIMATION RESORT

Based on the overwhelming popularity of the handful of family suites at the All-Star Music Resort, Disney radically expanded the concept with the Art of Animation Resort. The resort has four sections, each themed around a popular Disney film.

The first three sections are Finding Nemo, Cars, and The Lion King, which collectively add almost 1,200 value-priced family suites to the Disney lineup. The fourth and final section, The Lit-

---

HELPFUL HINT

So, which on-site hotel is best for you? It comes down to four questions:

✦ How much are you willing to spend?

✦ What park do you want to be closest to?

✦ Are there must-have amenities (like dining or sporting options, or villa-style accommodations)?

✦ What theme seems the coolest?

tle Mermaid, holds regular guest rooms. The Art of Animation is adjacent to Pop Century, and the two resorts are connected by a bridge.

The suites are popular because they offer more space and comfort, and many families consider them a far more workable option than two adjoining rooms. They include a master bedroom, two bathrooms, a kitchenette, and three separate sleeping areas—meaning that six people can stay comfortably. The movie-based theming is also far more intense and immersive than in the older Disney resorts, making the resort tremendous fun for kids. Suites start at $299 a night; standard rooms start at $118. Once again, as with all large value resorts, either use advance online check-in or brace yourself for a potentially lengthy check-in process.

Proximity to the Magic Kingdom:	Fair, via bus
Proximity to Epcot:	Fair, via bus
Proximity to Hollywood:	Good, via bus
Proximity to the Animal Kingdom:	Fair, via bus

Pluses

+ Value-priced suites like these, which may be the wave of the future in family travel, offer undeniable bang for the buck.

+ The rooms are new and themed to the max. The Finding Nemo pool area is especially fun for kids; it offers one big, bright photo op after another. A separate water-play area caters to smaller guests.

+ A large food court and gift shop offer a reasonable range of shopping and dining options on-site.

Minuses

− Disney's newest suites are designed to make maximum use of space: They feel, as one Florida mother wrote, "more like a cruise cabin than being in an apartment." Although the suites do have three sleeping areas, that doesn't mean three bedrooms with closing doors; one of the beds might be a converted dining table, another a couch. So don't expect the same level of privacy you'd find in suites at an older resort like Old Key West.

— While the suites at the Art of Animation are value priced, the location on Disney property and the perks of being on-site mean they are still more expensive than those at similar hotels in the Orlando area.

— The same über-theming that delights kids may overwhelm parents. "I can understand the giant statue of Crush by the pool," said a dad from Ohio. "But do the rooms have to look like a giant cartoon?"

— The location means a longer commute time to the parks.

Overall Grade: Art of Animation, which combines family-size suites at a value price point, is a welcome addition to the Disney family. Our early mail on this resort has been positive. ✉ *1850 Animation Way* ☎ *407/938–7000* ↪ *1,984 rooms, 1,120 suites.*

$$
★

DISNEY'S POP CENTURY RESORT

At Pop Century, each pair of buildings is themed to a different decade, from the 1950s to the 1990s. Expect the same larger-than-life icons that mark the All-Stars. Cultural touchstones from each decade—including giant yo-yos, Big Wheel bikes, and Rubik's Cubes—mark the entrances, and the roofs are lined with catchphrases from each era. As with the other value resorts, advance online check-in is a must. ■**TIP→ Request placement in the 1960s section when you make your reservation at Pop Century. It's a bit louder—and during the on-season they may charge you $10 more per night—but you're close to the bus stops, food court, and the fun Hippie Dippy pool. The 1980s and '90s sections are a long walk from most of the hotel amenities.**

Proximity to the Magic Kingdom:	Fair, via bus
Proximity to Epcot:	Fair, via bus
Proximity to Hollywood:	Fair, via bus
Proximity to the Animal Kingdom:	Fair, via bus

Pluses

+ Affordable, starting at $106 a night.

+ Free transportation, a rarity in this price range.

+ Since there's only one bus stop all your commutes are reasonably efficient.

Minuses

- Food options are limited to a fast-food court.

- This resort is a special favorite for cheerleading competitions, bands, and other teenage groups. It can get loud and rowdy in the pool areas.

- Sporting options are limited to swimming.

- The rooms are small; they sleep four, but you'll be crowded.

Overall Grade: The value resorts offer numerous perks at a reasonable price and are a great option for on-the-go families who primarily use their hotel as a place to shower and sleep. ⊠ *1050 Century Dr.* ☎ *407/938-4000* ⤴ *2,880 rooms.*

About Off-Site Non-Disney Hotels

If you are going to stay off-site, then you have considerations you might not have if you are staying in a Disney on-site hotel. We've tried to highlight the important pieces of information to help you make the choice that's right for your family.

Choosing the Perfect Location

The three main off-site areas that Disney visitors frequent are Exits 62 and 68 off Interstate 4 and International Drive.

Exits 62 and 68 are within a 10-minute drive of the theme parks. Exit 68 (U.S. 535) has a vast number of chain hotels and eateries and is your best bet if you want to get close to Disney without paying Disney prices.

Exit 62, which leads to U.S. 192, has similar chains represented, but the rates are about $30 less per night. Why? The hotels are, in

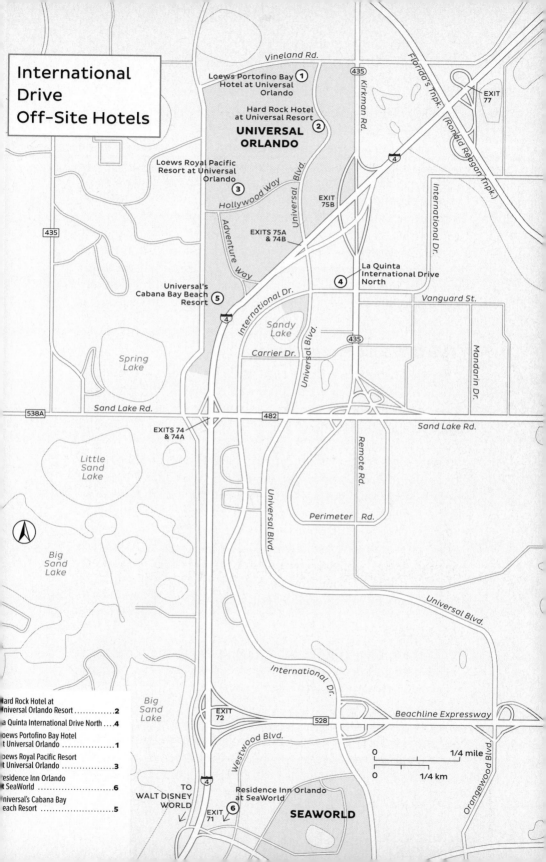

International Drive Off-Site Hotels

Vineland Rd.

Loews Portofino Bay Hotel at Universal Orlando ①

Hard Rock Hotel at Universal Resort ②

UNIVERSAL ORLANDO

Loews Royal Pacific Resort at Universal Orlando ③

Hollywood Way

Adventure Way

Universal Blvd.

Kirkman Rd.

435

Florida's Tpke. (Ronald Reagan Tpke.)

EXIT 77

I-4

EXIT 75B

EXITS 75A & 74B

La Quinta International Drive North ④

Vanguard St.

International Dr.

Universal's Cabana Bay Beach Resort ⑤

I-4

International Dr.

Sandy Lake

Carrier Dr.

Universal Blvd.

435

Mandarin Dr.

Spring Lake

Sand Lake Rd.

538A

482

Sand Lake Rd.

EXITS 74 & 74A

Little Sand Lake

Remote Rd.

Perimeter Rd.

Universal Blvd.

Big Sand Lake

Universal Blvd.

International Dr.

Beachline Expressway

Big Sand Lake

Westwood Blvd.

EXIT 72

528

I-4

TO WALT DISNEY WORLD

EXIT 71

Residence Inn Orlando at SeaWorld ⑥

SEAWORLD

Orangewood Blvd.

0 — 1/4 mile
0 — 1/4 km

general, older than the hotels off Exit 68. The whole area is a little less spiffy but still close to Disney property.

International Drive is farther out, about 20 minutes from the Disney theme parks. This area has representatives from every chain restaurant and hotel you've ever heard of, as well as entertainment options like malls and miniature golf. International Drive is the conduit that runs between the convention center and Universal Orlando, so it's a smart central location if you're planning to visit those parks as well as Disney. Note that the more upscale end of International Drive is near the convention center, to the south. As you head north toward Universal Studios, it gets a little shabbier, so be wary of any "seems too good to be true" deal unless you're already familiar with the property.

Top Off-Site Hotel Issues

There's a wide range of amenities and perks among the hundreds of hotels in the Orlando area. To make sure you're getting top value for your dollar, take nothing for granted. Some $250-a-night hotels charge you for breakfast; some $75 ones do not. Some hotels count 12-year-olds as adults; others consider 19-year-olds to be children. Some relatively inexpensive hotels have kids' clubs; some larger and more costly ones are geared to convention and business travelers and don't even have an arcade. To minimize the time you have to spend in rush-hour traffic, only choose a hotel between Exits 55 and 75 off Interstate 4. The moral is, always ask. ■TIP➜ **An extremely cheap hotel rate, say $55 or less, generally means that the hotel is in a less desirable part of town than those we recommend, both in terms of theme-park proximity and general security.**

Child Care

Does the hotel provide in-room babysitters? Is there an on-site child-care center or kids' club? What's the cost? How far in advance do you have to make reservations?

Hotel-Sponsored Transportation

Does the hotel provide direct shuttle service to the theme parks? How often do the buses run? How early do they begin and how late do they run? How many stops do they make? Do you share the shuttles with other hotels? Do they run to the theme parks directly or make a circuit of all four? Is there a fee?

Meals and Dining

Does the hotel have any suites with kitchens? If not, can you rent refrigerators or microwaves? Does the hotel provide a free buffet breakfast as part of the regular room rate? What fast-food or family-style restaurants are nearby?

> **HELPFUL HINT**
>
> If you're staying off-site and will be eating at least some of your meals outside of Disney property, pick up a few of the free tourist magazines available in the airport and all around Orlando. They're full of dining discount coupons, many for family-oriented restaurants near the theme parks.

Other Issues

Do kids stay free? Up to what age? Are there laundry facilities on the premises?

Saving Money on Off-Site Hotels

Orlando has more hotel rooms than any other U.S. city besides Las Vegas, so there are plenty of beds out there for the taking. Here are a few tips to make sure you're getting the most for your money.

The Orlando Magicard

The Orlando Magicard is free and offers 20% to 30% discounts on area hotels, as well as restaurants and non-Disney attractions. You can download a card by visiting ⊕ *www.orlandoinfo.com/ magicard.*

Calling the Hotel Directly

Try calling both the hotel chain's toll-free number and the direct line to the particular hotel. You may be quoted different rates.

If you especially like a particular hotel chain, you can simply call its toll-free number and ask for the hotel nearest Disney World. This strategy eliminates the element of surprise because one Hampton Inn looks pretty much like another. Big chains have multiple Orlando locations, so stress that you'd like to be as close as possible to the Disney gates, preferably near Exit 62 or 68. Proximity to Disney raises the rate about 20%, but location is impor-

Hotel-Operated Park Shuttles

Many off-site hotels claim to run shuttles to the theme parks, but beware. Relying on off-site transportation can sometimes make for a long commute. The worst situations are when two or three hotels share a shuttle and you have to stop at all of them. Even if a resort has its own shuttle, it may stop at all of the major parks on each run or sometimes drop all its passengers at the Magic Kingdom, forcing them to use Disney's transportation to reach the other parks. This can mean commutes of up to an hour just to get from your hotel to the theme park of your choice. A lengthy bus ride is maddening in the morning when the kids are eager to get to the rides; at night, when you're all exhausted, it can be disastrous.

A mother of three had this story: "We loved our resort along Highway 192 (Exit 62); very nice, with good amenities. But the shuttle was awful. It was hot, crowded, and took two hours to get back from the Magic Kingdom on a night after the fireworks. The hotel advertises that it is '4 miles from Disney' but it doesn't tell you that its shuttle stops at five other hotels and all four theme parks. We like the hotel well enough to go back, but next time we'll get a rental car."

To make matters worse, some off-site hotels charge you for shuttle rides. They may tell you that by buying shuttle tickets you'll save the "horrendous" cost of Disney parking, but the truth is that Disney parking is $17 no matter how many people are in a car, the shuttle-bus tickets can range from $5 to $12 per person, and it still may take you forever to get there!

I suggest that families staying off-site either drive to Orlando or get a rental car. If you do decide to use an off-site resort shuttle, be sure to ask if it's a private shuttle and if service to theme parks is direct. If you don't like what you hear, rent a car or call a cab.

tant; if you end up in a hotel near the airport or downtown, that means a major daily commute, and Orlando traffic can be brutal.

Finally, six little words can save you major bucks. When talking to a reservation clerk, always ask, "Do you have any discounts available?" Remember that the reservation clerk works for the hotel, so if he can sell you a room at $95 a night there's no incentive for him to tell you how you can drop the rate to $79. But if you specifically inquire about discounts, he has to tell you.

Great Off-Site Hotels for Families

The listed properties that follow are tried-and-true family favorites based on proximity to Disney World, amenities, and value.

Two notes: The hotels listed here receive the same kind of star ratings as an on-site hotel. And since Walt Disney World is so huge and spread out, our "proximity to Disney" rating is based on the distance between the hotel and Disney's main entrance gate.

There are plenty of great hotels in the Orlando area, but based on our visits and comments from readers, we've narrowed down the choices considerably in each category: luxury, mid-priced, condos, and budget.

Recommended Off-Site Luxury Hotels

Orlando has its share of understated, classy hotels where you can swap the Disney vibe for tranquillity and adult-oriented amenities.

$$$
★★★

B RESORT AND SPA

Conveniently located on Hotel Plaza Boulevard, the B Resort is within walking distance of Downtown Disney and provides easy access to all the Disney theme parks. The hotel has just undergone a massive refurbishment and emerged with a bright, futuristic techno-vibe that will especially appeal to teens and preteens. As a Disney partner hotel, the B brings you as close to Disney as an off-site hotel can be and has upscale amenities: a full spa, convention facilities, an on-site Disney store, and American Q, which has a terrific breakfast buffet literally served out the back of a flatbed truck. The lanai rooms, some of which have patios opening directly onto to the pool area, are great fun choices for families.

Proximity to Disney World: Good, via a complimentary shared bus. One bus runs exclusively to Downtown Disney in the afternoon and evenings. The other buses run to two parks each.

Proximity to Universal: Fair, via a 15-minute drive

Pluses

+ Complimentary shuttle service to all Disney parks.

+ Family-friendly lodging options, such as a king bed and two bunk beds (many rooms have pullout couches as well).

+ Full-service spa, which includes a teen menu.

+ Zero-entry pool and kids'-zone area with toys and games.

+ The digital "monscierge" gives you quick, real-time info on the theme parks, weather, and information on all Orlando area attractions.

+ Accommodations are reasonably priced for the area, with basic rooms starting at $95 in the off-season and $165 in the on-season.

Minuses

− The Disney shuttles are shared with the other hotels of Hotel Plaza Boulevard, which means a longer commute time.

− The convention space and sleek decor give the property a more adult feel than at many Orlando resorts.

− More elaborate accommodations can be quite expensive, with the lanai-style suites ranging from $300 to $420 depending on the season.

Overall Grade: A good choice for families with older kids who want to be close to the theme parks while not immersed 24/7 in the Disney vibe. ✉ *1905 Hotel Plaza Blvd.* ☎ *407/828–2828 or 888/662–4683* ⊕ *www.BResortLBV.com* ✈ *394 rooms.*

$$$
★★

HARD ROCK HOTEL AT UNIVERSAL ORLANDO RESORT

Fun, flashy, and funky, the nearly 650-room Hard Rock has a broad and eclectic collection of rock memorabilia. If you like the idea of a 7 am serenade from Elvis, you can even ask for a rock-star wake-up call in the morning. Music plays continually throughout the beautifully landscaped grounds and sophisticated lounges. The dramatic pool area has a 260-foot waterslide, plus a 12-speaker underwater sound system, so you can get your aural fix even while taking a swim. There are three bars, a gym, and two restaurants, including an Orlando version of the well-known Palm Restaurant. The children's program center, called Camp Lil' Rock, is open year-round in the evening, with extended daytime hours during the on-season.

The Hard Rock Hotel is the perfect choice for families with older kids and teens who can appreciate the hipper-than-thou ambience. Rates range from $239 to $404 per night, and some of the pricier rooms have kids' suites. If money isn't an object, you can live like the King in the $2,000-per-night Graceland Suite, whose flamboyant amenities include a piano.

Proximity to Disney World: Fair, via a 20-minute drive
Proximity to Universal: Excellent, via water taxi

Pluses

+ Cool ambience and interesting dining options.

+ Great choice for teens and tweens.

+ The most fun and funky of the Universal resorts.

Minuses

− Price. Rates average $300 a night.

− The hipster vibe isn't always family-friendly.

Overall Grade: If you want a bit of Vegas in Orlando, this is your kind of place. ✉ *5800 Universal Blvd.* ☎ *407/503–7625 or 800/232–7827* ⊕ *www.hardrockhotelorlando.com* ⤳ *621 rooms, 29 suites.*

$$$
★★★
HYATT REGENCY GRAND CYPRESS

This beautiful hotel has expansive grounds, lush landscaping, spiffy restaurants, and numerous sporting options. It's a serene oasis and a great choice for families who want the option to escape from Disney in the evening and yet remain conveniently close to the parks. Prices start at about $195 in the off-season, $225 in the on-season. There is a discount for advance booking.

A $25 surcharge per room per day is automatically added and covers a plethora of extras: shuttle transportation to the TTC, where you can catch the monorail or buses to all Disney parks; bike and watercraft rental; poolside activities for the kids; Internet access; an elaborate pitch-and-putt golf course; a climbing wall; and access to the health club.

Proximity to Disney World: Excellent, via a 5-minute drive or shuttle service

Proximity to Universal: Fair, via a 15-minute drive

Pluses

+ The pool area is gorgeous, with 12 waterfalls and several very secluded hot tubs. There's a terrific slide for kids, and a section of the pool is heated, if you're traveling off-season.

+ You can golf, play tennis, and enjoy a far wider than normal range of resort activities. Pleasant trails wind through the grounds for walkers and runners. If you're looking to schedule a day off from theme-park touring, simply hanging around the Hyatt can keep you more than entertained.

+ Camp Hyatt has great activities for kids 3 to 12, such as pool games, nature walks, poolside movies, canoeing, tennis lessons, fire-pit marshmallow roasting, and pitch-and-putt golf. It runs daily during the summer and holidays as well as weekends throughout the off-season. Prices are $90 a day and $60 for evenings and include meals. A half-day session with no meals is $45. (Children must be toilet trained; the resort will help you arrange in-room sitting if you need child care for babies or toddlers.) Check to make sure Camp Hyatt is running and confirm prices when you make your reservation.

✦ Sophisticated dining options include Hemingway's, dramatically perched atop one of the pool waterfalls, and La Coquina's Chef's Table, which offers a seven-course tasting menu served in a luxurious nook in the kitchen.

Minuses

— Price: Both the rooms and restaurants can be expensive, especially during the on-season or if you upgrade to suite-style accommodations. Keep in mind that in addition to an automatic resort fee, you're on your own for breakfast, and there's a fee to park your car.

— The Hyatt frequently hosts conventions and attracts a more adult crowd than other area hotels. But since 2012, it has added more family-oriented activities and reports that its leisure guests now outnumber its business guests.

Overall Grade: The resort is a world unto itself, with ample ways to entertain families planning to spend a lot of time at their hotel. ✉ *1 Grand Cypress Blvd.* ☎ *407/239-1234 or 800/233-1234* ⊕ *www.hyattgrandcypress.com* ⇥ *815 rooms.*

$$$
★★
LOEWS PORTOFINO BAY HOTEL AT UNIVERSAL ORLANDO

The Portofino Bay is modeled after the Italian seaside village of Portofino. From the outside you see quaint, colorful row houses that are actually all connected on the inside. The 750 elegant rooms include 18 children's suites. Portofino Bay has eight restaurants and lounges, a full-service spa, three swimming pools, and Campo Portofino, a supervised children's activity center that is open in the evenings year-round, with extended daytime hours during the on-season.

Like the other luxury hotels at Universal, this is a Loews resort, so the service is top-notch. Of the three resorts, Portofino Bay is the most posh, with the most amenities geared to adults who want to relax in a beautiful environment. Rates for regular rooms range from $274 to $439 a night, while suites, including the roomy kids' suites, are higher, averaging about $700.

Proximity to Disney World: Fair, via a 20-minute drive

Proximity to Universal: Excellent, via water taxi

Pluses

+ Elegant and understated.

+ This is the most "honeymoon" like of the Universal Orlando Resorts.

Minuses

– Most of the amenities are adult-oriented.

– Expensive, especially the suites.

Overall Grade: This is the most adult-oriented of the Universal hotels, so it may not appeal to families. ✉ *5601 Universal Blvd.* ☎ *407/503-1000 or 800/232-7827* ⊕ *www.loewshotels.com/ Portofino-Bay-Hotel* ↘ *750 rooms, 49 suites.*

$$$
★★

LOEWS ROYAL PACIFIC RESORT AT UNIVERSAL ORLANDO

The Royal Pacific is the largest of the three Universal resorts, with 1,000 guest rooms on 53 acres. The lush grounds, thickly planted with tropical plants and trees, have a distinct South Pacific flair, and they're connected to CityWalk and the theme parks via water taxi and a series of winding, well-manicured pathways. There are two restaurants and two lounges, plus a luau party area, a fitness center, a children's activity center, and a massive pool area.

Perhaps most significant, the Royal Pacific is Universal's convention hotel, with 80,000 square feet of meeting space. This doesn't mean the resort won't be comfortable for families—the enormous pool and the children's center indicate that the resort is family-friendly—but you may find a lot of businesspeople mixed in with the vacationing crowd.

Rates range from $219 to $349 a night, making the Royal Pacific the most affordable of the three on-site resorts.

Proximity to Disney World: Fair, via a 20-minute drive
Proximity to Universal: Excellent, via water taxi

Pluses

✦ The best access to Universal Studios and Islands of Adventure.

✦ It's walkable if you have older kids.

Minuses

— Lots of conventioneers give the hotel an adult feel that may be off-putting for families.

Overall Grade: Unparalleled location for Universal Orlando and CityWalk. ✉ *6300 Hollywood Way* ☎ *407/503-3000 or 800/232-7827* 🌐 *www.universalorlando.com* 🔁 *1,000 rooms, 113 suites.*

Recommended Off-Site Mid-Priced Resorts

Orlando is full of family-friendly, mid-priced hotels. Here are our favorites.

$$
★★

EMBASSY SUITES LAKE BUENA VISTA

The Embassy Suites chain is very popular with our readers, especially this location. The suites include kitchenettes, the hotels are generally well maintained, and a bountiful breakfast is included in the price. There are seven Embassy Suites in Orlando; rates at the Lake Buena Vista location, which is the closest to Disney World, range from $113 to $146 during the off-season and $147 to $177 during the on-season.

Note: The two International Drive locations—Embassy Suites International Drive–South and Embassy Suites International Drive Jamaican Court—are also convenient to area theme parks, being reasonably close to Disney World and very close to Universal Orlando. A newer location, Embassy Suites Lake Buena Vista South, located off Exit 62, is also close to Disney and thus almost as convenient as the Lake Buena Vista location.

Proximity to Disney World: Good, via a 10-minute drive
Proximity to Universal: Fair, via a 15-minute drive

Pluses

✦ You can access Disney property through the Downtown Disney gate without the hassle of getting on Interstate 4.

+ Complimentary breakfast buffet with made-to-order pancakes and an omelet station.

+ Kitchenettes make it easy to keep snacks and sandwich supplies on hand.

+ A shopping center with a grocery and fast-food restaurants is nearby, and there is a Pizza Hut Express in the lobby.

+ The heated indoor–outdoor pool is an asset in the winter.

+ Lots of sports options: a gym, tennis courts, basketball, shuffleboard, and volleyball.

+ Although the resort isn't new, the grounds have been well maintained.

Minuses

– Proximity to Interstate 4 means a consistently high noise level.

– This Embassy Suites is on Palm Parkway, surrounded by many other hotels, which means you may hit traffic getting to the parks—another reason to start early.

Overall Grade: Reasonably priced and comfortable. ✉ *8100 Lake St.* ☎ *407/239-1144, 800/257-8483, or 800/362-2779* ⊕ *www.embassysuites.com* ⇗ *334 suites.*

$$
★★

RESIDENCE INN ORLANDO AT SEAWORLD

The suites at the Residence Inn are especially homelike, and you can choose among one- to three-room units, all with separate areas for eating and relaxing. Plus, Disney World and Universal Studios are almost equidistant, about 5 miles away. Prices begin at $94 for a studio, $149 for a one-room suite with sofa bed, and go up to $229 for a three-room (two bedrooms and a living room with sofa bed) suite. During peak times the prices rise about $20 a night. The property features a heated outdoor pool, a game room, a sports court with basketball and tennis, a health club, and a children's playground. "My husband hates crowds and noise and was very skeptical about taking a vacation in Orlando," a woman from Michigan wrote to us. "But even he had to admit that the Residence Inn was very relaxing."

Proximity to Disney World: Good, via a 10-minute drive
Proximity to Universal: Good, via a 10-minute drive

Pluses

+ Suites are spacious, and the kitchens are well equipped.

+ Complimentary hot breakfast buffet.

+ Packages including theme park tickets are available.

+ Complimentary theme-park transportation.

Minuses

- The bigger the suite, the higher the price.

- The hotel is a bit off the main drag of International Drive. For families seeking peace and privacy, that actually may be a plus, but you'll have to drive for every meal unless you're eating in your own kitchen.

Overall Grade: A good mid-priced option, with good access to Universal and Disney as well. ✉ *11000 Westwood Blvd., I–4 Exit 72* ☎ *407/313–3600 or 800/331–3131* ⊕ *www.residenceinnseaworld. com* ⬎ *350 suites.*

$$
★★★
$$

UNIVERSAL'S CABANA BAY BEACH RESORT

This new mid-priced resort adds a much-needed option to Universal's hotels with competitive pricing and plenty of family-friendly perks. Based on beach resorts of the 1950s and '60s, Cabana Bay is retro done right. The attractive property is dotted with amenities: two large pool areas, complete with a lazy river and waterslide, pool bars, posh cabanas to rent, and poolside "Dive In" movies each evening; a game room; a Jack LaLanne fitness studio; sand play areas and splash zones for toddlers; fire pits for relaxing. A 10-lane, bowling alley is also on-site and features the hotel's only full-service restaurant, the Galaxy Bowl Restaurant. Bayliner Diner, the hotel's quick-service dining option, offers tons of kid-friendly food options and surprisingly reasonable prices. Both standard rooms, with two queen-size beds and a mini-refrigerator, and family suites are available. The family suites can sleep up to six, with two queen beds and a pullout couch, a separate living space with its own TV, and a convenient split bathroom with sinks on both sides and the toilet in a separate room from the tub.

Free shuttles run to Universal Orlando run every 10 minutes from 6 am to 2 am, when the clubs of CityWalk finally shut down. And, as of this writing, a very special perk is in place: Hotel guests may enter the Diagon Alley section of Harry Potter a full hour before day visitors. Given the popularity of the Harry Potter sections of Universal Studios and Islands of Adventure, this is a perk worth its weight in gold. (Be sure to ask if this offer is still in effect when you book. It may be a limited-time offer.)

Proximity to Disney World: Fair, via a 20-minute drive
Proximity to Universal: Excellent, via shuttle

Pluses

+ Family-oriented suites with a convenient layout and more room than is typical of many Orlando hotels.

+ Guests get the extra hour in Diagon Alley section of Harry Potter. Mondo perk!

+ An insane amount is going on at this resort, with pools that border on being water parks, bowling, movies, play areas, and a great family-friendly feel.

+ Complimentary transportation to both Universal Orlando.

+ Good value for what you get. Rooms range from $93 to $134 depending on the season, while suites range from $169 to $224.

Minuses

− No Express Pass for guests here as you get at the more expensive Loews resorts (just the extra hour with Harry Potter).

Overall Grade: Cabana Bay impressed us very favorably on our inaugural visit. We expect it to be a great favorite with our readers. ✉ *6550 Adventure Way* ☎ *407/503-4000 or 800/232-7827* 🌐 *www.universalorlando.com* 🛏 *900 rooms, 900 suites.*

Recommended Off-Site Budget Hotels

Budget can mean grimy and cheap, or it can mean practical and convenient. Here are some properties our readers have recommended that offer true value for the money.

$
★★

COMFORT SUITES AT MAINGATE EAST

This hotel is cheaper than most of the area suites-style hotels, largely because of its location off Route 192, also known as Irlo Bronson Memorial Highway. Route 192 isn't as upscale as International Drive, but this hotel is clean and comfortable, the staff are pleasant, and the price is definitely right. Maingate East is a mere 2 miles from Disney property, and if you're looking for a location that's both affordable and close enough to be able to return to your hotel for a midday break, the Comfort Suites at Maingate East is a good option. Prices range from $89 to $149 during the off-season and $119 to $189 during the on-season.

Proximity to Disney World: Excellent, via a 5-minute drive

Proximity to Universal: Fair, via a 20-minute drive

Pluses

+ With the smallest suites starting at $89, it's hard to beat the price.

+ Suites have either partial dividers or separate rooms, plus microwaves, refrigerators, coffeemakers, and sleeper sofas.

+ A deluxe continental breakfast is included.

+ This is as close as you'll get to Disney property at this price; the Maingate East entrance means you can skip Interstate 4 traffic altogether.

Minuses

− The one-bedroom suites are comfortable for families of four at most. Although the website says the suites can accommodate a family of six, you'll be cramped.

− Route 192 may be the least scenic part of Orlando. You're close to a funky little amusement park, endless chain restaurants, and big-box discount stores. But one of the reasons we recommend the Comfort Suites over other properties in the area is that it's pretty far off the main drag and thus quieter and more secluded than the others. In fact, keep your eyes peeled, as it's easy to miss the hotel entrance altogether.

Overall Grade: Fancy? No. Clean, convenient, and friendly? Yes. ✉ *11000 Westwood Blvd., I–4 Exit 72* ☎ *407/397–7848* ⊕ *www.comfortsuitesfl.com* ⤳ *350 suites.*

$ ★★ LA QUINTA INTERNATIONAL DRIVE NORTH

There are plenty of La Quintas in Orlando, but this location is especially appealing to families who are headed to Universal Studios. Rooms begin as low as $74 in the off-season. During peak times prices climb to the $79–$120 range, which is still a deal.

Proximity to Disney World: Fair, via a 20-minute drive

Proximity to Universal: Excellent, via a 5-minute drive

Pluses

+ It's an easy drive to Universal and a bit farther to Disney. The hotel runs complimentary shuttles to the theme parks.

+ There are plenty of family-friendly chain and budget restaurants along I-Drive.

+ Complimentary breakfast is included, and there are laundry facilities on-site.

Minuses

− The commute to Disney can be problematic if you're traveling at peak traffic times.

− The I-Drive location, while bringing you close to services, means you'll also have to deal with traffic and noise.

Overall Grade: An unbeatable location for cost-conscious families who want to visit Disney and Universal Orlando. ✉ *5825 International Dr., I–4 Exit 75A* ☎ *407/351–4100* ⊕ *www.lq.com* ⤳ *155 rooms.*

Recommended Condo Properties

Sometimes families want to get far, far away from the crowds and bustle, retreating to a homelike atmosphere each evening. A condo offers more space and a kitchen. Due to the wide range of lodging options, we offer no star rating for condo properties.

$$ **MAGICAL MEMORIES VILLAS**

One can only imagine how thrilled Disney is that this independent rental agency has adopted the word "magical"—perhaps the most frequently employed word in Disney promotional materials. Magical Memories can offer good deals for families. The company handles both condo and house rentals in nine different neighborhoods throughout Orlando. If you want to pay for a home with a private pool in a gated community, that's certainly available, but most of the rentals are clean, simply furnished, safe apartments in condo complexes. Rates start surprisingly low: During the off-season you might find yourself paying as little as $109 for a two-bedroom condo and $179 for a five-bedroom house with a private pool. During the on-season, condos begin at $129 a night and houses at $224 a night. Be sure to browse the website to see all your options. There's a substantial range of amenities and prices.

The benefits can be substantial, as outlined by a mother from Canada: "Because we have a family of six, we would have had to rent two hotel rooms, so renting a house was ideal for our situation—not to mention that we split the cost with another family. We ended up with a five-bedroom, five-bath house with all the perks. They said it was minutes from Disney, and it really was."

Proximity to Disney World: Minimum 5 miles, maximum 8 miles

Proximity to Universal: Maximum 16 miles

Pluses

+ Good choice for large families and groups because you can get a multibedroom house or condo with a well-equipped kitchen and all the conveniences of a hotel.

+ If you're staying at one of the condo-style Magical Memories Villas, you'll also have use of the villa clubhouse. Some have amenities such as Wi-Fi, exercise rooms, and larger pools. The Magical Memories Villas encompass 15 different villa sites, and each clubhouse is different, so if you're seeking a specific amenity, be sure to ask when reserving.

Minuses

- This isn't like a familiar hotel chain where you know what to expect. There's a range in the quality of accommodations.

- For rentals of four nights or fewer you'll be charged a cleaning fee based on the size of your unit.

- A stay of three nights is required for the villas and five nights for the houses.

- There's a very strict reservation and payment policy. This isn't something you can cancel at the last minute, like a hotel, so make sure your plans are firm before you book.

Overall Grade: An excellent choice for larger families. ☎ *407/390–8200* ⊕ *www.magicalmemories.com.*

$$ ## SHERATON VISTANA RESORT AND SHERATON VISTANA RESORT VILLAGES

Both of the Sheraton Vistana properties have been favorites with our readers since we first began doing resort surveys. One mom wrote, mirroring many other letters, "We found the Villages to be very pretty, very quiet, and very clean. And it took us only 15 minutes to drive to Disney World."

The two properties are fairly close to each other, with the older Sheraton Vistana Resort slightly more convenient to Disney, and the Villages located on International Drive. The Villages is the newer and more upscale of the two, but the Resort is the favorite of many families with older children, who report it has more activities. One grandfather of five, who stayed at both properties in the course of a single week, distinguishes them this way: "Both properties were a good value, but when we had all the kids down we preferred the Resort, which had a lot going on. When we put the kids on the plane and settled down to relax by the pool, the Villages were the better choice."

One-bedroom villas begin at $140 in the off-season and $189 in the on-season; two-bedroom villas begin at $177 off-season and $219 on-season.

Proximity to Disney World: Fair, via a 15-minute drive
Proximity to Universal: Fair, via a 15-minute drive

Pluses

+ Activities offered in the game room during the day and in-room babysitting at night allow parents to have some private time. Some of the activities have modest fees, but many are free.

+ Adults have their own choice of activities, which might include karaoke, a mix 'n' mingle, or setting sail on a casino cruise.

+ A central location near both International Drive and Interstate 4 makes it easy to get to all the theme parks and to family-friendly restaurants and minor attractions along International Drive.

+ The villas are larger and more comfortable than those in most other all-suites hotels.

+ Excellent guest service, including a remarkably efficient check-in process. On our last visit, even though the lobby was full, we were checked in within 10 minutes and were sent off with a list of local shops, restaurants, medical centers, and grocery stores, as well as GPS directions to all the parks.

Minuses

− On-property food options are limited, although there's a casual deli-style restaurant and pool bar. Since most families take advantage of the villa kitchenettes and there are plenty of family-friendly restaurants in the area, the lack of on-site dining options is rarely a problem.

− The entrance to the Sheraton Vistana is a bit difficult to get to, especially at night. There's no light, and the multiple entrances do not connect to each other, so you may end up making a few U-turns.

- The condos are spread out at both locations, so it really does feel like you're more at home than on vacation. This is an advantage for families who are seeking normalcy at the end of an active day, but a disadvantage for families who like to keep the rah-rah vacation feel going 24/7.

Overall Grade: A great home-away-from-home that offers many activities and adventures. ✉ *8800 Vistana Centre Dr., I–4 Exit 68 (Resort), 12401 International Dr., I–4 Exit 71 (Villages)* ☎ *407/239–3100 (Resort), 407/238–5000 (Villages)* ⊕ *www.starwoodhotels. com* ⤴ *1,680 units (Resort), 1,037 units (Villages).*

CHAPTER 3

ONCE YOU GET THERE

You say you've done all the preplanning? Good for you. But there are still a few last-minute factors to consider, from the possibility of a thunderstorm to an upset tummy to happier unforeseen issues. Like maybe your two-year-old develops an absolute obsession with Minnie and has to see her Every Single Day.

It can be fun to plan certain parts of a vacation—looking over hotel pictures and restaurant menus, plotting how to meet the characters. But knowing how to handle those less-fun details, such as stroller rental and finding a place to change the baby, can make sure your time in the parks runs smoothly.

Few vacations go off without a single hiccup, but if you're prepared, a dead car battery or the loss of a MagicBand won't ruin your whole day. And if you're even slightly in doubt as to how to best handle an unforeseen problem, ask the nearest cast member for assistance. Disney does a wonderful job at helping guests in need.

Bare Necessities

Whether you're pregnant, traveling with a baby, or nursing a sore ankle, Disney World is prepared to accommodate your needs.

Strollers

Strollers are available for rent at each theme park for $15 (single) and $31 (double). (If you book one for multiple days, the price per day drops to $13 for a single and $27 for a double.)

At these rates, if you need a stroller every day it's obviously most cost-effective to bring one from home. If you have an older child who will only need a stroller at Epcot, a rental isn't a bad option. All kids three and under will need a stroller for napping as well as riding and resting. For kids four to six, the general rule is that strollers are a must at Epcot, nice in the Magic Kingdom, and less needed at Animal Kingdom or Hollywood, where the walkable areas of the parks are smaller and you spend a lot of time sitting in shows.

On busy days the Magic Kingdom opens an additional stroller-rental stand outside the main gate, before you enter the bag-check area. This location is never as crowded as the rental stand inside the park.

If you plan to park hop at Disney in a single day, you don't have to pay for a stroller twice: Keep your receipt and show it for a new stroller on arrival at the next park.

At Epcot, if your five-year-old swears she doesn't need a stroller at 8 am, but at noon she collapses in a heap halfway around Epcot's World Showcase, head for the World Traveler shop. The World Traveler is also the place to rent a stroller if you're coming from the Yacht and Beach clubs, BoardWalk, or the Swan and Dolphin hotels and using the "back-door" entrance.

Families staying at one of the more sprawling resorts, such as Pop Century, Caribbean Beach, Coronado Springs, Art of Animation, Port Orleans, Fort Wilderness, or the All-Star resorts, should bring a stroller from home for any child under four. You'll need it just to get from your room to the food court or shuttle-bus stop.

■TIP→ If you're renting a stroller for more than one day, you don't have to get in line every morning. On your first park visit, tell the cast member at stroller rental that you want, for example, a four-day stroller rental, and you'll be given coupons for four days. After that, you can skip the rental line and go directly to the stroller pick-up booth.

Do be aware that there are Disney cast members whose sole duty is to collect and rearrange strollers, lining them up outside rides and packing them as close together as possible. Just because your stroller isn't where you left it, keep looking—you'll likely find your stroller a few yards away. It may simply have been moved aside. Families often stop in mid-stride when they see an appealing attraction and abandon their stroller on the sidewalk, and cast members try to deal with these immediately.

Replacement Strollers

Still can't find your stroller? In Animal Kingdom replacement strollers are at Mombasa Marketplace, and in Hollywood they can be found at Tatooine Traders. In the Magic Kingdom, check in at Tinker Bell's Treasures in Fantasyland, the Frontierland Trading Post in Frontierland, or Buzz Lightyear's Space Ranger Spin in Tomorrowland. At Epcot you can get a new stroller at the World Traveler shop between France and the United Kingdom or the Glas und Porzellan shop in Germany. As long as you've kept your receipt there's no additional charge for a new stroller; however, the shops don't have many spare strollers and those they do have are given out on a first-come, first-served basis.

■**TIP→ If you're flying and would like a stroller for the resort as well as the parks, consider an independent rental company such as Kingdom Strollers or Orlando Stroller Rentals. Prices are lower, and the strollers can be dropped off and picked up at most hotels in the Orlando area.**

Baby Care

Each park has a Baby Care Center where rockers, bottle warmers, high chairs, and changing tables are available; diapers, formula, and jars of baby food are for sale.

In the Magic Kingdom, Baby Care is beside the Crystal Palace Restaurant. In Epcot it's on the bridge that connects Future World to the World Showcase. At Hollywood it's in the Guest Relations (a.k.a. Guest Services) building; and in the Animal Kingdom it's behind the Creature Comforts gift shop.

Disposable diapers are available in the larger gift shops, but they're kept behind the counter, so you'll have to ask for them. Changing tables are provided in most women's restrooms and some men's. If fathers have trouble locating a changing table in a men's room, they can always make a stop at Baby Care.

Nursing Moms

Disney World is so casual and family-oriented that you shouldn't feel self-conscious about nursing anywhere that's comfortable. The main problem is that the noise and sound of other children's voices often pull babies "off task." If your child is easily distracted, try the rockers in the Baby Care Center.

One tip though—don't think moving out from the crowd will guarantee privacy. On a recent trip Leigh found a perfectly secluded spot in the Magic Kingdom only to find that other guests wandered over, thinking there was a show or restrooms just because they saw someone sitting there.

First Aid

First-aid clinics are beside the Baby Care Center in each park. Although the clinics mostly treat patients with minor problems such as sunburn, motion sickness, and boo-boos, they're equipped for major emergencies and, when necessary, can arrange for ambulance service to an area hospital. Seek medical advice the moment you suspect there may be a problem. Waiting it out only makes the solution more painful and more expensive.

If you do suffer a medical emergency, take comfort in the fact that dozens of families that we've interviewed have given ringing endorsements to Disney cast members in times of crisis. We've gotten emails and letters from people who have broken their arms, fainted from heat, gone into premature labor, come down with chicken pox, and everything else you can imagine—and each person has lauded the Disney cast members for their quick medical response and emotional support. One mother of two from Maryland wrote, "We visited Walt Disney World with our son, who has cystic fibrosis, and found everyone there to be extremely helpful and aware of what our needs might be. In fact, they often anticipated our needs before we did."

General First-Aid Tips

Keep these suggestions in mind if something goes wrong:

✦ If someone begins to feel ill or suffers an injury while in the parks, head for the nearest first-aid clinic. If the nurses there can't fix the problem, they'll find someone who can.

✦ All on-site hotels and many off-site hotels have physicians on call 24 hours a day. Contact either the Guest Relations desk at your own hotel or Centra Care Walk-In Medical Care (⊕ *www. centracare.org*), which, as the name implies, accepts walk-in patients and has in-house pharmacies. There are two locations near Disney World. Most area hotels provide courtesy transport to medical clinics and pharmacies for guests in need.

> **INSIDER'S SECRET**
>
> If anyone in your family has a recurring medical condition—your son often gets ear infections, for example—bring a copy of any prescriptions you generally use from home in case you need medication while in Orlando.

✦ If you need a pharmacy, try the **Walgreens** (☎ *407/253-6288*) on Kirkman Road or the **CVS** (☎ *407/390-9185*) on U.S. 192. Both are open 24 hours a day.

✦ Of course, in a true emergency call 911. Within the parks, any cast member can summon an ambulance for you.

✦ Electric Convenience Vehicles (ECVs; $50 with an additional $20 deposit) and wheelchairs ($12 a day or $10 a day for multiday use) are available at all theme parks, so if you're traveling with an older family member, a woman in the late stages of pregnancy, or anyone who might be laid low by the heat, don't hesitate to rent a little transportation assistance—especially at Epcot, which has the largest walking area of any Disney park. Also, ECVs are rented out on a first-come, first-served basis, so during the on-season, be sure to get one in the morning if you think there's a good chance you'll need it later in the day.

Child Care

Why might any decent parent seek a sitter while on a family vacation? Consider this scenario: Meaghan's sucking the inside of her mouth. Loud. Mom keeps making everyone stop while she readjusts the strap of her shoe to accommodate the blister she picked up halfway around the World Showcase Lagoon. You spent more than $200 to get through the Magic Kingdom gates—and Devin spends two hours feeding quarters into the same arcade game that's in the mall back home. Dad has been singing the first line—and only the first line—of "Zip-a-Dee-Doo-Dah" since Thursday. You've asked to see the kiddie menus from nine different restaurants in nine different Epcot countries, and you end up at

the American pavilion fast-food joint because Kristy won't eat anything but a hot dog. It's 100°F, this trip is costing at least $100 an hour, and that infernal sucking sound is getting on your last nerve.

Although it may seem un-American to suggest building time apart into the middle of a family vacation, the truth is that everyone will have more fun if you occasionally break up the group for a while. Even the most devoted of families aren't accustomed to being together 24 hours a day—for every meal, every ride, every potty stop. Every minute.

Some hotels in Orlando have responded with programs designed to get the kids involved with other children while parents have a night on the town. The idea is that everyone returns refreshed and recharged, with some happy stories to tell, and you can start the next day actually glad to be together again.

Quite a few off-site hotels have their own kids' clubs. Visit and tour the club before you drop your children off, and make sure that the place seems clean, safe, and has an appropriate child-to-caregiver ratio.

On-Site Kids' Clubs

Disney's on-site kids' clubs generally run in the evening for children ages 3 to 12, but they're most interesting for the 3 to 8 set. The older the child, the more likely he or she is to be bored. The clubhouses are well stocked with toys, computers, video games, and big-screen TVs. Make reservations by calling Guest Relations at the appropriate hotel; on-site guests get first crack at the available slots, but if the clubs don't fill up, space is available to off-site visitors. Note that children must be toilet trained.

Prices, policy, and planned entertainment change quickly at the kids' clubs, so confirm everything when you make your reservations.

The clubs usually open at 4 or 4:30 pm and close at midnight. Obviously, if you'll be dining at a Disney resort, it makes sense to try to book your kids into that hotel's child-care program so that you can drop them off, go on to your restaurant, and return easily to pick them up. Parents are given pagers in case of emergency, so you can truly relax while you enjoy your time alone. Rates average about $15 per hour per child with a two-hour minimum, and a credit-card guarantee is required when you make your reservation; if plans change, be sure to cancel or you'll be charged.

To get current pricing or make reservations at a kids' club, dial ☎ *407/939–3463* (☎ *407/WDW–DINE*). The following on-site hotels have kids' clubs:

Animal Kingdom Lodge	☎ *407/938–3000*
Beach Club	☎ *407/934–8000*
Dolphin	☎ *407/934–4000*
Polynesian	☎ *407/824–2000*
Wilderness Lodge	☎ *407/824–3200*

In-Room Sitters

Kids' clubs aren't always the right choice. Sometimes you'll need to arrange for an in-room sitter, especially if any of the following conditions apply:

✦ You have a child under the age of three. That's the cutoff point for most group programs.

✦ You plan to be out after midnight. Most kids' clubs close down before then, some as early as 10 pm.

✦ Your kids are exhausted. If you know in advance that you plan to employ an all-out touring schedule or your kids fall apart after 8 pm, hire an in-room sitter who can make sure they're in bed by their usual time. Most of the kids' clubs try to put preschoolers down in sleeping bags by 9 pm, but this involves moving them, and probably waking them, when parents return.

✦ You have a big family. Even with the add-on per-child rate, you can come out cheaper with an in-room sitter than by booking four kids into a group program.

For those staying on-site, one company, **Kid's Nite Out** (☎ *407/828-0920* ⊕ *www.kidsniteout.com*), provides trained sitters for all the Disney hotels; the service suggests calling two weeks in advance, but can sometimes accommodate more last-minute requests. Just prepare for sticker shock. The rate is $18 an hour for one child, plus $3 per hour for each additional child, with a four-hour minimum. A $10 transportation fee is also common, meaning that in-room sitting for two kids for four hours runs about $85—not cheap, but for many parents it's well worth the cost.

If you're staying off-site, you can also call either Kid's Nite Out or **Fairy Godmothers** (☎ *407/277-3724*), another service that has received consistent praise from readers. Or simply contact your hotel for help with in-room sitting. Most Orlando properties have relationships with reputable services. Not only does this save you a bit of hassle, but the person at the Guest Relations desk is also apt to know a lot more about whom to call than you do; if former guests haven't been pleased with a sitter, the hotel was undoubtedly the first to hear about it, so most family-oriented hotels use the same services over and over.

Things You'd Rather Not Think About

We've anticipated the problems you are most likely to encounter, and these are our best suggestions for what to do in less-than-ideal situations.

Rainy Days

Unless there's a full-out hurricane headed inland, the parks operate as usual. If there's an electrical storm, outdoor rides and shows are suspended until the weather clears, and water parks may close down for the day.

If you just run into one of those afternoon cloudbursts so common to Florida, soldier on. Rain slickers are available throughout the parks for $9, and they're much more practical than umbrellas because your hands are free to hang on to your kids. The only problem is that on a rainy day half the people in the park are wearing the slickers and everyone looks alike, making it easier to lose your kids in the crowd, so stay especially alert.

Here are some additional tips to make sure that a rainy day doesn't turn into a total washout.

✦ Disney's Hollywood Studios is a good choice when the weather is iffy because most of the rides and shows are indoors. The Animal Kingdom has mostly outdoor attractions, but if it's just misty and not pouring, it can also be a good choice because the animals are more active when a little rain cools off the air. The Magic Kingdom, where many rides are outside, and Epcot, which requires a lot of walking, are a bit tougher to navigate.

✦ There's always plenty to do at Downtown Disney: shop-ping, movies, Cirque du Soleil, and DisneyQuest. But be fore-warned—DisneyQuest is especially swamped when the weather turns bad.

✦ Remember, a rainy morning doesn't necessarily mean a rainy day. Weather conditions can change rapidly in Orlando, and if it clears up later in the day the parks will be less crowded than usual. If you see a storm approaching, duck into a show or in-door attraction and give it some time. You may walk out to find sunny skies.

Lost Kids

Obviously, your best bet is not to get separated in the first place. Savvy families set up prearranged meeting places. We also sug-gest that you stop by Guest Relations in the morning and get a tag where you can put your cell phone number on the inside of your child's clothing. ■**TIP➜ Where and when are kids most apt to get lost? During character signings, in play areas, and just after parades.**

If you do get separated and your kids are too young to un-derstand the idea of a meeting place, act fast. Disney employees are well briefed about what to do if they encounter a lost child, so the odds are good that if your preschooler has been wandering around on her own for more than a couple of minutes, she's been intercepted by a Disney cast member. The cast member has been trained to walk around the area with the child for about 10 minutes and, if they don't find you, take the child to the Baby Care Center in that park. So if you've been wandering around looking for longer than 10 minutes, flag down the nearest person you see wearing a Disney name tag, and ask him or her to call Baby Care and see if the child has been reported found. You can also make things easier if you wear colorful clothing and explain to any child old enough to remember that "Mom is wearing a bright blue shirt today." This increases the chances a cast member or your child will be able to spot you in the crowd.

INSIDER'S SECRET

Ironically, lost kids at Disney are often so entertained by the environment that they aren't crying and don't look lost, so no Disney employee intercepts them. Explain to your kids that if you get separated, they should approach anyone wearing a Disney name tag. That person can call in their name and, assuming you've also reported the child as missing, you can easily be reunited.

In real emergencies—when the child is very young or disabled, or when you're afraid she's been nabbed—bulletins are put out among employees. So if you lose a child, don't spend a half hour frantically searching on your own. Contact the nearest Disney employee and let the system take it from there.

Lost Cars

It's embarrassingly easy to forget where you parked, so be sure to write down your row number (or take a picture of it with your phone) as you leave your car in the morning. Aladdin 36 seems easy to remember at 8 am, but you may not be able to retrieve that information 14 brain-numbing hours later. If you forget to do this and can't find your car, tell a parking attendant the approximate time you arrived. Since the trams service parking-lot sections in a predictable sequence, if the attendant knows the general time you arrived, he or she can help you at least narrow the search.

Auto Breakdowns

As the tram drops people off at the end of the day, security vehicles are parked at the end of rows in anticipation of the fact some unlucky family is going to find that their battery is dead, a tire's gone flat, or they've locked their keys inside. This once happened to me on a rainy night, and I returned to the tram drop-off site and flagged down security to tell them our battery was dead. The young woman inside followed me back to the car and had the battery recharged within seconds. Then she was off to help a frantic family who couldn't remember what their rental car looked like. It's these little "we take care of you" touches that make Disney so special.

Closed Attractions

Because Disney World is open 365 days a year, there's no downtime for repainting and repairing rides. Ergo, two or three attractions throughout Disney World may be closed for refurbishment on any given day. They try hard to keep major attractions up and going for summer and holidays, so refurbishment is more likely to be an issue in the off-season. You can check to see which attractions are scheduled to be closed for maintenance during the time you'll be in Orlando by visiting ⊕ *www.disneyworld.com*. There's still a slight chance that a ride will be malfunctioning and temporarily closed when you visit, but this situation is relatively rare, and the rides usually come back on line quickly.

Other Unexpected Problems

No matter how carefully you plan your vacation, the unforeseen can always occur. Your best bet when trouble brews is to go straight to the nearest Disney cast member and report your problem. There's a reason you're paying these high prices, and one of the biggest is that Disney has created a very responsive team whose highest priority is to help you have a great experience. Our mail is absolutely full of stories about Disney cast members who have gone above and beyond the call of duty. Here are some examples from our readers:

✦ "My father lost his cell phone in the Animal Kingdom, and a cast member called every single attraction we had ridden that day until they found the phone. I can't say enough about the help-fulness of Disney employees!"

✦ "Our family missed the last bus leaving the Fantasia Gardens miniature golf course, and we had no idea how we were going to get back to Fort Wilderness. Panic was setting in when an out-of-service bus passed by. My dad flagged him down, and, to our surprise, the driver told us to get aboard, and he would take us there himself. He even calmed my little sister down by singing to her through the loudspeaker. It was the end of his shift, and he could have easily driven by, but that's not the Disney way."

✦ "We had a Princess dinner at Epcot scheduled for our first night, and my daughter's princess dress was packed in our luggage, which hadn't yet been delivered through Magical Express. We called the bell captain at our hotel, who was able to track the bag and get it to our hotel. He had it waiting for us when we got to the bell desk and let my daughter change in the luggage holding room! Then, since by that time we were running late, he even arranged for a special car to take us to Epcot so we wouldn't have to wait on the bus. It was a shining example of Disney customer service."

✦ "One day our 4-year-old was crying hysterically—I think it was because his sister drank the last of the pineapple juice. A street sweeper on Main Street asked us what was wrong, and then said 'Follow me,' and led us into Casey's where he got my son a Sprite. I was blown away. Such a kind gesture, especially considering how many crying kids that man probably sees in a day."

✦ "We had arranged to attend the Perfectly Princess Tea Party to celebrate my daughter's birthday. They called our room to tell us the event had been cancelled at the last minute—evidently Sleeping Beauty called in sick—but my daughter overheard the phone call and collapsed into tears. It was too late to get into any other character meals, but I remembered reading in an earlier version of your book that you should ask for help when you need it. We were staying at the Caribbean Beach Resort and a wonderful woman in Guest Relations not only got us into a Princess Breakfast at Epcot, which we all enjoyed, but sent a special little gift to the room for our daughter every single day for the rest of our trip."

Got the picture? If a problem develops, let the Disney cast members try to sort it out. And even if things are going smoothly, stop and chat with them. Many of our readers report that cast-member interactions are some of the highlights of their Disney stay.

Saving Money

Saving money at Disney World is something of an oxymoron, but there are ways to contain the damage.

Be aware that once you cross the Florida state line, there seems to be an inverse relationship between time and money. You have to be willing to spend one to save the other. It's worth taking a few minutes to analyze if cost-cutting measures are really worth it; given the high cost of tickets, it doesn't make sense to spend hours trying to save a few bucks.

Saving on the First Day

How should you spend your arrival day at Disney World? It's tempting to rush straight to the parks, but that's rarely the best use of your money. Because it will probably be at least afternoon before you arrive and settle into your hotel, you'll be using a full day of your expensive ticket for only a few hours in the park. Instead, relax around your resort pool or spend the evening at Downtown Disney, which offers lots of Disney-theme fun but doesn't require a ticket. You can start your first full day rested and raring to go.

Saving on Drinks

Staying hydrated is essential—and expensive—so bring your own bottles and refill them at fountains. All fast-food places provide free cups of ice water on request. Also, on-site hotels offer a deal where you can buy a souvenir beverage mug the first day of your trip and get free refills at the resort for the remainder of your stay. (These mugs can also be rented on a daily basis, so it's an especially great option for your "off" day when you're hanging around the hotel pool all afternoon and can take advantage of the free refills.) Because soft drinks and coffee are so costly, families who plan to eat a lot of meals at their hotel can save as much as $20 per person with the souvenir mugs.

Saving on Food

If you're not on the dining plan, try to eat at least some of your meals outside the parks. If you get a suite, it's easy to keep breakfast food and snacks in your room. Many off-site Orlando hotels offer free breakfast buffets to their guests, and there are numerous fast-food and family-friendly chain restaurants along the Interstate 4 exits that flank Walt Disney World.

Dining in Epcot's World Showcase can be very special, but book those restaurants for lunch, when prices are considerably lower than at dinner. And remember that portions are huge, even for kiddie meals. Consider splitting a meal with a family member or toss a few sandwich bags in your tote and save some of those chips or grapes for a later snack.

Dinner shows are expensive, costing a family of four about $150; even a character breakfast can set you back $70 or more. If the budget is tight, skip those extras and concentrate on ways to meet the characters inside the parks.

Saving on Extras

Except for maybe an autograph book and a T-shirt, hold off on souvenir purchases until the last day. By then the kids will really know what they want and you won't waste money on impulse buys.

Buy memory cards or film, diapers, foldable rain ponchos, and sunscreen at home before you leave. These things are all for sale in the parks, but you'll pay dearly for the convenience.

Saving on Parking

Guests staying off-site pay a lot to bring their car to Disney ($17 per day at this writing). If you move from park to park in the course of a day, save your parking receipt so you'll only have to pay the fee once. And remember that parking is free for on-site guests.

Saving on Park Tickets

Getting discounts on park tickets is difficult because Disney doesn't really discount. But you can certainly buy your tickets when you make your hotel reservations, so you'll have them before Disney decides it's time for another price increase before you leave.

Meeting the Disney Characters

Meeting the characters is a major objective for some families and a nice diversion for all. If your children are young, prepare them for the fact that the characters are big and often overwhelming in person. I once visited Disney World with a toddler whose happy babble of "my Mickey, my Mickey" turned into a wary "no Mickey, no Mickey" the minute she entered the Magic Kingdom gates and saw that everyone's favorite mouse was much, much larger than he appears on TV.

That reaction isn't unusual. Many kids panic when they first see the characters, and pushing them forward only makes matters worse. The characters are trained to be sensitive and sensible (in some cases more so than the parents) and will always wait for the child to approach them.

On the other hand, some kids fall in love with the characters from the start. A father from Ohio said, "We were really surprised at how fast our 3½-year-old daughter became a character groupie. Even when in her stroller she could spot them from a mile away, and she loved getting autographs. This took a lot of time but was worth it just to see the excitement on her face." And a mom from Tennessee reported that the first thing her four-year-old son said upon entering the Magic Kingdom gates was "I see the real Mickey and he is awesome."

Many children, even older ones, enjoy getting character autographs, and an autograph book can become a cherished souvenir. Before lining up, prepare the kids for the fact that the characters (except for those without masks) don't talk. As many as 30 young people in Mickey suits (mostly women because the suits are pretty small) might be dispersed around Disney World on a busy day, and they can't all be gifted with that familiar squeaky voice. Instead, they communicate through body language. (The exception is

Mickey at the Magic Kingdom, who can chat with all his guests. If this is a must-see, make sure to get a FastPass+.)

Times and places for meeting the characters are listed on theme-park maps, tip boards, and entertainment schedules.

Top 12 Tips for Hanging with the Characters

✦ Short on time? Character meals are a low-stress way to meet several characters at once. They're popular, so make reservations in advance, and if you can't get a reservation at Cinderella Castle, don't despair. There are princesses aplenty at the Akershus Royal Banquet Hall in the Norway pavilion at Epcot, which is much easier to book.

✦ What about the boys? In response to princess fever, Disney has done more to emphasize the pirates, especially at the Pirate League, where swashbuckling kids can get in face paint, eye patches, and costumes, and the Pirate Tutorial Session starring Captain Jack Sparrow. Both are located near the Pirates of the Caribbean ride in Adventureland.

✦ If you're scheduling a character breakfast, save it for the last day of your vacation. By this time kids have seen the characters plenty of times in parades and shows and even the most nervous toddler has usually relaxed enough to give Mickey a hug. If you choose a restaurant inside a resort, you can see the characters without having to burn a day of your ticket, and it's a great send-off for the trip home.

✦ Let the kids wear their costumes to the character meals, especially little girls with their princess regalia. What could be cuter than a miniature Belle meeting the real thing?

✦ Character dining can be pricey, so if money is an issue, skip the meals and use your entertainment schedule to find out where the characters will be inside the parks. The characters are usually available in greeting locations for about 20 minutes before they're whisked away to another spot. There's always an escort close at hand, so if the line to meet a certain character is long, check with the escort before you line up. He or she can tell you approximately how much longer the character will be there and save you from waiting patiently only to have Woody and Buzz leave just as your child makes it to the front of the line.

✦ If your child is nervous about meeting the characters, start with the so-called face characters, like Elsa or Peter Pan, who don't wear masks and can talk. They're far less intimidating to young children than "mask" characters like Goofy and Mickey.

✦ If the kids are still freaked out, remember not to push them forward. The characters are good at gently urging shy children to approach them. That said, because of the construction of their costumes, the mask characters can't always see what's happening beneath them too clearly. Donald and Daisy, for example, have a hard time looking over their bills, and small children standing at their feet might be ignored. If this appears to be happening, lift your child to the character's eye level. You can also make Mickey's day a little easier if you provide a thick marker for him to grasp and hold the pen and autograph book right in front of his face.

✦ Older kids especially love chances to interact with the characters, such as at the Jedi Training Academy outside of Star Tours in Hollywood or the aforementioned Pirate Tutorial Session in the Magic Kingdom.

✦ When the parks are crowded, you might need to go high-tech to assure that your kids see their favorites. The My Disney Experience app gives you the time and location of character appearances in every park, and guests are now able to get FastPass+ for some character greetings, which allows them to enter a shorter queue.

✦ Princess Fairytale Hall in the Fantasyland section of the Magic Kingdom offers a beautiful new venue for royal audiences. Cinderella and Rapunzel are available on one side to greet their subjects, while Elsa and Anna from Frozen are on the other. The Frozen princesses are the most popular characters in the Disney universe, often posting wait times of up to two hours. The good news is that once you finally get to the front of the line, you have plenty of time for pictures and autographs, but a FastPass+ reservation is an absolute must for this attraction. A similar situation exists at Enchanted Tales with Belle. Although it is a show and not just a meet and greet, the lines move slowly, so FastPass+ really helps.

✦ But, princesses aside—don't automatically assume that the best place to meet a character is the Magic Kingdom. The stars of Disney–Pixar films and Disney Junior are exclusively available at Hollywood Studios. The lines at the Animal Kingdom are rarely unmanageable, and the characters are doubly adorable outfitted in their safari gear. Not only are the classic characters always on hand in Epcot's Future World, but the World Showcase can be a character bonanza; meeting Mulan in China, Belle in France, Aladdin in Morocco, or Mary Poppins in the United Kingdom makes the experience that much more special.

✦ Wherever you are, don't get so involved in the hoopla that you lose your kids. When the kids are excited and dashing from one character to the next and parents are preoccupied with getting the perfect photo, it's easy to look up and realize little Jeremy has slipped out of sight.

CHAPTER 4

TOURING
TIPS &
PLANS

Disney World can be overwhelming for first-time guests, but these tips will turn even a group of overwhelmed newbies into a Disney-savvy family.

The size of Walt Disney World is often a shock to first-time visitors, many of whom arrive with vague notions that they can walk from Epcot to the Magic Kingdom or even that they are separate sections of the same theme park. There can also be confusion over the names: Some people use "Walt Disney World" and "Magic Kingdom" synonymously; in reality, the Magic Kingdom is a relatively small part of the much larger Disney World complex. There's more to this place than Cinderella Castle and Space Mountain. It's vital that you have at least a basic understanding of the Disney World layout and transportation system before you leave home.

Many of the tips in this chapter encourage you to visit more than one park a day—to follow a morning hitting the waterslides at Blizzard Beach, for example, with an afternoon taking in the shows at Hollywood. The best way to avoid overstimulation and burnout is to work a variety of experiences—some active, some passive, some educational, some silly—into each day. (Note that this strategy requires you to have a Park Hopper Pass.)

General Disney World Touring Tips

When it comes to touring, families tend to fall into three groups. The first group sleeps in, has a full-service meal at their hotel, and lollygags over to the parks around 11 am. They wander around, finding the lines for major rides so long that their only choices are either to wait 90 minutes for the Seven Dwarfs Mine Train or to spend the whole afternoon riding minor attractions. By the time they begin to get in a groove (for example, they figure out time-saving systems like FastPass+), it's 5 pm and they're exhausted. They retreat to their hotel room frustrated at how little they've seen, irritated by how much they've spent, and carping at each other. This is a vacation?

The second group is what I call Disney World Commandos. These hyper-organized types have elaborate tour plans and march determinedly from ride to ride, checking off their "to do" list as they go. Amanda wants to ride Dumbo twice in a row? No way! It'll throw them off schedule. Jeffrey wants to play one of the interactive games like Agent P's World Showcase Adventure at Epcot? Sorry, it's not on the list. If anything unforeseen happens—Space Mountain opens late or there's a glitch in the bus system—the whole group goes into a psychological meltdown. This is a vacation?

Disney-savvy families find the sweet spot between the two extremes. They have an overall plan but make sure to leave empty spaces in the day to allow for spontaneity. They get an early start each morning but factor in plenty of downtime to rest, particularly in the afternoon. Most important, they're familiar enough with each park and its attractions that they arrive with a clear idea of what they want to see but don't feel compelled to do it all. One father of four from Washington wrote, "Disney World is so big and so overwhelming that the first time we went down we spent hours just aimlessly drifting around. People need some kind of plan."

The following tips should help you make the most of your time without pushing parents or kids past their endurance level.

For families with kids, it's especially important to avoid the exhaustion that comes with just trying to get to one of the parks. If you're visiting at a crowded time and staying off-site, it can take two hours from the time you leave your hotel until you board your first ride, which is enough to shatter the equanimity of even the most well-behaved kid. Your children have been waiting for this vacation a long time, and now they've been flying and driving for a long time. You owe it to them to get into the parks quickly.

Understanding FastPass+

Use your FastPass+ options and use them wisely. They are a gift from the Disney gods and should not be squandered but used only for the most popular and slow-moving attractions. This might mean rides or it might mean character interactions, especially those that involve the princesses.

As of this writing, guests are allowed to make three Fast-Pass+ reservations per day in advance, and those three reservations must be used in the same theme park on three different rides. Thereafter, you can make as many FastPass+ reservations as you have time for and use them for any rides in the park (including multiple trips through the same attraction), but they can only be made one at a time through a kiosk. Your FastPass+ selections will be linked to your ticket, whether it is your MagicBand or a plastic ticket.

And while the first three reservations all have to be within the same park, the subsequent reservations you get through a kiosk can be from any park. For example, if you make three reservations in the Magic Kingdom in the morning, you can go to Animal Kingdom in the afternoon and make more FastPass+ reservations there. Note that these "once you're in the park" FastPass+ reservations probably won't be for the most popular attractions. The really primo FastPass+ reservations are snatched up 60 days in advance by on-site guests. But they can save you some time otherwise spent waiting for a second-tier ride or show.

A guest with a FastPass+ is allowed to enter a shorter line, whether it is for a ride or a character experience. A guest with a FastPass+ for a parade or show will be directed toward a reserved section in the theater or along the parade route. Note that this reserved section isn't necessarily in the front row—you just get guaranteed access to the event without having to line up an hour early. In other words, with parades and shows, the primary thing your FastPass+ gains you is time, not to mention eliminating the risk that you won't be seated at all.

Also remember that each family member needs his or her own FastPass+ reservation. One FastPass+ won't get all four of you onto Space Mountain.

As great as the FastPass+ is, you don't always need one. Don't bother using a FastPass+ for an attraction that routinely only draws moderate lines, such as "it's a small world" in the Magic Kingdom, or if the attraction in question is a theater-style show, such as Beauty and the Beast at Hollywood Studios, which admits hundreds of people at once. Essentially, you want to use your FastPass+ privilege where it will be most valuable—at the attractions that draw the largest crowds. This book—or the My Disney Experience app—can direct you toward the attractions where FastPass+ is at its most useful.

Best of all, if you change your mind—or if you discover that the wait time for a popular ride isn't so bad after all—you can change the FastPass+ reservations on the fly, as long as you do so before your ride time expires. So, if you have a FastPass+ reservation for Splash Mountain at 10 am but find that you can ride quickly after the rope drop, you can cancel that one and get a new FastPass+ reservation for a different ride, either by using the app on your smartphone or a FastPass+ kiosk.

Arriving

Every Disney World guidebook on the market tells people to come early, so it's no shock that in the 27 years since this book's first edition, the mornings have become more crowded. The good news for you is that most people visiting Disney World still arrive between 10 and 11 am, many of them proudly announcing that this is their vacation and they'll sleep in if they want. (These same people seem to take a strange inverse pride in bragging about how long they stood in line and how little they saw.) Arriving early is like exercising regularly: Everyone knows you should do it, but most people don't. An early start is still the best way to ride major attractions with little or no wait time.

If, for example, the Magic Kingdom is scheduled to open at 9 am, be at the gate by 8:30. At least part of the park is usually open early and you can be at the end of Main Street awaiting

INSIDER'S SECRET

Come early! If you follow only one tip in the whole book, make it this one. Although in recent years the mornings have become more crowded than they used to be, you'll still find far shorter waits for big-deal rides than you will in the afternoon. How important is an early arrival? During a recent October visit we got to the Magic Kingdom about 30 minutes before the stated 9 am opening time, and it took us approximately 10 minutes to get through the bag check and entrance gate. The next day we arrived at the Animal Kingdom 30 minutes after the stated 9 am opening time, and it took us over 20 minutes to get through the bag check and entrance gate. In other words, even an hour delay in arriving can double the amount of time it takes you to do a routine task. And when it comes to rides, the difference is even greater.

the rope drop while the other 50,000 poor saps are still crawling along Interstate 4.

If you're indeed allowed to enter the first section of the park early, use your time wisely. Take care of any business—get maps and entertainment schedules, rent strollers, take a potty break—before the main park opens. If you haven't had breakfast, there's always some sort of quick-service place where you can grab juice and muffins. The characters are usually on hand to greet kids, which is a fun way to start the day. But be sure to be at the ropes about 10 minutes before the stated opening times.

Planning Your Ride Time

To keep guests from stampeding after the rope drop, Disney controls how fast you can enter the main body of the park. Once the whole park opens, proceed quickly but calmly (they'll nab you if you run) to the first ride you'd like to board.

For those who are unable to use the My Disney Experience app, kiosks have been set up throughout the park. Lines shouldn't be terribly long, but if you are planning on using a kiosk, head there immediately upon entering the park. Here you will use a touch screen to select your FastPass+ times for the day, much like you would through the My Disney Experience app. A Disney cast member is always on hand to help you use the kiosks if you're having any trouble understanding FastPass+.

But it's an even smarter use of your time to move to your top-priority attraction first, then return to the kiosk after taking advantage of the relative emptiness of the early-morning hours.

Plan to see the most popular attractions either early in the day, late at night, or during a time when a big event siphons off other potential riders (such as the afternoon parade in the Magic Kingdom).

Kids usually want to revisit their favorite attractions, and parents who overschedule to the point where there's no time to go back risk a mutiny. One way to handle this is to save the entire last day of your trip for "greatest hits," and go back to all your favorites one more time, even if this means maximum park hopping.

∎TIP➜ **The single most important thing you can do to make your Disney visit go more smoothly? Use FastPass+ for the most popular attractions.**

Planning Your Meal Breaks

If you can, eat at "off" times. Some families eat lightly at breakfast, have an early lunch around 11 am, and supper at 5 pm. Others eat a more substantial breakfast and then a late lunch around 3 pm and have a final meal back at their hotel after the parks close. If you tour late and you're really bushed, all on-site hotels and many off-site hotels have in-room pizza delivery service.

∎TIP➜ **To maximize your time in the parks, either eat breakfast at your hotel or buy fast food while you're waiting for the rope drop. There's always at least one sit-down place to get breakfast in each park, but you don't want to waste the relatively uncrowded morning hours in a restaurant.**

Creating a Touring Plan

Use the touring plan to cut down on arguments and debates. It's a naive parent indeed who sits down at breakfast and asks, "What do you want to do today?" Three different kids will have three different answers. Here are some of the issues to consider when making those plans.

INSIDER'S SECRET

When scheduling your FastPass+ reservations, use a bit of reverse psychology. Use them when the park is at its most crowded, in the late morning and early afternoon. Also, space your FastPass+ times at least an hour apart. Some of the attractions where they are most valuable—Enchanted Tales with Belle and Princess Fairytale Hall—are time-consuming experiences even if you don't have to wait in a long line.

Finally—and most importantly—remember that FastPass+ works on a first-come, first-served basis. Only a certain number are available per attraction, so make your choices well in advance, preferably before you leave home. The most popular experiences—such as the Frozen princess meet-and-greets in Princess Fairytale Hall in the Magic Kingdom—fill up weeks in advance during the on-season.

Park Size

When making plans, keep the size of the parks in mind. Hollywood is small and can be easily crisscrossed to take in various shows. Likewise, the Animal Kingdom can be toured in five or six hours. The Magic Kingdom has more attractions and more crowd density, slowing you down; although some cutting back and forth is possible, you'll probably want to tour one land fairly thoroughly before heading to another. Epcot is so enormous that you're almost forced to visit attractions in geographic sequence or you'll spend all your time and energy in transit.

Park Hopping

If your kids have the stamina for it, try park hopping. Families with a multiday pass might figure: We'll spend Monday at the Magic Kingdom, Tuesday at Hollywood, Wednesday at Blizzard Beach, Thursday at Epcot, and Friday at the Animal Kingdom. It sounds logical, but a day at the Magic Kingdom is too much riding, 14 hours at Epcot is too much walking, the Animal Kingdom simply doesn't require that much time, a whole day at Hollywood is too many shows, and anyone who stays at Blizzard Beach from

Planning for Wait Times

If you're trying to predict how crowded a ride or show will be, five factors come into effect:

NEWNESS

In general, the newer it is, the hotter it is, which is why the expanded section of Fantasyland, which hosts a variety of relatively new attractions, such as the Seven Dwarfs Mine Train, is always busy.

QUALITY

Space Mountain, Fantasmic!, and other Disney classics will still be mobbed years from now.

SPEED OF LOADING

Continuous-loading attractions such as Pirates of the Caribbean and Under the Sea: Journey of the Little Mermaid can move thousands of people through in an hour. The lines at start-and-stop rides such as Dumbo move much more slowly, as do the lines for character-interaction experiences, such as Enchanted Tales with Belle or Princess Fairytale Hall.

CAPACITY

Shows like Festival of the Lion King, Beauty and the Beast, and Mickey's PhilharMagic have theaters that can accommodate large crowds. For this reason, theater-style attractions are good choices in the afternoon, when the park is at its most crowded and you need a rest.

CHARACTER INTERACTION

Any attraction where you are meeting a character, such as Enchanted Tales with Belle or Princess Fairytale Hall, both in the Magic Kingdom, will automatically have slow-moving lines. People love these interactive experiences because the characters take a lot of time with their kids. Trouble is, they're taking a lot of time with everyone else's kids, too. The line to meet Anna and Elsa, the Frozen princesses, at Princess Fairytale Hall moves at an especially glacial speed. Make a FastPass+ reservation (as far in advance as possible) if you can. Otherwise, try to arrive early.

dawn to dusk will wind up water-
logged. Mix it up a bit.

Transportation

Take some time to familiarize
yourself with the sprawling WDW
transportation system. If you're
staying on-site you'll be given a
transportation guide at check-in,
and Guest Relations (a.k.a. Guest
Services) can help you decide the
best route to take to out-of-the-
way locations.

> **HELPFUL HINT**
>
> Go digital. The My Disney
> Experience app provides
> real-time info about line
> lengths, FastPass+ return
> times, and even the loca-
> tions of the characters for
> meet and greets. It's also
> GPS enabled to keep you
> oriented and to help when
> you need to find a charac-
> ter, a hamburger, or a rest-
> room—and fast.

Meeting Characters

For families with young children,
seeing the characters is a major part of what makes Disney World
special, so don't overplan to the point where you have no time
to hang with Mickey and the gang. Your theme-park map and the
My Disney Experience app indicate when and where they'll appear, but the one place you probably won't see them is just walking down the street. At Disney, the characters are the equivalent
of rock stars, and security around them is tight. If you want that
photo, autograph, or hug, you'll need to line up or schedule a
character meal.

Open Hours

In the off-season, the Magic Kingdom, Hollywood, and the Animal Kingdom sometimes close at 5 or 6 pm, but Epcot always
stays open later, even during the least-crowded days of the year.
So spend your days at one of the parks that closes early and your
evenings at Epcot. This buys you more hours in the parks for your
money and, besides, many of the best places for dinner are at Epcot.

Splitting Up

If there's a wide gap in the ages of your kids, be aware of which
attractions are so intense that you'll need to split up. There are
plenty of places throughout all four parks where Disney has put
kiddie attractions next to rides that appeal to older kids. For ex-

ample, the Beauty and the Beast show at Hollywood Studios is just down the block from the Tower of Terror and Rock 'n' Roller Coaster. One parent can take the younger kids to the show while the other takes the older kids to the thrill rides. Likewise, at the Animal Kingdom, the Dinosaur ride scares the willies out of youngsters, but the nearby Boneyard is a great place for them to play while their older siblings are on the ride. Other attractions—such as Mickey's PhilharMagic, Soarin', and Kilimanjaro Safaris—are designed for all ages to experience together.

Taking a Day Off

If you'll be at Disney World for more than four days, consider planning a day off in the middle of your vacation. A day in the middle of the trip devoted to sleeping in, hanging around the hotel pool, shopping at Downtown Disney, and maybe taking in a character breakfast at an on-site hotel can make all the difference. Not only will you save a day on your multiday ticket, but you'll also start the next morning refreshed and energized.

Closing Time

You need a strategy for closing time. The major parks have nighttime extravaganzas that result in logjams as nearly every guest in the park convenes for the show and then mobs the exits when it's over. See the "Exit Strategies" section in each park for specific information on how best to exit.

Tips for Visitors Staying On-Site

If you're staying at a Disney resort, count yourself lucky and take advantage of all the perks and shortcuts you can.

Down Time

One of the greatest advantages of staying on-site is the shortened commute to the theme parks, making for an easy return to your hotel for a mid-afternoon nap or swim. You can reenter the parks in the early evening. Remember the mantra: Come early, stay late, and take a break in the middle of the day.

Extra Magic Hours

Take advantage of the Extra Magic Hour program. You're given a brochure at check-in telling you which park is featured on which day of your visit. This information is also incorporated into the My Disney Experience app. If you want to use this information in your pretrip planning, visit 🌐 *www.disneyworld.com* to verify which park will have extended hours on which day.

FastPass+

If you are staying on-site, you can make FastPass+ reservations 60 days in advance, which means if you plan your trip carefully, you can make your selections a full month before guests staying off-site. That means you'll have far more choices.

Tips for Visitors Staying Off-Site

While it's often easier to bite the bullet money-wise and stay on-site, that's not always possible. Saving on accommodations (and even some meals) is a good thing, and you can still have fun even if you aren't spending every single moment of your vacation on Disney property.

Time Your Commute

If you can make it from your hotel to the theme-park gates within 30 minutes, it may still be worth your while to return to your hotel for a midday break. If your hotel is farther out and your commute is longer, it's doubtful you'll want to make the drive four times a day.

Find a Place to Rest

If it isn't feasible to return to your hotel, find afternoon resting places within the parks. *(See the sections headed "Afternoon Resting Places.")* Sometimes kids aren't so much tired as full of pent-up energy. If that's the case, take them to the play areas in each park (Tom Sawyer Island in the Magic Kingdom; the play fountains in Epcot; the Honey, I Shrunk the Kids Movie Set Adventure at Hollywood; and the Boneyard at the Animal Kingdom) and let them run around for a bit.

Eat at the Resorts

The restaurants in the Magic Kingdom resorts are rarely crowded at lunch, and dining there is much more relaxed and leisurely than eating in the park. An early dinner can also effectively break up a summer day, when you'll be staying at the park until late. If you do take the monorail to a Magic Kingdom resort, be sure to line up for the train marked "Resort Monorail" and not the express back to the Transportation and Ticket Center (TTC).

Get Strollers

Off-site visitors tend to tour all day, so either bring or rent strollers for preschoolers. Few four-year-olds can walk through a 14-hour day.

FastPass+

Disney is still tinkering with changes to the FastPass+ system. As of this writing, off-site visitors with tickets in hand can reserve three FastPass+ selections (per day, but only in a single park) up to 30 days in advance. This might change, but even if it doesn't, not all off-site visitors get their tickets in advance. If you arrive at a theme park with no FastPass+ reservations and without access to the My Disney Experience app, hotfoot it to the first kiosk you see and make your choices. And be prepared for the likelihood that the most popular times and attractions may no longer be available thanks to on-site visitors who made their FastPass+ reservations weeks in advance.

Use Park Hopper

If you have the Park Hopper option on your ticket, spend the morning in a park where you'll be active (like the Animal Kingdom or the Magic Kingdom) and in the afternoon transfer to a park (such as Epcot or Hollywood) that has more shows and, thus, more places to sit and rest.

Money-Saving Tips

It isn't easy to save money at Disney, but the following tips will help.

Disney Dining Plans

By turning your vacation into more of an all-inclusive, the plans help you better gauge the cost of your trip in advance, a planning tool that some families prefer to showing up and winging it.

Hotel Choice

Choose wisely when it comes to your hotel. A more expensive hotel with lots of family-friendly perks might end up being more cost-effective than a hotel with a lower nightly rate but no extras.

Maximizing Tickets

Tickets are expensive, so use them only on days when you can maximize your hours in the park. This might mean not visiting a park on the first or last day of your vacation, when your travel schedule cuts into your available time; instead, use these days for a character breakfast at a Disney hotel, a visit to Downtown Disney, miniature golf, or just to relax at the hotel pool.

Controlling Extra Charges

Be aware of how little things add up, especially now that the MagicBands make it oh-so-easy to charge even the smallest item back to the room. Bring strollers, sunscreen, water bottles, diapers, and so on, from home. Make lunch your big meal of the day. Let two family members share a drink or a meal. Ask for a cup of ice water instead of buying bottled water at quick-service venues. And bring resealable plastic bags so that you can save leftover chips and fruit for a later snack.

One savvy mom from Wisconsin suggested that you hold souvenir shopping to a minimum by giving each child a gift card with a reasonable amount of money on it the first day you arrive. "If they know they have $40 to spend for the whole trip," she wrote, "they may decide on their own that they don't really need that $20 toy. It keeps them from begging and whining for every little thing you pass."

When it comes to character mania, cut corners where you can. If you figure out ways to meet the characters inside the park, you won't have to pay for a character breakfast. One mother from Florida reported that she bought her daughter's Cinderella dress on sale at the Disney Store before they left home and then did her own version of the Bibbidi Bobbidi Boutique in their hotel room on the morning of their character lunch. "I dabbed on a little makeup and put her hair in an updo with glitter hairspray," she said. "This alone saved us a hundred dollars."

On the other hand, when faced with a preschooler determined to have one of those $15 Mickey balloons they sell on Main Street in the Magic Kingdom, there are times that you just have to take a deep breath and get over it. "Choose your battles carefully," advised an Oklahoma mom. "It's their vacation, too. Buy them the balloon already."

Tips to Save Your Sanity

Pardon us if we are repeating ourselves with some of these tips, but good advice sometimes bears repeating.

Use Your Time Wisely

This boils down to one thing: Avoid the lines.

Head for the most crowded, slow-loading attractions first. In the Magic Kingdom that's Splash Mountain, Space Mountain, and Big Thunder Mountain, and any attraction within the new Fantasyland section, especially Enchanted Tales with Belle, Princess Fairytale Hall, and the Seven Dwarfs Mine Train. In Epcot it's Soarin' and Test Track. At Hollywood it's Toy Story Mania, the Rock 'n' Roller Coaster, and the Tower of Terror. At the Animal Kingdom it's Expedition Everest and Kilimanjaro Safaris.

Ride as many of the big-deal rides as you can in the morning, when waits are shorter. In general, save theater-style attractions for the afternoon. And if you can't get to all the big-deal rides in the first couple of hours the park is open, try again during the parades or the last hour before closing.

Be Willing to Split Up

By this point in the planning process, it's probably beginning to dawn on you that every member of your family expects something different from this vacation.

Discuss which attractions you'll enjoy as a family; some rides, shows, restaurants, and parades will be a blast for everyone. But there are also bound to be some attractions that won't have universal appeal, especially if there's a significant gap in the ages of your children.

If only one or two members of the family are into a certain show or ride, there's no need to drag the whole crew along. Preteens and teenagers, in fact, often like to split off for an hour or two. Security in Disney parks is tight, so this is an option worth considering. Just make sure to have a clearly designated meeting time and place or remind them to keep checking their cell phones for your calls or texts.

Know When You Don't Need FastPass+

As great as FastPass+ is, you don't always need one. Don't use the FastPass+ system if (a) the wait time in the general-admittance line is 20 minutes or less, (b) the attraction in question is a theater-style show that admits hundreds of people at once, or (c) you plan to ride an even more popular attraction later. Essentially, you want to use your FastPass+ privilege where it's most effective: for the big-deal rides that get the largest crowds.

Tips for Big Families

The official Disney website (⊕ *www.disneyworld.com*) offers special planning advice for large families, including a list of resorts with the sort of accommodations you'll likely need. The following tips may also make things a little less hectic. ■**TIP➔ The My Disney Experience app allows families to share information (such as reserved dining times or FastPass+ info) as well as pictures, and thus can serve as a sort of "group memo" to remind everyone of upcoming events.**

Dining

If you have a large group all on the dining plan, you may qualify for a special dining experience. These experiences vary, but in the past have included an IllumiNations reception at Epcot, a safari-theme meal at the Animal Kingdom, and a character breakfast at the Magic Kingdom. Your options will be explained to you when you add the dining plan to your package.

It's approximately, um, three times harder to get a table for 12 than one for 4, so make dining reservations early. If you have trouble getting bookings, eat at off times (say, 3 pm for lunch or 5 for dinner) or stick to resort restaurants, which are generally less crowded than those in the parks. Note: A gratuity of 18% is added for parties of eight or more—even at buffet restaurants.

Lodging

Consider renting a villa or condo. Many have kitchens, so you can save on eating out. On-site resorts with villa-style lodging include Old Key West, Saratoga Springs, BoardWalk Villas, the Beach Club Villas, the Grand Floridian Villas, the Bay Lake Towers at the Contemporary, the Villas at Wilderness Lodge, and the soon-to-open Polynesian Villas. There are also plenty of off-site condos and villas for rent; check out the Off-Site Hotels section in Chapter 2 for ideas.

If you'd like a little less togetherness, book more rooms but ask that they be adjoining.

Transportation

Transportation can be an issue, especially if there's a wide variation in the ages, stamina, and risk tolerance of the family members. Older kids will probably want to stay at the park all day, while toddlers and great-grandparents might be burned out and ready to rest by noon. Either way, stay on-site so you can use the Disney transportation system at your leisure, or, if you're driving, bring more than one vehicle to the parks so that family members have the option to leave early.

Tips for Guests with Disabilities

Sadly, for years, some visitors have looked for ways to take unacceptable advantage of Disney's generous policy toward guests with disabilities. Able-bodied people would rent Electric Convenience Vehicles (ECVs) simply to avoid walking and for the free front-of-the-line access. This glut of ECVs, often badly driven by theme-park guests who were clearly using them for the first time, really held up the system, especially on buses, where it takes considerable effort to load and unload them. Ergo, Disney has tightened the system.

Disability Access Service Cards

Guests needing extra help, including those with Down syndrome and autism, now visit Guest Relations upon arrival at the theme park to pick up a Disability Access Service card. A cast member will take the guest's picture to be placed on the pass, thus ensuring that the card can only be used by the person who needs it, and by those traveling with him or her. You then show the pass to the cast member standing at the entrance to each attraction. Most lines have now been altered to cater to guests in wheelchairs or with disabilities, so expect to sometimes use the normal queue. Otherwise the cast member will hand you a ticket that will in effect hold your place in line. For example, if the line to Space Mountain is 30 minutes long, you will receive a special type of FastPass+ to return 30 minutes later.

The Disability Access Cards, especially when held by children, guarantee you a little special treatment. One mother of a special-needs child wrote that her four-year-old son was nervous about meeting Captain Hook, but she told him to show the villain his "special card." Hook rose to the occasion, dramatically blowing his nose on the card before returning it to the child with great ceremony. "Andrew was laughing by then," the mother said, "and didn't worry about meeting characters for the rest of the trip."

Wheelchair Rentals

You can rent wheelchairs ($12 per day, $10 per day for multiday use) and Electric Convenience Vehicles (ECVs; $50 per day plus an additional refundable $20 deposit) on a first-come, first-served basis.

Download a copy of the official *Guidebook for Guests with Disabilities* at ⊕ *www.disneyworld.com* when you book your room. It offers detailed information on how to approach each attraction. You can also get the guidebook at any Disney hotel and Guest Relations window, but having it in advance will help you know what to expect.

Accessible Guest Rooms

People with disabilities give the Disney resorts high marks for convenience at reasonable prices. The All-Star resorts, for example, have several wheelchair-accessible rooms that begin as low as $109 a night. Most of the on-site resorts offer rooms with specially equipped bathrooms and extra-large doors, and, if you request it, you can have a complimentary wheelchair waiting for you upon check-in.

For more detailed information on hotel options for people with disabilities, call Central Reservations at ☎ 407/934-7639 (☎ 407/W-DISNEY) and ask for the Special Reservations Department.

Accessible Transportation

The monorail, buses, boats, and other forms of transportation are all wheelchair accessible.

Storage for Medications

You can refrigerate insulin and other medications at first-aid stations, all on-site hotels, and most off-site hotels.

Tips for Guests with Visual Disabilities

Guests with visual disabilities should be aware that guide dogs are welcome at all parks and many area hotels. You can also borrow a wireless-enabled Assistive Technology Device describing the attractions at each park or a Braille guidebook with a refundable deposit. Just visit Guest Relations.

Tips for Guests with Hearing Disabilities

Guests who are deaf can pick up a handheld captioning device at Guest Relations. This device works on many attractions. Guests with some hearing loss can rent listening devices that amplify attraction music and words. The devices are available through Guest Relations with a refundable deposit.

TTYs are available throughout Disney World, and guests can also contact Disney Reservations via TTY at ☎ 407/939-7670.

Tips from Our Readers

Finally, here are some words of reassurance. If you're traveling with someone who has a health problem or disability, rest assured that the Disney World cast members will help you in any way they can. Because Disney World is frequently visited by children sponsored by the Make-A-Wish Foundation and other programs like it, the Disney staff is accustomed to dealing with

a wide range of situations, even cases in which visitors are seriously ill. The key is to make sure that Disney employees both
at your hotel and within the parks are aware of your presence
and that you may need assistance. With a few preliminary phone
calls, you'll find that Disney World is one of the best possible
travel destinations for such families.

A dad of three, including a special-needs eight-year-old,
wrote, "We heard how Disney cast members go out of their way
to accommodate special children. We found this to be absolutely
true. For any ride that William could go on, we got front-of-line
privileges. We also were escorted to special viewing areas for
shows and parades."

A mom from Connecticut wrote, "We informed our hotel (the
Contemporary), in advance, of our daughter's health problems and
when we checked in, we were delighted to learn that our family
had been invited to ride in the first car of the afternoon parade
at the Magic Kingdom. The cast member told us that there is no
way to guarantee such an invitation, but that if they know a special-needs child is visiting, they try to offer some treats. Riding in
the convertible and waving to the crowd was the highlight of our
daughter's week."

"My 6-year-old daughter has some usable vision but is legally
blind," wrote another mom. "We knew she wouldn't be able to
enjoy most of the shows, so we stopped by Guest Relations, and
they gave us [our special card]. Any time we approached a show,
she held out the card and a cast member would escort us to [up-
front] seating. This meant the world to all of us. She was able to
actually *see* Belle dancing with the Prince."

Tips for Pregnant Guests

Talk about the circle of life. Kim, this book's original author, first
toured Disney World three decades ago, when she was pregnant
with her daughter Leigh. Leigh has recently welcomed her own
first child. So we're proof that it is possible to have a great time in
the parks while pregnant—as long as you take a few precautions:

✦ Make regular meal stops. Instead of buying a turkey leg from
a vendor, get out of the sun and off your feet at a sit-down
restaurant.

✦ If you aren't accustomed to walking the typical Disney trek of 7 miles a day, begin getting in shape a couple of months before the trip by taking 30- to 40-minute walks. Make sure to "train" outside if possible—the Florida heat and humidity make touring Disney much different from walking the treadmill inside a gym.

✦ Dehydration is a real danger. Keep water in your tote bag and sip frequently. You can refill your bottle at water fountains throughout the parks or ask for free refills at any counter-service location.

✦ Consider staying on-site so that you can return to your room in the afternoon to rest.

✦ Mothers-to-be are welcome to rest in the rocking chairs inside Baby Care.

✦ The most important tip of all if you're pregnant: Check out restroom locations in advance.

Birthdays and Special Occasions

Celebrating a birthday? Anniversary? Graduation? Is it your first visit? Drop by Guest Relations in each park and pick up a free pin announcing your status. Cast members keep an eye out for special visitors and will make an extra effort to acknowledge them, especially a child wearing a birthday pin. One mother reported that when the characters in the afternoon parade saw her daughter's birthday pin, they made a point to come over and high-five her or shake her hand.

If you're celebrating a special occasion, the general rule is "Ask and you shall (probably) receive." If you're staying at a Disney resort, inform Guest Relations or the concierge in advance if you'd like flowers or a gift delivered on a special day. Rooms can also be decked out with confetti, balloons, and banners while you're in the park so that the celebrant returns to find a decorated room. If you want to celebrate with a special meal, make reservations at your restaurant of choice weeks in advance and let the manager know your preferences. You can arrange for a special cake that's themed to the occasion and the likes of the birthday boy or girl. (And if you want to have a full birthday party on-site, there are locations for that as well.)

One mother wrote that her son celebrated his birthday at a character breakfast featuring Pooh and friends. The cake was delivered to the table by Tigger, the child's favorite character, who then led the birthday guests in an impromptu parade around the restaurant. Or consider the young man who proposed to his girlfriend at the Coral Reef in the Seas pavilion at Epcot. The couple was having dinner next to the mammoth glass aquarium when, at the key moment, one of the divers swam by the table carrying a sign that read, "Will you marry me?" When the girl turned to look at her boyfriend, he was on one knee with the ring—and the whole restaurant stood up and cheered when she said yes.

If you'd like to add some treats and surprises to a special occasion, contact the management at the hotel or restaurant. With their help, you should have no trouble finding a way to make the day memorable.

Customizing Your Touring Plan

Gather Information

Both Disney's website, ⊕ *www.disneyworld.com,* and the app My Disney Experience are good sources of preliminary information, including theme-park hours during the time that you'll be visiting, the times for Extra Magic Hours, and any attractions scheduled to be closed for refurbishment.

Ask Yourself Some Basic Questions

Consider how long you'll want to stay at each park. If your kids are under eight, you'll probably want to spend more time in the Magic Kingdom. Older kids? Plan to divide your time fairly equally among the major parks and save some time for the water parks and Downtown Disney.

The time of year you'll be visiting is a major factor, too; although you may be able to tour Hollywood thoroughly in a single day in October, it will take you twice as long to see the same number of attractions in July. In summer the combination of the

INSIDER'S SECRET

If you're a single parent, consider vacationing with one of your siblings or another single parent. "My daughter is 11 and my son is 4," wrote one mother from Texas. "They like totally different things, and it would have been impossible to give them both the Disney experience they wanted if we'd gone to Orlando by ourselves. So we went with my sister and nephew, rented a nice condo, and had a great time. I did the wild rides with my daughter and meanwhile my sister, who is so prone to motion sickness that she once threw up in an elevator, took the boys around to meet all the characters."

"It's never a good idea to let the kids outnumber the adults," added another single mother, from New Jersey. "My friend Jenny, who doesn't have kids but who loves being an unofficial aunt, has gone down to Disney with us twice. Otherwise, I don't think I'd have the guts to try it."

crowds, the heat, and extended park hours means you'll need to build in more downtime.

Plan at least one evening each in the Magic Kingdom, Hollywood, and Epcot, so that you can see all the closing shows. If you're traveling during the off-season, when Hollywood Studios' Fantasmic! and the Magic Kingdom parades only run on some nights, make sure you're in the right park on the right night.

Set Your Priorities

Poll your family on what attractions they most want to see and build these priorities into the plan. I'd let each family member choose three must-sees per park. For example, at Hollywood, 10-year-old Jeremy wants to ride Toy Story Mania, the Tower of Terror, and the Rock 'n' Roller Coaster. His six-year-old sister, Elyce, chooses Muppet*Vision 3D, the Frozen Singalong, and Voyage of the Little Mermaid. Mom thinks the '50s Prime Time Café sounds like a hoot and wants to ride the Great Movie Ride and Toy Story Mania. Dad is all over the Tower of Terror/Rock 'n' Roller

Coaster thing and thinks the Lights, Motors, Action! Extreme Stunt Show sounds interesting.

Because of some overlap, you have nine items on this family's personal must-see list. They should make sure that they experience these attractions even if they don't do anything else. With any luck, they'll have some extra time and may be able to work in a few other things as well, but the key is to make sure you honor everyone's top three choices.

And, of course, this customized "must-see" list then becomes the basis of your FastPass+ list. Use the individual park chapters in this book to determine which attractions on your list are most apt to draw a long line or move slowly and then use FastPass+ to guarantee you get to enjoy them with minimal waits.

Cut Some Deals

Building each family member's must-sees into the touring plan has many advantages. You're seeing the best of the best, you've broken out of that "gotta do it all" compulsion, and the kids feel that they're giving input and are full partners in the vacation planning.

There's another huge advantage: A customized touring plan minimizes whining and fights. Your 12-year-old is more apt to bear a character breakfast with good grace if she knows that you'll be spending the afternoon at Blizzard Beach, one of her top choices. Kids understand fair. They might fidget a bit in Chefs de France, but if you've already covered Soarin' and Mission: SPACE, you're perfectly justified in saying, "This is Mom's first choice in Epcot, so be quiet and eat your *croquette de boeuf*."

Break Up the Days

Divide each day of your visit into three components: morning, afternoon, and evening. It isn't necessary to plan where you'll be every hour on the hour—that's way too confining—but you need some sense of how you'll break up the day. (Note: This plan assumes you have the Park Hopper option on your tickets.)

Pencil in things that have to be done at a certain time. You have a character breakfast for Wednesday morning, for example, or you must be in the Magic Kingdom on Friday night because that's the only time the evening parade is scheduled during your visit.

Monday

- **Morning:** Magic Kingdom
- **Afternoon:** Rest by hotel pool
- **Evening:** Epcot

Tuesday

- **Morning and afternoon:** Animal Kingdom
- **Evening:** Hollywood

Wednesday (rest day)

- **Morning:** Character breakfast
- **Afternoon:** Downtown Disney, then early to bed

Thursday

- **Morning and afternoon:** Blizzard Beach
- **Evening:** Epcot

Friday

- **Morning:** Hollywood
- **Afternoon:** Rest by pool
- **Evening:** Magic Kingdom

CHAPTER 5

THE
MAGIC
KINGDOM

* * *

Opened in 1971, the Magic Kingdom was the first park in Walt Disney World, and it's still the most popular (and crowded!) of the four main theme parks. The Magic Kingdom is broken into six sections, arranged in a circle around Cinderella Castle. This mecca for the under-10 crowd is full of kiddie rides and character sightings as well as parades and shows.

The Magic Kingdom is the park that best embodies the Disney spirit, because it is home to many of the classic rides like Dumbo and the Mad Tea Party that are so much a part of our collective Disney consciousness. Since the attractions here are almost exclusively designed for families, there are relatively few rides that will scare off kids under eight. Prepare to tour mostly as a family, enjoying the shows, parades, and classic attractions together.

You will enter the Magic Kingdom by walking down Main Street U.S.A, an idealized replica of Walt Disney's own hometown of Marceline, Missouri, complete with shops, ice-cream parlors, and a cinema. At the end of Main Street is Cinderella Castle, the Magic Kingdom's primary landmark.

From there, take one of the bridges into either Adventureland, Liberty Square, Fantasyland, or Tomorrowland. Pirate wannabes should head to Adventureland, home of the Jungle Cruise and Pirates of the Caribbean. Liberty Square pays homage to America's beginnings and leads into Frontierland, which features Splash Mountain and Big Thunder Mountain Railroad, the wildest ride in the wilderness. Fantasyland is home to Disney's popular princesses and has recently almost doubled in size to include new attractions and restaurants. (This expanded area is usually referred to as "new Fantasyland" while the section just behind the castle is often referred to as "classic Fantasyland.") Tomorrowland portrays a retro-style future that never was, complete with Space Mountain. Plan to finish off your night back where you began, watching the Main Street Electrical Parade and the nightly fireworks spectacular.

Magic Kingdom Touring Tips

Getting Here

If you're staying off-site, prepare for a complicated journey. Either drive or take your hotel shuttle to the Transportation and Ticket Center (TTC) inside the Magic Kingdom parking lot. From the TTC you can cross the Seven Seas Lagoon by ferry or monorail. Both deliver you to the Magic Kingdom front gates.

If you're staying on-site, getting to the Magic Kingdom is a lot easier. From the Contemporary Resort, you can bypass the TTC and take the monorail to the Magic Kingdom or simply walk to the park. From the Grand Floridian, you can either take the monorail or ferry. From Fort Wilderness Campground or Wilderness Lodge, take the ferry. Polynesian guests have all the options: the monorail, a water taxi, or the ferry.

Guests at Disney hotels that aren't Magic Kingdom resorts take shuttle buses that deliver them directly to the Magic Kingdom's front gates, bypassing the TTC. Sometimes families who stay on-site but have a car prefer to drive to the parks, which can save time at every park except the Magic Kingdom. If you're headed there, take Disney transportation even if you have your own car, just so you can avoid the TTC.

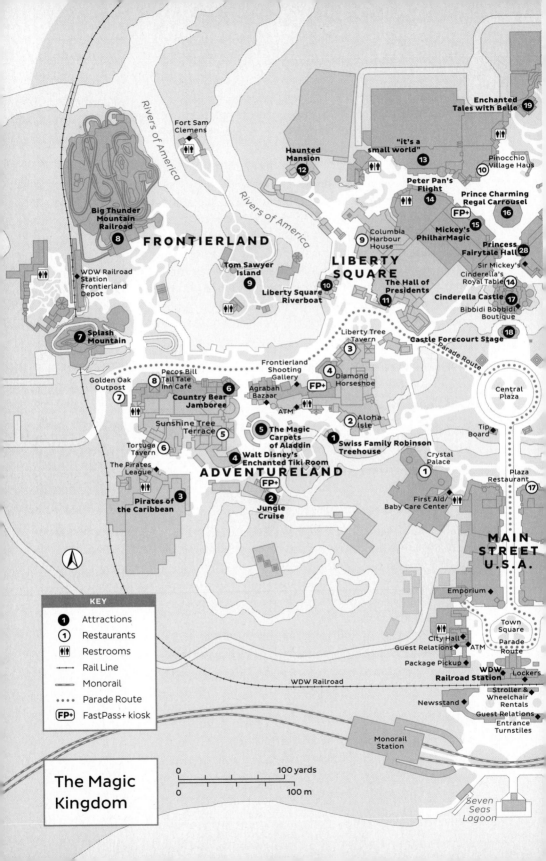

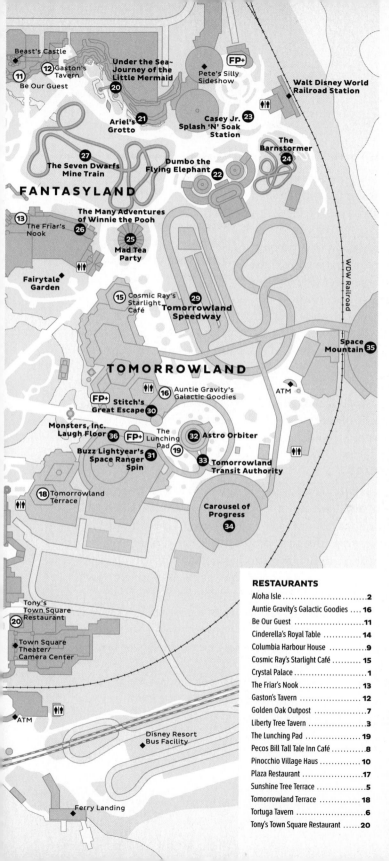

Beast's Castle

⑪ ⑫ **Gaston's Tavern**

Be Our Guest

⑳ **Under the Sea~ Journey of the Little Mermaid**

◆ **Pete's Silly Sideshow** FP+

Walt Disney World Railroad Station

㉑ **Ariel's Grotto**

◆ ㉓ **Casey Jr. Splash 'N' Soak Station**

㉔ **The Barnstormer**

㉗ **The Seven Dwarfs Mine Train**

㉒ **Dumbo the Flying Elephant**

FANTASYLAND

⑬ **The Friar's Nook**

The Many Adventures of Winnie the Pooh ㉖

㉕ **Mad Tea Party**

◆ **Fairytale Garden**

⑮ **Cosmic Ray's Starlight Café**

㉙ **Tomorrowland Speedway**

Space Mountain ㉟

TOMORROWLAND

⑯ **Auntie Gravity's Galactic Goodies**

ATM

FP+ **Stitch's Great Escape** ㉚

Monsters, Inc. Laugh Floor ㊱ FP+ **The Lunching Pad** ⑲ ㉜ **Astro Orbiter**

Buzz Lightyear's Space Ranger Spin ㉛ ㉝ **Tomorrowland Transit Authority**

⑱ **Tomorrowland Terrace**

Carousel of Progress ㉞

Tony's Town Square Restaurant ⑳

Town Square Theater/ Camera Center

◆ **Disney Resort Bus Facility**

ATM

Ferry Landing

WDW Railroad

Morning Tips

Through the Turnstiles

The bag check is a necessary nuisance, but it moves quickly. To save time, have one adult go through with all the bags while the other takes the kids through the "no bag" entrance. Then on to the turnstiles.

If you're staying on-site or have purchased them in advance, you have the option to choose the colors of your MagicBands. Your theme-park tickets—if you opt to go old school—will each have a different scene or character on the front. This is to help you remember whose ticket is whose. Disney's security system requires ticket holders to place their second finger into an electronic reader as they go through the turnstiles. Disney makes a quick electronic measurement of the finger, allowing the system to link your park ticket or MagicBand to you and you alone.

Getting Around

The Disney World Railroad leaves from Main Street with stops in Frontierland and Fantasyland. A lap around the park takes 20 minutes; trains depart from Main Street every 4 minutes at busy times and every 10 minutes at slower times. Even so, this isn't the fastest way to get around the park. In the morning, when crowds are heaviest, you may have to wait for a second or even third train; by that time, you could have walked.

Walking, in fact, is the fastest means of transport in the Magic Kingdom. The train, vintage cars, and horse-drawn carriages are cute, but think of them as rides, not as a serious means of getting around the park.

Be prepared to make frequent rest stops in the Magic Kingdom. You won't walk as much as you do in Epcot, but you're likely to spend more time standing in line. This is ultimately harder on the feet—and the nerves—than walking.

Your First Hour in the Magic Kingdom

Be through the gates 30 minutes earlier than the stated opening time. Rent strollers if needed and pick up a map and entertainment schedule as you enter. The entertainment schedule gives you showtimes and character meeting times for that day.

- **Guest Services.** Early morning is a great time to visit Guest Relations (a.k.a. Guest Services) inside Town Hall. If anyone in your party has something to brag about—a birthday, an anniversary, or just being a first-time visitor—you can pick up a pin announcing the news and guaranteeing you a little extra attention from cast members.

- **Character Meet and Greets.** There are usually characters waiting to interact with you in the Town Square section of Main Street. If the park hasn't officially opened and the ropes haven't dropped, let the kids stop by and say "hi." But if the park is open, you need to move ahead to the rides, which will draw long lines later in the day. You can always return to Main Street in mid-afternoon to meet the characters.

- **Busy Days.** On days that are expected to draw large crowds, you can travel the length of Main Street before the Magic Kingdom officially opens. On less crowded days, early arriving guests are usually held in the Town Square just in front of the railroad.

- **Extra Magic Hours.** On Extra Magic Hour mornings, Fantasyland and Tomorrowland open first. Older kids should head straight for Space Mountain and Buzz Lightyear's Space Ranger Spin, while younger kids should start with Enchanted Tales with Belle, the Seven Dwarfs Mine Train, and Princess Fairytale Hall.

- **Splitting Up.** If there's a gap in the ages of your children and the nine-year-old is ready for a coaster but the five-year-old isn't, split up during the crucial first hour, when popular attractions have relatively short waits. Mom can take one child, Dad the other, and you can meet back up in an hour.

- **Setting Up FastPass+.** Day guests who have arrived at the Magic Kingdom without making FastPass+ reservations should find the nearest kiosk and choose three FastPass+ options for the day. FastPass+ kiosks are located in Tomorrowland near Stitch's Great Escape, in Adventureland near the Jungle Cruise, and in Fantasyland near Mickey's PhilharMagic. Remember that each member of the family will need his or her own FastPass+.

✦ **Maximizing FastPass+.** We've talked about this special perk for on-site guests before. FastPass+ can be used for any ride or character meet and greet—but make sure to use these judiciously. Families with little princesses will do best to sign up for Princess Fairytale Hall (both sides) and Enchanted Tales with Belle. If princesses aren't your thing, get a FastPass+ reservation for the Mickey line in Town Square Theater and the Seven Dwarfs Mine Train. For older kids, set up FastPass+ for Space Mountain, Big Thunder Mountain, and Splash Mountain.

Afternoon Tips

Afternoon Resting Places

When you don't want to return to your hotel room but still need a short, air-conditioned break, here are your best bets:

- ✦ Country Bear Jamboree
- ✦ The Disney World Railroad (you can rest while you ride)
- ✦ The Enchanted Tiki Room
- ✦ Hall of Presidents
- ✦ Mickey's PhilharMagic
- ✦ Monsters, Inc. Laugh Floor

Best Vantage Points for Watching the Parades

The Magic Kingdom has two basic parades: the afternoon parade (usually 3 pm), which runs daily, and the evening parade, which runs nightly in the on-season and periodically during the off-season. All parades begin by City Hall and finish beside the gate just to the left of Splash Mountain.

INSIDER'S SECRET

Sorcerers of the Magic Kingdom is a park-wide interactive experience, where guests collect magic-spell cards that help them fight Disney villains. Visit one of the training centers in Fantasyland, Liberty Square, or Main Street to receive a packet of six magic cards and a specialized key card. Then travel around to different locations throughout the Magic Kingdom, hold up your key card, and use the spell cards to fight off villains. Sound complicated? Cast members are all around to help, but kids always pick it up faster than adults. Be warned, though: This game can become addictive and will take away from valuable time in the parks. Try to steer the kids clear if this is your first visit to the Magic Kingdom.

The new afternoon parade, called Festival of Fantasy, has become a big hit by featuring a mix of classic and contemporary characters. Because Disney changes its parade very rarely, this is big news with locals and loyalists. Expect even larger-than-average crowds.

Stake your curb space about 30 minutes before the parade is due to start. If you show up an hour early, you might snag a seat on the second floor of the railway station. For some families the bird's-eye view more than makes up for not being able to interact with characters.

Best Vantage Points for Watching the Fireworks

The evening fireworks include a nifty little extra called Tinker Bell's Flight. Look toward the castle and you'll see a young gymnast dressed like Tink descend via wire from the top of the castle.

FastPass+ gives families the option of reserving a special viewing spot, and this may be worth it if you haven't already used your three extras up. But most people would rather use their extra passes on rides and character experiences—and indeed, that is probably the smarter move. The "special viewing" spot isn't all that special.

Fireworks Tips

The best place to watch the Magic Kingdom fireworks isn't actually in the Magic Kingdom at all. It's at the California Grill, high atop the Contemporary Resort. The California Grill is a beautiful upscale restaurant that offers some of the best cuisine in all of Orlando. Despite the restaurant's reputation, it isn't formal or stuffy. Kids are welcome.

To see the fireworks, reserve a time about 30 minutes before the evening parade, which is followed by the fireworks, is due to start. (You must do this before you leave home. First call ☎ 407/824–4321 or visit ⊕ www.disneyworld.com to determine the evenings and times the parade is scheduled, and then reserve a table by calling ☎ 407/939–3463.) Since so many guests have been showing up at the restaurant just to see the fireworks, the restaurant has implemented a policy that only diners are allowed to view the show. (Can't get a perfectly timed reservation? If you dine at California Grill earlier that evening, ask if you can return at fireworks time. Some families have reported that if they kept their dining receipt they were allowed back for the viewing. A large outdoor walkway area keeps the restaurant from getting too packed.)

Once the fireworks begin, the restaurant dims its lights and pipes in the theme music from the fireworks show. You have a fabulous view of the pyrotechnic display and a bona fide magical moment.

Although the vantage point isn't quite as perfect, you can also see the fireworks from Narcoossee's and Cítricos, two restaurants in the Grand Floridian, and at 'Ohana in the Polynesian.

If you're willing to part with a few doubloons, there's even the Pirates & Pals Fireworks Voyage on the Seven Seas Lagoon that gives you a terrific view of the fireworks and lots of fun extras. It sails on select dates, usually departing around 8:45, and costs $59 for adults, $34 for kids. For more information call ☎ 407/939–7529.

Evening Tips

Your Last Hour

Wishes, the present manifestation of the fireworks display in the Magic Kingdom, is beautiful, with pyrotechnics perfectly synchronized to a musical score. It's presented nightly at closing

Magic Kingdom Don't-Miss List

IF YOUR KIDS ARE 8 OR OLDER:

✦ Any Fantasyland rides that catch their fancy

✦ Big Thunder Mountain Railroad

✦ Buzz Lightyear's Space Ranger Spin

✦ Haunted Mansion

✦ Mickey's PhilharMagic

✦ The parades

✦ Pirates of the Caribbean

✦ The Seven Dwarfs Mine Train

✦ Space Mountain

✦ Splash Mountain

IF YOUR KIDS ARE UNDER 8:

✦ Buzz Lightyear's Space Ranger Spin

✦ Dumbo

✦ Enchanted Tales with Belle

✦ "it's a small world"

✦ Mad Tea Party

✦ The Magic Carpets of Aladdin

✦ The Many Adventures of Winnie the Pooh

✦ Mickey's PhilharMagic

✦ The parades

✦ Peter Pan's Flight

✦ Pirates of the Caribbean

✦ Princess Fairytale Hall

✦ The Seven Dwarfs Mine Train

✦ Splash Mountain and Big Thunder Mountain, if they're bold enough and if they pass the height requirement

✦ Under the Sea–Journey of the Little Mermaid

Quick Guide to Magic

Attraction	Location	Height Requirement
Astro Orbiter	Tomorrowland	None
Barnstormer	Fantasyland	35 inches
Big Thunder Mountain Railroad	Frontierland	40 inches
Buzz Lightyear's Space Ranger Spin	Tomorrowland	None
Carousel of Progress	Tomorrowland	None
Country Bear Jamboree	Frontierland	None
Dumbo the Flying Elephant	Fantasyland	None
Enchanted Tales with Belle	Fantasyland	None
The Enchanted Tiki Room	Adventureland	None
The Hall of Presidents	Liberty Square	None
Haunted Mansion	Liberty Square	None
"it's a small world"	Fantasyland	None
Jungle Cruise	Adventureland	None
Liberty Square Riverboat	Liberty Square	None
Mad Tea Party	Fantasyland	None
The Magic Carpets of Aladdin	Adventureland	None
The Many Adventures of Winnie the Pooh	Fantasyland	None

This chart does not include Magic Kingdom character meet-and-greets, many of which accept FastPass+.

Scare Factor
0 = Unlikely to scare any child of any age.
! = Has dark or loud elements; might rattle some toddlers.
!! = A couple of gotcha! moments; should be fine for school-age kids.
!!! = You need to be pretty big and pretty brave to handle this ride.

Kingdom Rides

Speed of Line	Duration of Ride/Show	Scare Factor	Age Range
Slow	2 min.	!	5 and up
Moderate	1 min.	!	4 and up
Moderate	3 min.	!!	5 and up
Fast	6 min.	O	3 and up
Fast	22 min.	O	10 and up
Moderate	15 min.	O	All
Moderate	1 min.	O	All
Slow	20 min.	O	All
Fast	20 min.	O	All
Fast	20 min.	O	10 and up
Slow	9 min.	!!	7 and up
Fast	11 min.	O	All
Slow	10 min.	O	All
Fast	15 min.	O	All
Slow	2 min.	O	4 and up
Moderate	1 min.	O	All
Moderate	5 min.	O	All

Quick Guide to Magic

Attraction	Location	Height Requirement
Mickey's PhilharMagic	Fantasyland	None
Monsters, Inc. Laugh Floor	Tomorrowland	None
Peter Pan's Flight	Fantasyland	None
Pirates of the Caribbean	Adventureland	None
Prince Charming Regal Carrousel	Fantasyland	None
Seven Dwarfs Mine Train	Fantasyland	38 inches
Space Mountain	Tomorrowland	44 inches
Splash Mountain	Frontierland	40 inches
Stitch's Great Escape	Tomorrowland	40 inches
Swiss Family Robinson Treehouse	Adventureland	None
Tomorrowland Indy Speed way	Tomorrowland	32 inches
Tomorrowland Transit Authority	Tomorrowland	None
Tom Sawyer Island	Frontierland	None
Under the Sea—Journey of the Little Mermaid	Fantasyland	None

This chart does not include Magic Kingdom character meet-and-greets, many of which accept FastPass+.

Scare Factor
0 = Unlikely to scare any child of any age.
! = Has dark or loud elements; might rattle some toddlers.
!! = A couple of gotcha! moments; should be fine for school-age kids.
!!! = You need to be pretty big and pretty brave to handle this ride.

Kingdom Rides

Speed of Line	Duration of Ride/Show	Scare Factor	Age Range
Moderate	20 min.	0	All
Moderate	22 min.	0	All
Moderate	3 min.	0	All
Fast	8 min.	!!	6 and up
Slow	2 min.	0	All
Moderate	3 min.	!	5 and up
Moderate	3 min.	!!!	7 and up
Moderate	10 min.	!!	5 and up
Moderate	15 min.	!!!	7 and up
Slow	n/a	0	4 and up
Slow	5 min.	0	2 and up
Fast	10 min.	0	All
Slow	n/a	0	4 and up
Moderate	6 min.	0	All

time, even when the parade isn't scheduled to run, and it's visible from any location. But because it's a popular nighttime attraction, that means that crowds remain in the park right up until closing. Disney has expanded the viewing area in front of Cinderella Castle, which should help to alleviate some of the crowds and allow those not watching the parade to exit the park faster.

In the meantime, here are some suggestions for how to deal with crowds and get back to your hotel in one piece.

- ✦ If you're visiting on an evening when the parade is scheduled, make sure you're stationed as close as possible to the beginning of Main Street. This way you can get a snack and make a final potty run before the parade begins, then make a quick exit after the fireworks end. Otherwise you risk being stuck in the exiting crowds, which can be really difficult to navigate, especially if you're trying to carry small children or push a stroller.

- ✦ Not watching the evening parade? It pulls almost everyone in the park to one place at one time, so about an hour before the parade starts you'll notice a definite shift in the crowd. This is a great time to squeeze onto a couple of rides that had long lines earlier in the day. Some rides—most notably Big Thunder Mountain Railroad, the Carousel, Astro Orbiter, Dumbo, the Seven Dwarfs Mine Train, and Splash Mountain—are particularly beautiful at night.

- ✦ If you want to avoid being caught in the exit crowd, leave 15 minutes before the parade starts. "People who aren't watching the evening parade really do need to get out before it begins," confirms one mother from New York. "The kiddie rides in Fantasyland get less crowded before the parade starts so we decided to ride a few one night and then slip out before the parade began. Bad idea. We lost track of time and it took us literally 45 minutes to get from Fantasyland to the front gate, pushing two strollers through crowds of people who were standing still in the middle of the sidewalks, looking up at the fireworks. After that we started setting our phone alarm to ring for 30 minutes before the parks were scheduled to close."

- ✦ The rides stop running at the park's official closing time, but Main Street stays open for up to an hour longer. If the crowd looks bad here, you can be sure it looks even worse at the bus stop or monorail station. Pause, have a snack, and let the crowds thin before you exit.

Exit Strategies

How you exit the Magic Kingdom after closing depends on where you are staying.

- ✦ Upon exiting, visitors staying off-site should pause and survey their options. If a ferry is approaching or in dock at your far left, that's your fastest route back to the TTC. Otherwise, queue for the express monorail back to the TTC.

- ✦ Guests of the Contemporary Resort should either take the monorail or, if stamina permits, the footpath.

- ✦ Guests of Wilderness Lodge and Fort Wilderness should take the water-taxi launch.

- ✦ Guests of the Polynesian or Grand Floridian resorts should glance down at the launch dock. If a water taxi is in sight, take it back to your hotel. Otherwise, head for the resort monorail.

- ✦ Guests of other Disney hotels should return to the shuttle-bus station.

Food Choices in the Magic Kingdom

Let's face it, the Magic Kingdom isn't known for fine dining. Even so, some options are better than others.

Character Meals

If you want to have a sit-down meal and see the characters, consider Cinderella's Royal Table, which is inside the castle. The princess breakfasts and lunches are especially popular with young girls (generally ages 10 and under) who want to meet Cinderella, Snow White, Belle, and some of the other princesses. (Characters vary in the evening; check when you book.) Reservations are always snapped up months in advance, so be sure to reserve early, preferably 180 days ahead of time, by calling ☎ *407/939-3463* (☎ *407/WDW-DINE*).

Meeting the Characters

Character meetings are a hot ticket, and kids can easily spend the entire day collecting autographs. Consider suggesting kids pick only their top five characters to meet or, if they are intent on collecting every autograph, set aside a day to dedicate to autographs. Here is where characters can be found in the Magic Kingdom. (There might also be additional characters on busy days, so check your map and entertainment guide.)

- ✦ **Mickey Mouse:** Town Square Theatre (FastPass+ available)

- ✦ **Minnie Mouse, Daisy Duck, Goofy, and Donald Duck:** Pete's Silly Sideshow

- ✦ **Anna and Elsa:** Princess Fairytale Hall (FastPass+ available)

- ✦ **Cinderella and Rapunzel**: Princess Fairytale Hall (FastPass+ available)

- ✦ **Ariel:** Ariel's Grotto by Under the Sea

- ✦ **Belle:** Enchanted Tales With Bell (FastPass+ available)

- ✦ **Tinker Bell:** Town Square Theatre (FastPass+ available)

- ✦ **Aladdin and Jasmine:** Adventureland

- ✦ **Pooh and Tigger:** The Many Adventures of Winnie the Pooh

- ✦ **Merida:** Fairytale Garden

- ✦ **Tiana:** Liberty Square

- ✦ **Alice and the Mad Hatter:** Mad Tea Party

This is such a tough ticket to get that we thought the following note from a conscientious mom of two hit the nail on the head: "The one thing we learned about the Magic Kingdom princess breakfast is not to promise this treat unless you already have reservations. It took us six days of getting up at 6:30 am to start trying to get through the phone line at 7 before we got lucky enough to get seats. I was already trying to figure out how to tell my then–5-year-old daughter there wasn't room for us at the castle." ■**TIP**➔ **Closed out of the princess character meals at Cinderella Castle? Try the lesser-known princess meals at Akershus Royal Banquet Hall in the Norway Pavilion of Epcot.**

Little girls like to wear their princess regalia when they dine in the castle, so pull out those tiaras and magic wands before you go. One mother reported that she brought her daughter's princess gear with her and let her change in a nearby bathroom just before her character meal. "I noticed a lot of families doing the same," she said. "It makes sense because afterwards you can change your child back into play clothes for the rest of the day."

Other character options include the Crystal Palace, where Winnie the Pooh and his friends circulate among diners for breakfast, lunch, and dinner. There's a wide debate on the quality of the Crystal Palace experience; while one mom considered it "perfect for our family since we love the Pooh characters, and the food selection was really nice," another mom described the food as "inedible, even by theme-park standards." The food is served buffet style, so at least there's no waiting and plenty of variety.

Full-Service Dining

Willing to dine without the characters? At Liberty Tree Tavern, expect an all-you-can-eat dinner with down-home cooking like turkey, pork chops, mashed potatoes, and macaroni and cheese. The Plaza Restaurant on Main Street, thematically the plainest of all Magic Kingdom restaurants, provides a variety of salads and sandwiches, along with elaborate ice-cream-based desserts. Tony's Town Square, also on Main Street, offers generous servings of Italian food and a charming *Lady and the Tramp* theme.

The hottest ticket in town is the Be Our Guest Restaurant in Fantasyland. At breakfast and lunch it's a counter-service location, offering salads, soups, sandwiches, and other standard lunch fare ordered from electronic kiosks. Each family is given a rose-shape marker that they take to a table; the food is then served to them there via a rather elegant food trolley. Note that this is not a character-dining venue, so don't expect to meet Belle or any of her princess friends.

Another caveat: The word is out that Be Our Guest is a gorgeously themed venue, so a lot of people eat here primarily to see the place. (They won't let you just walk in and look around, so the dining line is the only way to get in.) As a result, the marvelous setting is somewhat marred by constant bedlam as diners wander from room to room gawking over the details of the castle.

> ## INSIDER'S SECRET
>
> You can now reserve lunch or dinner at Be Our Guest up to 180 days in advance of your trip and pre-order your lunch 30 days in advance (breakfast reservations can only be made 90 days in advance). Without advance reservations, be prepared for an average wait of 45 minutes to an hour just to get through the door for lunch. The line can be somewhat shorter for breakfast. The restaurant closes at 3 pm to set up for the table-service dinner.

At dinner there's table service and a more elaborate French-themed menu, and the setting is considerably calmer. Make reservations well in advance. Another bonus: At Be Our Guest, Disney has lifted its Magic Kingdom alcohol ban to serve beer and wine in the evening.

Fast Food

In terms of fast food, your choices abound, but Cosmic Ray's Starlight Café in Tomorrowland is the largest fast-food spot in the park, and the lines move fast. For snacks, try the fruit cobblers or chicken and waffles at Sleepy Hollow in Liberty Square or the pineapple whips at Aloha Isle in Adventureland.

Main Street

Main Street is where the stage is set. The pristine sidewalks, Victorian shops, flower stalls, and antique cars make a stroll down Main Street like a walk through an idealized circa-1890 American town. It also provides a transition from the unglamorous parking lots and buses to the charms of the park, and people visibly relax as they move toward Cinderella Castle. Usually by the time they arrive, they're thoroughly Disney-fied.

Main Street Tips

Although you might spend a few minutes mingling with characters as you enter, don't take too much time in the shops of Main Street. One mom, who made the mistake of shopping too early, said, "We bought souvenirs on the way into the park, and I spent the whole day dragging things around. I looked like a Disney bag lady!" Instead, focus on getting to the major rides.

INSIDER'S SECRET

Not sure about how to use your MagicBand or the FastPass+ reservation system to its maximum benefit? Encountering some sort of technical issue? Never fear, all your questions can be answered at the My Magic Service Center in the Town Square Theater on Main Street, where cast members are always on hand to talk guests through the new technology.

✦ **Get the Current Scoop.** Consult the My Disney Experience app to keep informed about current wait times and character meeting locations.

✦ **Get Your Picture Taken.** You may be waylaid by a Disney photographer wanting to snap a family shot with the castle in the background. Do it. If you have a MagicBand, all of your photos will be linked to it. If you don't have a MagicBand, you'll get a PhotoPass card, which looks like a credit card and will track all your official photos from your trip. Once you get home, use the number on the card to access all the pictures at ⊕ *www.disneyphotopass.com*. After deciding which ones you like, consolidate all of your pictures onto a PhotoCD or order individual prints. Families who plan on using PhotoPass will want to look into the Memory Maker Service, which is a single price for the entire PhotoPass service. There are significant savings if you book in advance, so if your family plans to rely heavily on the Disney photographers, this could be a great deal.

✦ **Avoid Post-Lunch Crowds.** You might want to return to Main Street around noon for lunch or shopping, when the stores

FastPass+ Attractions

The Magic Kingdom has more FastPass+ rides than any park.

✦ Ariel's Grotto

✦ The Barnstormer

✦ Big Thunder Mountain Railroad

✦ Buzz Lightyear's Space Ranger Spin

✦ Dumbo the Flying Elephant

✦ Enchanted Tales with Belle

✦ Festival of Fantasy Parade

✦ The Haunted Mansion

✦ "it's a small world"

✦ Jungle Cruise

✦ Mad Tea Party

✦ The Magic Carpets of Aladdin

✦ Main Street Electrical Parade

✦ The Many Adventures of Winnie the Pooh

✦ Mickey's PhilharMagic

✦ Monsters, Inc. Laugh Floor

✦ Peter Pan's Flight

✦ Pirates of the Caribbean

✦ Princess Fairytale Hall: Cinderella, Rapunzel, or Anna and Elsa

✦ Seven Dwarfs Mine Train

✦ Space Mountain

✦ Splash Mountain

✦ Tomorrowland Speedway

✦ Town Square Theater Mickey Mouse and Tinker Bell Meet and Greet

✦ Under the Sea–Journey of the Little Mermaid

✦ Wishes Nighttime Spectacular

are relatively uncrowded. But if you're not planning to see the parade, be off Main Street by 2:30 pm. After that, it's a mob scene.

✦ **Store Your Goods.** Anyone can stow any purchases in the lockers beneath the main railroad station—or have them sent to Package Pick-Up next to Guest Relations. Disney resort guests can have packages sent directly to the gift shop in their resort.

✦ **Enjoy the Parades.** The Magic Kingdom has interactive parades throughout the day. The parade theme changes periodically, but the daytime parades are designed to get you into the action, sometimes inviting you to dance or interact with the characters. It's all great fun, but keep an eye on your kids. It's easy to lose track of them in the celebration.

✦ **Pick a Meeting Place.** If you're touring the Magic Kingdom late and your party splits up, choose a spot on Main Street as your meeting place. Disney cast members clear people out of other sections of the park at closing time, but Main Street stays open at least an hour after the rides. It's the best place to reassemble the family before heading home.

Fantasyland

Fantasyland, directly behind Cinderella Castle, is home to many of the Magic Kingdom's classic kiddie rides. It's also the most congested section of the park. The attractions of the new Fantasyland section are incredibly popular and, thus, should be experienced early in the day.

Highlights of the new Fantasyland include (1) Under the Sea–Journey of the Little Mermaid; (2) Enchanted Tales with Belle, an interactive storytelling experience, with Belle and Lumière from *Beauty and the Beast*; (3) Princess Fairytale Hall, a special area for character greetings; (4) a new, double Dumbo attraction on the site of the old Mickey's Toontown; (5) a full-service *Beauty and the Beast*–themed restaurant called Be Our Guest, and an adjacent quick-service restaurant called Gaston's Tavern; (6) Storybook Circus, a big-top-themed section of Fantasyland that includes a fountain play area based on Casey Junior from *Dumbo,* a clever new meet and greet where you can find the characters costumed as circus heroes, and a revamped Barnstormer with flights piloted by the Great Goofini; and (7) a completely new coaster, the Seven Dwarfs Mine Train.

Fantasyland Tips

With its new expansion, Fantasyland has quickly become more popular than it ever was before. Still, there are some ways to make your visit more enjoyable.

- ✦ **Come Early or Come Late.** Visit Fantasyland either before 11 am, after 7 pm, or during the parades. These are the only times it's even moderately less crowded.

- ✦ **Know What's Popular.** Expect Princess Fairytale Hall, the Seven Dwarfs Mine Train, and Enchanted Tales with Belle to be mobbed. Use FastPass+ or visit early.

- ✦ **Eat Elsewhere.** Unless you are headed for the one-of-a-kind Be Our Guest, don't eat or shop in Fantasyland. Similar foods and souvenirs are available elsewhere in less crowded areas of the park.

Fantasyland Attractions

☀ Ariel's Grotto

As Ariel points out, "flipping your fins you don't get too far," and as a result she's been one of the most rarely seen characters in the Magic Kingdom. But Ariel now has her own little grotto for meet and greets, located beside the entrance of Under the Sea. The line moves more slowly than that for Under the Sea, so catch her in the morning before you board the ride. Scare Factor→ **It's not scary.**

☀ The Barnstormer

This zippy little coaster, a great "first coaster" experience for young riders, has been rethemed and is now piloted by the Great Goofini. Guests must be 35 inches tall to ride. Scare Factor→ **The ride is short but lively, so watch it make a few revolutions before you decide if it's a good choice for your kids.**

☀ Casey Jr. Splash 'N' Soak Station

This bright and adorable little play area gives kids the chance to run, play, and get really, really wet. The train itself stands at the center of the action, holding any number of animals, such as spitting camels and elephants eager to spray you from their trunks. It's a good place to cool off on a hot day; some parents bring swimsuits, acknowledging that kids won't get merely splashed but soaked. Scare Factor→ **It's not scary.**

☀ Castle Stage Show

The characters come out in full force for these 20-minute stage shows, which run several times daily in front of the castle. Although the premise changes every year or so, the productions are always full of songs, dancing, and fun. Consult your map for showtimes, and if you want the best view, try to arrive 15 minutes in advance. Everyone stands, and it can be tiring, especially on a hot day, so don't worry if you arrive late and have to watch from the sidelines. These shows are entertaining, but it's not worth missing other Magic Kingdom attractions to see them. Scare Factor→ **It's not scary.**

☀ Dumbo the Flying Elephant

There's something very special about Dumbo; every kid who visits Disney wants to ride it. For decades, this attraction boasted some of the longest lines in Fantasyland. Because of the Fantasyland expansion, Disney has dramatically cut down on the lines by both adding an additional, identical ride (dueling Dumbos?) and creating an interactive queue. When families arrive, they are given a pager much like you might receive at some restaurants. Kids are then invited to play in a circus-themed play area. When the pager goes off, an attendant will hand you a pass, so that families only have to wait for a few cycles of Dumbo before boarding. The ride is just as classic and infectiously fun as it ever was. Scare Factor→ **You control the height of your Dumbo flight via a joystick, so the** ride is appropriate for any age. All the elephants do rise for a couple of high-flying laps at the end, but by then kids are generally used to the sensation.

☀ Enchanted Tales with Belle

Imagineers have drastically expanded this interactive show, which was once a sleeper known as Story Time with Belle, to include some of Disney's neatest special effects to date. As a result, Enchanted Tales with Belle is very popular and has a slow-moving queue, a combination that often results in hour-long waits in a line that is almost completely exposed to the sun. FastPass+ is a must, unless you get there first thing after park opening.

As you enter Belle's cottage, keep your eyes open for her favorite book and a portrait of her mother. Next it's on to Maurice's workshop to witness his enchanted mirror at work. With a simple wish to return to the day Belle and Beast met, the mirror crackles to life and expands to become a doorway into the Beast's castle.

Once you're inside the castle, cast members ask for volunteers from the audience to help Belle tell the story. Madame Wardrobe herself holds the costumes used in the simple play. Don't worry—if your child isn't chosen for a role initially, additional volunteers are added at the end as enchanted objects, ensuring that everyone who wants a part gets one.

The final scene is in the library at the Beast's castle. A very lifelike Lumière calls in Belle and then everyone, including the audience, helps reenact the story. At the end, the "cast" receives a photo op with Belle. It's a quick visit, with no time for autographs, but you do get a souvenir bookmark. Scare Factor→ **It's not scary.**

☀ "it's a small world"

During this 11-minute boat ride, dolls representing children of all ages greet you with a song so infectious that you'll still be humming it at bedtime. (Which may or may not be a good thing.) The line moves steadily, even during the most crowded parts of the afternoon. Babies, toddlers, and preschoolers seem to be especially enchanted.

Although beloved by preschoolers, the ride can be torture for older siblings. One 10-year-old wrote that Disney should offer an "I Survived 'it's a small world'" T-shirt similar to those they sell outside of Splash Mountain or the Twilight Zone Tower of Terror. In other words, if older kids opt to skip the ride, don't press the point. Scare Factor→ **It's not scary.**

☀ Mad Tea Party

Spinning pastel cups, propelled by their riders, swirl around the Soused Mouse, who periodically pops out of his teapot. Because you largely control how fast your teacup spins, this ride can be enjoyed by all ages. Just don't go right after lunch. Scare Factor→ **It's not scary.**

☀ The Many Adventures of Winnie the Pooh

This upbeat attraction follows Pooh and friends through a "blustery" day, so be prepared for your honey-pot-shape car to swirl and sway along the way. Designed especially for younger kids, the ride is gentle and fine for any age. FastPass+ is a good idea on crowded days. Hundred Acre Goods, at the exit, has great souvenirs for Pooh fans.

Many Disney purists mourned the passing of Mr. Toad's Wild Ride, an original Fantasyland attraction that was torn down to make way for Pooh. In a nod to the dear departed amphibian, there's a painting inside the ride that shows Mr. Toad passing along a deed to Owl. Scare Factor→ **Some toddlers can become unnerved by the brief nightmare scene in The Many Adventures of Winnie the Pooh but will love the rest of the ride.**

☀ Mickey's PhilharMagic

A 3-D show projected onto a mammoth screen, Mickey's PhilharMagic, which rates high with all age groups, is one of the best attractions in Walt Disney World.

The story begins when maestro Mickey is called away from the stage and Donald steps in as conductor. He promptly loses control of the orchestra and is whisked away on a madcap journey. Lots of other Disney characters get into the act—you see Donald falling in love with Ariel, dancing with Simba, and sailing through the skies with Aladdin. The show is funny, the 3-D effects are breathtaking, and the music is stirring; in short, it's a great introduction to the 3-D experience for kids. "It was our 4-year-old's favorite attraction at the Magic Kingdom," concurred one dad from Ohio. "We were surprised at how much she enjoyed all the shows (even more than the rides), but this was the best." **Scare Factor→ Although the theater is dark and some special effects startling—Donald leaps right out of the screen at you—the presence of beloved Disney characters usually calms the kids. Unless you have a baby or toddler who's afraid of the dark or loud noises, children of any age will love the show.**

☀ Peter Pan's Flight

Tinker Bell flutters overhead as you board miniature pirate ships and sail above Nana's doghouse, the night streets of London, the Indian camp, and Captain Hook's cove. Of all the Fantasyland attractions, this one is most true to the movie that inspired it, and the level of detail is so captivating that even older kids tend to enjoy the ride. It lasts only 3 minutes, though, so if the wait's longer than 30 minutes, use FastPass+ or come back during the parade. **Scare Factor→ It's not scary.**

☀ Prince Charming Regal Carrousel

Seventy-two white horses prance while a pipe organ toots out "Chim Chim Cheree" and other classic Disney songs. The carousel is especially gorgeous at night. **Scare Factor→ It's not scary.**

☀ Princess Fairytale Hall

The former site of Snow White's Scary Adventures has become the spiffy new area where Disney princesses meet their loyal subjects. As of this writing, Cinderella and Rapunzel await at the end of one queue, while Anna and Elsa from *Frozen* are at the end of the other. In other words, you meet two princesses at a time; after going through one queue, you can enter the other. FastPass+ is available for each queue, but if you want to see all four princesses, you'll need two separate FastPass+ reservations.

The waiting gallery is castlelike, with portraits of Disney royalty. Visitors are taken back in small groups to chambers, where the princesses receive them in a quiet, cool, calm environment. This is definitely a step up from your typical meet-and-greet venue!

Due to the individual attention paid to each guest, lines are long all day. **Scare Factor→ It's not scary.**

☀ The Seven Dwarfs Mine Train

The capstone of the new Fantasyland is a coaster suitable for the whole family. Guests ride through scenes from Snow White and the Seven Dwarfs in a specially designed mine train that rocks and pivots and sways and rattles as it moves in and out of the mountain. The ride contains a couple of medium-size drops.

The height requirement is 38 inches, indicating a family-friendly experience. The music is upbeat, the scenes feature the dwarfs, of course, as well as "playful forest critters," and the movement of the train is intended to be fun, not terrifying. In short, they've learned their lesson from the late, not especially lamented, Snow White's Scary Adventures. The wicked witch does appear at the end—remarkably lifelike but in an outdoor setting that dilutes the intensity. The mood here is more "Heigh-ho" than "Oh no!"

Though there is an interactive queue with mining-themed games, the ride is new and, thus, extremely popular. FastPass+ is a must. **Scare Factor→ It's a zippy coaster but not scary and in general a perfect first coaster for kids. The back of the train receives a lot more whipping action than the front, so if in doubt, ask to be seated near the front.**

☀ Under the Sea–Journey of the Little Mermaid

Fans of *The Little Mermaid* will love this picture-perfect portrayal of Prince Eric's castle. Guests move from scene to scene in a clamobile listening to (and sometimes singing along with) Ariel, Sebastian, and even big, bad Ursula.

Under the Sea is a typical dark-ride experience, albeit one with some very advanced Audio-Animatronics. Everything from Sebastian's eyes to the moving waves in Ariel's hair is carefully detailed. In short, Under the Sea is a faithful retelling of a beloved Disney story, appropriate for any age. **Scare Factor→ The 7½-foot replica** of Ursula the Sea Witch is imposing but not "on stage" too long. Most kids take her in stride.

Tomorrowland

Tomorrowland has a 1930s sci-fi look of "the future that never was." We're talking metal, chrome, robots, and neon.

Tomorrowland Tips

Tomorrowland has a few big-deal rides, but it's not usually as busy as some of the other areas.

✦ Ride Space Mountain early—by 9:15 it has substantial lines. Or you can use one of your FastPass+ options.

✦ Looking for fast food during peak dining hours? Tomorrowland stands are rarely as busy as those in other lands. Cosmic Ray's Starlight Café, the largest such place in the Magic Kingdom, moves you in and out fast.

Tomorrowland Attractions

☀ Astro Orbiter

This circular thrill ride, similar to Dumbo, is a bit too much for preschoolers and a bit too little for teens. If you ride at night, the astro-ambience is more convincing. Scare Factor➔ **Astro Orbiter is a good choice for children ages 5 to 10 who might not be quite up for Space Mountain, but it's not for anyone prone to motion sickness or with a fear of heights.**

☀ Buzz Lightyear's Space Ranger Spin

This attraction is an "interactive fantasy in which riders help Buzz save the world's supply of batteries." Huh? The ride transports you into the heart of a video game, where you pass through various scenes, spinning your cars and shooting at targets. Your car tallies your score and you learn whether you're a Space Ace or a lowly Trainee. Buzz is addictive, but the lines move swiftly and FastPass+ is available. "Buzz Lightyear is great for all ages," wrote a mother from Texas. "Our family members ranged from 2 to 83, and this was one ride everybody got into. Of course, we all got a little too competitive...."

INSIDER'S SECRET

Princess alert! The Bibbidi Bobbidi Boutique, fashioned on the popular Downtown Disney location, is appropriately situated inside Cinderella Castle. A variety of packages starting at $50 let young princesses receive fairy-tale makeovers: glittery new hairstyles, shimmering makeup, and sparkly nails. The complete Castle Package includes all of the above plus a costume and photos starting at $190. (Note: Several parents have written to complain that it's nearly impossible to get the glitter out of their children's hair.)

One mother got a little snippidi snappidi at my suggestion, in a previous edition of this book, that parents would have to have lost their minds to spring for the full package. "Yes, we paid almost $200 to have our daughter transformed into Princess Tiana," she wrote, "but they did it like only Disney can do it, and it was her favorite experience of the trip. Besides, they gave me all the leftover hair and makeup supplies, and I was able to reuse them when we got home. She ended up with the best Halloween costume ever."

In a gesture toward gender equality, boys can get the $15 Knight Package, which translates to hairstyling and a plastic sword and shield. Children must be at least three years old and, for the Magic Kingdom salon, theme-park admission is required. Reservations, which can be made 180 days in advance, are a must. Call ☎ 407/939-7895 (☎ 407/WDW-STYLE).

One thing for cost-and-time-conscious parents to note: It takes a while for the hairstyling and makeup, and that's an hour that you won't be riding rides and exploring the park. Considering the price of Disney tickets, you might want to let the girls get the princess treatment at the Bibbidi Bobbidi Boutique in World of Disney at Downtown Disney. You don't need a theme-park ticket for that.

Attention Space Ace wannabes: The tougher the target, the higher the points, so don't waste all your time taking cheap shots. There are 100,000-point targets on the palm of the orange robot's left hand in the Robot Attack scene and on the bottom Z of the spaceship in Zurg's Secret Weapon. If you hit a target multiple times, it gives you more points. **Scare Factor→ It's not scary.**

✸ Carousel of Progress

This is a fairly long show (22 minutes) and a high-capacity attraction, so it's good for the crowded times of the afternoon. Kids might be bored by this salute to modern inventions, especially once they've seen the more high-tech presentations of Epcot. That said, it has a nostalgic appeal; Carousel of Progress was one of Walt's contributions to the 1964 World's Fair. Note: Carousel of Progress is often closed during the off-season. **Scare Factor→ It's not scary.**

✸ Monsters, Inc. Laugh Floor

This show lets you laugh, joke, sing, and interact right along with your one-eyed "monster of ceremonies" Mike Wazowski and other characters from *Monsters, Inc.* Although the show technology is highbrow, the humor is lowbrow. Children as young as five should be able to enjoy the silly jokes and slapstick, and even if they miss a joke here or there, they'll still have fun. If the spotlight doesn't fall on you, you can still get in on the action—while you're waiting, you can text-message jokes for possible use in the show.

Monsters, Inc. was created in response to the way-popular Turtle Talk with Crush in the Seas at Epcot. Kids love shows in which characters on-screen interact with people sitting in the audience. It's high-tech with heart. **Scare Factor→ It's not scary.**

✸ Space Mountain

This three-minute roller-coaster ride through inky blackness is one of the few scream-rippers in the Magic Kingdom. The cars move at a mere 32 mph, a tame pace compared to other monster coasters, but as the entire ride takes place in the dark, it's almost impossible to anticipate the turns and dips. Space Mountain is perennially popular. Use FastPass+ to cut down on your wait time. **Scare Factor→ Space Mountain is the most intense ride in the Magic Kingdom, with a 44-inch height requirement. Most** kids aged 3 to 8 find it too scary, but the 9 to 11 age group gives it a solid thumbs-up. It's the highest-rated attraction in the park among teens.

☀ Stitch's Great Escape

Stitch's Great Escape tells the story of what Stitch was like before he came to Earth in the hit movie *Lilo & Stitch*. Stitch is captured by the Galactic Federation and taken to a prisoner-processing facility. As Stitch's reputation as a troublemaker precedes him, visitors to the attraction are recruited to provide additional security. But you can't keep a good alien down, and Stitch eludes security, causing mayhem everywhere he goes. The show features sophisticated Audio-Animatronics, including the remarkable three-dimensional Stitch figure. It's also loud, dark, and far more forbidding than the advertisements indicate. **Scare Factor→ We receive a lot of mail about Stitch's Great Escape—most of it negative. Although the height requirement to see Stitch is only 40 inches, the prevailing complaint is that the darkness and volume of the ride are simply too scary for many preschoolers.**

☀ Tomorrowland Indy Speedway

Tiny sports cars circle a nifty-looking racetrack, and although the ride itself isn't anything unusual, kids under 11 rate it highly, perhaps because young drivers can steer the cars themselves. (Kids 52 inches and taller can drive solo; others must be at least 32 inches tall and accompanied by an adult.) **Scare Factor→ It's not scary.**

■TIP→ Persuade your child not to rush through the Indy Speedway; loading and reloading the cars takes time—better to drive slowly than sit for five minutes in the pit waiting to be unloaded.

☀ Tomorrowland Transit Authority

This little tram circles Tomorrowland and provides fun views, including a glimpse inside Space Mountain and the Buzz Lightyear attraction. The trip lasts 10 minutes, and the ride is never crowded, so the attendant usually lets you stay on for more than one cycle. The rocking of the train has lulled many a cranky toddler into a nap; cast members report that the ride is often full of parents holding sleeping youngsters. **Scare Factor→ It's not scary.**

Adventureland

Thematically the most bizarre of all the lands—sort of a Bourbon Street meets Trinidad by way of Congo—Adventureland definitely conveys an exotic mood.

Adventureland, Frontierland, and Liberty Square Tips

✦ If you aren't up for Space Mountain, begin your day in Frontierland, at Splash Mountain. Move on to Big Thunder Mountain, then the Haunted Mansion in Liberty Square. All three attractions are relatively easy to board before 10 am.

✦ These lands stay crowded between noon and 4 pm, when the crowds line up to watch the afternoon parade disperse. If you miss Splash Mountain, Big Thunder Mountain, or the Haunted Mansion early in the morning, wait until early evening to visit them.

✦ Should you find yourself stuck in these lands in the afternoon, you'll find a bit of breathing space on Tom Sawyer Island or in the Enchanted Tiki Room or the Hall of Presidents. Surprisingly, Pirates of the Caribbean can be a smart choice even when the park is crowded. At least you wait inside, and this is one of the fastest-loading attractions in Disney World.

Adventureland Attractions

☀ Jungle Cruise

You'll meet up with headhunters, hyenas, water-spewing elephants, and other varieties of frankly fake wildlife on this 10-minute boat ride. It's dated looking in comparison to the attractions in the Animal Kingdom, but it's still fun, thanks largely to the amusing patter of the tour guides, who tell jokes and puns

---

INSIDER'S SECRET

If you've visited the Magic Kingdom before and want to try something a little different, consider the Family Magic Tour. This adventure is designed for kids 4 to 10 and their families. You follow clues throughout the park and end by solving the mystery and finding a character. See Chapter 10 for details.

HIDDEN MICKEY

When you and the kids are keeping an eye out for Mickey Mouse, you may not realize that you're walking right past him. No, we're not talking about the life-size Mickeys, we're talking about those silhouettes and abstract images that are cleverly tucked throughout Walt Disney World. These "Hidden Mickeys" began as an inside joke among the Imagineers and artists who design theme-park attractions. Spotting a Hidden Mickey is a real treat.

Ready for your first test? When you pass a group of three beached canoes halfway through the Jungle Cruise, look carefully at the carvings. You'll see not only Mickey, but Donald and Goofy, too.

so corny that you're groaning and laughing in the same breath. FastPass+ is available but is rarely necessary. **Scare Factor→ The cruise isn't at all scary and is fine for any age.**

☀ The Magic Carpets of Aladdin

This colorful, appealing attraction is a circular aerial ride similar to Dumbo. The twist is that you can make your carpet tilt, rise, or drop on command—evasive maneuvers that are necessary if you wish to avoid the spitting camels that guard the ride. **Scare Factor→ Because the carpets pitch around a bit, the Aladdin ride is slightly more intense than Dumbo, but most kids love it.**

☀ A Pirate's Adventure: Treasures of the Seven Seas

In this new interactive attraction guests participate in virtual "pirate raids" throughout Adventureland, helping Captain Jack Sparrow fight off a host of enemies. There are five different adventures, each requiring a series of tasks, and at the end successful buccaneers are welcomed into Sparrow's crew. Although the family can play together, the Adventure is designed with pirate-crazed kids 5 to 12 in mind. **Scare Factor→ It's not scary.**

☀ Pirates of the Caribbean

This attraction inspires great loyalty, and because of the success of the movie series of the same name, the pirates are hotter than ever, especially Captain Jack Sparrow. If you've been on the

ride before, you'll notice an updated twist to the story as Sparrow races to a cache of plundered treasure. It's a kick to see the
relatively new figures interacting with some of the older Audio-
Animatronics buccaneers. All the Audio-Animatronics figures are
remarkably lifelike, right down to the hair on their legs, and the
theme song is positively addictive. Even though the story is dark,
violent, and brutal, in the hands of Disney it all somehow manages to come off as a lighthearted, happy adventure.

Near the entrance of Pirates of the Caribbean, look for the fun,
lively, interactive Captain Jack Sparrow's Pirate Tutorial. A Johnny
Depp look-alike and his mangy sidekicks pull young volunteers
from the audience and give them a crash course in everything it
takes to be a swashbuckling buccaneer. Check your entertainment
schedule for showtimes. Scare Factor→ **The queue winds through
a dark, drafty dungeon, so many kids are nervous before they
even board. After that, the scariest elements of the ride occur
in the first three minutes—there are skeletons, cannons, periods
of shadowy darkness, and a manifestation of Davy Jones in the
mist. This ride is fine for most kids over six, unless they're afraid
of the dark.**

☀ Swiss Family Robinson Treehouse

There's a real split of opinion here—some visitors revel in the details and love climbing through this replica of the ultimate tree
house, while others rate it as dull. Kids who have seen the movie
tend to like it a lot more. Note: There are lots of steps, and this
can be an exhausting attraction to visit with preschoolers, who
often start out with enthusiasm and then clamor to be carried.
There's been a persistent rumor that the Swiss Family Robin-
son Treehouse is due for a major revamp to tie the theme in to a
more contemporary movie and make it more interesting to the
younger set. Stay tuned. Scare Factor→ **It's not scary.**

☀ Walt Disney's Enchanted Tiki Room

Due to a number of guest complaints, the Enchanted Tiki Room
has gone through an "anti-refurbishment"—in other words,
Imagineers have removed Zazu and Iago and returned the Tiki
Room to its original show. The singing-and-talking Tiki Room
birds represent Disney's first attempt at the Audio-Animatronics that are now such an integral part of theme-park magic. Al-

INSIDER'S SECRET

The Pirate League in Adventureland begins with the spin of a chest to reveal your pirate name. (Kim is Charlotte Crestpaddler, and Leigh is Scarlett Spiderwick.) From there, young buccaneers can choose a pirate makeover (beginning at $30), but there are also empress and mermaid packages for girls. Kids can also go the full Johnny Depp route. After their transformations, the freshly minted pirates are taken into a private room for the swearing of an oath, the presentation of their pirate credentials, and a picture-taking session before being released back into Adventureland. The cool thing about the Pirate League is that it isn't just an imitation of the Bibbidi Bobbidi Boutique; the setting is terrific and the cast members enter into the pirate theme with great enthusiasm. Call ☎ *407/939-2739* (☎ *407/ WDW-CREW*) for reservations.

though not the most exciting show in the Magic Kingdom, it's an easy place to sit and rest for a few minutes on a hot afternoon. Grab a Dole pineapple whip at the nearby Aloha Isle to help you get in a tropical mood. Scare Factor→ **The Enchanted Tiki Room show is loud. When the Tiki gods are angered, the theater darkens and lightning and thunder begin. The noise level frightens some toddlers.**

Frontierland

Kids love the rough-and-tumble Wild West feel of Frontierland, which is home to several of the Magic Kingdom's most popular attractions.

For Adventureland, Frontierland, and Liberty Square Tips, see Adventureland, above.

Frontierland Attractions

☀ Big Thunder Mountain Railroad

A roller coaster designed as a runaway mine train, Big Thunder Mountain is one of the most popular rides in the park with all age groups. The glory of the ride is in the setting. You zoom through a deserted mining town and, although the details are best observed by day, the lighting effects make this ride especially atmospheric after dark. Be warned that the ride is very bouncy and jerky, but the effects are more apt to make you laugh than scream. Scare Factor➜ **When it comes to coasters, Big Thunder Mountain is more in the rattle-back-and-forth style than the lose-your-stomach-as-you-plunge style. Most children over seven should be able to handle the dips and twists, and many preschoolers adore the ride as well. The height requirement is 40 inches.**

☀ Country Bear Jamboree

Younger kids usually enjoy the furry, funny, Audio-Animatronics critters featured in this 15-minute show. From the coy Trixie, who enters via a ceiling swing, to the wincingly off-key Big Al, each face is distinctive and lovable.

The Jamboree seats large numbers of guests for each show, and it's a good choice for the afternoon when you'll want to sit and rest. Kids 10 and up often think the bears are hokey, so parents can take younger kids to the Jamboree while their older siblings visit Splash Mountain and Big Thunder Mountain Railroad. A clock outside the Country Bear Jamboree tells you how long you have until the next show. Don't enter the waiting area until the countdown is 10 minutes or less. Scare Factor➜ **It's not scary.**

☀ Splash Mountain

Based on *Song of the South* and inhabited by Br'er Rabbit, Br'er Fox, and Br'er Bear, Splash Mountain takes riders on a winding watery journey through swamps and bayous.

Because it's the first thing you see as you approach, most of the attention is given to that 40-mph drop over a five-story waterfall, but there's a great story to the ride as well. You get into a log boat and follow Br'er Rabbit's adventures throughout the attraction, and each time he gets into trouble, you get into trouble,

too. In other words, each dangerous moment is followed by an escape through a water drop, and the
ultimate danger culminates in the
ultimate water drop. The interior
scenes are delightful, and "Zip-a-
Dee-Doo-Dah," perhaps the most
hummable of all Disney theme
songs, fills the air.

> ## HIDDEN MICKEY
>
> In the final scene of Splash Mountain, as you pass the *Zip-a-Dee Lady* paddleboat, look for a pink cloud floating high in the sky. It's a silhouette of Mickey lying on his back.

Splash Mountain can get very
crowded; ride early in the morning or
in the last hour before closing. You can get really soaked, especially if you're in the front-row seats on the right of the log. This
can be great fun at noon in June, less of a kick at 9 am in January.
Some people bring ponchos or big black garbage bags for protection and discard them after the ride.

Just because your toddler can't ride Splash Mountain doesn't
mean she can't get a thrill. There's a great spot where you can
stand to watch the log boats on their final drop. The shrieks combined with the sprays of water will delight any child. A father of
three from Florida agreed: "Our 2-year-old's favorite ride was
Splash Mountain. She couldn't ride it, of course, but she stayed
outside with Dad while Mom and her brothers rode and she loved
watching the boats splash down. Water shoots up after the boats
and she squealed every time." **Scare Factor→ The intensity of
Splash Mountain's last drop, which gives you the feeling that
you're coming right out of your seat, along with the 40-inch
height requirement, eliminates some preschoolers. Watch a few
cars make the final drop before you decide. Our mail indicates
that most kids over five love the ride.**

☀ Tom Sawyer Island

A getaway playground full of caves, bridges, forts, and windmills,
Tom Sawyer Island is the perfect destination for kids full of pent-
up energy who just need to run wild for a while. You'll want to
accompany them through the Mystery Cave and Injun Joe's Cave,
however; both can be dark, confusing, and a little scary. Across
the bouncy suspension bridge is Fort Sam Clemens, the perfect
spot to play cowboy.

The big drawback is that the island is accessible only by raft, so you often have to wait to get there and back. If your kids are under five, don't bother. The terrain is too wild and widespread for preschoolers without careful supervision. Likewise, there's little on the island for teenagers and adults. But for kids 5 to 12, a trip to Tom Sawyer Island is the ideal afternoon break. "Tom Sawyer Island was my 6-year-old's favorite place in the Magic Kingdom," wrote a mom from Texas. "It's so detailed, with a lot for a boy his age to do. We definitely thought it was worth the wait to catch the raft." Scare Factor➔ **It's not scary.**

Liberty Square

As you walk between Frontierland and Fantasyland, you find yourself transported back in time to colonial America, strolling the cobblestone streets of Liberty Square.

Liberty Square Attractions

☀ The Hall of Presidents

The residents of the Hall of Presidents are so lifelike that it's a bit eerie (and Disney cast members report that this attraction is very "interesting" to clean at night). The show opens with a film about the history of the presidency (otherwise known as "nap time" for the preschool set) and moves on to the highlight, the presidential roll call. Each chief executive responds to his name with a nod or similar movement, while in the background the other presidents fidget and whisper.

The hall seats 700, with shows every 20 minutes, and thus is a good choice during the most crowded parts of the afternoon. Ask an attendant at the lobby doors how long it is before the next show and amble in five minutes early. Scare Factor➔ **It's not scary.**

☀ Haunted Mansion

More apt to amuse than to frighten, the recently revamped mansion is full of clever special effects—there's a fascinating ballroom scene where spirits waltz, and, at one point, a ghost hitchhikes along in your "doom buggy." The cast members have great costumes (including the bat-in-a-hat that ladies wear), and they add to the fun with their morticianlike behavior and such instructions as "Drag your wretched bodies to the dead center of the room." The mansion is full of clever inside jokes. For example, the tombstones outside feature the names of Imagineers who designed the ride; keep watching Madame Leota's face and you may be surprised; and be sure to take a glance at the pet cemetery when you leave.

HIDDEN MICKEY

As you're passing above the dining room, look at the arrangement of dishes on the table in the Haunted Mansion banquet scene. Do any of the place settings look like you-know-who?

The mansion draws long lines in the afternoons, especially just before and after the parade. Try to see it mid-morning, or—if you have the courage—after dark. **Scare Factor→ Many kids 7 to 11 list the Haunted Mansion as a favorite attraction. Although some in this age group are frightened by the opening story, the setting, and the darkness, once they get going, they're usually okay. The attraction is richly atmospheric, but the spooks are mostly for laughs. In contrast, many toddlers are intimidated. One mother said that her daughter, age three, referred to "that ugly house with the bad people" for weeks after their Disney visit.**

✹ Liberty Square Riverboat

The second tier of this paddle-wheel riverboat offers nice views of the Rivers of America, but the 15-minute cruise is a bit of a snooze for kids. It would be fine if they could really nap, but there are few seats on the boat, so most riders stand. Board only if you have time to kill and the boat is at the dock. **Scare Factor→ It's not scary.**

CHAPTER 6

EPCOT

Walt Disney envisioned Epcot (an acronym for "Experimental Prototype Community of Tomorrow) as the centerpiece of Walt Disney World, and the park is a tribute to his optimism about a great, big, beautiful tomorrow. Walt's original vision was to build a community where people actually lived, and he hoped that countries from around the world would send their citizens to live in this community and to share their culture while looking for innovative solutions for the future.

While that never quite happened, what we're left with is a pretty amazing theme park. Future World is home to some of Disney's most innovative rides, such as Soarin' and Mission: SPACE, and the entertainment and restaurants of the World Showcase, which promotes the idea of global harmony, can make anyone feel like a citizen of the world.

The Epcot Disney actually built follows more closely the form of a permanent World's Fair. Spaceship Earth (or "the big ball") is Epcot's park icon, visible immediately upon entering, and it sets the tone for Future World, which shows off the latest in technology and invention. The World Showcase, where country pavilions are located around a pretty lagoon in the back of the park, has a much more mellow mood. Eleven countries from around the globe are featured, so guests can shop the bazaars of Morocco, taste a true Italian pizza, and stroll along a Parisian boulevard. The pavilions are staffed by representatives from the host countries, and Disney does an excellent job of pulling together architecture, music, entertainment, and food to truly give each pavilion its own unique flavor.

Epcot Touring Tips

Getting Here

Many off-site hotels and all on-site hotels offer shuttle buses to Epcot, and it is also easy to reach by car. If you arrive early in the morning, you can park close to the entrance gate and forego the tram. If you arrive a bit later, however, the trams do run quickly and efficiently. Just be sure to note the number of the row where you parked your car.

If you're staying at the Contemporary, Polynesian, or Grand Floridian resorts, your fastest route is to take the monorail to the Transportation and Ticket Center (TTC) and then transfer to the Epcot monorail.

The Yacht Club, Beach Club, BoardWalk, Swan, and Dolphin resorts are connected by a bridge to a special "back-door" entrance that leads directly into Epcot's World Showcase. You can get there either by water taxi or by foot.

Getting Around

Some Disney insiders insist that Epcot really stands for "Every Person Comes Out Tired." The park is indeed sprawling—more than twice the size of the Magic Kingdom. It's composed of two circular sections, Future World and the World Showcase, which form a basic figure-eight shape. The only in-park mode of transportation is the FriendShip (there are actually two) that crosses the World Showcase Lagoon; most of the time, you'll walk.

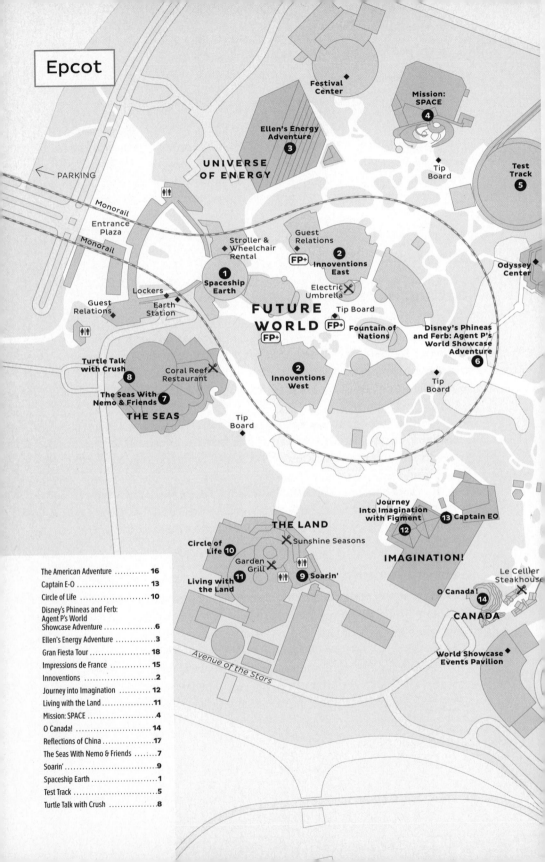

Epcot

PARKING →

Monorail

Entrance Plaza

Monorail

UNIVERSE OF ENERGY

Festival Center

Ellen's Energy Adventure **3**

Mission: SPACE **4**

Tip Board

Test Track **5**

Stroller & Wheelchair Rental

Guest Relations

FP+ Innoventions East **2**

Electric Umbrella

FUTURE WORLD

FP+

FP+ Fountain of Nations

Tip Board

Odyssey Center

Guest Relations

Lockers

Earth Station

Spaceship Earth **1**

Disney's Phineas and Ferb: Agent P's World Showcase Adventure **6**

Tip Board

Innoventions West **2**

Turtle Talk with Crush **8**

Coral Reef Restaurant

The Seas With Nemo & Friends **7**

THE SEAS

Tip Board

Journey Into Imagination with Figment **12**

13 Captain EO

THE LAND

Sunshine Seasons

IMAGINATION!

Circle of Life **10**

Garden Grill

Living with the Land **11**

9 Soarin'

Le Cellier Steakhouse

O Canada! **14**

CANADA

Avenue of the Stars

World Showcase Events Pavilion

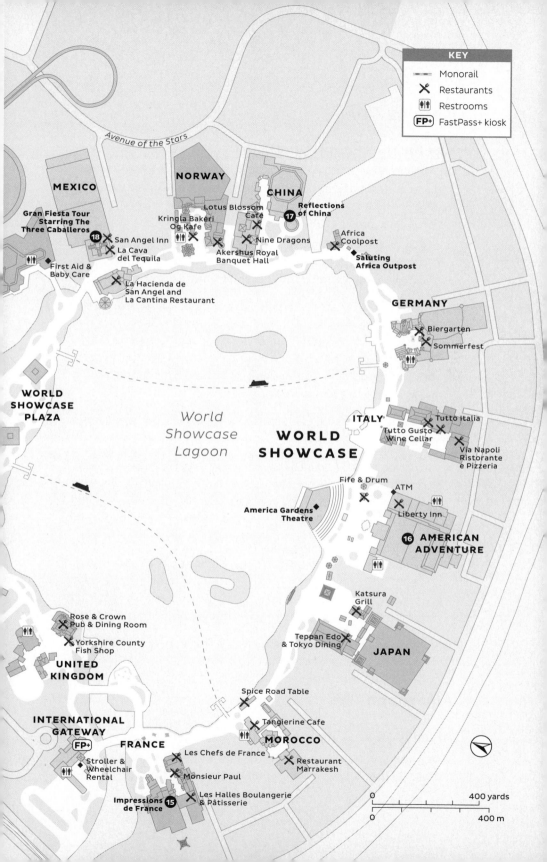

KEY

- ⊶ Monorail
- ✕ Restaurants
- 🚻 Restrooms
- **FP+** FastPass+ kiosk

Avenue of the Stars

MEXICO

Gran Fiesta Tour Starring The Three Caballeros

18

First Aid & Baby Care

San Angel Inn
La Cava del Tequila

La Hacienda de San Angel and La Cantina Restaurant

NORWAY

Kringla Bakeri Og Kafe

Lotus Blossom Café

Akershus Royal Banquet Hall

Nine Dragons

CHINA

17 Reflections of China

Africa Coolpost

Saluting Africa Outpost

GERMANY

Biergarten

Sommerfest

WORLD SHOWCASE PLAZA

World Showcase Lagoon

WORLD SHOWCASE

ITALY

Tutto Italia

Tutto Gusto Wine Cellar

Via Napoli Ristorante e Pizzeria

Fife & Drum

ATM

America Gardens Theatre

Liberty Inn

16 **AMERICAN ADVENTURE**

Katsura Grill

Rose & Crown Pub & Dining Room

Yorkshire County Fish Shop

UNITED KINGDOM

Teppan Edo & Tokyo Dining

JAPAN

INTERNATIONAL GATEWAY

FP+

Stroller & Wheelchair Rental

FRANCE

Spice Road Table

Tangierine Cafe

MOROCCO

Les Chefs de France

Monsieur Paul

Restaurant Marrakesh

Impressions de France **15**

Les Halles Boulangerie & Pâtisserie

0 — 400 yards
0 — 400 m

Morning Tips

Tips for Your First Hour at Epcot

On regular mornings, you're usually allowed into the entrance plaza around Spaceship Earth before the rest of the park officially opens. You'll have time to get a map and entertainment schedule and rent a stroller before the ropes drop.

- ✦ If you're an on-site guest and visiting Epcot on an Extra Magic Hour morning, only a few attractions will be open, but those will have a significantly reduced wait time.

- ✦ If you're staying at the Yacht or Beach club, BoardWalk, Swan, or Dolphin and thus entering through Epcot's back-door entrance, walk through the United Kingdom and Canada until you get to the rope. It's a bit of a hike to start the day, but the payoff is that you're in a good position to beat the main crowd to Soarin' once the ropes drop.

- ✦ If you haven't made your FastPass+ selections, find a kiosk and make them now.

- ✦ Once you're allowed into the main body of the park, ride Soarin' first. This attraction, popular with all age groups, can draw long lines later in the day. Many guests prefer to ride twice, so head here even if you have a FastPass+ for later.

- ✦ After Soarin', assuming your kids are up for it, cross Future World and head for Test Track. If you didn't get a FastPass+ at Soarin', get one for Test Track. These two rides are the ones most apt to get crowded later in the day, so you want to ride them relatively early and use your FastPass+ option judiciously.

- ✦ Next, visit The Seas with Nemo & Friends; after you disembark, head for Turtle Talk with Crush.

Afternoon Tips

Afternoon Resting Places

When you don't want to return to your hotel room but still need a short, air-conditioned break, here are your best bets:

- The American Adventure

- Captain E-O

- Circle of Life in the Land pavilion

- Impressions de France

- Universe of Energy

Epcot has many shows, so if the kids need to run off a little energy between presentations, check out the play fountains. One set is near Mission: SPACE, and the others are just to the right of the bridge leading to the World Showcase. They're a great place to cool off on a hot afternoon, especially if you bring along bathing suits or waterproof diapers.

Evening Tips

Best Spots for IllumiNations

- If you're staying for IllumiNations, find a spot around the World Showcase lagoon 30 minutes in advance during the off-season, 45 to 60 minutes in advance during the on-season. Have a snack to help pass the time.

- When staking out the perfect spot to watch IllumiNations, remember that much of the show takes place above you. If you sit beneath a tree or awning you'll have trouble seeing the fireworks in their full glory.

Your Last Hour

- Not staying for IllumiNations? Just be sure you're at the exit gates by the time the fireworks end and the onslaught of people begins.

Exit Strategies

- Lights are kept low during closing time to accentuate the effects of IllumiNations. This makes it easy to get separated from your party, so hang on tight to younger kids and make plans to meet at a certain place in case you lose each other in the exiting crowd.

Food Choices

Epcot is *the* food park. It has such an embarrassment of riches that it's hard to choose.

Character Meals

The princess character meals at Epcot are popular but not as well-known as those in the Magic Kingdom. They are held at the Akershus Royal Banquet Hall in Norway, and at present the princesses show up at breakfast, lunch, and dinner. They stay for only about an hour, though, so be sure to verify that you're booking your meal at the time the characters are slated to appear. Also note that you may see Belle, Snow White, Mulan, or Sleeping Beauty, but Cinderella appears only in the Magic Kingdom. Reservations are a must; call ☎ *407/939–3463* (☎ *407/ WDW–DINE*) up to 180 days before the date you wish to attend. The earlier the better!

The princess meals aren't just for girls. Consider this note from a mother of two in Delaware: "Even though it's somewhat geared toward girls, my 7-year-old son really enjoyed the princess breakfast in the Norway pavilion. The waiter greeted him by calling him 'Prince,' which he loved, and the princesses treated him like royalty throughout the whole meal. He seemed quite smitten with them."

Full-Service Dining

For sit-down dining, one perennial favorite is the San Angel Inn in Mexico, which is a great place to escape on a hot, sunny day. A shadowy waterway gurgles by, and the scene is that of an evening marketplace, romantically dark even at high noon. Another popular spot is Chefs de France in—you guessed it—France. Here the feel is of a Parisian sidewalk café, with white tablecloths and bustling waiters. Le Cellier in Canada is perhaps the most popular Epcot restaurant, due to its tasty steaks and elaborate desserts, and the Tutto Italia Ristorante in Italy serves up delicious clas-

sics. Kids enjoy the show-style tep-
panyaki dining at the Teppan Edo
in Japan, and the food—which includes such upscale items as Kobe
beef—is outstanding.

One of the greatest recent additions to Epcot dining, believe it or
not, is a pizzeria. But what a pizzeria!
Via Napoli is a great lunch stop.

Fast Food

Not up for full-service dining? For a
quick casual meal in Future World,
head for the Sunshine Seasons
food court in the Land, where you
can choose from healthy salads,
hearty sandwiches, and a variety of
well-prepared ethnic dishes at different counters.

INSIDER'S SECRET

Disney has made great strides in providing more nutritionally conscious options throughout all the parks. It's no longer hard to find carts selling fruit or to opt for veggies and fruit as a side rather than chips or fries. And on menus at full-service restaurants, look for items with the "Mickey check," indicating they are especially healthy choices.

In terms of World Showcase fast food, you have plenty of possibilities. If you're concerned about how the kids will react to un-
familiar cuisine, not to worry. On kiddie menus the food is a nod
to the country in question—for example, skewered chicken in Morocco or fish-and-chips in the United Kingdom—but the entrées
are smaller and less spicy than the adult meals and look enough
like chicken nuggets and fish sticks that the kids will eat them.

The Tangierine Café in Morocco has Mediterranean wraps,
hummus, salads, and platters of chicken and lamb. The food is
served in a pretty patio area with a perfect view of the pavilion.
Don't miss the pastry counter in the back for baklava and other
honeyed delights, not to mention Turkish coffee so strong that
you may set a land-speed record on your next lap around the
World Showcase.

While the Tangierine Café is right in the middle of the action, the Yakitori House in Japan is tucked away in the back of
the pavilion, with a soothing view of the manicured gardens and
koi ponds. The food—especially the broiled skewers of chicken,
shrimp, and beef—is tasty and a bit lighter than many of the
counter-service options. Another good choice is Kringla Bak-

eri Og Kafe in Norway, which has wonderful open-face salmon sandwiches and delicious pastries.

The Yorkshire County Fish and Chips stand in the United Kingdom is always popular. Carry your food into the back garden and sit on a park bench while you listen to the British Revolution band sing rock 'n' roll classics.

The Les Halles Boulangerie & Pâtisserie in France emits such phenomenal aromas of coffee and croissants that there's always a line, even though the café is in an out-of-the-way back alley. Drop by for sandwiches, quiche, and a wide selection of decadent pastries, which are so good that they make the Boulangerie a favorite with Disney cast members. *Bon appétit!*

■**TIP→ Not on the dining plan but you'd still like to size up a few of Epcot's posh restaurants? To save both time and money, stick to fast-food places for meals, and make reservations at a sit-down restaurant for a truly off time, like 3 pm or 10 pm, and just have dessert. You can soak up the ambience for an investment of 30 minutes and 20 bucks. Alternatively, as the average Epcot dinner for four costs about $100 without wine or beer, you can slice that bill in half if you visit the sit-down restaurant of your choice at lunch.**

Unique Offerings

The Magic Kingdom isn't the only place to see the characters, catch a show, watch fireworks, or buy souvenirs. Epcot provides a whole range of entertainment, but with an international spin.

World Showcase Performers

Singers, dancers, jugglers, and artisans from around the globe perform throughout the World Showcase daily. Times are outlined on your entertainment schedule.

Some of these presentations are more child-oriented than others. Children especially enjoy the young acrobats in China, the balancing act in France, and the British Revolution, a talented rock 'n' roll group that plays in the United Kingdom.

The shows are set up so that you can pretty much flow from one to the other as you work your way around the World Showcase. If you're there 10 minutes before showtime you can usually get a decent spot.

MEETING THE CHARACTERS

The character meetings and shows at Epcot are rarely as crowded as those at the Magic Kingdom. A well-marked character spot to the right of the fountains in Future World is your best bet to meet Mickey and his pals; other characters appear in World Showcase country pavilions. Check your entertainment schedule for times.

Mickey Mouse, Minnie Mouse, and Goofy: Character Spot in Future World

Mary Poppins: England

Alice in Wonderland: England

Aladdin and Jasmine: Morocco

Snow White: Germany

Belle and the Beast: France

Donald Duck: Mexico

Mulan: China

Duffy Bear: the bridge between Future World and the World Showcase

IllumiNations

This display of lasers, fireworks, syncopated fountains, and stirring music is a real-life fantasia and an unsurpassed Disney World classic. Very popular, very crowded, and the perfect way to end an Epcot day, IllumiNations takes place over the World Showcase lagoon at the 9 pm closing time. If you watch from the Mexico or Canada pavilions, you'll be able to beat the crowd to the exits afterward. Guests staying at the Yacht or Beach club, or the BoardWalk, Swan, or Dolphin resorts, and thus leaving via the back-door exit, can watch from the bridge between the United Kingdom and France pavilions.

Shopping

You'll see things in Epcot that aren't available anywhere else in Disney World: German wines, Chinese silk robes, Mexican piñatas, Norwegian sweaters, and English teas are all within strolling distance of each other. Once you've made your purchases, either

Quick Guide to

Attraction	Location	Height Requirement
The American Adventure	World Showcase	None
Captain E-O	Future World	None
Circle of Life	Future World	None
Gran Fiesta Tour	World Showcase	None
Ellen's Energy Adventure	Future World	None
Impressions de France	World Showcase	None
Innoventions	Future World	None
Journey into Imagination	Future World	None
Living with the Land	Future World	None
Mission: SPACE	Future World	44 inches
O Canada!	World Showcase	None
Reflections of China	World Showcase	None
The Seas with Nemo & Friends	Future World	None
Soarin'	Future World	40 inches
Spaceship Earth	Future World	None
Test Track	Future World	40 inches
Turtle Talk with Crush	Future World	None

Scare Factor
0 = Unlikely to scare any child of any age.
! = Has dark or loud elements; might rattle some toddlers.
!! = A couple of gotcha! moments; should be fine for school-age kids.
!!! = You need to be pretty big and pretty brave to handle this ride.

Epcot Attractions

Speed of Line	Duration of Ride/Show	Scare Factor	Age Range
Fast	30 min.	0	All
Fast	17 min.	!	5 and up
Fast	20 min.	0	All
Fast	9 min.	0	All
Slow	30 min.	!!	3 and up
Fast	20 min.	0	10 and up
n/a	n/a	0	3 and up
Fast	13 min.	0	3 and up
Fast	10 min.	0	All
Slow	15 min.	!!!	7 and up
Fast	20 min.	0	10 and up
Fast	20 min.	0	10 and up
Moderate	8 min.	0	All
Moderate	15 min.	!	5 and up
Moderate	15 min.	0	All
Moderate	25 min.	!!!	7 and up
Fast	15 min.	0	3 and up

have them sent to Package Pick-Up near the front gate and retrieve them as you exit or, if you're staying on-site, have them delivered to your hotel. Both services are free.

Epcot International Food & Wine Festival

Dining your way around the World Showcase is always a treat, but it gets even better during one of the park's premier special events, the annual Epcot International Food & Wine Festival. It runs for approximately eight weeks, from late September through November. You can get exact dates, a list of prices, reservations, and information by calling ☎ 407/939–3378 (☎ 407/WDW–FEST). Details are also at ⊕ www.disneyworld.com.

Open-air booths serving the food, wine, and beer of more than 60 nations are set up around the World Showcase, offering everything from New Zealand lamb chops to Bavarian strudel. The sample-size servings range from $2.50 to $6.50, so you can happily nosh your way around the world, indulging in Walt Disney World's biggest buffet. If you want to learn more about what you're eating and drinking, cooking demonstrations and wine tastings are scheduled daily and are often free or at least reasonably priced.

True foodies and wine enthusiasts should consider one of the special-event dinners. The Party for the Senses, Winemaker Dinners, and Reserve Dinners are very heady events, held in secluded glamour points all around Disney property, and they sell out weeks in advance.

General Epcot Advice

In the off-season, Epcot hours are often staggered. Future World is generally open from 9 am to 7 pm (although Soarin', Test Track, and Mission: SPACE generally remain operative until Epcot closes), and the World Showcase is open from 11 am to 9 pm. Keep the size of the park in mind, and follow these tips to make your visit more enjoyable.

INSIDER'S SECRET

IllumiNations produces a lot of smoke. Before you select your vantage point, note which way the wind is blowing. If you have a pleasant breeze in your face now, you can be sure you'll catch the full brunt of the smoke during the show.

EPCOT DON'T-MISS LIST

✦ IllumiNations

✦ Mission: SPACE (if the kids are old enough and pass the 44-inch height requirement)

✦ Soarin' (if the kids pass the 40-inch height requirement)

✦ Spaceship Earth

✦ Test Track (if the kids pass the 40-inch height requirement)

✦ Turtle Talk with Crush

✦ World Showcase entertainment

✦ Take Epcot in small doses if you're traveling with young kids; four hours at a time is enough.

✦ Tour Future World in the morning and then drift toward the World Showcase in the afternoon. You can escape to the films and indoor exhibits during the hottest and busiest times of the day.

✦ On entering a World Showcase pavilion that has a show or film—France, Canada, America, or China—ask the attendant how long until the show begins. If your wait is 10 minutes or less, go on inside. If the wait is longer, browse the shops or take a bathroom break and return 10 minutes before showtime. Epcot theaters are so large it's rarely a problem to get in.

✦ Check your entertainment schedule and save time for some of the shows that take place in the pavilions of the World Showcase. Shows like the Chinese acrobats have major kid appeal.

✦ If you miss Soarin', Mission: SPACE, or Test Track in the morning, return in the evening. Although they're packed throughout the afternoon, it's often easier to slip onto these popular rides while everyone else is eating dinner in the World Showcase or watching IllumiNations.

✦ If you're touring off-season and plan to spend mornings in the other parks and evenings at Epcot, make your dinner reservation times early (for example, at 5 pm), which will leave you several hours to tour after dinner.

✦ Restaurants are open late, so if the kids have had a good afternoon nap and can keep going until 11 pm, arrange your dinner reservations for 8:30. The restaurants keep serving as the park closes down, so eating late buys you maximum hours in the park—assuming your kids can handle the schedule, that is, and assuming that you'll be seeing IllumiNations on another night.

✦ If you're not staying for IllumiNations, begin moving toward the exit gates while the show is in progress.

Future World

Future World comprises nine large pavilions, each containing at least one major attraction, and it is very much like a permanent World's Fair, mixing educational opportunities with pure entertainment.

Future World Attractions

Standalone Rides

☀ Captain E-O

In 2010, *Captain E-O,* a circa-1986 film starring Michael Jackson, returned to the Disney parks for the first time in 15 years. The 17-minute presentation—which has silly characters, great dancing, and seat-grabbing 3-D effects—appeals to all ages. The basic plot is that Captain E-O, as a down-on-his-luck space commander with a misfit crew, uses music to transform a colorless planet into a world of peace and happiness. But it's really all just an excuse to remember what a phenomenal performer Michael Jackson was. Scare Factor→ **In Captain E-O volume is loud, the seats rumble a bit, and the supreme commander starts out pretty darn ugly, but there's little doubt that Michael and the gang will ultimately carry the day, so the show won't scare most kids.**

FastPass+ Attractions

Unlike at the Magic Kingdom, rides and attractions at Epcot are grouped into two tiers, and you can get only one Tier One FastPass+ among your first three. This means that you can't get both Soarin' and Test Track. ■TIP→ Epcot has FastPass+ kiosks in Future World in the breezeways at both Innoventions East and West and at the International Gateway, located at the entrance to the World Showcase. By far the most valuable FastPass+ in the park is for Soarin', but they go fast.

TIER ONE

✦ Epcot Character Spot

✦ IllumiNations: Reflections of Earth

✦ Soarin'

✦ Test Track

TIER TWO

✦ Captain E-O

✦ Journey Into Imagination with Figment

✦ Living with the Land

✦ Mission: SPACE

✦ The Seas with Nemo & Friends

✦ Spaceship Earth

✦ Turtle Talk with Crush

☀ Ellen's Energy Adventure

Universe of Energy features Ellen DeGeneres, Alex Trebek, and Jamie Lee Curtis. Ellen has a dream in which she's a contestant on the game show *Jeopardy!*, and when she's thoroughly skunked by smarty-pants Jamie Lee, she realizes she needs to know a lot more about energy. Luckily for her, neighbor Bill Nye the Science Guy is happy to help.

> ### INSIDER'S SECRET
>
> A persistent Disney rumor is that Innoventions might be closed as part of a larger Epcot overhaul. Also, Ellen's Energy Adventure is often closed in the off-season, and there are also rumors that it, too, might close permanently.

The Disney twist comes when the 97-seat theater begins to break apart in sections that align themselves in sequence and form a train. A curtain lifts and you begin to move through a prehistoric scene that carries you back to the era when coal deposits first formed on Earth. All around you are those darn dinosaurs, among the largest Audio-Animatronics figures Disney has ever created. After your train has once more morphed into a theater, there's a final film segment in which a newly educated Ellen gets her *Jeopardy!* revenge.

When entering the Universe of Energy, ask the attendant how long it is until the next show begins or check the digital clock. Don't enter sooner than 10 minutes before showtime; this is a 30-minute presentation, and there's no point in wearing out the kids before you begin. The theater can seat many people, so there's rarely a reason to line up and wait.

Despite its proximity to the front gate, Universe of Energy isn't a good choice for the morning; save it for the afternoon, when you'll welcome the chance to sit down for 30 minutes. **Scare Factor→ The dinosaurs are big and can be scary to younger kids.**

☀ Innoventions

Innoventions is a pavilion with many interactive exhibits, but it doesn't contain a big-deal ride or attraction. Rather, it lets you experience virtual reality, learn through hands-on games, and experience products and games before they hit the market. The Imagineers even make fire safety, saving money, and weather fun.

Don't be overwhelmed by the options at Innoventions—just wander over to a kiosk and start playing. Cast members can answer questions or help you get the hang of the games and experiments. Exhibits change frequently, keeping things fresh, and many of the stations are kid-friendly. Even preschoolers will find plenty to do.

One of Innoventions' best exhibits, the Sum of All Thrills, lets theme-park guests play the role of Imagineer and build their own ride. The experience begins with a tutorial in a design room. A few lessons on math and engineering sneak in along the way as participants use a touch-screen computer to pick a vehicle shape and determine how fast the ride can and should go. The information is saved on a magnetized card that is fed into a simulator; visitors then get to experience the track they just created. Kids get to take the cards home where they can be used on a website sponsored by attraction developer Raytheon to access more fun math and science games. **Scare Factor→ It's as scary as you make it.**

☀ Journey into Imagination

The ride's premise is that Dr. Nigel Channing (Eric Idle), the rather stuffy head of the Imagination Institute, must be broken out of his shell and taught the true meaning of imagination, and the lovable purple creature known as Figment is just the dragon for the job. The ride is pretty simple, especially in contrast to other Future World attractions, but younger kids like it, and there's rarely a wait. After the ride, stop off at the interactive exhibits in the ImageWorks labs. **Scare Factor→ It's not scary.**

☀ Mission: SPACE

Epcot's most technologically advanced thrill ride launches guests into a simulated space adventure, from the excitement of liftoff to the wonder of flight. To develop the story and design, Disney Imagineers worked with 25 space experts from NASA, and the result is completely immersive and interactive.

You're grouped into teams of four, and each person is given a crew position—Commander, Navigator, Pilot, or Engineer—and assigned the tasks that go along with that role. Once you board your

pod, everything happens fast. If you've opted for the spinning version of the ride, the motion is so rapid that it really feels like flight.
The sustained g-forces during the launch are by far the most intense part of the ride. And before you fully recover, you're required
to take on your crew role and push a few buttons (made somewhat
more difficult by the gravitational pull of the ship's movement) as
directed by mission control. (These "tasks" engage the kids, especially if they're a bit nervous about flying, but if you mess up, not to
worry. You'll land safely back in Orlando just the same.)

Disney offers a tamer—in other words, nonspinning—version
of the ride for younger children and anyone with health concerns.
As you approach the attraction, signs direct you toward either the
orange team, which boards the spinning capsules, or the green
team, which boards the nonspinning capsules. If you opt not to
spin, you have the same engaging preshow and postshow and the
same visual effects; the main difference is you don't feel the dramatic g-forces during the liftoff portion of the ride.

In motion simulators you can avoid motion sickness by looking away from the screen, but on the spinning version of Mission:
SPACE, where your cabin is actually moving, the opposite is true.
If you begin to feel queasy, keep your head back against the seat
and focus intently on the screen. Shutting your eyes is the worst
thing you can do.

As you exit, there's a small Space Base crawl area for younger
kids and a cool, competitive group game called Space Race for
older kids. Scare Factor→ **The height requirement is 44 inches for
either version (spin or no spin), which will weed out the younger
kids. But take Disney's safety recommendations seriously: no
pregnant women, children under seven, or anyone with high
blood pressure or back, neck, or motion-sickness problems, especially on the spinning version of the ride. That said, there's a
fair amount of bouncing around in both sets of capsules.**

☀ Spaceship Earth

Whatever their age, few travelers can remain blasé at the sight
of Spaceship Earth, the most photographed and readily recognizable symbol of Epcot. Even preschoolers rate it highly, probably
because of the excitement of actually entering the "big ball."

The ride inside, which coils toward the top of the 17-story
geosphere, traces developments in communication from cave

drawings to computers. You climb past scenes of Egyptian temples, a Greek classroom, and the invention of the Gutenberg press. A simple interactive game near the end lets you answer some questions and then see your own "future"—complete with your own face.

> **HIDDEN MICKEY**
>
> We all know Mickey is a star, and he actually has his own constellation in Epcot's Spaceship Earth. Look for him in the starry sky at the beginning of the ride, just after you load.

Take a few minutes to check out the postshow as you exit the ride. Most of the exhibits are technology based and geared toward older kids, but children of any age will enjoy watching their image flash on the screen and their hometown light up on a global map that indicates those of past guests. Scare Factor→ **It's not scary.**

☀ Test Track

Test Track is the fastest ride in all of Disney World—we're talking 34 separate turns, 50-degree banking, and speeds of 65 mph. In other words, this isn't the Tomorrowland Speedway.

The ride begins in the queue. Guests are invited to create their own vehicle using a touch-screen computer. Every choice used to build the car, from the tires to the shape, will affect its ultimate performance. Up to three people can design a car together, or everyone can design his or her own.

As you board the real Test Track vehicle, your design is downloaded into the car's computer system. This allows you to test your personal car in a variety of simulations, measuring it in terms of efficiency, responsiveness, capability, and power.

Thanks to an onboard computer, the cars constantly adapt to road conditions, vehicle weight, and the location of the other 28 cars on the track.

You go through various tests inside, but the real excitement comes when your car emerges onto the outdoor track that circles the building. Here cars reach their top speeds—they could go higher than 65 mph, but Imagineers didn't think it would be prudent to break the Florida speed limit—as they go through a mile of curves, hills, and turns. It's one powerful ride.

Test Track can draw long lines and frequently runs out of FastPass+ times. If your kids are old enough to handle the intensity, consider going through the Singles Line. You won't get to ride together, but your wait time will be cut significantly. **Scare Factor→ Children must be 40 inches tall to ride Test Track. It's all about speed, with no flips or plunges, so kids five and up should be fine.**

The Land

This cheerful pavilion, devoted to the subjects of food production and the environment, is home to three attractions, a rotating restaurant, and one of Epcot's most elaborate fast-food courts. Because there are so many places to eat here, the Land is crowded from 11 am to 2 pm, when everyone heads in for lunch.

☀ Circle of Life

This 20-minute film stars Simba, Pumbaa, and Timon from *The Lion King,* and the beloved characters do a terrific job of pitching the conservation message. Simba explains how humans affect their environment, both positively and negatively, so the show is educational and entertaining. Because the Harvest Theater is large, with comfortable seats, Circle of Life is a smart choice for afternoon. Scare Factor→ **It's not scary.**

☀ Living with the Land

You travel by boat past scenes of farming environments, ending with a peek at fish farming, drip irrigation, and other innovative agricultural technologies. It's a fairly adult presentation, but it moves swiftly, so kids shouldn't be too bored. If you have older kids who might benefit from doing a school project on the subject of futuristic farming, consider the hour-long "Behind the Seeds" greenhouse tour. The sign-up booth is tucked away near the entrance to Soarin', and the price is $20 for adults and $16 for kids. Scare Factor→ **It's not scary.**

☀ Soarin'

Soarin' provides a bird's-eye view on an exhilarating flight above the beautiful state of California. It works like this: You're lifted 40 feet off the ground inside a giant dome. The interior of the dome is actually an enormous screen with images of redwood forests, Napa Valley, Yosemite, and the Golden Gate Bridge. You'll feel like you're hang gliding as you gently climb, bank, and descend your way through the scenery. The details make the ride: You'll feel the wind blowing through your hair and smell orange blossoms and pine trees. One mother of three from New York raved about the experience: "Soarin' was the favorite of everyone in our family, including our 5-year-old. She is normally afraid of heights but insisted on riding it three times, and the last time she actually wanted to sit on the highest row so she could see better!"

Soarin' may be the most popular ride in all of Walt Disney World, both in terms of being highly rated and in terms of the ride volume. Perhaps it's because the ride appeals to all age groups, preschoolers to grandmas (though guests must still be 40 inches to ride). Scare Factor➔ **It's not scary unless you are especially bothered by heights.**

■**TIP➔ Soarin' is madly popular (and in fact is due for an expansion to somewhat help cope with the crowd flow). A FastPass+ reservation here will help you save more time than at any other attraction in all of Epcot; if you don't have one, come first thing in the morning.**

The Seas

The focal point of the Seas pavilion is a saltwater aquarium so enormous that Spaceship Earth could float inside it. It also has popular restaurants and two attractions.

☀ The Seas with Nemo & Friends

The Finding Nemo ride within is a hit with preschoolers. You board "clamobiles" (similar in shape to the Haunted Mansion "doom buggies") and travel through a coral reef looking for Nemo. On the way, you meet Dory, Bruce, and other stars from the film. At the end of the ride, you disembark at Sea Base, where there are interactive exhibits. Scare Factor➔ **It's not scary.**

☀ Turtle Talk with Crush

Don't miss the lighthearted and funny Turtle Talk with Crush, in which the laid-back animated turtle interacts with kids in the audience through real-time animation technology. Encourage your child to sit up front on the floor and ask Crush questions. We get tons of positive mail about this show. "Adorable," wrote a mom from Canada. "Our children considered it one of the highlights of the day." Turtle Talk with Crush is far more popular than its out-of-the-way location and small seating area would indicate. If you have preschoolers, try to get here before 11:30 am. Afternoon shows can be crowded. Scare Factor→ **It's not scary.**

World Showcase

Pretty by day and gorgeous by night, the World Showcase comprises the pavilions of 11 nations: Mexico, Norway, China, Germany, Italy, America, Japan, Morocco, France, the United Kingdom, and Canada. The countries are like links in a chain that stretch around a large lagoon. Really large. Making a full circle is a 1.2-mile trek.

Some of the pavilions have full-scale attractions, while others have only shops and restaurants. Wonderful live entertainment is also available; check your entertainment schedule for showtimes.

Each pavilion is staffed by citizens of the country it represents. Disney goes to great pains to recruit, relocate, and if necessary, teach English to the shopkeepers and waiters here, bringing them to Orlando for a year and housing them with representatives from the other World Showcase nations. It's a cultural-exchange program on the highest level. These young men and women save the World Showcase from being merely touristy, and provide your kids with the chance to rub elbows, however briefly, with folks from other cultures.

World Showcase Attractions

☀ The American Adventure

This multimedia presentation, combining Audio-Animatronics figures with film, is popular with all age groups. The technological highlight comes when the Ben Franklin robot walks up the stairs to visit Thomas Jefferson, but the entire 30-minute presentation is packed with elaborate sets that rise from the stage, film montages, and moving music.

INSIDER'S SECRET

If you really want to experience the Seas, a program called DiveQuest ($175) lets visitors 10 and over scuba dive in the aquarium, while the Epcot Seas Aqua Tour ($140) lets guests 8 and up snorkel. Whether you go under the sea or stay on top, these three-hour programs give you bragging rights and a cool T-shirt. Call ☎ *407/939-8687* (☎ *407/WDW-TOUR*) if you're interested.

It's worth noting that some guests find the patriotism of the American Adventure a little heavy-handed. There seem to be two primary reactions to the show—some people weep through it, and some people sleep through it. Most of our readers rate it as one of the best attractions in Epcot. **Scare Factor→ It's not scary.**

☀ Disney Phineas and Ferb: Agent P's World Showcase Adventure

This interactive game, which leads you all around the countries of the World Showcase looking for clues, is a great way to encourage kids to explore the nooks and crannies of the various pavilions. The idea is that you're helping Agent P, a.k.a. Perry the Platypus from the popular *Phineas and Ferb* TV show, in a secret-agent adventure.

> ### INSIDER'S SECRET
>
> Get your kids involved in the World Showcase by visiting the Kidcot Fun Stops. Children begin a craft project (at present it's Perry the Platypus, but sometimes they make a mask or musical instrument) at the first booth you encounter, and as they move to each country, they receive another element to add to their project. It's a great ice-breaker to help them interact with cast members.

You can register to play by stopping by the kiosk on the bridge between Future World and the World Showcase. (If you're entering from the back-door entrance, there's a location there, too, as well as ones near the Norway and Italy pavilions.) Missions may take you to Norway, China, Japan, France, Germany, Mexico, or the United Kingdom. After signing up, you're issued a FONE (or Field Operative Notification Equipment) that will provide you with clues to help capture the villains.

Following the clues is fairly difficult, so this is a good game to play as a family. It takes about 30 minutes to complete a mission—those in the know claim Germany is the best. If you get hooked, you can go immediately to another country and start a new mission. "My 11-year-old son loved it," said a mom from Texas. "It did just what the designers of the game undoubtedly intended—make him actually excited about visiting the World Showcase pavilions." But be careful. One mother of two reported that "it was all our kids wanted to do. We had trouble getting them to Future World for any of the rides!" **Scare Factor→ It's not scary.**

☀ Gran Fiesta Tour

This mild little boat ride stars the Three Caballeros. The story has Donald skipping out on a singing gig and José and Panchito searching throughout Mexico for their friend. The Gran Fiesta Tour is a very simple ride, somewhat reminiscent of "it's a small world" on a more limited scale, but younger kids like it. Scare Factor→ **It's not scary.**

> **INSIDER'S SECRET**
>
> Maelstrom in Norway is closed at this writing to make way for a new attraction starring Elsa and Anna from *Frozen*. Stay tuned for details!

☀ Impressions de France

What a difference a seat makes! Like all the Epcot films, *Impressions de France* is exceedingly well done, with lush music and a 200-degree widescreen feel. It's easy to get in, even in the afternoon, and no one minds if babies take a little nap. The 20-minute film shows on the hour and half hour. Scare Factor→ **It's not scary.**

☀ O Canada!

This 20-minute Circle-Vision 360 film, starring Martin Short, is gorgeous and stirring but difficult to view with kids under six. To enjoy the effect of the circular screen, you must stand during the presentation, and no strollers are allowed in the theater. This means babies and toddlers must be held, and preschoolers, who can't see anything in a room full of standing adults, often clamor to be lifted up as well. Scare Factor→ **It's not scary.**

☀ Reflections of China

Another lovely 360-degree film. But again, it's not an easy attraction to view with young children. Scare Factor→ **It's not scary.**

CHAPTER 7

DISNEY'S

HOLLYWOOD STUDIOS

Have you ever wanted to see how Disney movie magic is made? Well, here's your chance! Disney's Hollywood Studios is a tribute to film, from the golden age of the silver screen to the age of modern digital, Pixar-style animation.

Visiting Hollywood Studios is like walking right onto a Hollywood soundstage. Hollywood Boulevard leads to a replica of Grauman's Chinese Theatre, which houses The Great Movie Ride, a journey that will take you into some of the most famous movies of all time. Streets of America is a conglomeration of mock-ups of some of America's most famous cities, so you can stroll from New York to San Francisco within the course of a minute.

This park is all about peeking behind the scenes and getting a glimpse of how films are made. The Lights, Motors, Action! Extreme Stunt Show illustrates how special effects are created, and the Magic of Disney Animation not only lets you see animators at work, but offers a class in how to draw a character. There are thrill rides in the form of the Tower of Terror and the Rock 'n' Roller Coaster, both among Disney's best. And there's no better way to wrap up a day recalling the glitz and glamour of Hollywood than to dine at the world-famous Brown Derby restaurant.

Hollywood Studios Touring Tips

Getting Here

Compared with the Magic Kingdom, getting to Disney's Hollywood Studios is a snap. Shuttle buses run approximately every 15 to 20 minutes from all on-site hotels. Guests staying at the Swan, Dolphin, and BoardWalk resorts or the Yacht or Beach club are a 15-minute water-taxi ride from the Hollywood gate.

If you're driving to the parks, note that the Hollywood parking lot is small. If you get there at opening time and park close to the entrance, you can forgo the parking-lot tram and walk to the front gate.

Getting Around

Hollywood is a relatively small park with no trains, boats, or buses. In other words, you'll walk.

Morning Tips

Tips for Your First Hour at Hollywood

Pick up a map and entertainment schedule as you enter. If you need a stroller, rent one at Oscar's Super Service Station.

✦ Toy Story Midway Mania! appeals to all age groups, so if you haven't reserved it via FastPass+, visit as early as you can.

✦ Do your kids want to be Padawan trainees and fight Darth Vader? Of course they do. The Jedi Training Academy is so popular that slots fill up quickly, even on busy days when they offer as many as 15 training sessions. Drop by the recruitment center (located just before you get to the Star Tours ride) to see what times are still available.

✦ Next ask yourself: Are your kids old and bold enough for a couple of big-deal rides? If so, turn onto Sunset Boulevard and head straight toward the Rock 'n' Roller Coaster and the Twilight Zone Tower of Terror. Waits are usually tolerable in the morning, but if it's a busy day, plan on using FastPass+ here.

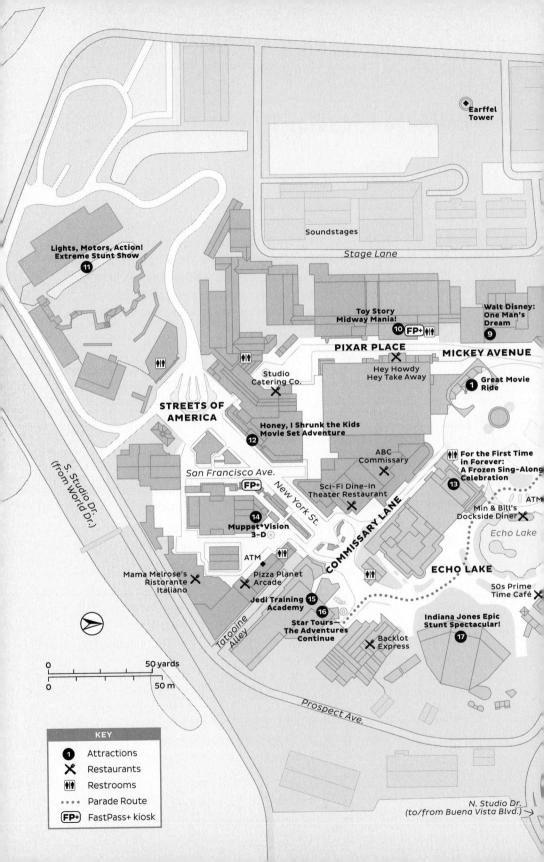

Earffel Tower

Soundstages

Stage Lane

Toy Story Midway Mania!
10 FP+ 👫

Walt Disney: One Man's Dream
9

PIXAR PLACE

MICKEY AVENUE

Hey Howdy Hey Take Away ✕

1 **Great Movie Ride**

Lights, Motors, Action! Extreme Stunt Show
11

👫

Studio Catering Co. ✕

STREETS OF AMERICA

Honey, I Shrunk the Kids Movie Set Adventure
12

👫

ABC Commissary ✕

👫 **For the First Time in Forever: A Frozen Sing-Along Celebration**
13

ATM

San Francisco Ave.

FP+

Sci-Fi Dine-In Theater Restaurant ✕

Min & Bill's Dockside Diner ✕

Echo Lake

S. Studio Dr. (from World Dr.)

14 **Muppet*Vision 3-D**

New York St.

COMMISSARY LANE

ECHO LAKE

👫

Mama Melrose's Ristorante Italiano ✕

ATM 👫

Pizza Planet Arcade ✕

50s Prime Time Café ✕

Jedi Training Academy
15

Star Tours— The Adventures Continue
16

Indiana Jones Epic Stunt Spectacular!
17

Tatooine Alley

Backlot Express ✕

0 ——— 50 yards
0 ——— 50 m

Prospect Ave.

N. Studio Dr. (to/from Buena Vista Blvd.)

KEY
1 Attractions
✕ Restaurants
👫 Restrooms
···· Parade Route
FP+ FastPass+ kiosk

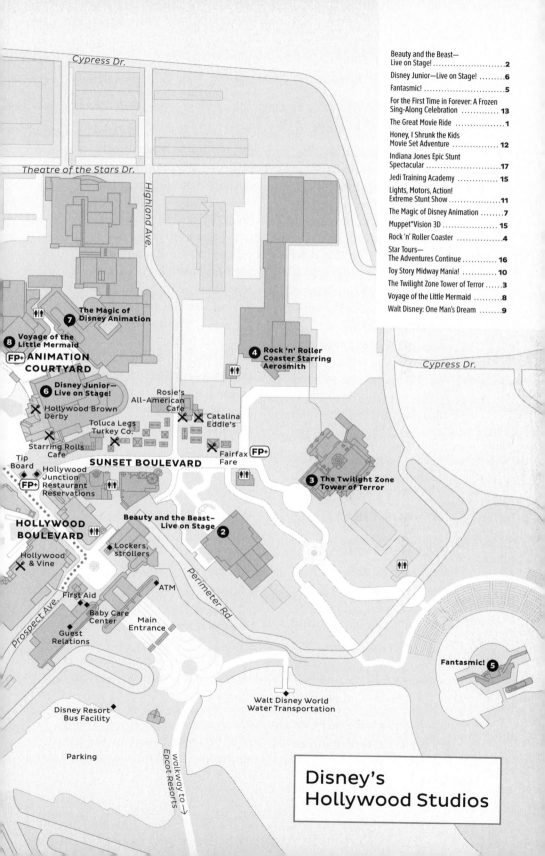

Cypress Dr.

Theatre of the Stars Dr.

Highland Ave.

Cypress Dr.

7 The Magic of
Disney Animation

8 Voyage of the
Little Mermaid

FP+ ANIMATION
COURTYARD

4 Rock 'n' Roller
Coaster Starring
Aerosmith

6 Disney Junior—
Live on Stage!

Rosie's
All-American
Cafe

Hollywood Brown
Derby

Toluca Legs
Turkey Co.

Catalina
Eddie's

Starring Rolls
Cafe

Fairfax **FP+**
Fare

Tip
Board

SUNSET BOULEVARD

3 The Twilight Zone
Tower of Terror

FP+ Hollywood
Junction
Restaurant
Reservations

**HOLLYWOOD
BOULEVARD**

Beauty and the Beast—
Live on Stage

2

Hollywood
& Vine

Lockers,
strollers

First Aid

ATM

Baby Care
Center

Main
Entrance

Guest
Relations

Prospect Ave.

Perimeter Rd.

Fantasmic! **5**

Disney Resort
Bus Facility

Walt Disney World
Water Transportation

Parking

walkway to
Epcot Resorts →

Disney's
Hollywood Studios

INSIDER'S SECRET

Disney wouldn't be Disney without the constant rumor of changes, and the biggest is that Hollywood Studios is on the verge of a major revamp, which will eventually engulf the entire back-lot area, either closing or making major changes to a large number of attractions.

There are rumors that a few attractions, such as the venerable Indiana Jones Stunt Show and Muppet*Vision 3D, are on the chopping block. Both of these attractions are still open at this writing and are still included in this chapter, but be aware that they may be phased out to make way for a whole new section based on . . . (rumbling theme music) . . . *Star Wars*!!! We will provide details on the projected Star Wars attractions as we can verify them. Additionally, the Sorcerer's Hat has been taken out, and the park's name will likely be changed once the revamp starts.

Star Tours, which is popular with all ages, is another good choice for morning.

Evening Tips

Your Last Hour

Fantasmic! always draws big crowds, and that is a blessing if you aren't seeing the show, but can be a pain if you are.

✦ To guarantee yourself a seat for Fantasmic!, you'll need to enter the stadium at least an hour in advance, 90 minutes during the on-season. That's quite a wait, so you may want to eat dinner while you hold your seat. The stadium sells hot dogs and the like, but if you want a more elaborate meal, you can buy fast food from anywhere in the park and carry it in.

✦ If you're not watching Fantasmic!, the last hour before closing is a great time to hit any attraction you missed early in the day or to revisit favorites. Just be sure to be out of the park before the show wraps up. The big fireworks salvo at the end is your cue to get moving toward the exits.

Exit Strategies

Although it's a terrific show that more than justifies any inconvenience, Fantasmic! draws virtually everyone in the park to one spot at closing. Ergo, exiting afterward is a nightmare.

✦ Try to sit near the back of the Mickey section so you'll not only have the best view but also the best shot at getting out fast and beating the crowds to the buses, trams, or water taxis. Be forewarned—this is prime real estate and fills up early.

✦ If you end up near the water or in one of the sections to the extreme right or extreme left of the stadium, you've got no choice but to deal with the crowd. One option is to sit tight and wait for the stadium to empty at least partially, then eat or shop your way through the park, allowing most of the people to exit ahead of you.

Character Meet and Greets

You'll find some Disney celebs in Hollywood that you can't meet anywhere else. Either consult your map and entertainment schedule or visit the My Disney Experience app to confirm the times and places they'll appear. You can also reserve some meet and greets through FastPass+.

Food Choices at Hollywood Studios

Hollywood Studios has some of the better sit-down options in any of the Walt Disney World parks.

Character Meals

The stars of Disney Junior appear for breakfast and lunch at the Hollywood & Vine buffeteria. Reservations are definitely a good idea for this one.

MEETING THE CHARACTERS

Several characters are nearly always on hand, but Hollywood is also the park where Disney Pixar stars make their debut, so character offerings change often. Consult the My Disney Experience app or check out your entertainment schedule to make sure you don't miss anyone.

- **Buzz and Woody:** Woody's Picture Shooting Corral by Toy Story Midway Mania!
- **Phineas and Ferb:** Streets of America
- **Lightning McQueen and Mater:** Streets of America
- **Mike and Sulley:** Streets of America
- **Mr. Incredible and Frozone:** The Magic of Disney Animation
- **Mickey Mouse:** The Magic of Disney Animation
- **Disney Junior stars:** Animation Courtyard

Full-Service Dining

The Hollywood Brown Derby is one of the best restaurants inside a Disney theme park—or any theme park, for that matter. Although it has gourmet cuisine and a beautifully urbane setting, it's still casual and friendly enough to take the kids. The menu changes seasonally and is frequently updated, but one thing that's always available is the signature Cobb salad.

Other Hollywood restaurants offer big doses of fun for kids. The '50s Prime Time Café plunks you down in the middle of a television sitcom and serves comfort food like meat loaf, milk shakes, and mac and cheese. TVs play nonstop, you're seated in replicas of baby-boomer kitchens, and the waitress pretends to be your mom. Before the meal is over, everyone gets into the act, and "Mom" is likely to inspect your hands for cleanliness before she'll feed you, or she may force the kids to finish their green beans using the dreaded airplane technique.

Equally campy is the Sci-Fi Dine-In Theater Restaurant, where you eat sandwiches, salads, and pasta in cars as if you were at a drive-in movie. Your waiters are carhops, the film clips are cheesy, and the waiters add to the fun by presenting your bill as a speeding ticket. Drinks even come with glow-in-the-dark ice cubes. The one drawback to the Sci-Fi is that the monster clips shown on the drive-in screen are so graphic and so huge that they alarm some children, and the creepiness is accentuated by the fact that the restaurant is extremely dark.

Due to its out-of-the-way location near Muppet*Vision 3D, Mama Melrose's Ristorante Italiano is definitely the least crowded and the fastest of the sit-down places. The veal saltimbocca and penne *alla vodka* are excellent.

Fast Food

If you just want a quick nosh, the Backlot Express lives up to its name and serves burgers and salads fast. Pizza Planet gets consistently high marks from our readers for both its *Toy Story* ambience and kid-friendly plain cheese pizza. If your party can't agree on what to eat, head for the open-air food court called the Sunset Ranch Market on Sunset Boulevard. You can each go in different directions for pizza, hot dogs, turkey legs, ice cream, and fruit, then all meet back at your table.

Other Hollywood Touring Tips

✦ **Do Big Rides First Thing.** Tour continuous-loading attractions such as the Tower of Terror, The Great Movie Ride, Toy Story Midway Mania!, the Rock 'n' Roller Coaster, and Star Tours early in the day. The exception to this is For the First Time in Forever: A Frozen Sing-Along Celebration, which should be seen in the morning.

✦ **Sit in the Afternoon.** In general, you should save theater-style presentations—Disney Junior; Beauty and the Beast; Voyage of the Little Mermaid; Muppet*Vision 3D; Indiana Jones; and Lights, Motors, Action!—for the afternoon, when other rides are getting busy.

DISNEY'S HOLLYWOOD STUDIOS DON'T-MISS LIST

✦ Beauty and the Beast–Live on Stage!

✦ Disney Junior–Live on Stage! (if your kids are under six)

✦ For the First Time in Forever: A Frozen Sing-Along Celebration (if your kids are under eight)

✦ The Great Movie Ride

✦ Lights, Motors, Action! Extreme Stunt Show

✦ Muppet*Vision 3D

✦ Rock 'n' Roller Coaster (if your kids are eight and up)

✦ Star Tours—The Adventures Continue

✦ Toy Story Midway Mania!

✦ Twilight Zone Tower of Terror (if your kids are eight and up)

✦ Voyage of the Little Mermaid

Sunset Boulevard

✴ Beauty and the Beast—Live on Stage!

The Theater of the Stars is modeled on the Hollywood Bowl, and it's the perfect setting for this appealing 30-minute show. The costuming, choreography, and production are first-rate. The plot is drastically compressed, but because about 99.9% of the audience has seen the movie, it's not a problem. Beauty and the Beast is a good choice for the afternoon. The theater is covered and large enough to seat 1,500, so if you show up 20 minutes before showtime you should easily get a seat. Scare Factor→ It's not scary.

✴ Fantasmic!

Fantasmic! may be the best closing show in any Disney park. It has everything—lasers, fireworks, lighting effects, music, fountains, a 6,900-seat amphitheater, 1.9 million gallons of water, 45 cast members, and a 50-foot fire-breathing dragon. The show plays at closing every night during the on-season and twice nightly on extremely busy days. During the off-season, it may play as rarely as twice a week, so make sure to arrange your tour-

INSIDER'S SECRET

In Hollywood Studios, Fast-Pass+ kiosks are located at the corner of Hollywood Boulevard and Sunset Boulevard, outside the Tower of Terror, and in the Animation Courtyard. The service center, where you can go with all your FastPass+ and My Disney Experience questions, is located immediately to the left as you enter the park.

The most valuable Fast-Pass+ reservations for Hollywood are Toy Story Midway Mania! (where it's essential), For the First Time in Forever: A Frozen Sing-Along Celebration, and (if your kids are old enough and bold enough) Rock 'n' Roller Coaster and Tower of Terror.

ing plan so that you'll be in Hollywood Studios on a night when Fantasmic! is scheduled.

Mickey performs in his role as the Sorcerer's Apprentice, fighting off a horde of evil Disney characters with a variety of special effects, including the projection of film images onto a screen of water. For a while it looks like the bad guys are winning, and these dark scenes are upsetting for some children. In due time, however, Mickey's imagination conjures up images of happiness, love, and friendship, and the good-guy characters show up in force. Children of all ages rate the show highly, and it's surprisingly moving, even for adults.

Fantasmic! is always packed, but one surefire way to guarantee you get in is to purchase a Fantasmic! dinner package. It includes a meal at one of three Hollywood restaurants (the Hollywood Brown Derby, Mama Melrose's Ristorante Italiano, or Hollywood & Vine) plus access to a priority-seating area of the Fantasmic! theater. Prices depend on the restaurant you choose, and the dinner package is included in the Disney Dining Plan.

As you pay for your meal, you're given a voucher that lets you into the priority-seating area. Don't arrive at the last minute—you aren't guaranteed a specific seat, just a seat within that area. Make reservations by calling ☎*407/939-3463* (☎*407/WDW–DINE*).

Be sure to sit at least 15 rows back from the front to avoid being sprayed with water. Scare Factor→ **In Fantasmic! every Dis-**

ney villain you can think of shows up for the cartoon Armageddon, and the middle scenes of the show are emotionally wrenching for preschoolers. Mickey saves the day, of course, and most kids adore the show. The noise is enough to frighten some babies and toddlers.

> ### HIDDEN MICKEY
>
> As you walk through the rotunda area before boarding the Rock 'n' Roller Coaster, check out the floors; if you look carefully, you'll see two Hidden Mickeys in the tiles.

☀ Rock 'n' Roller Coaster

The Rock 'n' Roller Coaster is one of the best rides in Disney World. The sound track, featuring Aerosmith, is perfectly synchronized to the movements of the coaster, and the volume is cranked to the max.

The premise is simple. You play the part of fans that have shown up at an Aerosmith taping, but unfortunately the group is in the process of leaving for a concert. They insist you come along to the show, so you're boarded into 24-passenger stretch limos, which their manager promises are "real fast," and you're off on a rock-and-roll trip through the highways of L.A.

Takeoff is amazing—0 to 60 in 2.8 seconds—and then you're quickly thrown into your first total flip. The mazelike track makes a total of three inversions, and at one point you rip through an "O" in the "Hollywood" sign. The coaster is smooth and fast and offers uneasy riders one comfort: Since the whole ride takes place inside a building, you never go very high, so there's no plunging sensation. Rock 'n' Roller Coaster is more about speed than big drops. Scare Factor→ **Loud, fast, and wild, especially at takeoff, Rock 'n' Roller Coaster is for older kids and teens. With a 48-inch height requirement, it will be much too much for kids under eight.**

☀ The Twilight Zone Tower of Terror

The Twilight Zone Tower of Terror combines the spooky ambience of a decaying, cobweb-covered 1930s-style Hollywood hotel with sheer thrills. For the clever preshow, Imagineers spliced together clips from the old *Twilight Zone* TV series, bringing back the long-deceased Rod Serling as narrator.

The story begins on a dark and stormy night in 1939 when five people—a movie star and starlet, a child actress and her nanny, and a bellboy—board a hotel elevator. The hotel is struck by lightning, the elevator drops, and the five passengers are transported into the Twilight Zone. One of the cast members who works at the attraction reports that the most common questions people ask her are "Is this a real hotel?" and "Am I going to die?" (The answer to both is "No.")

> **HIDDEN MICKEY**
>
> During the Tower of Terror preshow, look closely as the group of five unfortunate passengers boards the elevator. You'll see that the child actress is holding a Mickey Mouse toy.

Your car moves out of its elevator shaft and through a hallway with holographic images before eventually settling into a second elevator shaft. (This is all drawn out with agonizing slowness.) When the car reaches a height of 150 feet, you begin your series of free falls.

That's right. Free falls is plural. When the ride first opened, you dropped only once, but Imagineers have since introduced a random drop pattern, which means that computers controlling the ride select from several possible drop sequences. You may be hauled up and dropped as many as seven times, and the trip up is as exhilarating as the one down. **Scare Factor→ Tower of Terror has a 40-inch height requirement, which means that many preschoolers are tall enough to ride. Nonetheless, our suggestion is eight and up, because of both the spooky setup and the drop. The expanded drop sequence means you're bouncing around in the shaft for a good 20 to 30 seconds, which can feel like forever to a terrified child.**

Hollywood Boulevard

✳ The Great Movie Ride

Beginning in the Chinese Theatre at the end of Hollywood Boulevard, The Great Movie Ride is a bona fide classic. Disney's largest ride-through attraction, it loads steadily and fairly swiftly and is best toured either mid-morning or in the last hour before the park closes.

Your tour guide provides an amusing spiel as you glide past soundstage sets from *Casablanca, Alien, The Wizard of Oz,* and other great films. The Audio-Animatronics figures of Gene Kelly, Julie Andrews, and Clint Eastwood are among Disney's best. But

Quick Guide to Hollywood

Attraction	Location
Beauty and the Beast—Live on Stage!	Sunset Blvd.
Disney Junior—Live onstage!	Animation Courtyard
Fantasmic!	Sunset Blvd.
For The First Time In Forever: A Frozen Sing-Along Celebration	Echo Lake
The Great Movie Ride	Hollywood Blvd.
Honey, I Shrunk the Kids Movie Set Adventure	Streets of America
Indiana Jones Epic Stunt Spectacular	Echo Lake
Lights, Motors, Action! Extreme Stunt Show	Streets of America
The Magic of Disney Animation	Animation Courtyard
Muppet*Vision 3D	Streets of America
Rock 'n' Roller Coaster	Sunset Blvd.
Star Tours	Echo Lake
Toy Story Mania	Pixar Ave.
Twilight Zone Tower of Terror	Sunset Blvd.
Voyage of the Little Mermaid	Animation Courtyard
Walt Disney: One Man's Dream	Pixar Ave.

Scare Factor
0 = Unlikely to scare any child of any age.
! = Has dark or loud elements; might rattle some toddlers.
!! = A couple of gotcha! moments; should be fine for school-age kids.
!!! = You need to be pretty big and pretty brave to handle this ride.

Studio Attractions

Height Requirement	Speed of Line	Duration of Ride/Show	Scare Factor	Age Range
None	Fast	30 min.	0	All
None	Moderate	15 min.	0	All
None	Fast	25 min.	!!	3 and up
None	N/A	20 min.	0	All
None	Fast	25 min.	!	5 and up
None	Slow	n/a	0	2 and up
None	Fast	30 min.	!	All
None	Moderate	25 min.	!!	All
None	Moderate	35 min.	0	All
None	Fast	20 min.	!	2 and up
48 inches	Moderate	3 min.	!!!	8 and up
40 inches	Moderate	10 min.	!!	5 and up
None	Moderate	12 min.	0	All
40 inches	Moderate	10 min.	!!!	8 and up
None	Fast	20 min.	!	3 and up
None	Moderate	20 min.	0	8 and up

FastPass+ Attractions

Like Epcot, Hollywood Studios groups its rides and attractions into two tiers for FastPass+, and you can only get one FastPass+ from the Tier One group. During the on-season, the park could add more attractions to this list.

TIER ONE

✦ Beauty and the Beast—Live on Stage!

✦ Fantasmic!

✦ The Great Movie Ride

✦ Rock 'n' Roller Coaster

✦ Toy Story Midway Mania

TIER TWO

✦ The Comedy Warehouse Holiday Special

✦ Disney Junior–Live on Stage!

✦ For the First Time in Forever: A Frozen Sing–Along Celebration

✦ Indiana Jones Epic Stunt Spectacular

✦ Lights, Motors, Action! Extreme Stunt Show

✦ Muppet*Vision 3D

✦ Star Tours—The Adventures Continue

✦ The Twilight Zone Tower of Terror

✦ Voyage of the Little Mermaid

INSIDER'S SECRET

A problem that arises with Disney's theater-style attractions is especially acute in huge venues like the Theater of the Stars, where Beauty and the Beast—Live on Stage! plays, and the Fantasmic! theater. Let's say you arrive before the stated showtime and find yourself a terrific seat. As others file into the theater, cast members encourage you to move over and make room so, ironically, those who came earliest often end up politely sliding their way into the far corners of the theaters, while stragglers end up with the best seats. And if you try to avoid this by swooping in at the last minute, you may not get a seat at all. Solution? Instead of staking out aisle seats in side sections (where you'll find yourself being pushed to the walls), arrive early and sit along one of the aisles in the center section. You'll still be asked to keep sliding, but at least you'll end up near the middle of the theater.

things suddenly turn ugly as your car stalls and the movie scenes come to life. Depending on which car you've boarded, you're about to be overrun by either a Mafia-style gangster or a Western desperado. Your tram will be taken hostage, but don't fret too much. In a later scene, drawn from *Indiana Jones and the Temple of Doom*, justice prevails. Was there ever any doubt there would be a happy ending? Scare Factor→ **On The Great Movie Ride you'll encounter the Alien from** *Alien,* **the Wicked Witch from** *The Wizard of Oz,* **and any number of bad guys on your trip. Some of the scenes are startling for preschoolers—the pretend gunfire as well as the confrontations, however campy, can be jarring to some—but the fact that your tram driver disappears and reappears does underscore the fact that it's all "just pretend."**

Echo Lake

☀ For the First Time in Forever: A Frozen Sing-Along Celebration

Based on the hit movie *Frozen,* Disney has added a simple show that highlights the music from the film and encourages guests to sing along—as loudly as they can! Anna, Elsa, and Kristof make appearances, but the majority of the show is led by the "royal historians," who gloss over most of the plot and focus on why the kids are really there—to sing and dance. The show has taken up residence in the theater that previously held American Idol. Videos are played along in the background with the words, but as the historians point out, you're really only there if you know the words already.

Young fans of the movie will love this attraction, and the banter from the historians is enough to keep the adults engaged. Watching the little ones sing can be entertaining in and of itself; on our last trip we sat next to a real diva-in-training. An indoor snowstorm at the end whips everyone into a frenzy. Scare Factor→ **It's not scary.**

☀ Indiana Jones Epic Stunt Spectacular

This stunt show is loud, lively, and full of laughs. Audience volunteers are a key part of the action, and your odds of being tapped improve if you show up early and are near the front of the line. Professional stunt people re-create daring scenes from the Indiana Jones movies in this 30-minute show that is a great chance to see how some of those difficult and dangerous stunts wind up on film.

It's a huge theater, so even people who show up right at showtime are still usually seated. Scare Factor→ **The gunfire and explosions in the Indiana Jones show startle some kids, but the fact that the theater is outdoors dilutes the intensity.**

☀ Jedi Training Academy

Younglings will jump at the chance to participate in the Jedi Training Academy, held several times a day on a stage outside of Star Tours. A Jedi knight selects audience volunteers (ages 4–12) and is leading them through some basic light-saber moves when suddenly (who could have seen this coming?) Darth Vader and his

Storm Troopers show up looking for trouble. Each young Jedi-in-training gets a chance to show off his or her fighting skills in defense of the Force. "My 6-year-old son loved this attraction," reported one father from Michigan. "We ended up coming back for another show."

The Academy, which started out as a simple sidewalk show, has become so popular that Padawan hopefuls need to sign up first thing in the morning or risk disappointment. The sign-up site is right in front of Star Tours, in the former of site of Sounds Dangerous. It's a little extra effort, but as a mom from Florida explained, it's all worth it. "My daughter loves Star Tours. A lady in Guest Relations told us we'd have to rush over to get her signed up, and we barely got her on for the last show of the day. A bonus is that the PhotoPass photographer was there. He got some great up-close shots of her fighting Darth Vader. She still talks about the experience, and the photos are among her most prized possessions."

> ## INSIDER'S SECRET
>
> If the Jedi Training Academy washes out due to a sudden rainstorm, this can be a good time to ride Star Tours. Not only is the attraction inside and thus safe and dry, but sometimes Darth Vader and his Storm Troopers find themselves dressed up with nowhere to go and are on hand to greet guests.

The Jedi Training Academy can be great fun to watch even if you don't have a child in training. The young Padawans are adorable, and it's pretty exciting when Vader shows up. The best place to watch is from the elevated and shady patio of the nearby fast-food spot, the Backlot Express. Scare Factor→ **It's not scary.**

☀ Star Tours—The Adventures Continue

Motion-simulation technology and a jostling cabin combine to produce the real feel of flight in Star Tours. The ride is the best of both worlds—the 3-D effects are so convincing that you'll clutch your arm rails, but the actual rumbles are so mild that only the youngest children are eliminated as passengers.

The ride has 54 possible story lines. You read that right: 54. There are three possible opening sequences, three possible closing sequences, and between them you might travel to any variety of destinations from the movies. Ergo, the experience is a little different every time, so ardent fans opt to take multiple trips.

Scare Factor→ **Most kids love Star Tours, and the new 3-D technology has actually cut down on the problem of motion sickness, which was formerly a complaint from some riders. The height requirement is 40 inches.**

Animation Courtyard

☀ Disney Junior—Live on Stage!

Younger kids love this stage show where they sing, dance, and play along with puppets and costumed cast members from Disney Channel shows. (Characters are updated periodically to make sure they're from currently popular programs.) The performance space holds large crowds, with the children (largely preschoolers) grouped on the floor where they can participate in the show: They can stand, jump, sing, and shriek within the confines of your claimed spot on the carpeted floor.

Although the show is simple, it's a big hit with toddlers and preschoolers, and substantial lines begin forming about 30 minutes before showtime. Visit whenever your kids are at their happiest and most rested.

Your first instinct will be to sit as close to the stage as possible—but don't. Due to the height of the stage the puppets can be difficult to see from the front of the theater, so try sitting in the back or along the aisle for your toddler's best view.

There's more excitement as you exit. Characters are often on hand for meet and greets in the Animation Courtyard, and this is the only place you'll see Disney Junior stars. Scare Factor→ **It's not scary.**

☀ The Magic of Disney Animation

The Magic of Disney Animation opens with a fast and funny show starring Mushu, the pint-size dragon from *Mulan,* with the voice of Eddie Murphy, and a live Disney animator. The animator describes how a character evolves in the animation process, and

> **INSIDER'S SECRET**
>
> Whenever there are evening Extra Magic Hours at Disney's Hollywood Studios, a Disney Junior Dance Party is held in the Animation Courtyard, offering extra entertainment for kids.

Mushu learns, to his horror, that he originally wasn't destined to be a dragon at all.

After the show, it's on to the interactive exhibits. These are fun for all ages, and you can stay as long as you like. "You're a Character," a quiz that tells you which Disney character is most like you, will save you years of money otherwise spent on therapy. (Don't like your character? Try the test again!) Or you can insert your own voice into clips of animated classics, digitally color a cartoon, or—most exciting for youngsters—meet the stars of Pixar's latest film. Although stars from the Disney flicks circulate through all the parks, Hollywood is your best bet to meet the newest stars.

The best part of the attraction for older kids is the Animation Academy, where you can learn to draw a Disney character. Your drawing becomes a great free souvenir that you can take home. Many kids like to have the character they drew autograph the picture the next time they see him or her in the park. You can also buy a frame for your masterpiece as you exit the attraction. "Learning to draw Pooh was an unexpected highlight for our family," wrote one mom. "I think we may have discovered an unknown talent in our 8-year-old son!" **Scare Factor→ It's not scary.**

☀ Voyage of the Little Mermaid

Using puppets, animation, and live actors to retell the story of Ariel and Prince Eric, Voyage of the Little Mermaid remains one of the most popular shows at Hollywood.

The special effects in this 20-minute show are among the best Disney has to offer. You'll feel as if you're really underwater, and the interplay among the animation, puppetry, and live actors is ingenious. **Scare Factor→ Voyage of the Little Mermaid does have some frightening elements. The storm scene is dark and loud, and Ursula the Sea Witch is one big ugly puppet. That said, most kids have seen the movie and know enough to expect a happy ending, so they usually make it through the dark scenes without becoming too upset. Parents with toddlers will want to sit along the aisles if possible, in case they need to make a quick exit.**

Pixar Avenue

☀ Toy Story Midway Mania!

Ever fancied being one of the toys in *Toy Story*? Well, going on this ride may be the closest you ever get. Toy Story Midway Mania! combines a ride through a cartoon toy box with the challenge of playing carnival midway games. You put on 3-D glasses, and suddenly you've been shrunk into a toy spinning around with Woody, Hamm, Rex, and other familiar characters. Using spring-action shooters, you'll launch rings at aliens, shoot darts at balloons, and hurl eggs at barnyard targets. Best of all, the ride gauges your skill level during the practice round and then adjusts the difficulty for each rider to create a level playing field. So a 5-year-old can compete head-to-head with her 12-year-old brother.

Toy Story Midway Mania! is similar in concept to Buzz Lightyear's Space Ranger Spin in the Magic Kingdom, but the technology is considerably more advanced. As you play, you see the "virtual objects" you've launched from your shooters either hit or miss targets. At times it even seems as if objects are whirling past you as they pop out of the 3-D scenes. Like any attraction with scoring, Toy Story Midway Mania! is addictive, with riders coming back time after time to try and beat their own scores. "The best ride in Hollywood," enthused one mother of three, "and maybe in all of Disney World. The kids loved it and it took me and my husband back to our childhoods." Scare Factor➜ **It's not scary.**

■**TIP**➜ "Mania" is right. No matter what time of day or season, Toy Story Midway Mania! is the one Hollywood attraction where FastPass+ is most essential. And there are rumors that the stand-by queue will close completely on busy days.

☀ Walt Disney: One Man's Dream

This is more of an exhibit than an attraction, but it does remind you that almost everything in Disney World sprang from the extraordinary vision of a single man. There are plenty of artifacts and memorabilia, as well as a film about Walt Disney's life. Scare Factor➜ **It's not scary.**

Streets of America

☀ Honey, I Shrunk the Kids Movie Set Adventure

In this playground, based on the film, "miniaturized" guests scramble through a world of 9-foot Cheerios and spiderwebs three stories high. It's the perfect place for kids to blow off steam and very popular with the under-10 set. Scare Factor→ **It's not scary.**

☀ Lights, Motors, Action! Extreme Stunt Show

Based on the popular Moteurs...Action! Stunt Show Spectacular at Disneyland Paris, this show features special cars, motorcycles, and watercraft built to blow up, split in half, and perform other high-octane stunts. When the show starts you've been transported to a movie set, where the director is filming chase scenes and other daring feats with a cast and crew of 50.

"The Lights, Motors, Action! stunt show was incredible," wrote one mother of two from Massachusetts. "We saw it twice. It's an especially good show for boys, since some of the other shows at Hollywood are a little girly."

Showtimes for Lights, Motors, Action! will be listed on your entertainment schedule and on the tip board on Hollywood Boulevard. The performances are in a large arena, so generally everyone who comes within five minutes of showtime can be seated. Come 10 minutes early on crowded days. Scare Factor→ **The engines and pyrotechnics in Lights, Motors, Action! may startle babies and toddlers.**

☀ Muppet*Vision 3D

The Muppets combine slapstick and high wit, so everyone from preschoolers to adults will find something to make them laugh. Kids love the 3-D glasses and the eye-popping special effects. And the preshow is nearly as clever as the 20-minute main show. This is a good choice for early afternoon, when you've ridden several rides and would like to sit and laugh for a while. The 3-D effects are more convincing if you sit near the center toward the back of the theater. Scare Factor→ **Although Muppet*Vision 3D tested highly among kids ages two to five, some parents reported that children under two were unnerved by the sheer volume of the finale.**

☀ Snowground Playground

Located next to Wandering Oaken's Trading Post—a shop that sells exclusively Frozen-theme merchandize—is a fun little play area for younger kids. The kick is that it has real snow, so youngsters can build their own personal Olaf. It's a great place to let toddlers and preschoolers burn off some energy, and as an added bonus, it's always cool inside. ■**TIP➔ The snowground was obviously added to keep kids entertained while waiting for the popular Sing-Along and may be moved or closed if the Sing-Along does indeed move into the theater where American Idol used to be held.**

CHAPTER 8

THE
ANIMAL
KINGDOM

When building the original Disneyland in 1955, Walt Disney hoped to have live animals in his park—a dream that proved impossible at the time. But now it's a reality, here at the Animal Kingdom. This 500-acre park is far more than a zoo, encouraging the conservation and preservation of the world's natural habitats. You'll encounter animals from around the globe—and some pretty exciting rides as well!

The centerpiece of the Animal Kingdom is the Tree of Life, a mammoth artwork with more than 325 animals carved into its trunk, including a tiny ant, since the legend of the tree (as told by cast members) is that it was the ant who originally asked Mother Earth for friends. In response, she gave the ant a tiny seed to plant. That seed sprouted into the Tree of Life, which became the hub of the Animal Kingdom.

This story is a great metaphor for the message of the Animal Kingdom—that just a tiny seed can change the world. Lessons here focus on how families can make the world a safer place for animals, especially species that are endangered. Witness the true circle of life by walking along the lush habitat trails or by taking a jeep ride through the African savanna; or, you can simply stop by to see how the animals are cared for at Rafiki's Planet Watch. And, of course, there are plenty of thrills as well, such as Dinosaur and Expedition Everest, the park's most intense rides in the park.

Animal Kingdom Touring Tips

Getting Here

The Animal Kingdom parking lot is relatively small. All on-site hotels run direct shuttles, and many off-site hotels do as well. If possible, arrive by bus. If you're coming by car, try to arrive early, before the main parking lot is filled. Otherwise, you'll be directed to an auxiliary lot.

Getting Around

With more than 500 acres, the Animal Kingdom is the largest of all the Disney parks, but most of the space is earmarked for animal habitats, such as the huge 100-acre savanna featured in Kilimanjaro Safaris. The walkable part of the park is relatively compact—a good thing, since the only real means of getting around is on foot. The layout is basically circular, with the 14-story Tree of Life in the center.

At Disney World it's easy to fall into the trap of thinking "the faster you go, the more you'll see," but at the Animal Kingdom, the opposite is true. Slow your pace a little, because this park is designed for savoring. There are more than 1,700 live animals representing more than 250 species in the Animal Kingdom, and the park is also a botanical marvel, showcasing more than 3,000 species of plants. So, relax and enjoy the incredible natural beauty of the park and the many small-animal habitats tucked along the way. The Maharajah Jungle Trek and Pangani Forest Exploration Trail are major attractions, as well designed as any zoo, and there are other small enclaves of animal habitats around the Tree of Life.

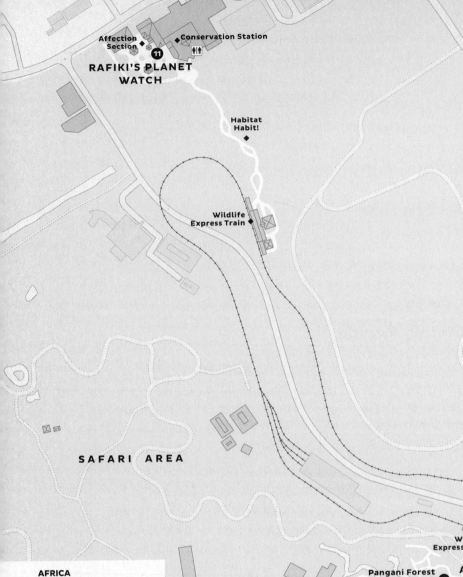

Affection Section

Conservation Station

RAFIKI'S PLANET WATCH ⑪

Habitat Habit!

Wildlife Express Train

SAFARI AREA

Wildlife Express Train

Pangani Forest Exploration Trail ⑫

AFRICA

Mombasa Marketplace

Kilimanjaro Safaris ⑬

Harambe Fruit Market

Kusafiri Coffee Shop & Bakery

Festival of the Lion King ⑭

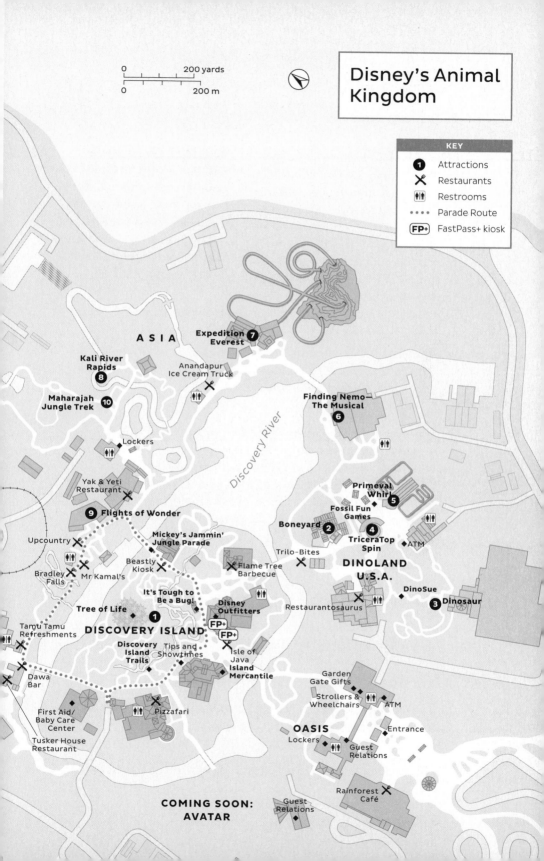

Disney's Animal Kingdom

Scale: 200 yards / 200 m

KEY
- **1** Attractions
- ✕ Restaurants
- 🚻 Restrooms
- ···· Parade Route
- **FP+** FastPass+ kiosk

ASIA
- **Expedition Everest** 7
- **Kali River Rapids** 8
- **Maharajah Jungle Trek** 10
- Anandapur Ice Cream Truck
- Lockers
- **Yak & Yeti Restaurant**
- **9 Flights of Wonder**
- Upcountry
- Bradley Falls
- Mr Kamal's
- Beastly Kiosk
- Mickey's Jammin' Jungle Parade

DINOLAND U.S.A.
- **Finding Nemo—The Musical** 6
- **Primeval Whirl** 5
- **Fossil Fun Games**
- **Boneyard** 2
- **TriceraTop Spin** 4
- Trilo-Bites
- ATM
- **3 Dinosaur**
- DinoSue
- Restaurantosaurus

DISCOVERY ISLAND
- **It's Tough to Be a Bug!**
- **Tree of Life** 1
- Flame Tree Barbecue
- Disney Outfitters
- Tips and Showtimes
- Isle of Java
- Island Mercantile
- Discovery Island Trails
- Tamu Tamu Refreshments
- Dawa Bar
- First Aid/Baby Care Center
- Pizzafari
- Tusker House Restaurant

OASIS
- Garden Gate Gifts
- Strollers & Wheelchairs
- ATM
- Entrance
- Lockers
- Guest Relations
- Rainforest Café

Discovery River

COMING SOON: AVATAR

Guest Relations

Morning Tips

Your First Hour

On Extra Magic Hour mornings only a few attractions will be operative during the first hour, but they will be indicated on a sign as you enter.

Because of their proximity, consider combining a morning visit to the Animal Kingdom and an afternoon visit to Blizzard Beach. The parks are five minutes apart by car and many hotel buses stop at both.

> **HELPFUL HINT**
>
> All families will want a FastPass+ for the über-popular Kilimanjaro Safaris. During the on-season also get a FastPass+ for Festival of the Lion King and, if your kids are old enough, Expedition Everest.

✦ The Oasis is the entry area, much like Main Street in the Magic Kingdom, and it often opens 30 minutes before the stated entry time. Characters are usually on hand to keep the kids entertained.

✦ The animal-habitat areas in the Oasis are charming, but don't visit them in the morning. You'll be stampeded by the people behind you hustling to get to the big rides—not to mention the fact that you need to hustle to the big rides yourself. It's better to visit the Oasis in the afternoon or evening, on your way out of the park. That way it's not a big deal if you stand there for 20 minutes waiting for the three-toed sloth to move.

✦ If you haven't made your FastPass+ selections, find a kiosk and choose them now, or scan your tickets with your smartphone and use the My Disney Experience app.

✦ Head first to Africa and ride Kilimanjaro Safaris. Then cross to Asia and ride Expedition Everest.

Afternoon Tips

✦ The Animal Kingdom closes early (between 5 and 7 pm depending on the season).

✦ Because of the relatively small number of attractions, you can tour the Animal Kingdom in about six hours. The park is often

INSIDER'S SECRET

Animal Kingdom offers mobile FastPass+ kiosks that can be added or eliminated based on crowd flow. You can normally find these extra kiosks located near Expedition Everest, Kali River Rapids, and in front of Disney Outfitters on Discovery Island. If you need help, either making FastPass+ reservations or navigating the system, stop by the service center near the Creature Comforts shop between Discovery Island and Africa. And remember that at Animal Kingdom, FastPass+ reservations are most helpful for Kilimanjaro Safaris, Festival of the Lion King, Dinosaur!, and Expedition Everest.

mobbed between 10 am and 3 pm, but it usually begins to clear out by mid-afternoon. If you can't be there first thing in the morning, consider arriving after lunch.

Evening Tips

Your Last Hour

A new closing show is planned for Animal Kingdom, which will take place along the Discovery River. Don't expect any fireworks or pyrotechnics though—they would scare the animals. The show is more likely to be a sort of floating parade. Find a good spot along the river outside of DinoLand or in the Oasis.

Exit Strategies

Until the new closing show begins, closing time at Animal Kingdom is not as hectic as at the other parks, but if you have split up to ride a last ride or two, make sure you have a clear meeting point.

Food Choices in the Animal Kingdom

As the Animal Kingdom closes the earliest of all the parks—usually between 5 and 7 pm, depending on the season—people rarely eat dinner there.

DISNEY'S ANIMAL KINGDOM DON'T-MISS LIST

- ✦ Dinosaur (if your kids are 7 or older)
- ✦ Expedition Everest (if kids are 8 or older and at least 44 inches tall)
- ✦ Festival of the Lion King
- ✦ Finding Nemo—The Musical
- ✦ Kali River Rapids
- ✦ Kilimanjaro Safaris
- ✦ Maharajah Jungle Trek
- ✦ Pangani Forest Exploration Trail
- ✦ Tree of Life—It's Tough to Be a Bug!

Character Meals

The Tusker House in Africa is the site of the Animal Kingdom's only character meals, Donald's Safari Breakfast and Donald's Safari Lunch. Reserve before you leave home by calling ☎ *407/939–3463* (☎ *407/WDW–DINE*). (After the character meals are over each day, the Tusker House serves a buffet and remains one of the few places in the Animal Kingdom where you can consistently count on finding fresh vegetables.) "The food at the Tusker House character breakfast was outstanding," said one mom of three. "We loved the Jungle Juice and the Mickey waffles. My daughter was so happy to finally meet Daisy Duck, and the characters do a little song that's really cute."

Full-Service Dining

There are three sit-down restaurants: Rainforest Café, which is just as you enter the park, and open for breakfast, lunch, and dinner; the Tusker House Restaurant, which features a buffet for breakfast, lunch, and dinner; and the Yak & Yeti, an Asian-fusion restaurant with table service, a full bar, quick-service options, and a beer garden that is open for lunch and dinner.

Fast Food

Pizzafari, between Discovery Island and Africa, and Flame Tree Barbecue, near the entrance to DinoLand, are also good lunch choices. All the restaurants have outdoor patios where you can take your food, find a pretty view, and really relax. These lush, shady eating areas in the Animal Kingdom help blur the line between fast food and sit-down dining.

The Dawa Bar, adjacent to the Tusker House patio, offers alcoholic beverages and entertainment in the afternoon.

Other Useful Information for Visiting Animal Kingdom

Unique Entertainment

The Animal Kingdom provides interactive entertainment throughout the park. Cast members are stationed with animals, and kids are welcome to ask questions and have up-close encounters with the bugs, birds, reptiles, and small mammals. At the Dawa Bar in the Africa section you'll find storytellers, music, African drumming, and acrobats.

Keep an eye out for DeVine, a moving human topiary, who can often be found literally hanging around the park. She blends in so well with the vegetation that she's been known to startle some guests.

Character Meet and Greets

The Animal Kingdom can be a good spot to meet the characters, with new indoor (and thus air-conditioned) meet-and-greet pavilions having opened since Camp Minnie–Mickey shut down and the Festival of the Lion King relocated. Check your map or the tip board for the times and places where the characters are set to appear.

Wilderness Explorers

Most of Disney's new interactive games, scattered throughout the four major theme parks, are pretty high-tech. But Wilderness Explorers, based on the movie *Up!,* is old-fashioned and hands-on. In fact, it's similar to the Boy and Girl Scouts, with kids earning "badges" in the form of stickers from "troop leaders"

WHERE TO MEET THE CHARACTERS

Here is where many of the characters can be found in the Animal Kingdom. Check the My Disney Experience app or your theme-park map for a complete listing.

✦ **Dug and Russell:** Dug & Russell's Wilderness Explorers Club House outside It's A Bug's Life

✦ **Pocahontas:** Discovery Island Trail

✦ **Baloo and King Louie:** Upcountry Landing

✦ **Rafiki:** Rafiki's Planet Watch

✦ **Donald, Pluto, and Goofy:** DinoLand

✦ **Mickey Mouse and Minnie Mouse:** Adventurer's Outpost (FastPass+ available)

stationed around the park. Kids will learn African currency, animal calls, and how to search for animals in the wild. To earn one of the more than 30 badges, a child must demonstrate knowledge of certain facts about the animal or its habitat. The tasks are designed to be age-appropriate for many levels and to encourage kids to take a brief break from the rides to focus on how cool the animals really are. This program is a welcome addition to the park!

Wilderness Explorers is not meant to be tackled in a single day: Any child who aims to gather all 30 badges will have to understand that fulfilling all the requirements for the entire program is something that's meant to happen over time and will require multiple visits to Animal Kingdom.

Animal Kingdom Attractions

The attractions may be few, but they're powerful. Most are designed for the whole family to enjoy together.

Asia

☀ Expedition Everest

Expedition Everest is one of the most exciting attractions in all of Disney World. The premise is that your mountain train is chugging up the snowy mountainside when it suddenly encounters a break in the track. Uh-oh. Wonder why? The trip back down not only involves wild plunges and even wilder speeds, but you also meet up with the yeti that lives in the mountain, and he's not in a good mood. Your train races both forward and backward as you attempt to escape his rage.

Expedition Everest draws major crowds. Although the ride boards quickly and the lines move fast, come in the morning or use FastPass+. The ride is a huge hit with our readers, with almost 80% of them listing it as their favorite attraction in the Animal Kingdom. "I expected my 11-year-old to like it," wrote one mom from Arizona, "but to my surprise my 6-year-old loved it just as much. Even my father-in-law insisted on riding twice!" Want the most intense ride? Be sure to sit at the front. Scare Factor→ **Although Expedition Everest doesn't have the corkscrews and flips of the Rock 'n' Roller Coaster, the yeti is indeed slightly more frightening than Steven Tyler. Also, the train moves at almost twice the speed of Space Mountain, which means the ride will probably be too intense for kids under eight. The height requirement is 44 inches.**

☀ Flights of Wonder

The Caravan Stage is home to this lovely display of birds in free flight. The show's premise is a bit silly, but you can count on seeing falcons, vultures, hawks, and toucans demonstrating their unusual talents. Several members of the audience, including kids, are invited onstage to interact with the birds. Showtimes are noted on your entertainment schedule; be there 10 minutes early to ensure a good seat, 20 minutes during the on-season. Flights of Wonder is a good choice for the most crowded times of the afternoon. Scare Factor→ **It's not scary.**

Quick Guide to Animal

Attraction	Location
The Boneyard	DinoLand
Dinosaur	DinoLand
Expedition Everest	Asia
Festival of the Lion King	Africa
Finding Nemo—The Musical	DinoLand
Flights of Wonder	Asia
It's Tough to Be a Bug!	Discovery Island
Kali River Rapids	Asia
Kilimanjaro Safaris	Africa
Maharajah Jungle Trek	Asia
Pangani Forest Exploration Trail	Africa
Primeval Whirl	DinoLand
Rafiki's Planet Watch	Africa
TriceraTop Spin	DinoLand

Scare Factor
0 = Unlikely to scare any child of any age.
! = Has dark or loud elements; might rattle some toddlers.
!! = A couple of gotcha! moments; should be fine for school-age kids.
!!! = You need to be pretty big and pretty brave to handle this ride.

Kingdom Attractions

Height Requirement	Speed of Line	Duration of Ride/ Show	Scare Factor	Age Range
None	n/a	n/a	0	All
40 inches	Moderate	10 min.	!!!	7 and up
44 inches	Moderate	10 min.	!!!	8 and up
None	Moderate	25 min.	0	All
None	Moderate	30 min.	0	All
None	Fast	25 min.	0	All
None	Slow	10 min.	!	All
38 inches	Moderate	7 min.	!	4 and up
None	Moderate	20 min.	!	6 and up
None	Fast	n/a	0	All
None	Moderate	n/a	0	All
48 inches	Slow	7 min.	!!	5 and up
None	Fast	20 min.	0	All
None	Slow	4 min.	!	All

FASTPASS+ ATTRACTIONS

FastPass+ rides and attractions at Animal Kingdom are not tiered, so you can choose three from this list:

- Dinosaur
- Expedition Everest
- Festival of the Lion King
- Finding Nemo—The Musical
- Kali River Rapids
- Kilimanjaro Safaris
- Meet Favorite Disney Pals at Adventurers Outpost
- Mickey's Jammin' Jungle Parade
- Mickey's Jingle Jungle Parade (seasonal)
- Primeval Whirl

☀ Kali River Rapids

For this water ride you board an eight-passenger raft for a descent down a meandering river through rapids, geysers, and waterfalls. Expect to get very wet, possibly soaked, depending on where you're sitting in the raft. (As the rafts are circular and constantly turning throughout the ride, it's impossible to predict which seats will catch the most spray.) Stow cameras and other water-sensitive valuables in lockers before you board, and bring your trusty poncho.

It's also good to keep your feet up on the center bar. A wet backside is an inconvenience, but wet shoes and socks can lead to blisters and ruin your whole day. Also consider bringing a change of clothes. One mom said her soaking-wet child burst into tears and had to be taken back to the hotel to change.

Are some of your kids too young or too short to ride? Let them man Kali's water cannons on the bridge as you approach the ride; there they can take aim against their older siblings as they pass in the rafts below. Revenge is sweet! And, to be honest, soaking strangers can be fun, too. Scare Factor→ **The height requirement is only 38 inches, reflecting the fact that Kali River Rapids is a very mild ride, with only one sizable descent along the way. It's** fine for anyone who isn't afraid of getting wet.

☀ Maharajah Jungle Trek

Another lovely walking path, this one goes through habitats of Asia. The Bengal tigers are the undisputed stars of the show, but you'll also encounter Komodo dragons, gibbons, and, most intriguing of all, giant fruit bats. Take time along the path to appreciate the glorious landscaping and the beauty of the architecture. Scare Factor→ It's not scary.

> **HIDDEN MICKEY**
>
> The Maharajah Jungle Trek is Hidden Mickey city. In fact, there are several in the drawings on the ruins just as you enter the tiger habitat. Still can't see them? Look at the earrings the royal couple is wearing.

DinoLand USA

DinoLand is a story unto itself. The official history of this section is that a giant collection of dinosaur bones was found in central Florida, and the scientifically minded Dino Institute built its headquarters next to the dig site. The Institute attracted so many interns that separate quarters had to be built—in what is now Restaurantosaurus—and this led to the Institute's becoming a tourist attraction. A Texan couple named Chester and Hester, never ones to let a good opportunity pass them by, bought up all the land surrounding the Institute to build a roadside attraction to entertain all those tourists. And thus the part-serious, part-wacky "DinoLand" was born.

☀ The Boneyard

A great attraction for kids seven and under, the Boneyard is a playground designed to simulate an archaeological dig. Kids can dig for "fossils," excavate "bones," and play on bridges and slides. The playground is visually witty—where else can you find slides made from what look like prehistoric animal skeletons?—and has fun surprises, such as a footprint that roars when you jump on it.

Visit the Boneyard after you've toured the biggies and the kids are ready to romp for a while. The play area can get very hot on a Florida afternoon, however, so remember the sunscreen and water bottles. If it's a really roasting day, head for the woolly mammoth dig-site area, which is covered and has large fans to cut down on the heat. "My 3-year-old loved the dig site," reported one father. "We hung out there for about an hour while my wife took the older kids on Dinosaur." **Scare Factor→ It's not scary.**

☀ Dinosaur

You're strapped into "high-speed" motion vehicles and sent back in time to the Cretaceous period to save the gentle, plant-eating iguanodon from extinction.

It's a noble mission, but it ain't easy. Along the way, Disney throws everything it has at you: asteroids, meteors, incoming pterodactyls, and ticked-off people-eating dino-

> ### HELPFUL HINT
>
> The good news is that kids can lose themselves in the Boneyard and happily play for an hour. The bad news is that parents can lose their kids as well. The Boneyard is sprawling, so keep your eyes on young children at all times, especially when they're playing on the slides. When they enter at the top, it's often hard to tell what chute they're in or where they'll emerge.

saurs. The dinosaurs are extremely lifelike, and in some cases extremely close. The jeeps bounce around like mad, so Dinosaur can be a bit rough—but it's also a powerfully fun ride. **Scare Factor→ Dinosaur combines atmospheric scariness with a wild-moving vehicle. The height requirement is 40 inches, which means that plenty of preschoolers qualify to board; nonetheless, based on the realism of the dinosaurs, we say wait until kids are at least seven to ride, and even then consider whether they're brave enough to handle very big, very loud dinosaurs jumping out at them while the car takes steep drops. "As much as our young son (age 7) loves dinosaurs, this ride proved to be too much for him," wrote a mom of two. "We are planning another trip to Disney this year, and he still reminds us that he is not going on the dinosaur ride again."**

☀ Finding Nemo–The Musical (In Theater in the Wild)

Based on the animated film *Finding Nemo*, this kid-pleasing musical combines performances by puppets, dancers, and acrobats, all choreographed to envelop you in Nemo's big blue world. The puppets, created by the same team who brought *The Lion King* to Broadway, are especially amazing, and the special effects are dazzling.

INSIDER'S SECRET

Really into animals? Willing to pay for a one-of-a-kind adventure? Consider the three-hour, family-friendly, behind-the-scenes **Wild Africa Trek,** which is suitable for ages eight and up. One highlight is crossing a rope bridge that sways 50 feet above a creek full of crocodiles. You're safely tethered with a bungee cord, of course, and the bridge is created only to seem precarious, but it's still exciting. You also hike through the bush, get up close to hippos, eat a stupendously good lunch from a deck in the savanna, and have access to guides who give far more info than you'd get on Kilimanjaro Safaris. In fact, the Trek is the perfect basis for a school project. Despite the $139–$249 per-person price, tours fill up fast. Make reservations at ☎ 407/939–8687 (☎ 407/WDW–TOUR) well in advance.

This show is a good example of why closer isn't always better. If you sit too close to the stage, you'll miss some of the action, which takes place on the catwalk behind the section closest to the stage. The best viewing is the center section, about two-thirds of the way back.

The story will be familiar to anyone who's seen the movie—Nemo and his father, Marlin, go on separate journeys that ultimately teach them how to understand each other. The catchy pop music and multigenerational humor are designed to appeal to all age groups, and the ending may cause you to shed a tear. Arrive at the theater 20 minutes ahead of showtime, 30–45 during the on-season, to guarantee good seats. Scare Factor➔ **It's not scary.**

☀ Primeval Whirl

The second ride in Chester and Hester's Dino-Rama is Primeval Whirl, a crazy mouse-style coaster with spinning cars, hairpin turns, and numerous dips. Primeval Whirl is a slow-boarding, low-capacity ride and can draw lines. Scare Factor➔ **A bit surprisingly, Primeval Whirl has a 48-inch height requirement. The ride is faster than it looks and has many spins. Most kids over five (assuming they make the height requirement) love it, but if you** have any doubts, watch it make a cycle or two before joining the queue. This is not a good choice for anyone prone to motion sickness.

☀ TriceraTop Spin

The kid-friendly TriceraTop Spin is a circular ride similar to Dumbo, except that you fly in dinosaurs, naturally. The beasts tilt back and forth as you climb or descend. **Scare Factor→ If they loved Dumbo, they'll love TriceraTop Spin.**

Discovery Island

☀ It's Tough to Be a Bug!

This state-of-the-art 3-D film is shown inside the Tree of Life, which is an amazing edifice with 325 animals carved into its trunk—perfect for pictures. The show combines visual, sensory, and tactile effects, and the cast of characters, including an accurately named Stinkbug, is so funny that everyone leaves laughing. The best effect of all is at the very end of the show.

Be aware that at one point large spider puppets dangle over your head. Later, the theater goes dark, you hear swarming wasps, and the back of your seat might give you a small electrical zap. (Not into pain? Simply lean forward in your seat.) **Scare Factor→ The show is a huge hit with most kids, who seem to find Flik and friends to be great fun, but the scary scenes mean that there's usually at least one child crying in the audience. If your kids are scared of the dark or bugs, skip the show. "My 7-year-old girl is normally a brave thing," wrote a mom from England. "She went on Tower of Terror, Space Mountain, Expedition Everest, etc., with no problem at all. But It's Tough to Be a Bug! scared her so badly she was ready to leave."**

Africa

☀ Festival of the Lion King

One of the best attractions in the Animal Kingdom has recently moved to a new theater in the Africa section of the park. Festival of the Lion King features what you might expect—singers, dancers, the characters—as well as acrobatic "monkeys," a "hyena" twirling a fire baton, and "birds" that dramatically take flight. The costuming is incredible, the music is wonderful, and the finale is guaranteed to give you goose bumps.

The performers interact directly with the audience, and at one point small children from the crowd are invited to join in a simple circular parade. Children sitting near the front are more apt to be tapped.

Showtimes are printed on your entertainment schedule; be there at least 30 minutes early if you'd like to sit near the front. Because of its popularity, Festival of the Lion King is one of the few theater-style attractions that justify using a FastPass+. **Scare Factor→ It's not scary.**

☀ Kilimanjaro Safaris

This is the Animal Kingdom's premier attraction, a 2-mile ride through the open bush that simulates an African photo safari. The animals have a great deal of open space around them and appear to be running free—although cleverly incorporated water and plant barriers ensure that the cheetahs don't meet up with the ostriches and graphically illustrate the circle of life right in front of the kids.

Your guide helps you tell the impalas from the gazelles and at times your vehicle (called a lorry) comes startlingly close to the wildlife.

Safari drivers say that the animals are often active in the morning but that you have a better chance of seeing cheetahs, rhinos, and warthogs later in the day. And because of the attraction's mammoth and unpredictable animal cast, Kilimanjaro is, in essence, a different adventure every time. You could go on one safari in the morning and return in the afternoon for a whole new show. As part of the Animal Kingdom expansion, a nighttime version of Kilimanjaro Safaris is expected to premier soon. **Scare Fac-**

tor➔ **It's not terribly scary, but the animal encounters could frighten some small kids.**

☀ Pangani Forest Exploration Trail

Near the exit of Kilimanjaro Safaris is this self-guided walking trail. The highlight is seeing the jungle home of Gino, the silverback gorilla, and his harem. (The dominant male in a gorilla troop is called the silverback because he is ordinarily older than the other males and often has gray hairs mixed in with the black.) Along the trail you also pass everything from mole rats to hippos to birds in an enclosed aviary, but children seem especially to enjoy the warthogs and meerkats in the savanna exhibit. Trail Guides are on hand to answer questions and help point out the animals. Scare Factor➔ **It's not scary.**

☀ Rafiki's Planet Watch

This attraction will answer many of the questions you may have about how Disney cares for animals in the park.

You board a nifty train called the Wildlife Express for a five-minute ride to Rafiki's Planet Watch. Along the way, you'll see where the animals sleep at night—a cool peek behind the scenes that older kids appreciate. You disembark at Rafiki's Planet Watch, a station in the farthest-flung section of the park. There you'll find exhibits on the subjects of conservation and animal endangerment. Kids especially enjoy touring the veterinary labs, where newborns and sick animals get a lot of attention, and the Affection Station, where they can pat and touch the friendly goats, llamas, and sheep.

Rafiki's Planet Watch is difficult to reach with small children, since getting from the train to the station is quite a hike. For kids under five, make sure to bring your stroller. The good news is that once you get there, you can park it and see everything relatively easily—including meet-and-greet opportunities with Rafiki and sometimes even the rarely seen Jiminy Cricket. Scare Factor➔ **It's not scary.**

CHAPTER 9

THE
DISNEY WORLD

WATER
PARKS

A chance to cool off is always welcome in the hot summer sun, and Disney has two distinct water parks—Typhoon Lagoon and Blizzard Beach—to help you do just that. Just like the four major parks, these two minor parks have their own themes, unique attractions, and plenty of surprises.

For those families looking for more than just a splash at the hotel pool, both Typhoon Lagoon and Blizzard Beach offer a fun, intense, and, yes, exhausting alternative. Each park has a section for preschoolers and elementary-school-age children, while offering plenty of wild rides for older siblings. Blizzard Beach is home to one of the world's tallest free-fall waterslides, while Typhoon Lagoon will literally let you swim with the sharks.

But don't think you won't get a chance to unwind. Both parks feature broad beaches and a lazy river, which lets you float around the park in lieu of walking—a nice switch after a few days in the theme parks! Older kids can take on the monster slides while parents relax in a lounge chair with a book, and younger kids will find plenty of sand toys to help make their own version of Cinderella Castle.

Water Park Touring Tips

Getting to the Water Parks

On-site visitors can take the bus to both Typhoon Lagoon and Blizzard Beach, but expect a long commute. Getting to Typhoon Lagoon may involve sitting through the stops at Downtown Disney, while getting to Blizzard Beach often involves a stop at the Animal Kingdom. In other words, bus travel can take a while. If you have a car, drive to the water parks.

For off-site visitors, a car is definitely the best option. If you don't have one, take a cab.

Try to arrive about 20 minutes ahead of the stated opening times for the parks, particularly if you're visiting in summer or during a major holiday. During midday and afternoon hours in peak seasons the parking lots often fill to capacity.

What You'll Need

- **Towels.** You can rent towels, but they're small, so it makes more sense to bring your own.

- **Swimwear.** Girls should wear one-piece swimsuits. More than one bathing suit top has been lost on the waterslides.

- **Footwear.** Bring rubber beach shoes with nonskid bottoms if you have them. They'll protect the soles of your feet from the hot sidewalks. Flip-flops aren't the best choice for kids because they are not allowed on the waterslides.

- **Life Vests.** You can borrow life vests for free at the locker-rental stand, although you have to leave your driver's license or a credit card as a deposit.

- **Snorkels, Fins, and Floats.** Snorkeling equipment can be picked up for no charge at Hammerhead Fred's near the Shark Reef at Typhoon Lagoon. There's no point in bringing your own fins and floats; only official Disney equipment is allowed in the pools.

Lockers

There are plenty of lockers, and the keys come on rubber bands that slip over your wrist or ankle, so you can keep them with you while you're in the water. If you arrive in the morning when a swarm of guests enters at once, getting a locker can be quite a hassle, with the rental lines sometimes 20 minutes long and the area around the lockers packed. Many families skip locker rentals and keep vitals such as room keys, charge cards, and a bit of cash in one of those flat plastic holders you wear around your neck. (They sell them in the water-park gift shops for about $7.)

> **INSIDER'S SECRET**
>
> During the most crowded days of the on-season, Extra Magic Hours sometimes allow on-site guests a little more time in the water parks. "Our extra magic evening at Typhoon Lagoon was the highlight of our entire week at Disney World," wrote one family from England. "It was a warm starry night and perfect for swimming in the big wave pool."

MagicBands are waterproof, so that's not an issue. By forgoing locker rentals, you can grab the best lounge chair locations and dash straight to the rides while everyone else is still trying to get a locker.

Other Things to Consider

✦ **Younger vs. Older Kids.** The water parks draw a rowdy preteen and teenage crowd, which means young kids and unsteady swimmers may get dunked and splashed more than they like. If your children are very young, stick to Ketchakiddee Creek in Typhoon Lagoon and Tike's Peak at Blizzard Beach. These kiddie sections are off-limits to older kids.

✦ **Weather.** Summer afternoons in Florida often mean thunderstorms, and even a rumble of distant thunder can lead to water-park closings. If you're visiting in summer and want to make sure you have time to try everything, visit the water parks first thing in the morning.

✦ **The Scare Factor.** If you have younger kids, consider the scare factor, because the attractions at both Typhoon Lagoon and

Blizzard Beach are more physically intense than most of the rides in the four theme parks. Most kids adjust quickly, especially if they're reasonably strong swimmers, but you might want to start the day on mild slides and gradually work your way up to the zippier rides.

✦ **Lost Kids.** The Lost Kids Stations at both parks are so far away from the main water areas that it's unlikely your children would find their way there. Instruct them, should they look up and find themselves separated from you, to approach the nearest person wearing a Disney name tag. A cast member will escort the kids to the Lost Kids Station, and you can meet them there. Because both of the parks are full of meandering paths with many sets of steps and slides, it's easy to get separated from your party. Set standard meeting places and times for older kids.

✦ **Eating.** There are fast-food restaurants at both water parks as well as places to picnic.

✦ **On-Season Visits.** If you're visiting in summer, consider dropping by both water parks. They offer very different experiences. Typhoon Lagoon has the better beaches and pools. Blizzard Beach is the pow! park, focusing on slides.

✦ **Off-Season Visits.** Typhoon Lagoon and Blizzard Beach are often closed for refurbishing in January and February, although it's rare for both to be closed at the same time unless the weather is truly cold or inclement. If you're planning a winter trip, visit ⊕ *www.disneyworld.com* to see which will be open during the time you're in town.

✦ **After the Parks.** Because you're climbing uphill all day, half the time dragging a tube or mat behind you, the water parks are exhausting. If you spend the day at one, plan to spend the evening at a film or show, or take the night off.

Typhoon Lagoon

Disney calls its 56-acre Typhoon Lagoon "the world's ultimate water park," and the hyperbole is justified. Where else can you float through caves, take surfing lessons, picnic with parrots, and swim (sort of) with sharks? Typhoon Lagoon is a replica of the perfect tropical isle—older kids can hit the thrill slides, younger kids can splash in the bays and dig in the sand, and parents can relax (at least in shifts) under a palm tree with a piña colada in one hand and a best seller in the other.

For anyone with a Water Park Fun & More option, entrance to Typhoon Lagoon is included. Otherwise, admission is $58 for adults and $50 for children ages three to nine, before sales tax.

Typhoon Lagoon Attractions

☀ Castaway Creek

Castaway Creek is a meandering 2,000-foot river full of inner tubes. You simply wade out, find an empty tube, and climb aboard. It takes about 30 minutes to circle the rain forest, with a bit of excitement at one point when riders drift under the waterfall. There are numerous exits along the creek, so anyone who doesn't want to get splashed can hop out before the falls. In fact, Castaway Creek serves as a means of transportation around the park; savvy guests who don't want to burn their feet on hot pavement or waste energy walking around often hop in and float their way from attraction to attraction. Scare Factor→ **Castaway Creek is a fun, relaxing ride appropriate for any age. The water is 3 feet deep throughout the ride, however, so keep a good grip on young kids or those who can't swim.**

☀ Crush 'n' Gusher

This thrill ride combines flumes, spillways, and steep drops, but the real kick is that you're hit so hard with pulsing streams of water that at one point in the ride your two-person raft is actually propelled back uphill. The concept is that you're lost in an abandoned fruit-processing facility. There are three paths out— the Banana Blaster, Coconut Crusher, and Pineapple Plunger— each about 420 feet long with plenty of twists and turns along the way. Scare Factor→ **The Crush 'n' Gusher is not for the faint of**

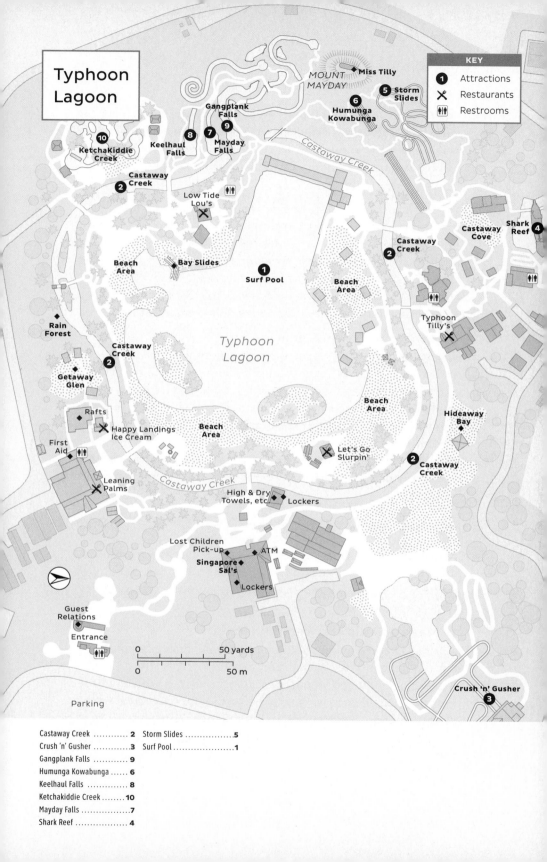

Typhoon Lagoon

KEY

- ① Attractions
- ✕ Restaurants
- 🚻 Restrooms

MOUNT MAYDAY

◆ Miss Tilly

⑤ Storm Slides

Gangplank Falls

⑥ Humunga Kowabunga

⑧ Keelhaul Falls

⑦ ⑨ Mayday Falls

⑩ KetchaKiddie Creek

Castaway Creek

② Castaway Creek

Low Tide Lou's ✕ 🚻

Castaway Creek

Castaway Cove

Shark Reef ④

🚻

Beach Area

Bay Slides

① Surf Pool

Beach Area

🚻

Typhoon Tilly's ✕

Rain Forest ◆

② Castaway Creek

Getaway Glen ◆

Rafts ◆

Happy Landings ✕ Ice Cream

Typhoon Lagoon

Beach Area

Beach Area

Hideaway Bay

First Aid 🚻

Leaning Palms ✕

Castaway Creek

Beach Area

Let's Go Slurpin' ✕

② Castaway Creek

High & Dry Towels, etc. ◆

Lockers

Lost Children Pick-up ◆

Singapore Sal's ◆

ATM

Lockers ◆

Guest Relations ◆

Entrance 🚻

0 ——— 50 yards

0 ——— 50 m

Crush 'n' Gusher ③

Parking

heart or anyone who is unnerved by water splashing directly in their face. The height requirement is 48 inches; even if younger children are tall enough for it, you should probably warm them up on Keelhaul Falls before tackling Crush 'n' Gusher.

☀ Gangplank Falls

You weather these white-water rapids in four-passenger rafts. Slower and calmer (but much bumpier) than Mayday or Keelhaul, Gangplank is a good choice for families with kids who are nervous about tackling a white-water ride on their own. Gangplank Falls does load slowly, however, and the ride is short, so hit it early in the morning before the line becomes prohibitive. **Scare Factor→ If the kids are nervous about the slides, this is a good starter.**

☀ Humunga Kowabunga

With three enclosed waterslides that drop you a stunning five stories in a matter of seconds, Humunga Kowabunga is definitely a thrill. Riders reach speeds of up to 30 mph! **Scare Factor→ Humunga is an intense ride that fully deserves its height requirement of 48 inches. Part of the scare factor is certainly the drop, but falling in complete darkness makes the experience even more intense. Nonetheless, once guests ride it and get over that initial trepidation, they usually climb right back up to do it again.**

☀ Ketchakiddee Creek

This water playground designed for toddlers and preschoolers has geysers and waterspouts in the shapes of crocodiles and whales as well as pint-size slides, a grotto with a waterfall, and a small white-water raft ride. No kids over 48 inches are allowed inside, which keeps the area safe for the younger ones. **Scare Factor→ It's not scary.**

☀ Mayday Falls and Keelhaul Falls

A Disney employee helps you climb into your inner tube and begin your winding journey down a white-water stream. The journey is fast, giggle inducing, and has enough turns that you often feel like you're about to lose your tube. **Scare Factor→ Keelhaul Falls is slightly milder than Mayday, so let younger children try it first. The park provides some smaller inner tubes with built-in bottoms. Kids as young as four have reported loving this ride.**

☀ Shark Reef

In this unusual attraction, snorkelers swim in a saltwater pool "among" exotic marine life, including small leopard and hammerhead sharks. The sharks are behind Plexiglas and aren't too numerous, so anyone expecting the *Jaws* experience will be disappointed.

Swimmers need to be able to cross a 60-foot pool confidently twice, a task that might preclude the participation of some young kids who find this too physically demanding even with a flotation vest. If older kids want to suit up, younger siblings can watch from an underwater viewing area that gives you a good view of the marine life and the snorkelers.

Disney provides the snorkeling equipment and a brief orientation on how to use it. Only official Disney equipment is allowed in the pool, so don't bother packing your own masks. **Scare Factor→ Shark Reef isn't scary per se, but young kids sometimes struggle with the equipment and panic when they either flood their masks or suck water through their snorkel.**

> **HELPFUL HINT**
>
> Trying to decide which Disney water park to visit? We agree with this father from Michigan: "Our extended family visited both water parks and concluded that Typhoon Lagoon was the favorite of the adults and the younger children because it's pretty, with nice beaches and shallow places for little ones to swim. Family members age 10 to 25 preferred Blizzard Beach because of the slides."

☀ Storm Slides

The Storm Slides are curvier and thus a little tamer than a straight plunge down the mountain. Each of the three slides offers a slightly different route, although none is necessarily wilder than the others. **Scare Factor→ Kids of any age can ride the Storm Slides, but they need to be fairly confident in the water. Although the pool you land in at the bottom isn't deep, you do hit the water with enough force to temporarily disorient a shaky swimmer. Most kids 7 to 11 love these zesty little slides, and even some younger kids can handle them.**

☀ Surf Pool

In this huge and incredible 2½-acre lagoon, guests can ride machine-made waves up to 6 feet high. The waves come at 90-second intervals and are perfectly sized for tubing and bodysurfing. A foghorn blast alerts you to when a big one is on its way; if you're bobbing around with young kids, stay in the shallow areas, where the swells won't be too overwhelming and you can avoid the surfers.

Toddlers and preschoolers can safely splash around in two small, roped-off coves called Blustery Bay and Whitecap Cove. **Scare Factor→ The Surf Pool's waves come with a lot of force, so make sure that you keep an eye on unsteady swimmers.**

Blizzard Beach

Blizzard Beach may have the cleverest theme of any Disney park. The tropical ambience of Typhoon Lagoon seems natural for a water park, but who could have predicted a melting ski lodge?

Blizzard Beach is built on the tongue-in-cheek premise that a freak snowstorm hit Orlando and a group of enterprising businesspeople built Florida's first ski resort. The sun returned in due time, and for a while it looked like all was lost—until someone spied an alligator slipping and sliding down one of the slushy slopes. Thus, Blizzard Beach was born. The snow may be gone, but the jumps, sled runs, and slalom courses remain, resulting in a high-camp, high-thrill ski lodge in the palms. The motif extends into every element of the park: There are Plexiglas snowmen, a chalet-style restaurant, even ski marks running off the side of the mountain. And the original skiing alligator, Ice Gator, is the park mascot.

At the center of Blizzard Beach is "snowcapped" Mt. Gushmore. You can get to the top via ski lift (long line, short ride) or a series of stairs (big climb, short breath), but how you get down is up to you.

Everybody Goes Surfing

At Typhoon Lagoon, guests can catch a wave at Craig Carroll's Cocoa Beach Surfing School. Because the park's 2.75-million-gallon wave pool is such a controlled environment, with a steady supply of 6-foot waves and top-notch instructors, almost everyone manages to catch a wave by the end of the class.

The 2½-hour program, for guests age eight and older, is available by reservation for $165 on select mornings prior to regular park hours. Since classes are capped at 12 students, make sure to call well in advance for reservations. The classes usually begin at 6:30 am (before buses start running), so you'll either have to drive to Typhoon Lagoon or arrange for a cab. Entrance to Typhoon Lagoon is not included in the price. Call ☎ 407/939-7529 (☎ 407/WDW-PLAY) for more information.

The bold descend via two wild water rides called Summit Plummet and Slush Gusher, but there are medium-intensity flumes, tube rides, and white-water rafts to take you down as well.

The water parks have a tight cap on how many people they can admit and tend to get quite crowded, at least during peak season in the summer. Showing up early is the only way you can ensure you'll get in at all and have some chance to sample all the rides. Like Typhoon Lagoon, Blizzard Beach is included in Water Park Fun & More; otherwise, admission is $58 for adults and $50 for children ages three to nine, not including sales tax.

Blizzard Beach Attractions

☀ Chair Lift

The Chair Lift offers direct transportation to the top of Mt. Gushmore, where Summit Plummet, Slush Gusher, and Teamboat Springs await. It's also a fun little diversion in itself, but lines can grow unbelievably long in the afternoon. Hiking up the steps is a lot faster. For a faster ascent, consider the singles line—you won't all ride together, but you can reach the top much faster.

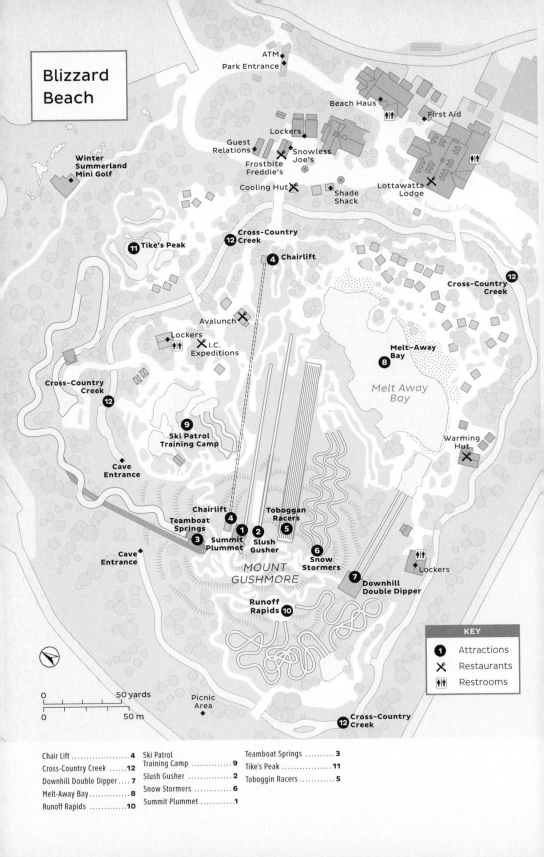

Blizzard Beach

ATM
Park Entrance

Beach Haus
First Aid

Lockers

Guest Relations
Snowless Joe's

Frostbite Freddie's

Cooling Hut
Shade Shack
Lottawatta Lodge

Winter Summerland Mini Golf

11 Tike's Peak

12 Cross-Country Creek

4 Chairlift

12 Cross-Country Creek

Avalunch

Lockers
I.C. Expeditions

Melt-Away Bay **8**

Melt Away Bay

12 Cross-Country Creek

9 Ski Patrol Training Camp

Warming Hut

Cave Entrance

Chairlift **4**
Teamboat Springs

Toboggan Racers **5**

3 Summit Plummet **1**

2 Slush Gusher

Snow Stormers **6**

Cave Entrance

MOUNT GUSHMORE

Lockers

Downhill Double Dipper **7**

Runoff Rapids **10**

Picnic Area

12 Cross-Country Creek

0   50 yards
0   50 m

KEY

1 Attractions

✕ Restaurants

🚻 Restrooms

Scare Factor→ **Although there's nothing scary about the ride, it's tough to hold on to a squirming toddler who's been slathered with sunscreen, so there's a height requirement of 32 inches.**

☀ Cross-Country Creek

Blizzard Beach has its own version of a lazy river. There are plenty of inner tubes, so all you have to do is wade in, climb on, and float along on a relaxing loop of the park. Oh, and watch out for the occasional blasts of "icy" water from the caves and cascades. Scare Factor→ **It's not scary.**

☀ Downhill Double Dipper

On this individual tube ride, you race the rider in the other chute, going through water curtains and free falls during your descent. At one point in the ride you're completely airborne. The Double Dipper is fun and addictive, albeit a bit more jarring than some of the other rides at Blizzard Beach. Test the kids on nearby Runoff Rapids before you tackle it. Scare Factor→ **Downhill Double Dipper is a bit rougher than it looks, and has a 48-inch height requirement.**

☀ Melt-Away Bay

Unlike the huge surfing pool at Typhoon Lagoon, this swimming area is relatively small and offers mild swells instead of big waves. Fed by "melting snow" waterfalls, the pool is perfect for young kids and unsteady swimmers. There are plenty of chairs and shady huts nearby for relaxing, but these tend to be claimed early in the day. Scare Factor→ **It's not scary.**

☀ Runoff Rapids

You take a separate set of stairs up the back of Mt. Gushmore to reach these three inner-tube rides. To start, you get to choose between tubes that seat either one or two people. Just remember, the heavier the raft, the faster the descent, so don't assume that two family members in one raft will tone down the experience. The rapids are great fun, and each of the slides provides a slightly different thrill so you can try it over and over. The only downside is that each time you have to troop up the 7 zillion stairs (157, to be exact); visit early in the morning before your stamina fails. Scare Factor→ **Most kids love this ride, but if little** ones are nervous, being able to ride together lessens the intensity.

☀ Ski Patrol Training Camp

This special play area is designed for kids 5 to 11 who are too old for Tike's Peak but not quite ready for the big-deal rides. They can walk across icebergs, swing from T-bars, test their mountaineering skills, and ride medium-intensity slides. **Scare Factor→ It's not scary.**

☀ Slush Gusher

This is another monster slide but with a couple of bumps along the way to slow you down. Akin in intensity to Humunga Kowabunga at Typhoon Lagoon, Slush Gusher is so much fun that many kids insist on doing it more than once, despite the climb to the top and the long line. **Scare Factor→ Kids must be 48 inches tall to ride Slush Gusher. Try it as a plunge test before you queue up for Summit Plummet.**

☀ Snow Stormers

This is a mock slalom run that you descend on your belly as you clutch a foam-rubber "sled." The three slides are full of twists and turns that splash water into your face, and if you'd like, you can race the sledders on the other two slides to the bottom. It's so much fun that hardly anyone does it just once. **Scare Factor→ Although not a wild ride, it can be a bit hard to see where you're going. Try Toboggan Racers first.**

☀ Summit Plummet

The icon of the park, Summit Plummet is 120 feet tall, making it considerably longer than Humunga Kowabunga at Typhoon Lagoon. From the outside, it looks like Summit Plummet riders are shooting out of the side of the mountain into midair. In reality, the ride includes a 60-degree, 60-mph drop that's almost twice as fast as Space Mountain—and here you're not even riding in a car. **Scare Factor→ The height requirement for Summit Plummet**

INSIDER'S SECRET

If you're riding either Summit Plummet or Slush Gusher, don't forget to cross your legs as you descend. Your bathing suit will still ride up, but at least you'll have some protection against the Mother of All Wedgies. Women and girls should wear one-piece swimsuits unless they want their tops up by their ears as they land.

is 48 inches. Although it's a very short experience—less than four seconds from top to bottom—the drop feels like a free fall and may be the most intense sensation in all of Disney World. In short, this flume is the real deal, and best saved for kids eight and up.

☀ Teamboat Springs

In one of the best rides in the park, the whole family can join forces to tackle the white water as a group. The round boats, which you board at the top of Mt. Gushmore, carry up to six people, and the ride downhill is zippy, with lots of splashes and sharp curves. Teamboat Springs draws an enthusiastic thumbs-up from all age groups, from preschoolers to grandparents. It's much longer, wilder, and more fun than Gangplank Falls, the comparable white-water ride at Typhoon Lagoon. Scare Factor→ **Riding together makes even nervous kids feel at ease.**

☀ Tike's Peak

Toddlers and preschoolers gather here to play on small slides and flumes, in igloo-style forts, and in a wading pool that looks like a broken ice-skating rink. No kids over 48 inches tall are allowed. Scare Factor→ **It's not scary.**

☀ Toboggan Racers

Eight riders on rubber mats are pitted against one another on a straight ride down the mountain. The heavier the rider, the faster the descent, so the attendant at the top of the slide will give kids a head start over adults. Not quite as wild as Snow Stormers, Toboggan Racers lets kids get used to the sensation of sliding downhill on a rubber sled. Scare Factor→ **Kids as young as four have reported loving this ride.**

CHAPTER 10

········ THE ········

REST

OF THE

WORLD

Disney World is more than theme parks. Way more. Savvy visitors have discovered a whole host of entertainment options available without setting foot in a park. Want to try surfing? A Hawaiian luau? A tea party with Alice and the Mad Hatter? An afternoon in the spa? Or even more shopping? Don't worry, Disney has you covered!

If you're looking for a unique blend of shops, restaurants, and entertainment that doesn't require a theme-park ticket, head to Downtown Disney. Here you'll find shopping, bowling, movies, and nightclubs—as well as DisneyQuest and Cirque du Soleil.

And if you're all too pooped to venture out or you have younger kids who need a rest, not to worry. The Disney hotels offer their own entertainment and sporting options. Water sports and boating can be enjoyed by all ages, and daredevils in the group can try parasailing along Bay Lake. There's also tennis, biking, and golf, including two of the most innovative miniature golf courses in the world.

Repeat visitors might be interested in trying something different within the theme parks, such as a tour that takes you behind the scenes or one of the special holiday parties held during

Halloween and Christmas. The point is that even when you're sure you've "done Disney," there's always still a little more Disney to do.

Getting to the Rest of the World

Staying on-site? Although the Disney transportation system does a good job of shuttling guests between the on-site hotels and the major theme parks, it slows down a bit when it comes to the minor parks. Consult the transportation guide you're given at check-in for the best route from your resort to anywhere on Disney property. If the trip involves two transfers and you don't have a car, consider taking a cab. They're easy to get from any on-site resort, and the cost of being hauled from one end of Disney property to another is around $15–$20.

Staying off-site? If you have your own car, use it. Off-site hotels rarely offer shuttle service to anything other than the major parks. If you don't have a car, call a cab.

Getting to Downtown Disney

On-site hotels have direct bus service to Downtown Disney. The buses make two stops, which means a fairly lengthy commute, especially to get to DisneyQuest or Cirque du Soleil, which are far from any bus stops. Those staying at Port Orleans, Saratoga Springs, or Old Key West have boat service directly to the Marketplace.

In addition, on-site and off-site guests with cars can drive directly to Downtown Disney. There's no charge for parking.

Getting to the ESPN Wide World of Sports Complex

The fastest route is to drive your own car. Buses are an option, but few run to this out-of-the-way location. Check your transportation guide for the best route from your resort; if more than two transfers are involved, take a cab.

Going Between Resorts

On-site guests with their own cars can simply drive to any other resort and inform the guard they're visiting for dinner or another activity. If you don't have your own car, your simplest option is to take a cab. Your cheapest option is to use the theme park that's closest to you as a transfer station. For example, if you're staying

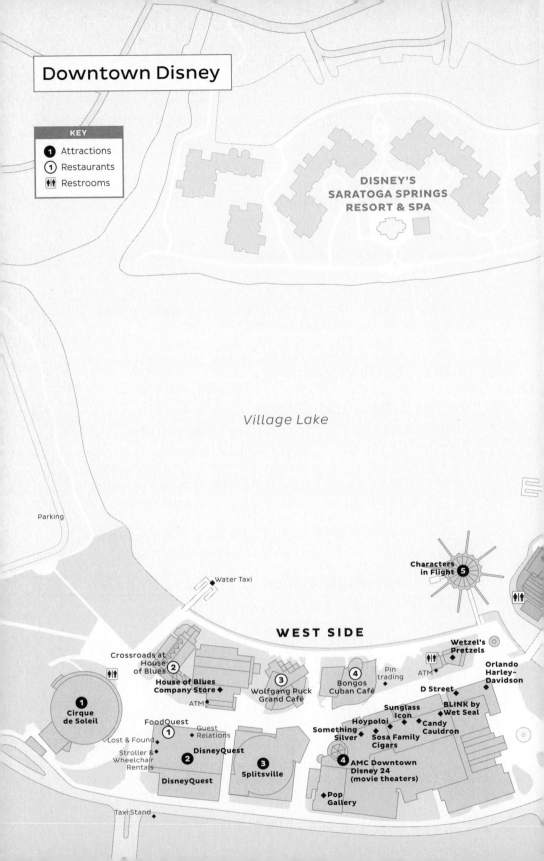

Downtown Disney

KEY
- **1** Attractions
- ① Restaurants
- 🚻 Restrooms

DISNEY'S SARATOGA SPRINGS RESORT & SPA

Village Lake

Parking

Water Taxi

Characters in Flight **5**

🚻

WEST SIDE

Wetzel's Pretzels

Crossroads at House of Blues

🚻

2

House of Blues Company Store ◆

Wolfgang Puck Grand Café **3**

Bongos Cuban Café **4**

Pin trading

ATM

ATM

Orlando Harley-Davidson

D Street ◆

ATM ◆

🚻

1 Cirque de Soleil

FoodQuest

◆ Guest Relations

Lost & Found ◆

Stroller & Wheelchair Rentals ◆

①

2 DisneyQuest

DisneyQuest

Splitsville **3**

Something Silver ◆

Hoypoloi ◆

Sunglass Icon ◆

Sosa Family Cigars ◆

BLINK by Wet Seal

Candy Cauldron ◆

4 AMC Downtown Disney 24 (movie theaters)

◆ Pop Gallery

Taxi Stand

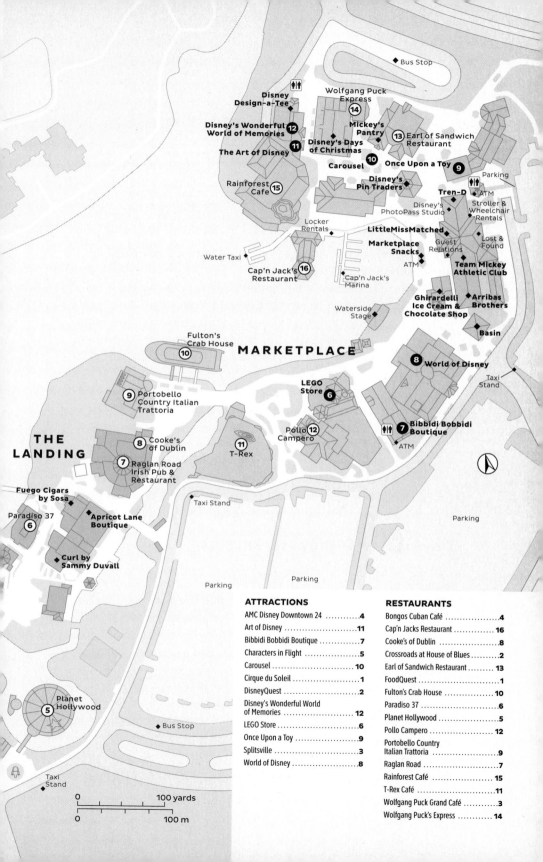

Bus Stop

Disney
Design-a-Tee

Disney's Wonderful
World of Memories **12**

The Art of Disney **11**

Rainforest
Cafe **15**

Wolfgang Puck
Express

Mickey's
Pantry **14**

Earl of Sandwich
Restaurant **13**

Disney's Days
of Christmas

Carousel **10**

Once Upon a Toy **9**

Disney's
Pin Traders

Parking

Tren-D

ATM

Disney's
PhotoPass Studio

Stroller &
Wheelchair
Rentals

Locker
Rentals

LittleMissMatched

Lost &
Found

Marketplace
Snacks

Guest
Relations

Water Taxi

ATM

Team Mickey
Athletic Club

Cap'n Jack's
Restaurant **16**

Cap'n Jack's
Marina

Ghirardelli
Ice Cream &
Chocolate Shop

Arribas
Brothers

Waterside
Stage

Basin

Fulton's
Crab House **10**

MARKETPLACE

World of Disney **8**

Taxi
Stand

Portobello
Country Italian
Trattoria **9**

LEGO
Store **6**

**THE
LANDING**

Cooke's
of Dublin **8**

T-Rex **11**

Pollo
Campero **12**

Bibbidi Bobbidi
Boutique **7**

Raglan Road
Irish Pub &
Restaurant **7**

ATM

Fuego Cigars
by Sosa

Paradiso 37 **6**

Apricot Lane
Boutique

Taxi Stand

Parking

Curl by
Sammy Duvall

Planet
Hollywood **5**

Parking

Parking

Bus Stop

Taxi
Stand

0 ——— 100 yards
0 ——— 100 m

at the Grand Floridian and have dinner reservations at the BoardWalk, take the monorail to the Magic Kingdom and catch a bus to the BoardWalk from there.

Downtown Disney

The enormous entertainment, dining, and shopping complex known as Downtown Disney is packed at night. Families who'd like to visit when there are fewer crowds should show up in the afternoon and eat dinner relatively early, like at 5 pm. It's a great spot for the first afternoon or evening of your vacation. It doesn't require a ticket but still has plenty of Disney spirit.

> **DON'T-MISS LIST**
>
> ✦ **Character breakfasts (if you have kids under 9)**
> ✦ **Cirque du Soleil**
> ✦ **DisneyQuest (if you have kids over 10)**
> ✦ **Downtown Disney**

"We didn't want to buy a ticket for our first day, since we were landing in Orlando around noon," reported one woman who visited with her husband and 14-year-old sister. "Instead we went to Downtown Disney, and had a great meal and then did some shopping. It was a low-key, perfect introduction to Disney World."

Off-season, Downtown Disney sections open at staggered times. If you have questions about hours, check with Guest Relations (a.k.a. Guest Services) at your hotel.

Downtown Disney Marketplace

The Marketplace section of Downtown Disney, not surprisingly, is full of shops. A good place to start is the World of Disney, the largest Disney store on Earth and the best place to find that perfect souvenir. Little girls will freak out at the sight of the **Bibbidi Bobbidi Boutique,** where they can purchase princess costumes, then have their hair, makeup, and nails done. Packages range from $55 for hairstyling and makeup to more than $195 for a complete photo portfolio and costume you can keep. Kids must be at least three years old to participate, and you can make appointments 180 days in advance by calling ☎ *407/939–7895* (☎ *407/WDW–STYLE*).

Warning: Once you go princess, it's hard to go back. "We were arriving in Orlando in the afternoon," wrote a mother from New

York, "and as you suggested we went to Downtown Disney, so we wouldn't burn a day on our theme-park tickets. We thought it would be cute to have our 5-year-old daughter Kate outfitted at Bibbidi Bobbidi Boutique to kick off her Disney vacation, but as it turns out, she was so enchanted with her new look that she refused to take down her hairdo, change clothes, or wash her face for the next seven days. In pictures we took near the end of vacation, Kate looks like Belle on crack."

> **INSIDER'S SECRET**
>
> Sometime in late 2015 or early 2016, Downtown Disney—which has been a bit of a construction site for years—will be renamed, rethemed, and rebranded as Disney Springs, with nearly double the number of restaurants and shops.

Another must-see is **Once Upon a Toy,** the ultimate shop for Disney-theme toys. Kids also enjoy Team Mickey's Athletic Club, which sells sporting equipment and clothes, and the Days of Christmas. The **LEGO Store** is just amazing, with enormous LEGO sculptures scattered around the lagoon, as well as a play area where kids can build their own models. Of course, without a budget, this can get out of control very fast. "I do have to take issue with your description of Downtown Disney as 'free,'" wrote one mother from Virginia. "We ended up spending more there than we did in any of the theme parks!"

Stop by the **Art of Disney,** where you can view limited-edition animation cels and other collectibles. Scrapbook hobbyists will enjoy **Disney's Wonderful World of Memories,** which is next door.

The **Rainforest Café** is great fun because birds and fish (real) and rhinos and giraffes (fake) surround your table while you eat. Check out the bar stools with their flamingo and zebra legs. **T-REX,** with a dinosaur theme (duh), is also oriented toward families. You're greeted by a life-size T-Rex as you enter and walk through a prehistoric environment with waterfalls, geysers, and a fossil dig site. Needless to say, these restaurants are wild and loud, more suited for a family meal than a parents' night out.

The part of Downtown Disney known as Pleasure Island is in transition while being prepared for the Disney Springs rebranding; the area will reopen in stages. Right now it looks a bit like a ghost town, but two restaurants—the popular Irish pub **Raglan Road** and the Latin-theme **Paradiso 37**—are both open and well worth the walk.

Also, between Pleasure Island and the West Side is a tethered hot-air balloon known as **Characters in Flight** as a tribute to Peter Pan, Mary Poppins, and some of Disney's other lofty stars. The balloon gently lifts 400 feet into the air for a great view of the surrounding area. Prices for a ride are $18 adult, $12 child. The cost is a bit steep (no pun intended) for the experience.

Downtown Disney West Side

The West Side is home to a variety of shops and restaurants, a 24-screen **AMC theater,** a 30-lane bowling alley called Splitsville, and two major attractions: DisneyQuest and Cirque du Soleil.

Bongos Cuban Café offers an Americanized version of Cuban dishes, a wild tropical decor, and throbbing Latin music. **Crossroads at House of Blues** serves up Cajun and creole cooking along with live jazz, country, and blues music. The Gospel Brunch at 10:30 am and 1 pm on Sunday is an especially good choice for families. Prices are $52.50 for adults and $32.25 for kids three to nine. Call ☎ *407/934-2583* (☎ *407/934–BLUE*) or visit ⊕ *www. ticketmaster.com* to buy tickets.

Wolfgang Puck Café serves terrific pizzas and sushi downstairs. Request the upstairs dining room for tonier adult dining. The giant blue globe of **Planet Hollywood** holds movie props, and even the menus—printed with high-school graduation pictures of stars—are entertaining.

Splitsville, in addition to its 30 bowling lanes, features billiards, live entertainment, and its own restaurant, which serves pizza, sushi, and sliders. One mother described Splitsville as "the nicest and most expensive bowling alley we've ever seen. An hour of bowling cost us $80." And be warned: After 8 pm Splitsville ca-

INSIDER'S SECRET

The Magic Kingdom's Bibbidi Bobbidi Boutique—while undeniably glamorous—requires theme-park admission. To maximize your expensive tickets, spend your day in the Magic Kingdom enjoying attractions, and visit the second Bibbidi Bobbidi Boutique at Downtown Disney on your day off or the first evening you arrive. That way you're not burning a day on your ticket.

ters to an adult crowd. Visit in the afternoon or early evening.

DisneyQuest

Most people call DisneyQuest an arcade—and within its five levels you will, indeed, see classic arcade games. But you'll also find high-tech interactive experiences that almost defy description.

HIDDEN MICKEY

As you get off the bus at Downtown Disney Marketplace, look closely at the water play area located near the bus drop-off entrance. Does the shape look familiar?

Favorite games include **Pirates of the Caribbean,** where you take to the deck to battle phantom buccaneers, and **Virtual Jungle Cruise,** an exhausting river-raft ride in which you paddle through the rapids of a prehistoric world. During your stay you can also fight comic-book villains, shoot foam balls at your competitors in a bumper-car war, and become a human joystick in a hockey-style pinball game.

■TIP➔ **DisneyQuest gets crowded in the evening, on weekends, and on rainy days. To make sure you have the chance to try out everything, visit at opening time on a weekday, which is usually around 11:30 am. The hours of operation vary seasonally, so check My Disney Experience for info on the date you'll be visiting.**

The centerpiece attraction of DisneyQuest is **CyberSpace Mountain,** in which you design your own virtual roller coaster. You can build in as many flips, spirals, and hills as time and distance allow; program in the speed of the car; and even get to name the sucker. When you're finished, your coaster is given a scariness rating from 1 to 5, meaning that you can either design a gentle, rolling, grade-1 coaster suitable for kids or a flip-you-over, slam-you-down, grade-5 coaster. (If your coaster gets a rating that's too mild or too wild, you can always redesign it.) Then you enter a booth where you're strapped into a capsule to ride a virtual re-creation of your design.

Needless to say, preteens and teens can get hooked on this stuff very fast, and DisneyQuest is primarily designed for the age 10–20 set. But there's entertainment for younger siblings as well, and any age can enjoy the arcade games or the Create Zone, where you can design your own toy or learn to draw a Disney character.

■TIP→ No strollers are allowed inside DisneyQuest, and there are a lot of stairs. Plan accordingly.

A single entry price ($47 for adults, $40 for kids 3 to 9) lets you play as long and as much as you like—an alarming thought for the parents of a 12-year-old boy. Admission is also included with the Water Park Fun & More option and, if you're willing to buy in advance, online discounts are often available as well.

> **HELPFUL HINT**
>
> DisneyQuest is large and loud, and each play zone has steps leading to other levels. In other words, it's easy to lose your kids. If you're going to let older kids and teens explore on their own, pick a designated time and place to regroup.

Cirque du Soleil

After a week at Disney World, probably the last thing you're itching to do is buy an expensive ticket to watch an acrobatic show, but the Cirque du Soleil show *La Nouba* positively wowed the families we surveyed.

Although the athleticism and agility of the troupe will amaze you, it's their ability to use props, sets, costumes, and their bodies to set a mood and tell a story that makes Cirque du Soleil unique. Don't expect any elephants or people being shot out of cannons—Cirque performances are more like theater than a traditional circus. Cirque du Soleil can best be appreciated by kids age eight and up.

Cirque du Soleil has a multitier pricing structure. Depending on where you sit and when you visit, general tickets range from $57 to $110 for adults and $47 to $92 for kids ages three to nine. The 90-minute show normally runs Tuesday through Saturday, twice daily at 6 and 9 pm. For reservations, details, and specific pricing for the dates you'll be visiting, visit ⊕ *www.cirquedusoleil. com* or call☎ *407/939-7600*.

It can take quite a long bus ride to get to Downtown Disney West Side (where Cirque du Soleil is located), even from an on-site hotel. Buses will drop you off at Pleasure Island and you then walk. Since the resorts often share buses to Downtown Disney, you'll have to sit through several stops before you arrive. The moral?

Drive if you can, but if you're taking a bus to Cirque du Soleil, leave your hotel an hour and a half before showtime.

The BoardWalk

Not up for the sprawl of Downtown Disney? At night, the shops, restaurants, and nightclubs in front of the BoardWalk Resort take on a whole new glitter. You can find plenty of low-key entertainment—face painting, hair braiding, midway games, and sometimes comedians and magic acts—along the waterfront. Eat dinner at the Flying Fish Café if you're feeling fancy, then rent a surrey bike ($20–$28 for 30 minutes, depending on bike size) for a lap around the lagoon.

The **ESPN Club** contains a broadcast and production facility, so celebrity athletes are sometimes on hand. It also serves up—and I quote—"the best ballpark cuisine from around the country." This bold claim translates into sandwiches, salads, and burgers, all sized for hearty appetites.

Two BoardWalk clubs are open strictly to adults 21 and older. The **Atlantic Dance Club** changes format frequently but is presently offering DJ-spun Top 40 dance music without a cover charge on some nights. **Jellyrolls** is a sing-along piano bar with lots of audience participation.

The fact that the BoardWalk isn't as vast and crowded as Downtown Disney appeals to many visitors; you can have a good meal and some entertainment without getting back into the mouse race. And at night, with the glowing Yacht and Beach clubs visible across the water and the fireworks of Epcot in the distance, the BoardWalk ranks as one of the most beautiful spots in Disney World. Pull up a rocker and let the world go by.

On-site guests can take monorails or buses to any theme park and then transfer to the BoardWalk bus. If you're staying at the Yacht or Beach clubs, the Swan, or the Dolphin, just walk. Off-site guests can either park in the BoardWalk lot or pay for the $12 valet parking, which is worth it on weekend evenings when the regular lot is crowded.

Disney Extras

Dinner Shows

Disney has three major dinner shows, some offered nightly and some a few times a week. Book any dinner shows you would like to attend before you leave home by calling ☎ *407/939–3463* (☎ *407/ WDW–DINE*). Reservations are accepted up to 180 days in advance and range in price depending on the time of year you're visiting.

Allow plenty of time to get to your dinner show. If you're relying on Disney transportation, your journey begins at the Magic Kingdom. For the luau, take the resort monorail from the Magic Kingdom to the Polynesian and follow the signs to the beach. For the Hoop-Dee-Doo or the barbecue, take the ferry from the Magic Kingdom to Fort Wilderness. Either way, you're in for a lot of walking. "It takes too much Hoop-Dee-Doo just to get there," wrote one reader from California, who is still steaming over missing her appetizer. If you have a car, obviously driving is easier. Or take a cab. ■**TIP→ Disney has recently required a credit-card guarantee for most of their sit-down restaurants, including dinner shows and character meals. You must cancel reservations at least 48 hours in advance to avoid being charged.**

☀ The Hoop-Dee-Doo Musical Revue

This show plays three times nightly (at 4, 6:15, and 8:30 pm) at Pioneer Hall in the Fort Wilderness campground. You can dine on ribs, fried chicken, and strawberry shortcake while watching a lovably hokey show that includes lots of audience participation. The cost is $59–$70 for adults, $33–$36 for children three to nine. ✉ *Fort Wilderness Resort, 3520 N. Fort Wilderness Trail* ☎ *407/939–3463* (☎ *407/WDW–DINE*).

☀ Mickey's Backyard Barbecue

Presented on select nights (usually Thursday and Saturday) at Fort Wilderness, the barbecue features a country band, line dancing with the characters, and picnic food such as barbecued ribs, roast chicken, and corn on the cob. Prices are $51–$60 for adults, $30–$36 for children three to nine. The barbecue is decidedly rowdier than other Disney dinner events. A mother of four from New York wrote, "The closest we came to a never-again moment was Mickey's Backyard Barbecue. It was a free-for-all with characters and kids running loose on the dance floor. On the other hand, the Polynesian luau was a delight, with plenty of entertainment for the kids but a much calmer atmosphere." ⊠ *Fort Wilderness Resort, 4510 N. Fort Wilderness Trail* ☎ *407/939–3463 (☎407/WDW–DINE).*

☀ The Spirit of Aloha

Disney's luau dinner is presented seasonally at 5:15 and 8 pm in the open-air theater in Luau Cove at the Polynesian Resort. The luau features hula dancing, music, and a "Polynesian feast," which translates as fruit, chicken, pork ribs, and pineapple bread. The cost is $59–$74 for adults and $30–$39 for children three to nine. "The Polynesian is a beautiful setting," wrote one family from Connecticut, "but we expected more of a traditional luau. Just be aware that this show has a modern story line." ⊠ *Disney's Polynesian Resort, 1600 Seven Seas Dr.* ☎ *407/939–3463 (☎407/WDW–DINE).*

> **HELPFUL HINT**
>
> Kids under three get into the parks for free, but what's the deal with character meals? Historically the buffets are more liberal than the sit-down venues about comping the under-three set, but don't assume: Anytime you book a character meal, ask the restaurant to spell out its policy about who, if anyone, eats for free.

Character Dining

The character meals are time-consuming and expensive, but families with young kids give them very high marks. It's not about the food, although that's usually fine; it's about the chance to have the characters actually visit your table so that there's plenty of time for pictures, hugs, and autographs. Reservations can (and should) be arranged 180 days in advance by calling ☎ *407/939–3463 (☎407/WDW–DINE).* Any character meal that takes place inside a theme park requires theme-park admission.

The character meal that gets the most attention is Cinderella's Royal Table, which is always booked months in advance—despite being by far the most expensive. Granted, there are some little extras (like a photo) included in the cost, but the drastic price jump is a clue to the popularity of this venue; people are willing to pay almost twice as much as for the typical character meal just to get their children inside the castle. During the on-season it is often sold out within minutes of the reservation line opening. Your best bet is to call ☎ *407/939–3463* (☎ *407/WDW–DINE*) *exactly* 180 days in advance and *precisely* at 7 am (EST). In general, dining reservations can be made online, but in the case of this popular venue, calling is best. And if you still can't get in, be prepared with a backup plan in the form of either the Princess Storybook Dining at Akershus in the Norway pavilion at Epcot, which features a variety of Disney princesses (except Cinderella), or 1900 Park Fare at the Grand Floridian, which offers Cinderella's Happily Ever After Dinner.

Don't forget: If you're going to dine with royalty, it's only fitting that little girls dress for the occasion. If you think the full princess outfit is too much for a day in the parks, change your girl back into casual clothes after the meal.

Character-meal times, places, prices, and the characters featured change often, so call to confirm the information before you book the meal. If your child has his or her heart set on meeting a particular character, be sure to verify that the character will actually be there when you visit. And confirm pricing when calling—meals are sometimes cheaper in the off-season.

The experience usually takes between 90 minutes and two hours, so plan accordingly. Families who have scheduled character breakfasts on the last day of their visits have also noted that a long breakfast coincides well with the usual 11 am check-out time at most Orlando hotels.

In the Resorts

☀ Cape May Café
Seaside picnic breakfast buffet with Goofy, Donald, and Minnie. Breakfast: adults $29, children (3–9) $16. ✉ *Beach Club Resort, 1700 Epcot Resorts Blvd.* ☎ *407/939–3463* (☎ *407/WDW–DINE*).

☀ Chef Mickey's
Party with Mickey, Minnie, Donald, Pluto, and Goofy. Breakfast: adults $38, children $20. Dinner: adults $50, children $26. ✉ *Contemporary Resort, 4600 N. World Dr., Magic Kingdom Resort Area* ☎ *407/939–3463* (☎ *407/WDW–DINE*).

☀ My Disney Girl's Perfectly Princess Tea Party

For the ultimate princess experience, pull out your wallet, take a deep breath, and head to the Grand Floridian for the Perfectly Princess Tea Party. The tea party includes a meet and greet with Princess Aurora from *Sleeping Beauty,* plus storytelling, sing-alongs, and a princess parade. (Needless to say, all little girls suit up in princess gear for this one.) Tea-party guests receive a special My Disney Girl doll dressed like Aurora, a ribbon tiara, bracelet, and princess scrapbook. The cost is $334 for one adult and one child aged 3–11. Additional adults are $99 each, and an additional child is $235. The tea party is offered from 10:30 to noon every day but Tuesday and Saturday. Lunch is served, but with all the excitement, don't be surprised if no one eats it. ✉ *Grand Floridian, 4401 Floridian Way, Magic Kingdom Resort Area* ☎ *407/939–3463* (☎ *407/WDW–DINE*).

☀ 1900 Park Fare

Breakfast with Mary Poppins, Alice in Wonderland, the Mad Hatter, and Winnie the Pooh and dinner with Cinderella, Prince Charming, the Evil Stepmother, and the Stepsisters. Several of our readers have given a special shout-out to Lady Tremaine and her daughters. "The evil stepmother is the only person in Disney who isn't constantly smiling," a dad from New York noted approvingly, while a mom from Virginia added, "The stepsisters were loud, obnoxious, graceless, and a lot of fun." Breakfast: adults $29, children $16. Dinner: adults $45, children $22. ✉ *Grand Floridian, 4401 Floridian Way, Magic Kingdom Resort Area* ☎ *407/939–3463* (☎ *407/WDW–DINE*).

☀ 'Ohana

Luau breakfast with Lilo and Stitch as well as Mickey and Pluto. Breakfast: adults $29, children $16. ✉ *Disney's Polynesian Resort, 1600 Seven Seas Dr.* ☎ *407/939–3463* (☎ *407/WDW–DINE*).

In the Magic Kingdom

☀ Cinderella's Royal Table

Medieval banquet meals in the perfect setting. Cinderella greets you downstairs and poses with you for a portrait, which is included in the price, along with wands for girls and swords for boys. After the royal greeting, you're escorted upstairs to meet the Fairy Godmother and at least two other princesses. Disney rotates them, but Snow White, Belle, Aurora, and Jasmine are often featured. Be sure to confirm all this when you book because of the insane popularity of Cinderella's Royal Table. Disney has changed this character meal more frequently than most, trying to figure out how to move people through more efficiently. It also keeps marching steadily upward in cost, with the price changing more frequently and more significantly than any other character meal on property. If it's any consolation, most of the families surveyed think it's worth the trouble, using terms like "magnificent" and "unsurpassed." Breakfast: adults $60, children (3–9) $38. Lunch: adults $63, children $40. Dinner: adults $75, children $45. ⊠ *Magic Kingdom, Cinderella Castle* ☎ *407/939–3463* (☎ *407/WDW–DINE*).

> ## INSIDER'S SECRET
>
> The fact that the 'Ohana breakfast is the only character meal featuring that prankster Stitch makes it especially lively—and a good choice for boys who may have seen one princess too many. "Stitch took my brother's Buzz Lightyear gun and engaged Pluto in a stickup," one boy happily reported. "It's a memory my family will cherish forever."

✳ Crystal Palace

Breakfast, lunch, and dinner buffets with Pooh and friends. "The food was OK," said one mother from New Jersey. "Nothing special, but they did have a separate buffet for the kids filled with things they would eat. What really made our character meal worth it is that the Pooh characters came around to our tables and our 3- and 5-year-olds didn't have to fight for their attention. The servers did a good job of keeping things orderly. When Tigger was visiting our table, a child from another family got so excited he ran up to join in. The server gently steered him back to his own seat, explaining Tigger would be there next." Breakfast: adults $29, children $16. Lunch: adults $32, children $17. Dinner: adults $45, children $22. ⊠ *Magic Kingdom, Main St.* ☎ *407/939–3463* (☎ *407/WDW–DINE*).

In Epcot

☀ Akershus Royal Banquet Hall

Norway—breakfast, lunch, and dinner buffets in a castle setting. At present, Snow White, Mulan, Mary Poppins, Belle, Aurora, and Jasmine show up at breakfast. At lunch and dinner you'll meet Belle, Jasmine, Aurora, Alice in Wonderland, Pocahontas, and Ariel—who, we're happy to report, is walking just fine in a ball gown. The princesses are sometimes reshuffled, so if your child has a preference, confirm who's expected to appear. Breakfast: adults $45, children (3–9) $27. Lunch: adults $46, children $28. Dinner: adults $52, children $28. ✉ *Epcot, Norway Pavilion* ☎ *407/939–3463* (☎ *407/WDW–DINE*).

■ **TIP→** When you enter a character meal, you'll probably be ushered into a line where families are waiting to have their pictures taken with the characters by a professional photographer. These shots can be added to your PhotoPass or, if you want to save a few bucks (not to mention the wait in line), ask to be shown directly to your seats. There will be plenty of time later for you to take your own pictures with the characters as they visit your table.

☀ Garden Grill

This rotating restaurant offers Epcot's only evening character dinner, with Mickey, Pluto, Chip, and Dale. They're dressed in cute farmer clothing, in a nod to the agricultural theme of the Land pavilion. Dinner: adults $41, children $20. ✉ *Epcot, The Land* ☎ *407/939–3463* (☎ *407/WDW–DINE*).

In Hollywood Studios

☀ Hollywood & Vine

A changing roster of current stars from Disney Junior television shows meet and greet guests during breakfast and lunch, so it's a good choice for the two-to-five set. Breakfast: adults $27, children (3–9) $15. Lunch: adults $34, children $18. Dinner: adults $45, children $24. ✉ *Hollywood Studios, Hollywood Blvd.* ☎ *407/939–3463* (☎ *407/WDW–DINE*).

In the Animal Kingdom

☀ Tusker House

Mickey, Donald, Daisy, and Goofy appear at a safari-themed breakfast. This one gets high marks from our readers for both the food and the general cuteness of the presentation. Breakfast: adults $32, children (3–9) $18. Lunch: adults $38, children $19. Dinner: adults $38, children $18. ⊠ *Animal Kingdom, Africa* ☎ *407/939-3463* (☎ *407/WDW-DINE*).

Special Holiday Parties and Events

Disney World is at its most magical during the holidays. Hours are extended, special parades and shows debut, and the parks and hotels are beautifully decorated.

The week between Christmas and New Year's is the absolute busiest of the year at WDW, but it's possible to celebrate the holidays at Disney without being caught in the crush. Decorations go up just before Thanksgiving, and the special shows and parades debut shortly thereafter. The first two weeks of December are among the least crowded of the year—perfect for celebrating Christmas at Disney (assuming that your child's school schedule can accommodate the trip).

Each resort puts up its own decorations—a nautical tree for the Yacht Club, seashell ornaments at the Beach Club, Native American tepees at the Wilderness Lodge, an enormous Victorian dazzler at the Grand Floridian. These decorations are so gorgeous that holiday tours of the Disney hotels are popular among Orlando locals.

☀ Mickey's Halloween Party

On select evenings during September and October the Magic Kingdom hosts Mickey's Halloween Party. As the name implies, this celebration is geared toward younger kids, with fortunetellers, face painters, and trick-or-treating throughout the park; parades featuring the characters in costume; and a special fireworks finale. Be sure to bring along everyone's Halloween costumes. Tickets for Mickey's Halloween Party ($62–$72 adults, $57–$66 children 3–9) are easily purchased at Disney during September but require advanced purchase during October. Purchasing in advance guarantees a $6 savings. Visit ⊕ *www.*

disneyworld.com or call ☎*407/934–7639* (☎*407/W–DISNEY*) for advance tickets and more information.

☀ Mickey's Very Merry Christmas Party

Christmas at Disney World is lovely all on its own, but Disney also offers a special ticketed party event on select evenings in the Magic Kingdom with holiday-themed shows and parades. Tickets for Mickey's Very Merry Christmas Party ($71–$74 adults, $66–$69 children 3–9) should be purchased well in advance, either online at ⊕ *www.disneyworld.com* or by calling ☎*407/934–7639* (☎*407/W–DISNEY*). Military discounts are sometimes available, so be sure to ask.

> **INSIDER'S SECRET**
>
> If you have preteens and teens who are up for a gorier scene, check out the super-scary Halloween Horror Nights event at Universal Studios.

Tours for Kids and Families

Most of Disney's behind-the-scenes tours require that guests be 16 and up to participate, but there are two programs at the Grand Floridian that are specifically for kids; one program each at Port Orleans Riverside, the Caribbean Beach, and the Yacht and Beach clubs; one tour in Animal Kingdom; and one tour in the Magic Kingdom designed for families.

☀ Family Magic Tour in the Magic Kingdom

Everyone gets into the act on this tour; although the activities are geared to kids ages 3 to 10, parents and both younger and older siblings can come along. The only rule is that you have to be willing to act silly.

Your tour guide meets you at Guest Relations in the Magic Kingdom and sets up the premise of the tour. Perhaps Peter Pan has stolen Captain Hook's favorite hook, and the captain is so furious that his band of buccaneers is threatening to take over the whole Magic Kingdom. To stop him, you must follow a map that takes you around the park—hopping, skipping, hiding, and keeping an eye out for each new clue.

At the final stop of the tour, you meet up with a character or two for a closing surprise. The tour is a great option for families who have been to the Magic Kingdom several times and are looking for a new spin. It's less appealing for first-time visitors who are itching to get on the rides.

The Family Magic Tour is held daily from 10 am to noon, and the cost is $34 per person, regardless of age. Call ☎ *407/939–8687* (☎ *407/ WDW–TOUR*).

☀ Pirate Adventure

This rollicking two-hour boat tour takes kids on a treasure hunt across the Seven Seas Lagoon with stops at all the Magic Kingdom resort marinas. Counselors help kids collect clues and complete a map that leads them to buried treasure. It's a good choice for active kids from age 4 to 12. A snack is served on the pontoon boat after the last stop, and everyone leaves with a bag of treasure. "My 6-year-old son loved the Pirate Adventure at the Grand Floridian," reported one mom from New York. "It's very reasonably priced, and since I'm a single parent, I have to confess it was wonderful to just have a couple of hours to lie by the pool while he was on tour."

The Adventure, which costs $37, currently departs the Grand Floridian marina at 9:30 am daily. Reservations are a must because this program fills up fast; call ☎ *407/939–3463* (☎ *407/WDW–DINE*) 90 days in advance.

The Pirate Adventure at the Grand Floridian is so popular that three more adventures have been made available. The Port Orleans Riverside now offers its own Bayou Pirate Adventure; Caribbean Beach features Tales of Old Port Royale; the Yacht and Beach clubs feature The Legend of the Albatross. The stories have different themes, but the rest of the excursion is very similar, and the price is the same.

☀ Wild Africa Trek in the Animal Kingdom

Kids eight and up who are really into animals (or who need to do a serious project to make up for the school days they're missing on this trip) will enjoy the Wild Africa Trek, which is offered daily in the Animal Kingdom. This three-hour tour takes you behind the scenes of the park, then on a special safari through the

savanna led by knowledgeable guides. Unlike the Kilimanjaro Safaris, which must keep moving, the Wild Africa Trek vehicles stop
at several points along the journey to allow plenty of time for
animal viewing and pictures.

The behind-the-scenes part of the Trek is really a blast, and
that's one of the reasons why this tour, despite the cost, has become so popular Disney is upping the number of trips per day. The
highlight is a shaky walk across a "broken-down" bridge extended
high in the air above a river full of dozing crocodiles. You're carefully tethered, of course, but it's still enough to get the pulse rac-
ing. And they serve you a truly terrific lunch on a viewing platform
right in the middle of the savanna.

The cost is $139–$225, and, owing to the construction of
some of the transportation vehicles and bridges, participants
must weigh between 45 and 300 pounds. The morning tours are
especially popular, since that's when the animals are most active.
Afternoon tours are a bit cheaper. Call ☎ *407/939–8687* (☎ *407/
WDW–TOUR*) for details or reservations.

☀ Wonderland Tea Party

Kids join Alice in Wonderland and the Mad Hatter for a tea party
held at 1900 Park Fare in the Grand Floridian. The table is festively appointed, and kids decorate their own cupcakes. Since
this is pretty much all they eat, expect an afternoon sugar high.
Afterward, the characters lead them in a variety of games, and
each child leaves with a souvenir photo of him- or herself with
the characters.

The Wonderland Tea Party is served weekdays from 2 to 3 pm
for kids ages 4 to 10 (no moms!), and the cost is $49. For reserva-
tions, call ☎ *407/939–3463* (☎ *407/WDW–DINE*) 90 days in advance.

Water Sports

Most on-site hotels have lovely marinas with a variety of watercraft for rent, but the major water-recreation area of WDW is the
Seven Seas Lagoon in front of the Magic Kingdom. Marinas at the
Grand Floridian, Polynesian, Contemporary, Fort Wilderness, and
Wilderness Lodge all service the lagoon, and you don't have to be
a guest of the resort to rent watercraft (although you'll need to
show either a driver's license or a resort ID).

Reservations are a good idea, especially in the on-season, and it never hurts to confirm prices before you go. Call ☎ 407/939-0754 for more information.

Boat Rentals

The Disney fleet includes mini-speedboats called Sea Raycers, canopy boats, sailboats, pontoons, pedal boats, and kayaks. The marina staff can help you decide which watercraft best fits your needs; pontoon boats are a good option for younger kids, and the whole family can take a 30-minute ride for $45.

The best place to rent the Sea Raycer mini-speedboats is the Seven Seas Lagoon. You have plenty of room to explore and can really pick up speed. The boats are for rent at the marinas in the Contemporary, Polynesian, and Grand Floridian resorts or Wilderness Lodge. At present prices are $32 for 30 minutes. Drivers must be at least 14 years old and 5 feet tall, although kids of any age will enjoy riding along with Mom or Dad.

Fishing

Fishing equipment for an afternoon of catch-and-release is for rent at Port Orleans and Fort Wilderness Campground starting at only $8 for 60 minutes or $14 for all day. If you'd like more action than simply dropping a line, fishing tours depart from water locations throughout WDW. Groups of up to five can book the elaborate two-hour tour for $270. Reservations can be made up to 180 days in advance; call ☎ 407/939-2277 (☎ 407/WDW-BASS) for exact times, locations, and prices.

Parasailing and Waterskiing

Another high-thrill activity is parasailing. Excursions leave daily from the Contemporary Resort marina, and the regular flights cost $95 for one person or $175 for two riders in tandem. That's enough for most people, but the truly adventurous can fly longer on the deluxe flight, which costs $130 for a single rider and $195 in tandem. At your top height of 600 feet above the lake you'll see all four parks. Sammy Duvall's Watersports Centre also offers waterskiing, wakeboarding, knee boarding, and tubing. For reservations or more information call ☎ 407/939-0754.

Specialty Cruises

Two of the greatest ways to spend an evening in Disney World are watching the Magic Kingdom fireworks or the pyrotechnics of IllumiNations at Epcot. And there's no classier viewing spot than aboard your private boat. "We called before we left home and rented a pontoon boat to see the Epcot fireworks," wrote one father. "What a treat. We had a great captain who drove us around then 'parked' under the bridge so we could see the show. It was great floating there, sipping a drink, while others were jam-packed in the park … and probably trying to figure out how they were going to exit along with thousands of others."

The fleet includes yachts and pontoons that can accommodate groups of 7 to 14 people. Factoring in the size of your party and where you'll be sailing from, the prices vary. To give you an idea, an hour-long cruise in a simple pontoon boat holding up to eight people may start at $299; in an elegant yacht that accommodates up to 12, it's $695. When you factor in how many people can participate in the experience, the specialty cruises are actually a (somewhat) cost-effective way to create a memorable evening for the whole family. Just be sure to reserve 90 days in advance by calling ☎407/939-7529 (☎407/WDW-PLAY).

Surfing

Surfing lessons are offered at Typhoon Lagoon on select mornings before the park opens. Participants must be at least eight years old and strong swimmers. For those up to the challenge, this clinic ($150 per person) is one of the most fun things to do in all of WDW. Call ☎407/939-7529 (☎407/WDW-PLAY) for details, and always confirm prices when booking.

Sports on Land

Biking

Bikes are for rent at most on-site hotels at a cost of $18 a day or $9 for an hour; helmets are included.

Golf

There are six courses on WDW grounds with twilight fees starting at $69 on weekdays for Disney World resort guests. The rates go straight up from there, topping out at $199. If you're beginning golfers who just want to give it a try, the Oak Trail, a 9-hole walking course, costs $38 for adults and $20 for kids three to nine. Clubs and shoes are available for rent. Visit ⊕ *www.disneyworld. com* or call ☎ *407/939–4653* (☎ *407/WDW–GOLF*) to reserve tee times and confirm rates.

Health Clubs and Spas

The Contemporary, Grand Floridian, Swan, Dolphin, Yacht and Beach clubs, BoardWalk, Animal Kingdom Lodge, Coronado Springs, Old Key West, and Saratoga Springs resorts all have health clubs. The most complete workout facility is at Saratoga Springs.

There are full-service spas at the Grand Floridian, Saratoga Springs, and Animal Kingdom Lodge. "My 7-year-old daughter had her first manicure at the Grand Floridian spa and was in heaven," a mom from New York wrote. "She felt very grown-up, and the manicurist was the sweetest cast member I've ever met—even at Disney World, where everybody is nice!"

Horseback Riding

Guided 45-minute rides circle the wooded trails of Fort Wilderness daily. Children must be at least nine to ride, but the horses are gentle and the pace is slow. The price is $46 per person, and the ride should be booked at least one day in advance.

Younger kids can ride around the stables at the Fort Wilderness Petting Farm while older siblings are on the trail ride. Children two and over and up to 80 pounds are welcome. Fort Wilderness also offers horse-drawn wagon rides departing from Pioneer Hall nightly, $8 for adults and $5 for guests three to nine.

During the holidays the options are jazzed up a bit. Nightly 25-minute "haunted carriage rides" are available during the month of October, and "sleigh rides"—sans snow, of course—are offered in December. Call ☎ *407/939–7529* (☎ *407/WDW–PLAY*) for prices and details.

Miniature Golf

Fantasia Gardens, just across from Disney's Hollywood Studios, is real eye candy—an 18-hole mini-golf tribute to the movie *Fantasia* with dancing hippos, orchestrated fountains, and the Sorcerer's Apprentice running the whole show. A second course, Fantasia Fairways, is a miniature version of a real golf course, with sand traps, water hazards, and roughs. Although you play with a putter, the holes are 100 feet long and difficult enough to drive a veteran golfer to curses.

> ### INSIDER'S SECRET
>
> Fantasia Fairways is too tough for golfers under 10, and even Fantasia Gardens is a fairly difficult course. Winter Summerland is a better choice for the preschool and grade-school set.

The second miniature golf complex at Disney World is Winter Summerland (beside Blizzard Beach), where you're greeted with the question "Would you like to play in snow or sand?" Your first clue that there's strange weather ahead is that Santa, his sleigh pulled by flamingos, has crash-landed on the roof and skidded through a snowbank–sandbank into the wackiest campground on Earth. You can opt to play either the icy white "greens" of the winter course, where you can find a hockey rink, a snow castle, and slalom ski runs, or the sandy shores of the summer course, where the Beach Boys serenade you amid pools, waves, and barbecue pits. Although both of the Winter Summerland courses are child-friendly, the summer course is harder. Must be all those sand traps.

Rates at Fantasia Gardens, Fantasia Fairways, and Winter Summerland are $14 for adults and $12 for kids ages three to nine. Reservations aren't necessary.

Running

Trails cut through the grounds of nearly every Disney resort. Consult Guest Relations for ideas on the best route around your particular hotel. Wilderness Lodge, with its invitingly shady trails, is an especially good choice if you're visiting in summer, when even morning runs can be steamy.

Tennis

Several on-site resorts (the Contemporary, the Grand Floridian, the Yacht and Beach clubs, BoardWalk, Old Key West, Saratoga Springs, the Swan, and the Dolphin) have tennis courts, and the Contemporary also offers clinics for guests 10 and older. There's considerable variation in rental rates and reservation policies, so call ☎ *407/939–7529* (☎ *407/WDW–PLAY*) for details.

ESPN Wide World of Sports Complex

This multimillion-dollar sports complex hosts competitions and tournaments, with facilities to accommodate 25 different kinds of sports, including the ever-changing roster of Disney-sponsored race events. It's also the spring training camp of the Atlanta Braves. You can have lunch or dinner at the ESPN Wide World of Sports Grille, a sports bar with multiple screens and interactive games.

Activities at the Wide World of Sports vary widely, so call ☎ *407/939–4263* or visit ⊕ *www.disneyworldsports.com* before you leave home to find out what will be going on during your visit. Admission varies with the event, but averages $14 for adults, $10 for kids ages three to nine.

CHAPTER 11

DINING AT DISNEY

Theme-park food used to be a terrifying concept, evoking images of endless hamburgers and chicken strips. Of course, fast-food staples are still available, but Disney has made a concerted effort to offer a wide variety of unusual—and yes, even healthy—dining options for families on the go. And when you're ready to sit down at night and really relax, the variety of specialty full-service restaurants is nothing short of astounding.

There are a bevy of dining options around Walt Disney World, so put your thinking cap on before you leave home. Will you want to concentrate on quick-service (fast-food) options, trying to make the most of your time in the theme parks? Or will you want to relax with a sit-down meal every day? Are you looking to eat healthy or is vacation a time to loosen all restraints? Do your kids want to meet a princess while they dine on mac 'n' cheese, or would they prefer watching fireworks while enjoying sushi? What's your idea of the perfect vacation meal?

Disney is prepared to offer it all, and choosing your restaurants will quickly become a big part of the planning process. It's best to check out food options from home, especially if your party includes picky eaters or those with dietary restrictions. For example, the best vegetarian quick-service meal in the Magic Kingdom is Columbia Harbor House's Lighthouse Sandwich. Knowing that in advance means a quick and easy stop in the middle of your touring. Not knowing it can mean you're searching for something suitable at 1:30 on a busy Sunday when everyone is famished. Not so fun.

Full-Service Restaurants at Disney

The biggest change in the Walt Disney World restaurant system in the past decade has been the Disney Dining Plan, which allows guests to include meals and snacks in their vacation packages and, thus, create the equivalent of an all-inclusive resort stay. The dining plan makes more sense for some families than others, but it has an effect on every family that visits Walt Disney World, even those who opt not to include it with their tickets.

Why? Because the popularity of the dining plan means that more restaurant reservations are being made and that they're being made earlier than ever. Unless you book your dinners and character meals well in advance, you may find yourself unable to get into the most popular restaurants, simply because families on the dining plan have beaten you to the punch. There's still a chance you can get a last-minute reservation if you're not picky about when and where you eat, but your selection will be curtailed. So even families opting not to participate in the dining plan still need to make their restaurant reservations as early as possible.

About the Disney Dining Plan

The Disney Dining Plan has been a runaway success—so much so that it's more important than ever to make advance reservations for character meals. The reason is this: Most families on the plan will be eating at least one full-service meal each day, which in itself means more general dining demand, since in the past many budget-conscious families stuck to counter-service meals. More families are also going for character meals under the plan; many of the character meals only count as one full-service credit, but others, such as those in Cinderella Castle, require you to combine two credits. Either way, it means that because character dining is more affordable under the plan, there are more people than ever trying to book those seats.

Quick Guide to

Restaurant	Description	Location
Magic Kingdom		
Be Our Guest	Incomparable setting. Quick-service lunch, full-service dinner	Fantasyland
Cinderella's Royal Table	Dine in the castle with the princess characters	Fantasyland
The Crystal Palace	Buffet dining with Winnie the Pooh and friends	Main Street
Liberty Tree Tavern	Thanksgiving-style feast	Liberty Square
The Plaza Restaurant	Don't miss the sundaes	Main Street
Tony's Town Square Restaurant	Lady and the Tramp theme and Italian classics	Main Street
Epcot		
Akershus	Authentic Norwegian cuisine and princess-character buffets	Norway
Biergarten	Rousing, noisy atmosphere, and live entertainment	Germany
Coral Reef	Great views of the Living Seas tank	Living Seas pavilion
Garden Grill Restaurant	American dishes and the Disney characters	Land pavilion
La Hacienda de San Angel	Upscale Mexican, waterfront dining	Mexico
Le Cellier	Great steaks, excellent salmon, huge desserts	Canada
Les Chefs de France	Like a Paris sidewalk café	France
Marrakesh	Exotic food and surroundings, belly dancers	Morocco
Monsieur Paul	Classic French cuisine—in an elegant setting	France
Nine Dragons	Cuisine representing every region in China	China

Disney Dining

Rating	Price	Advance Reservations for Peak Season	Suitability for Kids	Meals Served
★★★	$$$	6 months (L,D) 3 months (B)	High	B, L, D
★★★	$$$	6 months	High	B, L, D
★★	$$	4 months	High	B, L, D
★★	$$	4 months	Moderate	L, D
★	$$	4 months	Moderate	L, D
★★	$$	4 months	High	L, D
★★	$$	6 months	High	B, L, D
★★	$$	2 months	High	L, D
★★★	$$$	4 months	Low	D
★★	$$$	6 months	High	L, D
★★	$$	4 months	Moderate	D
★★★	$$$	6 months	Low	L, D
★★	$$$	2 months	Moderate	L, D
★★	$$	2 months	Moderate	L, D
★★	$$$	4 months	Low	D
★★	$$	2 months	Low	L, D

Quick Guide to

Restaurant	Description	Location
Rose & Crown Pub & Dining Room	Pub atmosphere and live entertainment	United Kingdom
San Angel Inn	Beautiful, romantic setting	Mexico
Spice Road Table	Mediterranean small plates in a waterfront setting	Morocco
Teppan Edo	Dining room chefs slice and dice before your eyes	Japan
Tokyo Dining	Casual with sushi and batter-fried entrées	Japan
Tutto Italia	Upscale Italian, lively service	Italy
Via Napoli	Best pizza in park; charming setting with equally charming service	Italy

Disney's Hollywood Studios

'50s Prime Time Café	Want to star in a 1950s sitcom?	Hollywood Blvd.
Hollywood & Vine	Large, attractive buffeteria, character meals with Playhouse Disney gang	Hollywood Blvd.
The Hollywood Brown Derby	Elegant and lovely with upscale cuisine	Hollywood Blvd.
Mama Melrose's Ristorante Italiano	Good food, good service, rarely too crowded	Streets of America
Sci-Fi Dine-In Theater	Campy; you eat in cars at a drive-in theater	Commissary Lane

Animal Kingdom

Rainforest Café	Large and lively	Park entrance
Tusker House	Buffet with great variety, character breakfast and lunch	Africa
Yak & Yeti	Asian fusion, complete with bar and beer garden	Asia

Disney Dining

Rating	Price	Advance Reservations for Peak Season	Suitability for Kids	Meals Served
★★	$$	4 months	Moderate	L, D
★★	$$	4 months	Moderate	L, D
★★	$$	4 months	Moderate	L, D
★★★	$$$	4 months	High	L, D
★★	$$	2 months	Moderate	L, D
★★★	$$$	4 months	Moderate	L, D
★★★	$$	2 months	High	L, D
★★★	$$	6 months	High	L, D
★★	$	4 months	High	B, L, D
★★★	$$$	4 months	Low	L, D
★★	$	2 months	Moderate	L, D
★★	$$	2 months	High	L, D
★★	$$	Not accepted	High	B, L, D
★★	$$	4 months	High	B, L, D
★★	$$	2 months	Moderate	L, D

Quick Guide to

Restaurant	Description	Location
WDW Hotels		
Artist Point	Fine dining in a rustic setting	Wilderness Lodge
Big River Grille & Brewing Works	Casual restaurant and brewpub	BoardWalk
Boatwright's Dining Hall	Southern dishes and Cajun food	Port Orleans, Riverside
Boma	African-inspired buffet and great breakfasts	Animal Kingdom Lodge
California Grill	The best of all	Contemporary
Cape May Café	Character dining at breakfast, clambakes in the evening	Beach Club
Captain's Grille	Cheery and bright—a cut above a coffee shop	Yacht Club
Chef Mickey's	Character dining while the monorail zooms by	Contemporary
Cítricos	Gourmet cuisine and an outstanding wine list	Grand Floridian
ESPN Club	The perfect place to watch the big game	BoardWalk
Flying Fish Café	Excellent seafood and steaks	BoardWalk
Grand Floridian Café	Great variety, Southern classics	Grand Floridian
Gulliver's Grill at Garden Grove	Whimsical decor, basic food	Swan
Il Milano	Gourmet Italian with wide variety of pastas	Swan
Jiko	African-influenced cuisine, South African wines	Animal Kingdom Lodge
Kimonos	Sushi in an elegant setting	Swan
Kona Café	Pacific Rim food with a tropical emphasis	Polynesian

Disney Dining

Rating	Price	Advance Reservations for Peak Season	Suitability for Kids	Meals Served
★★★	$$	4 months	Low	D
★★	$	Not accepted	Moderate	L, D
★★	$	1 day	Moderate	B, D
★★★	$$$	4 months	Moderate	B, D
★★★	$$$	6 months	High	D
★★	$$	2 months	High	B, D
★★	$$	2 months	Moderate	B, L, D
★★	$$	6 months	High	B, D
★★★	$$$	2 months	Low	D
★	$	Not accepted	Moderate	L, D
★★★	$$$	4 months	Low	D
★★	$$	1 day	Moderate	B, L, D
★★	$$	4 months	Moderate	B, L, D
★★	$$	4 months	Moderate	D
★★★	$$$	4 months	Moderate	D
★★	$$	2 months	Low	D
★★	$$	2 months	Moderate	B, L, D

Quick Guide to

Restaurant	Description	Location
Maya Grill	Latin American–inspired cuisine	Coronado Springs
Narcoossee's	Great fresh seafood; view of MK fireworks	Grand Floridian
1900 Park Fare	Buffet-style character dining	Grand Floridian
'Ohana	Family-friendly, with island entertainment	Polynesian
Sanaa	Indian food in a colorful setting with a view of the Savanna	Animal Kingdom Lodge
Shula's	Linebacker-size steaks in a dignified atmosphere	Dolphin
Shutters	Casual island fare	Caribbean Beach
Todd English's bluezoo	Fine seafood in a sleek, upscale setting	Dolphin
Trattoria al Forno	Authentic Italian with extensive regional wines.	BoardWalk
Victoria & Albert's	The most elegant restaurant on Disney property	Grand Floridian
The Wave...of American Flavors	Innovative regional cuisine	Contemporary
Whispering Canyon Café	Comfort food, family-style service	Wilderness Lodge
Yachtsman Steakhouse	One of the premier steakhouses in Disney World	Yacht Club

The Rest of the World

Bongos Cuban Café	Americanized versions of Cuban dishes	Downtown Disney West Side
ESPN Wide World of Sports Grill	Ultimate sports bar with cool games for the kids	ESPN Wide World of Sports Complex

Disney Dining

Rating	Price	Advance Reservations for Peak Season	Suitability for Kids	Meals Served
★	$	1 day	Low	B, D
★★	$$$	4 months	Low	D
★★	$$$	4 months	High	B, D
★★	$$	4 months	High	B, D
★★★	$$	2 months	Moderate	D
★★★	$$$	2 months	Low	D
★	$$	1 day	Moderate	D
★★	$$$	2 months	Low	D
★★★	$$$	1 month	Moderate	B,D
★★★	$$$	4 months	Low	D
★★	$$	1 day	Low	B, L, D
★★	$$	2 months	High	B, L, D
★★	$$$	2 months	Low	D
★	$$	Not accepted	Moderate	L, D
★★	$$	Not accepted	Moderate	L, D

Quick Guide to

Restaurant	Description	Location
Fulton's Crab House	Fine dining on a riverboat	Downtown Disney
House of Blues	Cajun and Creole cooking with live music	Downtown Disney West Side
Paradiso 37	Food from 37 different countries across the Americas, terrific tequila bar	Downtown Disney
Planet Hollywood	Always fun; film clips run constantly	Downtown Disney West Side
Portobello Country Italian Trattoria	Northern Italian cuisine	Downtown Disney
Raglan Road	Upmarket Irish pub with music and dance	Downtown Disney
Rainforest Café	Fun and funky atmosphere	Downtown Disney Marketplace
T-REX	Casual dining with a dinosaur theme	Dowtown Disney Marketplace
Wolfgang Puck Café	Terrific salads, pizza, and sushi	Downtown Disney West Side

Disney Dining

Rating	Price	Advance Reservations for Peak Season	Suitability for Kids	Meals Served
★★★	$$$	2 months	Low	L, D
★★	$$	Not accepted	Moderate	Sunday brunch, L, D
★★★	$$	2 months	Low	L, D
★★	$$	1 day	High	L, D
★★	$$	2 months	Low	D
★★	$$	4 months	Low	L, D
★	$$	Not accepted	High	B, L, D
★	$$	Not accepted	High	L, D
★★★	$$$	2 months (upstairs)	Moderate	L, D

The fact that the system allows guests to combine meals if they want to try a signature dining venue means that people who otherwise wouldn't have considered the California Grill or other upscale spots are trying to get in. The result? Guests on the Disney Dining Plan are flooding the full-service restaurants in such great numbers that all guests—including those who aren't on the plan or who aren't staying at Disney hotels—are feeling the squeeze.

Consider the experience of this grandmother from Rhode Island: "We have visited Disney World many times and have certain restaurants we know we enjoy. For our upcoming visit we decided against the dining plan but imagine my surprise when I called for reservations two months in advance and found that we could not get into eight of our ten favorites. Some of them were giving us ridiculous times like 10 pm for dinner, and others were simply saying there was nothing available at all. We were crushed!"

We'll go into this in more detail later, but here are the basics: The standard Disney Dining Plan includes one table-service meal, one quick-service meal, and one snack per person per day. If you plan carefully, you can have plenty of culinary adventures by using two of your table-service credits to experience (a) princess character dining, (b) a dinner show, or (c) one of Disney's signature restaurants, such as Cítricos, Flying Fish, or the California Grill. When you purchase the dining plan, you'll receive a brochure outlining all of your options.

"We were all about the credit combining," said a dad from Texas. "On a couple of days we ate fast food all three meals, so each member of our family had two table-service credits left over. We combined those for our breakfast in Cinderella Castle, which turned out to be a major cost savings. I almost passed out when I ran the numbers for how much that breakfast would have cost us otherwise."

The basic dining plan is the most popular, but there are other options. It's certainly possible to upgrade to the deluxe or wine-and-dine plans, but if your kids are young it's unlikely you'll want to spend that much time in restaurants. "In order to make sure our investment in the deluxe plan paid off, we scheduled lots of table-service meals," wrote one mother. "By the second day my husband was complaining that he felt like a slave to all of our reservations and we ended up canceling quite a few, which was disappointing.

But we decided as first-time visitors we'd be better off spending that time in the parks."

At the other end of the spectrum is the quick-service plan, which includes two quick-service meals and a snack per person per day. This plan is about 30% cheaper than the standard one, and some families prefer it, especially those with preschoolers who quickly grow impatient at full-service restaurants.

> **INSIDER'S SECRET**
>
> Disney's quick-service restaurant hours are sometimes changed or shortened during the off-season, but signature restaurants are always open.

Once you're in Orlando, your dining plan info is loaded onto your ticket/resort ID card or MagicBand, and the system keeps track of how you're doing—in fact, each time you use the card your server will give you a receipt showing the remaining balance. Remember that your number of meals is tied to the number of nights (not days) you're staying. If you remain all day on your last day, you'll probably run out of meals.

Making Reservations

The system works like this: A reservation doesn't hold the restaurant to a specific time for seating you, but rather guarantees you the next available table after you arrive. Let's say you made reservations for four people at 7 pm. When you show up at 7, your table won't be waiting with your name on it, but you will be given the next available table for four. Waits average between 10 and 20 minutes, but it's still far better than walking in with no prior arrangement.

But the reservations policy has also had some unintended side effects. Families not sure of exactly where they would be each night were making multiple reservations for each evening, resulting in a 30% no-show rate for many restaurants. The restaurants, thinking they were full, were turning away people and losing money. It didn't take Disney long to amend the policy. Now there's a new cancellation policy at the upscale restaurants and character meals. A credit card is required to make the reservation, and a $10 fee is charged for no-shows. If you cancel the reservation in advance, the fee is waived.

A mom from New Jersey offered this counsel: "Get to your reservation a few minutes early. They'll seat you in the order that you arrive and check in, so someone arriving at 5:50 for a 6 pm reservation gets the jump on the other six people who have reservations for the same time."

How do you make reservations? You can either call ☎ 407/939–3463 (☎ 407/WDW–DINE) or make them online up to 180 days in advance of the day for which you want reservations. Admittedly, this requires some planning. Ideally, you'll sketch out a general schedule for each day and evening of your vacation, so you'll know that on Tuesday you're having dinner at Epcot and on Saturday you're having a character breakfast.

If you've arrived at Disney without dining reservations, you can try to get last-minute slots by calling ☎ 407/939–3463 as soon as you know where you want to eat. Call with your cell phone while you're in line for a ride, or, if you're staying at an on-site hotel, you can press the dining button on your hotel-room phone. You won't get Saturday-night seating at California Grill by waiting until you get there, but if you're flexible about where and when you eat, finding last-minute reservations is possible. The My Disney Experience app is also helpful for finding restaurants on the fly.

A mom from Virginia added, "Even if the system tells you there's no availability, you can always just show up at the restaurant and talk to the hostess. What the dining line and Guest Relations [and app] can't know is if there have been any no-shows that night, but the hostess certainly knows, and sometimes they can work you in. Using this method on a recent trip, we were seated at two restaurants that the reservations guide had assured us were totally booked."

There are quite a few buffets at Disney World and, for families, they solve certain problems: The food is available immediately, and there are plenty of options for picky eaters. But consider working some full-service venues into your week as well. As one mother from Oregon wrote, "The fast-food and buffet venues have the same hectic atmosphere as the parks—you still have to stand in a line, carry things, and try to keep an eye on the kids in the meantime. And they're so loud, especially the character meals! We had an elegant, wonderfully relaxing lunch at the Brown Derby one day, and my husband said it was the perfect getaway from theme-park chaos—almost as if we'd gone back to our hotel room for a break."

If you're worried that the kids will get antsy during a full-service dinner, rest assured that Disney is all about getting the food out fast. The kiddie menus have games and puzzles, and waiters will bring out crayons, crackers, and drinks with lids to keep the kids busy while you wait.

Finding Healthy Food

Disney has removed trans fats from all of its meals, making it easier to feel better about grabbing snacks. You'll also find health-conscious choices in the kids' meals—fruit instead of chips and milk or water instead of soda, for instance. Healthy choices are clearly indicated on all menus, including quick service, with a "Mickey check," and there is at least one low-fat and one vegetarian entrée at every full-service restaurant.

Guests give Disney chefs major (trans-fat-free) brownie points for their willingness to address specific dietary needs. The chefs at full-service restaurants prefer advance warning (you can note any special dietary requests when you make your reservations) but they are also pretty adept at meeting guests' needs with shorter notice, as evidenced by this New Jersey mother's story. "I've been on a weight-loss plan for several months and am happy to have lost 50 pounds. But the very thought of going to Disney World terrified me. I pictured nothing but grease and sugar. Our very first meal was at the Brown Derby restaurant in Hollywood, and when I asked the server a question about how something was prepared she said 'Just a minute.' Almost immediately the chef came out and he practically created a new entrée for me on the spot. After that, I asked to speak to the chef every time we sat down for a meal. My son started calling me 'The Dining Room Diva.'"

Another mother wrote, "Both of my sons, ages 4 and 7, are allergic to dairy, eggs, and nuts, and dining out is usually a challenge for us. We had reserved a character dinner at the Crystal Palace, and after I spoke to the chef about our dietary restrictions, he couldn't have been more wonderful. He walked me through the buffet pointing out which foods would be safe and which were risky, and he made a special batch of pasta just for our boys. For dessert he brought them banana splits using the same soy ice cream we buy at home. They were in their glory!"

Rating the Disney Restaurants

The restaurant descriptions that make up the bulk of this chapter cover only full-service sit-down restaurants. We decided not to overwhelm you with full descriptions of all of the 100-plus food-service venues throughout Walt Disney World and to focus instead on restaurants where you're apt to be spending more time and more money and will thus have higher expectations.

Definition of Quick-Guide Ratings

Food Quality
★★★ Exceptionally good
★★   Tasty food
★   Okay in a pinch

Price for an Adult Meal (Main Course plus Appetizer)

$$$ Expensive; about $30 and up
$$ Moderate; about $15–$30
$ Inexpensive; about $15

🐇 Reservations

In most cases, full-service restaurants at Walt Disney World draw average-size crowds. In high season most will fill to capacity, so you should make reservations. If you're touring in the off-season or dining at off-hours, you should be able to make reservations at the last minute or be seated as a walk-in. (But at Walt Disney World there are still some restaurants where you simply will not get a table by showing up at the last minute without a reservation.)

For each restaurant, we have indicated the length of time in advance you should make a reservation. However, some restaurants do not accept reservations unless you have a party of 10 or more. Instead, you can show up at an off time and get a beeper, then shop nearby while you wait for a table. For these restaurants only, we indicate "Reservations not accepted."

Best Quick-Service Restaurants

IN THE MAGIC KINGDOM: BE OUR GUEST RESTAURANT

Be Our Guest, the newest restaurant in the Magic Kingdom, is delicious, elegant—and crowded. One visitor had this to say: "Service was slow, and the main dining room is noisy. But the food—mostly French-influenced soups and sandwiches—is good, and the atmosphere is nothing short of amazing!" To beat out the lines, make a reservation as far in advance as possible. Note that the quick-service menu is only for breakfast and lunch; at dinner, Be Our Guest turns into a sit-down restaurant. In early 2015, Disney started breakfast service here.

AT EPCOT: LES HALLES BOULANGERIE & PÂTISSERIE (FRANCE PAVILION)

The Boulangerie & Pâtisserie has always been a popular spot for delicious pastries and sandwiches, although the experience of dining there was marred by the almost insanely cramped location. A recent expansion has made the line more manageable and created additional seating, thus returning the patisserie to the top of our Epcot quick-service list.

AT DISNEY'S HOLLYWOOD STUDIOS: PIZZA PLANET ARCADE

One of the ironies of the Hollywood Studios is that it has some of the most interesting and cleverly themed full-service restaurants of any park, but the quick-service offerings have always been rather blah. Pizza Planet offers good standard pizza and fast service in a setting that will keep the kids happy.

IN THE ANIMAL KINGDOM: FLAME TREE BARBECUE

Smoked ribs, chicken, and sandwiches and—best of all—a large shady patio for dining.

Suitability for Kids

These ratings, found in the chapter's Quick Guide, will tell you how family-friendly a particular restaurant is. Even at Walt Disney World, some restaurants are not appropriate for kids.

🦢🦢🦢 The restaurant is informal, with food choices designed to appeal to kids. There may be some sort of entertainment going on, or perhaps the setting itself is interesting.

🦢🦢 This restaurant is casual and family-oriented.

🦢 This is one of WDW's more adult restaurants, with sophisticated menu choices and leisurely service.

🕐 Meals Served

B is for breakfast, L is for lunch, and D is for dinner.

Magic Kingdom Restaurants

$$$
★★★
🦢🦢🦢

BE OUR GUEST

Tucked away in Fantasyland, Be Our Guest doesn't look that imposing at first. But once you step through the castle doors, prepare to be amazed by the elegant chandeliers, the detailed statues, and an exact replica of the unforgettable ballroom from Disney's *Beauty and the Beast.* The West Wing is a real treat, covered with slashed tapestries, ripped curtains, and Beast's magic rose, which loses a petal amid simulated thunder every 20 minutes. The food gives a nod to its French setting, but there are plenty of options for kids or picky eaters. Reservations can be made for all meals served here. Note that this is also the only place in the Magic Kingdom where beer and wine are served, but they are only served when Be Our Guest becomes a full-service restaurant at night. In early 2015, Disney started breakfast service here. Bon appétit! ✉ *Magic Kingdom, Fantasyland* ☎ *407/939-3463 (* 📠 *407/WDW-DINE)* 🌐 *www.disneyworld.com* 🍽 *6 months* 🕐 *B, L, D.*

$$$
★★★

CINDERELLA'S ROYAL TABLE

High amid the spires of Cinderella Castle in Fantasyland, this restaurant offers the most dramatic views in the Magic Kingdom. The food, which is expensive, is admittedly elegantly presented—although the three-star rating is more the result of the overall experience than the cuisine. Cinderella's Royal Table is the home of the princess character meals, the toughest ticket in all of Disney World. A mother of two from Virginia reported, "It took us three days to get through the phone line for the princess breakfast in the Magic Kingdom, but it was well worth it! My 4-year-old daughter wore her Cinderella dress, and she loved all the special attention she received. It was a year ago and she still talks about it." "Too magical for words," agreed the mom of a five-year-old in Maine. ✉ *Magic Kingdom, Cinderella Castle* ☎ *407/939-3463 (☎ 407/WDW-DINE)* ⊕ *www.disneyworld.com* ⚐ *6 months* ⊙ *B, L, D.*

$$
★★

THE CRYSTAL PALACE

Winnie the Pooh and friends circulate among diners—and everybody agrees that that's cool, but there's a real difference of opinion on the quality of the food. Consider this report from a Texas mother of two: "In general I dislike buffets, but the food here was far better than I expected, and our children absolutely loved the ice-cream-sundae bar. (Even though things got so messy that we did have to change their shirts after lunch!) The Crystal Palace would be a good choice even if it didn't have the Pooh characters." But a mother from Florida was less pleased, writing, "You might want to reevaluate your rating on this one. We showed up starving but hardly anyone, including the children, found anything on the buffet they were willing to eat." ✉ *Magic Kingdom, Main Street* ☎ *407/939-3463 (☎ 407/WDW-DINE)* ⊕ *www.disneyworld.com* ⚐ *4 months* ⊙ *B, L, D.*

$$
★★

LIBERTY TREE TAVERN

In Liberty Square and decorated in a style reminiscent of Colonial Williamsburg, the Tavern serves salads, sandwiches, and New England clam chowder at lunch. The evening menu is an all-you-can-eat Thanksgiving-style feast with turkey and stuffing, flank steak, mac and cheese, and other family favorites. ✉ *Magic King-dom, Liberty Square* ☎ *407/939–3463* (🖷 *407/WDW–DINE*) ⊕ *www.disneyworld.com* ⚱ *4 months* ⏰ *L, D.*

$$
★
🐚🐚

THE PLAZA RESTAURANT

The salads, sandwiches, and burgers here are very filling—but also very bland. The restaurant has a wide selection of treats from the Ice Cream Parlor next door. ✉ *Magic Kingdom, Main Street* ☎ *407/939–3463* (🖷 *407/WDW–DINE*) ⊕ *www.disneyworld.com* ⚱ *4 months* ⏰ *L, D.*

$$
★★
🐚🐚🐚

TONY'S TOWN SQUARE RESTAURANT

Located in the Main Street Hub, this thoroughly enjoyable restaurant is dedicated to *Lady and the Tramp,* with scenes from the film dotting the walls and a statue of the canine romantics in the center. The cuisine, like that of the café where Tramp wooed Lady, is classic Italian, and the portions are generous. ✉ *Magic Kingdom, Main Street* ☎ *407/939–3463* (🖷 *407/WDW–DINE*) ⊕ *www.disneyworld.com* ⚱ *4 months* ⏰ *L, D.*

Epcot Restaurants

$$
★★
🐚🐚🐚

AKERSHUS ROYAL BANQUET HALL

This lovely castlelike restaurant in the Norway pavilion has a large buffet with some Norwegian food as well as some American staples. Even better, Akershus offers princess-theme character dining at breakfast, lunch, and dinner, which takes some of the pressure off the popular Cinderella Castle breakfast in the Magic Kingdom. But you'll still need to make reservations 180 days in advance. ✉ *Epcot, Norway* ☎ *407/939–3463* (🖷 *407/WDW–DINE*) ⊕ *www.disneyworld.com* ⚱ *6 months* ⏰ *B, L, D.*

$$
★★

BIERGARTEN RESTAURANT

There's plenty of room to move about in this German beer hall where yodelers and an oompah-pah band get the whole crowd involved in singing and dancing. The all-you-can-eat buffet features traditional Bavarian dishes: bratwurst, spaetzle, and various salads. ⊠ *Epcot, Germany* ☎ *407/939–3463 (☎ 407/WDW–DINE)* ⊕ *www.disneyworld.com* ⚑ *2 months* ⊙ *L, D.*

$$$ CORAL REEF
★★★

One whole wall of this restaurant is glass, giving you a remarkable view of the Seas' tank. Watching the fish keeps the kids entertained while parents browse the menu, which features, naturally, upscale seafood dishes. ⊠ *Epcot, The Seas* ☎ *407/939–3463 (☎ 407/WDW–DINE)* ⊕ *www.disneyworld.com* ⚑ *2 months* ⊙ *D.*

$$$ GARDEN GRILL RESTAURANT
★★

Easily recognizable American dishes make this a good choice for younger children. The restaurant is on a revolving platform, allowing you to observe scenes from the Living with the Land boat ride below. There's character dining in the evening. ⊠ *Epcot, The Land* ☎ *407/939–3463 (☎ 407/WDW–DINE)* ⊕ *www.disneyworld. com* ⚑ *6 months* ⊙ *L, D.*

$$ LA HACIENDA DE SAN ANGEL
★★

This restaurant offers more upscale Mexican cuisine than its sister restaurant, San Angel Inn Restaurante, featuring *parrillada* (mixed grills), short ribs, and create-your-own tacos. The best part of the dining experience is the perfect view the restaurant offers of the fireworks during IllumiNations! ⊠ *Epcot, Mexico* ☎ *407/939–3463 (☎ 407/WDW–DINE)* ⊕ *www.disneyworld.com* ⚑ *4 months* ⊙ *D.*

$$$ LE CELLIER STEAKHOUSE
★★★

Le Cellier is one of the most popular restaurants in Epcot, perhaps because there are relatively few steak houses in Disney World. The steaks here are excellent, as is the salmon, and the desserts are as big as the prairies of Alberta. ⊠ *Epcot, Canada* ☎ *407/939–3463 (☎ 407/WDW–DINE)* ⊕ *www.disneyworld.com* ⚑ *6 months* ⊙ *L, D.*

$$$
★★
👐👐

LES CHEFS DE FRANCE

Modeled after the sidewalk cafés of Paris, this restaurant bustles pleasantly. The classical French menu is a bit hit-or-miss in quality, but the waiters are charming, and you can gaze out at the World Showcase action. With any luck, you might even spot the charming Remy from *Ratatouille,* certainly one of the less frequently seen characters in the park. ✉ *Epcot, France* ☎ *407/939-3463 (*☎ *407/WDW-DINE)* 🌐 *www.disneyworld.com* 🍴 *2 months* 🕐 *L, D.*

$$$
★★
👐

MONSIEUR PAUL

Monsieur Paul, named after famed chef Paul Bocuse, is quieter, calmer, and more elegant than its sister restaurant, Chefs de France. It's also a tad too civilized for kids under 12, and thus perfect for an adult night out. Tucked away and accessible only by a staircase, Monsieur Paul is only open at night, when it offers beautiful views of the World Showcase Lagoon. Expect classic French cuisine—such as black-truffle soup, herb-crusted rack of lamb, and Grand Marnier soufflé—a wonderful wine selection, and Continental service. ✉ *Epcot, France* ☎ *407/939-3463 (*☎ *407/WDW-DINE)* 🌐 *www.disneyworld.com* 🍴 *4 months* 🕐 *D.*

$$
★★
👐

NINE DRAGONS RESTAURANT

Nine Dragons has taken the concept of an exhibition kitchen to new levels. Easily recognizable Chinese dishes are on the menu, along with more exotic offerings from five different cooking stations. ✉ *Epcot, China* ☎ *407/939-3463 (*☎ *407/WDW-DINE)* 🌐 *www.disneyworld.com* 🍴 *2 months* 🕐 *L, D.*

$$
★★
👐

RESTAURANT MARRAKESH

Ready for exotic surroundings and unusual entertainment? Kids enjoy the belly dancers, and the ladies sometimes invite them to enter into the act. The unfamiliarity of the food may pose a problem, but if the kids can be persuaded to give it a try, they'll find that roasted chicken tastes pretty much the same the world over. ✉ *Epcot, Morocco* ☎ *407/939-3463 (*☎ *407/WDW-DINE)* 🌐 *www.disneyworld.com* 🍴 *2 months* 🕐 *L, D.*

$$
★★

ROSE & CROWN PUB & DINING ROOM

This charming bar and restaurant has live entertainment, friendly service, and upscale pub grub such as fish-and-chips and meat pies. If you eat on the patio, you have a great view of the World Showcase Lagoon. ✉ *Epcot, United Kingdom* ☎ *407/939–3463 (☎ 407/WDW–DINE)* ⊕ *www.disneyworld.com* ⪡ *4 months* ⏲ *L, D.*

$$
★★

SAN ANGEL INN RESTAURANTE

A beautiful location inside the Mayan pyramid of the Mexico pavilion, with the Rio del Tiempo murmuring in the background, makes this restaurant a charming choice. The service is swift and friendly, and older kids can browse among the market stalls of the pavilion or even ride the Gran Fiesta Tour while waiting for their food. ✉ *Epcot, Mexico* ☎ *407/939–3463 (☎ 407/WDW–DINE)* ⊕ *www.disneyworld.com* ⪡ *4 months* ⏲ *L, D.*

$$
★★

SPICE ROAD TABLE

Spice Road Table serves Mediterranean tapas-style small plates in a beautiful waterside setting in Morocco. Look for lamb sliders, calamari, and other tasty tidbits. Because of the sophistication of the cuisine, this isn't the best choice for young kids, but it's a great spot for parents to take a break for a glass of wine in a relaxed and pleasant environment. ✉ *Epcot, Morocco* ☎ *407/939–3463 (☎ 407/WDW–DINE)* ⊕ *www.disneyworld.com* ⪡ *4 months* ⏲ *L, D.*

$$
★★★

TEPPAN EDO

In the Japan pavilion, Teppan Edo offers grilled specialties at large tables, in front of which the chefs slice and dice in the best Benihana tradition. Upscale options such as Wagyu and Kobe beef are available. It's terrifically entertaining for the kids—the chefs often jazz up the presentation even more in their honor—and the stir-fried, simply prepared food is a hit with all ages. A father of four from Ohio wrote a rave review: "Japan is a good choice if you want to eat out in Epcot with kids. The chefs toss food and catch it in their hats, make silly jokes like throwing the butter and saying 'butterfly.' And one time when we were in, they had a lady making origami animals for the children. Plus, since they cook at the table, you get your food really fast." ✉ *Epcot, Japan* ☎ *407/939-3463 (☎407/WDW-DINE)* ⊕ *www.disneyworld.com* ⌚ *4 months* ⏱ *L, D.*

$$
★★
👐

TOKYO DINING

Connected to Teppan Edo is a delightful sushi bar called Tokyo Dining, where you'll find great Japanese food without the fun but admittedly time-consuming ceremony of the full-fledged restaurant. Grilled steak and chicken are available for any sushi-shy members of the party. ✉ *Epcot, Japan* ☎ *407/939-3463 (☎407/WDW-DINE)* ⊕ *www.disneyworld.com* ⌚ *2 months* ⏱ *L, D.*

> **HELPFUL HINT**
>
> **Choose one of these great restaurants for a parents' night out away from the kids:**
> - ✦ California Grill
> - ✦ Cítricos
> - ✦ Jiko
> - ✦ Monsieur Paul
> - ✦ Victoria & Albert's

$$$
★★★
👐👐

TUTTO ITALIA RISTORANTE

Expect authentic Italian food, equally authentic waiters, and a lovely setting, which, because it's tucked away in the far reaches of the Italy pavilion, actually feels a little secluded, at least by Disney World standards. The food is top-notch, especially the calamari. ✉ *Epcot, Italy* ☎ *407/939-3463 (☎407/WDW-DINE)* ⊕ *www.disneyworld.com* ⌚ *4 months* ⏱ *L, D.*

$$
★★★
👐👐👐

VIA NAPOLI RISTORANTE E PIZZERIA

The pizzas emerge from giant wood-burning ovens—each oven named after a volcano—and they're incredibly tasty. The truffle-oil pizza alone is enough to induce a swoon. You sit at large tables, and the waiters bustle, so Via Napoli isn't exactly fine dining or a break from the stress of the theme parks, but the food is excellent and reasonably priced, and the servers are adorable. ✉ *Epcot, Italy* ☎ *407/939-3463 (☎407/WDW-DINE)* ⊕ *www.disneyworld.com* ⌚ *2 months* ⏱ *L, D.*

Hollywood Studios Restaurants

$$
★★★
☁☁☁

'50S PRIME TIME CAFÉ

With its kitschy decor and ditzy servers, this restaurant is almost an attraction in itself. Meat loaf, macaroni, milk shakes, and other comfort foods are served in a 1950s-style kitchen, while dozens of TVs blare clips from classic shows in the background. "Hi kids," says your waitress, pulling up a chair to the Formica-top table. "You didn't leave your bikes in the driveway, did you? Let me see those hands." Assuming you pass her clean-fingernails inspection, "Mom" will go on to advise you on your food choices. "I'll bring peas with that. Vegetables are good for you." The camp is lost on young kids, but they love the no-frills food and the fact that Mom brings around crayons and coloring books, then hangs their artwork on the front of a refrigerator with magnets. It's parents, raised on reruns of the sitcoms that the restaurant spoofs, who really adore this restaurant. "You just have to get in the mood of the place," advised a mother of one from Illinois. "The whole routine about being on a TV show is very corny and very funny, and the servers are great. We liked the food (chicken, pot roast, steak, salads, the basics), but when we left, my 8-year-old daughter said 'That was a good show,' and I think that's exactly the way you need to think of it." ⊠ *Hollywood Studios, Echo Lake* ☎ *407/939–3463 (*☎ *407/WDW–DINE)* ⊕ *www.disneyworld. com* ⌛ *6 months* ⊘ *L, D.*

$
★★
☁☁☁

HOLLYWOOD & VINE

This large, attractive, art deco "buffeteria" serves classic American dishes at breakfast, lunch, and dinner. Lines move quickly, and the variety makes this a good choice for families. It's the only character-dining venue in Disney World to feature characters from the popular Disney Junior television shows. That alone guarantees that you'll find plenty of toddlers and preschoolers at every meal. ⊠ *Hollywood Studios, Echo Lake* ☎ *407/939–3463 (*☎ *407/WDW–DINE)* ⊕ *www.disneyworld.com* ⌛ *4 months* ⊘ *B, L, D.*

THE HOLLYWOOD BROWN DERBY

$$$
★★★
🦐

A signature Cobb salad as well as veal, pasta, and fresh seafood are served at the Derby, where, just as you'd expect, caricatures of movie stars line the walls. The food is quite sophisticated considering that you're inside a theme park, and the restaurant itself is elegant and lovely, like stepping back into Hollywood in its heyday. The wine program, which offers suggested pairings by the glass with each entrée, is one of the best in Disney World. ✉ *Hollywood Studios, Hollywood Boulevard* ☎ *407/939–3463 (*☎ *407/WDW–DINE)* ⊕ *www.disneyworld.com* 🗓 *4 months* ⊙ *L, D.*

MAMA MELROSE'S RISTORANTE ITALIANO

$$
★★
🦐🦐

This restaurant is tucked away near the Muppet*Vision 3D plaza, and the out-of-the-way location means that you can sometimes squeeze in without advance reservations. Expect a casual New York feel and quick service. Mama's serves gourmet flatbreads from a wood-burning oven and a wide variety of pasta dishes; the penne *alla vodka* is a favorite. ✉ *Hollywood Studios, Streets of America* ☎ *407/939–3463 (*☎ *407/WDW–DINE)* ⊕ *www. disneyworld.com* 🗓 *2 months* ⊙ *L, D.*

SCI-FI DINE-IN THEATER RESTAURANT

$$
★★
🦐🦐🦐

At least as campy as the '50s Prime Time Café, the Sci-Fi seats you in vintage cars while hokey movie clips run on a giant screen. Offerings range from drive-in staples like milk shakes and popcorn all the way to seafood and St. Louis–style ribs. Older kids adore the setting and the funny waiters; in fact, they often get so absorbed in the old movie clips that they sit quietly while parents relax in the backseat. Younger kids, in contrast, might be spooked. "Only okay food but really very fun," said one mom, while another wrote, "My 4-year-old was so freaked out by the atmosphere we had to leave early." ✉ *Hollywood Studios, Commissary Lane* ☎ *407/939–3463 (*☎ *407/WDW–DINE)* ⊕ *www.disneyworld.com* 🗓 *2 months* ⊙ *L, D.*

Animal Kingdom Restaurants

$$ ★★ RAINFOREST CAFÉ

The jungle motif and large aquariums make the Rainforest Café fun for kids. The food is nothing special but tasty enough, with an emphasis on appetizers and other simple meals, like burgers, sandwiches, and huge salads. There are locations at both the Animal Kingdom and Downtown Disney. ⊠ *Animal Kingdom, Main Entrance* ☏ *407/939–3463* (☏ *407/WDW–DINE*) ⊕ *www.disneyworld. com* ⌖ *Reservations not accepted* ⊗ *B, L, D.*

$$ ★★ TUSKER HOUSE RESTAURANT

The Tusker House is a favorite with families, offering buffets with a lot of variety and popular character meals. "We tried this character breakfast when we got closed out of the ones at the Magic Kingdom," said one dad, "But it turned out to be a real treat. Good food, fun character presentation, and it moved fast—everything we needed." ⊠ *Animal Kingdom, Africa* ☏ *407/939–3463* (☏ *407/ WDW–DINE*) ⊕ *www.disneyworld.com* ⌖ *4 months* ⊗ *B, L, D.*

$$ ★★ YAK & YETI

This Asian-fusion restaurant in the Asia section offers full-service dining, casual outdoor dining, a full bar, and a beer garden. The food is quite good, and the setting, while campy, is the most adult and relaxing of all the Animal Kingdom restaurants. ⊠ *Animal Kingdom, Asia* ☏ *407/939–3463* (☏ *407/WDW–DINE*) ⊕ *www. disneyworld.com* ⌖ *2 months* ⊗ *L, D.*

Restaurants in the WDW Hotels

$$ ★★★ ARTIST POINT

The most upscale of the Wilderness Lodge eateries, Artist Point offers Pacific Northwest–theme food in a casual, faux-rustic setting. The cedar-plank salmon is the house specialty, and the wine list highlights excellent selections from the Pacific Northwest.

✉ *Wilderness Lodge, 901 Timberline Dr.* ☎ *407/939–3463 (☎ 407/ WDW–DINE)* ⊕ *www.disneyworld.com* ⌂ *4 months* ⊙ *D.*

$ ★★ 🐾🐾 BIG RIVER GRILLE & BREWING WORKS

WDW's only on-site brewpub is a good place to sample new beers and a couple of specialty ales. The food—mostly sand-wiches and salads—is pedestrian, but the pleasant patio allows you to take in the action of the BoardWalk while you sip your beer. ✉ *BoardWalk, 2101 Epcot Resorts Blvd.* ☎ *407/939–3463 (☎ 407/WDW–DINE)* ⊕ *www.disneyworld.com* ⌂ *Reservations not accepted* ⊙ *L, D.*

$ ★★ 🐾🐾 BOATWRIGHT'S DINING HALL

Boatwright's is the only full-service restaurant in Port Orleans, located in the Riverside section. The food is a mixture of Cajun specialties and American classics, and there are some interesting additions, such as a selection of microbrews from New Orleans. The Southern-inspired dessert menu—which includes an excel-lent pecan pie—rounds out the meal. One word of warning: Since the restaurant is adjacent to the food court and has an open-wall design, it's always loud. The designation "dining hall" is accu-rate. ✉ *Port Orleans, Riverside, 1251 Riverside Dr.* ☎ *407/939–3463 (☎ 407/WDW–DINE)* ⊕ *www.disneyworld.com* ⌂ *Reservations not necessary* ⊙ *B, D.*

$$$ ★★★ 🐾🐾 BOMA—FLAVORS OF AFRICA

This large family restaurant in the Animal Kingdom Lodge of-fers one of the best breakfast buffets in all of Walt Disney World. You can find the usual American classics, like eggs and pancakes, plus excellent grilled sausage and an outstanding selection of breads and pastries. The dinner buffet features African-inspired dishes, including wonderful grilled meats and a variety of whole-some grain dishes and salads. "The food was fresh and beauti-fully prepared," said a mom from Georgia. "Both the kids and the adults loved it." ✉ *Animal Kingdom Lodge, 2901 Osceola Pkwy.* ☎ *407/939–3463 (☎ 407/WDW–DINE)* ⊕ *www.disneyworld.com* ⌂ *4 months* ⊙ *B, D.*

CALIFORNIA GRILL

$$$
★★★

Widely acknowledged to be the best restaurant in all of Disney World, California Grill is very popular and always crowded. (One clue to the quality: Disney executives dine here.) "We used two dining plan table-service credits," reported one mother of three from Alabama, "but it was totally worth it. The only problem is we ate our first meal there and it set the bar so high that nothing else compared. We spent the rest of the vacation saying 'It's okay, but it's not the California Grill.'" Not only is the food excellent and stylishly presented, but the views from the top of the Contemporary are unparalleled, especially during the Magic Kingdom fireworks.

Note: Although fabulous to begin with, the California Grill has recently undergone a redesign of both the decor and menu. Disney chefs traveled to Napa and Sonoma to consult with some of the best chefs in the country to make sure the menu reflects authentic California cuisine. And the new layout of the tables and booths ensures even better views of the Magic Kingdom fireworks. ✉ *Contemporary Resort, 4600 N. World Dr.* ☎ *407/939–3463 (*☎ *407/WDW–DINE)* ⊕ *www.disneyworld.com* ⚓ *6 months* ☺ *D.*

CAPE MAY CAFÉ

$$
★★

Our readers give high marks to this bright and airy eatery in the heart of the Beach Club. It has an excellent seafood buffet at dinner, featuring shrimp, clams, mussels, and a couple of land-lubber choices. The breakfast buffet, during which the characters, dressed in adorable old-fashioned bathing attire, circulate among the diners, is very popular. Consider this report from a grandmother of four from Ohio: "We wouldn't consider it a trip to Walt Disney World without a stop at the Beach Club's Cape May Café. It's a family tradition, and the food is wonderful. We always leave the theme parks in the afternoon to take a nap, and Cape May is the perfect place to eat dinner before you go back into Epcot to see IllumiNations." ✉ *Beach Club Resort, 1700 Epcot Resorts Blvd.* ☎ *407/939–3463 (*☎ *407/WDW–DINE)* ⊕ *www. disneyworld.com* ⚓ *2 months* ☺ *B, D.*

$$ ★★ CAPTAIN'S GRILLE

This restaurant, off the main drag in the Yacht Club Resort, serves fish, chicken, and beef in a pleasant nautical-theme room. The enormous breakfasts offer hearty eaters the chance to load up for a day of touring. ✉ *Yacht Club Resort, 1700 Epcot Resorts Blvd.* ☎ *407/939–3463 (☎ 407/WDW–DINE)* ⊕ *www.disneyworld. com* ⚓ *2 months* ◷ *B, L, D.*

$$ ★★ CHEF MICKEY'S

The Contemporary Resort is one of the best places in Disney World for a character breakfast, lunch, or dinner. As Mickey and the crew wander among the diners, the monorail whisks by overhead. The buffet has classic American breakfast food in the morning and family-pleasing standards like pasta, chicken, and roast beef in the evening, plus a sundae bar for the kids. A father of three from New Jersey echoed the reports of many of our readers: "Chef Mickey's is definitely the way to go if you want to see the basic old-fashioned Disney characters like Mickey and Goofy. The buffet was great, and the characters spent plenty of time with our sons." ✉ *Contemporary Resort, 4600 N. World Dr.* ☎ *407/939–3463 (☎ 407/WDW–DINE)* ⊕ *www.disneyworld.com* ⚓ *6 months* ◷ *B, D.*

$$$ ★★★ CÍTRICOS

Cítricos offers Mediterranean cuisine in the Grand Floridian, and the restaurant is known for its outstanding wine list. Up to 20 labels are available by the glass, with a specific wine paired with each appetizer and entrée on the menu. A beautiful setting with consistently delightful cuisine, Cítricos is a real treat for a parents' night out. ✉ *Grand Floridian, 4401 Floridian Way* ☎ *407/939–3463 (☎ 407/WDW–DINE)* ⊕ *www.disneyworld.com* ⚓ *2 months* ◷ *D.*

$ ★ ESPN CLUB

Anchoring one end of the BoardWalk, the ESPN Club is better known for broadcasting sports events than for its food. "Our teenaged sons loved going to the ESPN Club on a Sunday during football season," wrote one mom of three from Pennsylvania. "The place was packed with people from all over the country, all wearing jerseys and screaming for their teams. We should have packed our Eagles jerseys—next time we'll know!" Menu choices include buffalo wings, burgers, nachos, and, of course, plenty of beer. There's an arcade next door to entertain the kids. ⊠ *BoardWalk, 2101 Epcot Resorts Blvd.* ☎ *407/939–3463* (☎ *407/WDW–DINE*) ⊕ *www.disneyworld.com* ⌂ *Reservations not accepted* ⊙ *L, D.*

$$$ FLYING FISH CAFÉ
★★★

The zany art deco decor is by Martin Dorf, who also designed the California Grill and Cítricos. The menu is updated frequently but generally includes wonderful seafood, delicious steaks, and excellent risottos. The service is outstanding, even by Disney standards. If you haven't made reservations, you can always dine at the bar and watch the chefs at work. ⊠ *BoardWalk, 2101 Epcot Resorts Blvd.* ☎ *407/939–3463* (☎ *407/WDW–DINE*) ⊕ *www.disneyworld.com* ⌂ *4 months* ⊙ *D.*

$$ GRAND FLORIDIAN CAFÉ
★★

If you'd like a good, solid meal of traditional favorites, simply served, with a pretty view of the Grand Floridian grounds, this place is for you. The menu tilts to the South—fried chicken, local fish, and key lime pie. ⊠ *Grand Floridian, 4401 Floridian Way* ☎ *407/939–3463* (☎ *407/WDW–DINE*) ⊕ *www.disneyworld.com* ⌂ *Reservations not necessary* ⊙ *B, L, D.*

$$ GULLIVER'S GRILL AT GARDEN GROVE
★★

This is the largest restaurant in the Swan, and it has a bit of a split personality. In the morning and at lunch it's an upscale coffee shop. In the evening it becomes Gulliver's Grill, with more elaborate dining. Weekend character breakfasts are also available, but they don't get very high marks from our readers. "Overpriced, with so-so food, and even the characters seemed bored," wrote one mom from Georgia. "Our other character meal was at Chef Mickey's, and there was no comparison." ⊠ *Walt Disney World Swan, 1200 Epcot Resorts Blvd.* ☎ *407/939–3463* (☎ *407/WDW–DINE*) ⊕ *www.disneyworld.com* ⌂ *4 months* ⊙ *B, L, D.*

IL MULINO

$$ ★★ ☾☾

The Swan Resort is home to this recently revamped trattoria, which serves a huge variety of upscale pasta in a pleasant, open setting. ✉ *Walt Disney World Swan, 1200 Epcot Resorts Blvd.* ☎ *407/939–3463 (☎ 407/WDW–DINE)* ⊕ *www.disneyworld.com* ⌂ *4 months* ⏲ *D.*

JIKO

$$$ ★★★ ☾☾

Jiko (Swahili for "cooking place") is the flagship restaurant of the Animal Kingdom Lodge, and the menu features contemporary African cuisine with an emphasis on fresh vegetables, grains, and game. Two wood-burning stoves simulate the effect of cooking in the open bush. "Very exotic with wonderful food and a lovely setting," reported a father of two from New York. "Our server was extremely knowledgeable about the South African wines. We'll be back!" ✉ *Animal Kingdom Lodge, 2901 Osceola Pkwy.* ☎ *407/939–3463 (☎ 407/WDW–DINE)* ⊕ *www.disneyworld.com* ⌂ *4 months* ⏲ *D.*

KIMONOS

$$ ★★

If you love sushi and sashimi, you'll adore this elegant restaurant in the Swan Resort. ✉ *Walt Disney World Swan, 1200 Epcot Resorts Blvd.* ☎ *407/939–3463 (☎ 407/WDW–DINE)* ⊕ *www. disneyworld.com* ⌂ *2 months* ⏲ *D.*

KONA CAFÉ

$$ ★★ ☾☾

The Kona Café offers Pacific Rim food with a tropical emphasis. The crab cakes are delicious, and the desserts alone make the Kona worth the trip. Situated in the Polynesian, this is also one of the best places among all the Magic Kingdom resorts for breakfast. ✉ *Polynesian Resort, 1600 Seven Seas Dr.* ☎ *407/939–3463 (☎ 407/ WDW–DINE)* ⊕ *www.disneyworld.com* ⌂ *2 months* ⏲ *B, L, D.*

MAYA GRILL

$ ★

Maya Grill, in Disney's Coronado Springs Resort, serves steak, pork, chicken, and seafood with a *nuevo* Latin touch. Many of the entrées are grilled over an open fire. Sadly, the quality doesn't always match the variety. ✉ *Coronado Springs Resort, 1000 W. Buena Vista Dr.* ☎ *407/939–3463 (☎ 407/WDW–DINE)* ⊕ *www. disneyworld.com* ♨ *Reservations not necessary* ◷ *B, D.*

$$$
★★
🐚

NARCOOSSEE'S

Inside the white octagonal building on the water at the Grand Floridian, Narcoossee's provides pretty views as well as fresh seafood. As a bonus, you can see the Magic Kingdom fireworks. ✉ *Grand Floridian, 4401 Floridian Way* ☎ *407/939–3463 (☎ 407/ WDW–DINE)* ⊕ *www.disneyworld.com* ♨ *4 months* ◷ *D.*

$$
★★★
🐚🐚🐚

1900 PARK FARE

This large, pleasant Grand Floridian restaurant is appealing to families because it offers character dining and large buffets with kid-pleasing food. Be forewarned—this place is always loud, even when the characters aren't in attendance. ✉ *Grand Floridian, 4401 Floridian Way* ☎ *407/939–3463 (☎ 407/WDW–DINE)* ⊕ *www. disneyworld.com* ♨ *4 months* ◷ *B, D.*

$$
★★
🐚🐚🐚

'OHANA

This fun, family-friendly place—the name, in fact, means "family" in Hawaiian—is in the Polynesian Resort. 'Ohana specializes in skewered meats, teriyaki- and citrus-based sauces, and tropical fruits and vegetables. The food is prepared in a large, open-fire pit, and there's often some sort of activity, such as limbo contests, to keep the kids entertained. "This place is a blast," a mom from North Carolina wrote. "The food is good, and they get it out fast, but the really nice thing is all the activities for the kids, like crazy relay races and hula lessons. We sat down at the table, ordered some of those big tropical umbrella drinks, and just relaxed and watched the kids have a ball." A mom from Massachusetts confirmed, "The service here is excellent. Our waiter was so busy trying to keep our 1-year-old entertained it was almost like having a babysitter." ✉ *Polynesian Resort, 1600 Seven Seas Dr.* ☎ *407/939–3463 (☎ 407/WDW–DINE)* ⊕ *www.disneyworld.com* ♨ *4 months* ◷ *B, D.*

SANAA

$$
★★★

Sanaa, which means "artwork" in Swahili, is one of the most beautifully decorated restaurants at Disney World. Located at Kidani Village, the Vacation Club side of the Animal Kingdom Lodge, it also offers diners a view of the animals on the savanna. The food here is African with a strong Indian influence, a nod to the large number of Indians who have emigrated to South Africa, bringing their delicious cuisine with them. A great choice for adventurous guests, it can be less popular with young children or picky eaters. ✉ *Animal Kingdom Lodge, Kidani Village, 2901 Osceola Pkwy.* ☎ *407/939–3463* (☎ *407/WDW–DINE*) ⊕ *www. disneyworld.com* ⚑ *2 months* ⊙ *D.*

SHULA'S STEAK HOUSE

$$$
★★★

The Dolphin's swankiest steak house is owned by the former Miami Dolphins coach Don Shula. (Nice tie-in!) The restaurant is quite dignified, despite the football theme, and you'll need an NFL-size appetite to finish the 48-ounce porterhouse or 4-pound lobster. Note: This is not, repeat not, a family restaurant. The menu pointedly states, "No children's menu available." ✉ *Walt Disney World Dolphin, 1500 Epcot Resorts Blvd.* ☎ *407/939–3463* (☎ *407/WDW–DINE*) ⊕ *www.disneyworld.com* ⚑ *2 months* ⊙ *D.*

SHUTTERS AT OLD PORT ROYALE

$$
★

Shutters, in the Caribbean Beach Resort, is a casual, island-theme restaurant serving prime rib, lamb chops, and jerk chicken. The food is nothing special, but if you just can't go to Florida without sampling a big, fruity rum drink, this is your kind of place. ✉ *Caribbean Beach Resort, 900 Cayman Way* ☎ *407/939–3463* (☎ *407/ WDW–DINE*) ⊕ *www.disneyworld.com* ⚑ *Reservations not necessary* ⊙ *D.*

TODD ENGLISH'S BLUEZOO

$$$
★★

Famed chef Todd English brought this sleek, contemporary seafood restaurant to the Dolphin. Although it's far too tony in atmosphere and eclectic in menu for most kids, bluezoo is a good spot for drinks or a parents' night out. The menu changes regularly but tends to feature upscale seafood dishes. ✉ *Walt Disney World Dolphin, 1500 Epcot Resorts Blvd.* ☎ *407/939–3463 (☎ 407/ WDW–DINE)* ⊕ *www.disneyworld.com* ⌂ *2 months* ⊙ *D.*

TRATTORIA AL FORNO

$$$
★★★
👶👶

The newest restaurant at the Boardwalk Resort offers an Italian menu featuring such dishes as baked lasagna, linguini alla vongole and T-bone steak Florentine. Expect authentic Italian flavors with plenty of familiar items for kids. Mozzarella is made fresh every day at 4 pm for that evening's dinner service, and 70 Italian wines are offered. ✉ *BoardWalk, 2101 Epcot Resorts Blvd.* ☎ *407/939–3463 (☎ 407/WDW–DINE)* ⊕ *www.disneyworld.com* ⌂ *1 month* ⊙ *B, D.*

VICTORIA & ALBERT'S

$$$
★★★
👶

Extraordinarily elegant cuisine and special attention to details, such as personalized menus, harp music, and roses for the ladies, are the hallmarks of this lovely restaurant in the Grand Floridian. The only AAA five-diamond restaurant in WDW (and the most expensive), V&A is the ultimate spot for a parents' night out. ✉ *Grand Floridian, 4401 Floridian Way* ☎ *407/939–3463 (☎ 407/ WDW–DINE)* ⊕ *www.disneyworld.com* ⌂ *4 months* ⊙ *D.*

THE WAVE ... OF AMERICAN FLAVORS

$$
★★
👶

Located in the Contemporary Resort, The Wave serves a seasonal menu featuring local and regional products as well as organic beers, trendy cocktails, and an international wine list that literally offers a twist: All of the wines have screw tops instead of corks. Breakfast here is terrific, but the other meals don't quite live up to the hype. ✉ *Contemporary Resort, 4600 N. World Dr.* ☎ *407/939–3463 (☎ 407/WDW–DINE)* ⊕ *www.disneyworld.com* ⌂ *Reservations not necessary* ⊙ *B, L, D.*

WHISPERING CANYON CAFÉ

$$
★★

Kids can saddle up and ride stick ponies to their table at this family-style eatery in the Wilderness Lodge. All-you-can-eat dinners are brought to the table in cast-iron buckets, or you can order à la carte. If you like home cooking in a casual atmosphere where the kids can get a bit rowdy, Whispering Canyon is a good bet. ✉ *Wilderness Lodge, 901 Timberline Dr.* ☎ *407/939–3463 (☎ 407/WDW–DINE)* ⊕ *www.disneyworld.com* ⚓ *2 months* ⊗ *B, L, D.*

YACHTSMAN STEAKHOUSE

$$$
★★

We're not sure how a yachtsman gets his hands on so much good beef, but this restaurant is one of the premier steak houses in Disney World. Hand-cut steaks and chops with your choice of sauces are served in a clubby dining room. ✉ *Yacht Club Resort, 1700 Epcot Resorts Blvd.* ☎ *407/939–3463 (☎ 407/WDW–DINE)* ⊕ *www.disneyworld.com* ⚓ *2 months* ⊗ *D.*

Restaurants in the Rest of the World

Except for the grill restaurant in ESPN Wild World of Sports, all these restaurants can be found in Downtown Disney.

BONGOS CUBAN CAFÉ

$$
★

Founded by the singer Gloria Estefan, Bongos delivers an Americanized version of Cuban dishes (for example, black bean soup and grilled pork), a wildly tropical decor, and loud Latin music. ✉ *Downtown Disney West Side, 1498 E. Buena Vista Dr.* ☎ *407/939–3463 (☎ 407/WDW–DINE)* ⊕ *www.disneyworld.com* ⚓ *Reservations not necessary* ⊗ *L, D.*

ESPN WIDE WORLD OF SPORTS GRILL

$$
★★

Televisions broadcast sporting events from every wall. Expect pasta, pizza, sandwiches, and burgers. ✉ *ESPN Wide World of Sports Complex, 700 S. Victory Way* ☎ *407/939–3463 (☎ 407/WDW–DINE)* ⊕ *www.disneyworld.com* ⚓ *Reservations not accepted* ⊗ *L, D.*

$$$
★★★

FULTON'S CRAB HOUSE

Fulton's, on the Empress Lilly riverboat, serves seafood flown in daily from all over the world. Try the raw oysters. ✉ *Downtown Disney Pleasure Island, 1670 E. Buena Vista Dr.* ☎ *407/939–3463* (☎ *407/WDW–DINE*) ⊕ *www.disneyworld.com* ≛ *2 months* ⊙ *L, D.*

$$
★★

HOUSE OF BLUES

The House of Blues serves up Cajun and creole cooking while a nightclub attached to the restaurant serves up jazz, country, rock and roll, and, yes, blues music. The gospel brunch on Sunday is an especially fun choice for families. To find out who's playing or to purchase tickets call ☎ *407/934–2583* (☎ *407/934–BLUE*). ✉ *Downtown Disney West Side, 1490 E. Buena Vista Dr.* ☎ *407/939–3463* (☎ *407/WDW–DINE*) ⊕ *www.disneyworld.com* ≛ *Reservations not accepted* ⊙ *B (Sun. only), L, D.*

$$
★★★

PARADISO 37

The "37" in the restaurant name refers to the fact that the menu features cuisine from 37 different countries in North and South America. The "Paradiso" no doubt refers to the tequila bar, which offers plenty of variety, too. The food here is ethnic-lite, hearty, and generally very good. The appetizers are designed for sharing tapas-style, which can be a fun way to sample several things. And because Paradiso 37 is in the perpetually under refurbishment section of Downtown Disney that was formerly known as Pleasure Island, it doesn't draw the crowds that are common at some other Downtown Disney restaurants. ✉ *Downtown Disney Pleasure Island, 1590 E. Buena Vista Dr.* ☎ *407/939–3463* (☎ *407/WDW–DINE*) ⊕ *www.disneyworld.com* ≛ *2 months* ⊙ *L, D.*

$$
★★

PLANET HOLLYWOOD

Planet Hollywood's giant blue globe holds numerous movie props, including the bus from *Speed*, which hovers menacingly overhead. Film clips run constantly, and even the menus, which are printed with the high-school-graduation pictures of stars, are entertaining. The food is just what you'd expect. ✉ *Downtown Disney West Side, 1490 E. Buena Vista Dr.* ☎ *407/939–3463* (☎ *407/*

WDW–DINE) ⊕ *www.disneyworld.com* ⚑ *Reservations not necessary* ⊘ *L, D.*

$$
★★

PORTOBELLO COUNTRY ITALIAN TRATTORIA

This restaurant is based on the idea of a Tuscan country trattoria, with an attractive interior and a wide variety of authentic Italian dishes. It's a bit quieter and more adult than many of the Downtown Disney restaurants. The patio is especially pleasant in spring and fall. ⊠ *Downtown Disney, 1650 E. Buena Vista Dr.* ☎ *407/939–3463 (*☎ *407/WDW–DINE)* ⊕ *www.disneyworld.com* ⚑ *2 months* ⊘ *D.*

$$
★★

RAGLAN ROAD IRISH PUB AND RESTAURANT

A life-size bronze statue of Irish poet Patrick Kavanaugh sitting lost in thought on a bench greets you outside this Downtown Disney Irish pub. Inside are four huge wooden bars crafted in Ireland in the 19th century. There's often live music, and there's never a cover. As for the food, it's pub classics gone upscale, with Angus-beef shepherd's pie and Colorado lamb in a sophisticated port-wine sauce. ⊠ *Downtown Disney, 1640 E. Buena Vista Dr.* ☎ *407/939–3463 (*☎ *407/WDW–DINE)* ⊕ *www.disneyworld.com* ⚑ *4 months* ⊘ *L, D.*

$$
★

RAINFOREST CAFÉ

This sister restaurant to the Animal Kingdom location serves casual food in a jungle-theme atmosphere. Most kids love the Rainforest Café, but the music and sound effects can get very loud, which may bother babies and toddlers. Take a buzzer and shop around the Marketplace while you wait. ⊠ *Downtown Disney Marketplace, 1780 E. Buena Vista Dr.* ☎ *407/939–3463 (*☎ *407/WDW–DINE)* ⊕ *www.disneyworld.com* ⚑ *Reservations not accepted* ⊘ *B, L, D.*

$
★★

T-REX

Managed by the same company that runs Rainforest Café, T-REX offers casual, family-friendly dining in the form of pasta, pizzas, seafood, and salads, plus giant Audio-Animatronics dinosaurs, geysers, waterfalls, and a fossil dig site. "A little wild," reported one father from Kansas. "We sat in the ice room, which was as cold as its name, and every 15 minutes there was a meteor shower with all these loud special effects. The kids loved it, but after a while my wife and I were ready to escape back into the hot Florida night." ✉ *Downtown Disney Marketplace, 1676 E. Buena Vista Dr.* ☎ *407/939–3463* (☎ *407/WDW–DINE*) ⊕ *www. disneyworld.com* ⚓ *Reservations not accepted* ☉ *L, D.*

$$$
★★★
◔◔

WOLFGANG PUCK GRAND CAFÉ

There are three parts to this restaurant: the ultracasual Express, which offers salads, sandwiches, and such; the inside restaurant, which provides Puck's signature pastas and pizzas, as well as outstanding sushi; and, upstairs, the formal dining room, serving the best Puck has to offer. Needless to say, the first two locations work best for families, and the latter is best reserved for a parents' night out. "The best meal we had during our entire time in Orlando was downstairs at Wolfgang Puck," said one father from Nebraska. "The kiddie food was a cut above average, and the adults thought the sushi was great." A father of three concurs that the inside restaurant is the perfect middle ground between the express and formal options, and that "the hoisin BBQ ribs are worth coming back for." ✉ *Downtown Disney West Side, 1482 E. Buena Vista Dr.* ☎ *407/939–3463* (☎ *407/WDW–DINE*) ⊕ *www. disneyworld.com* ⚓ *2 months* ☉ *L, D.*

CHAPTER 12
DISNEY
CRUISE LINE

In 1996 Disney stepped into the cruising industry, and a family cruise has never been the same since. World-class entertainment, fine dining, the Disney characters—everything you expect to find at Walt Disney World can now be discovered on the high seas. And with its growing fleet of ships, Disney is prepared to sail its guests to every corner of the globe.

Disney has four ships. The original two, the *Magic* and the *Wonder,* handle the longer sailings, which at present include Hawaii, Alaska, Mexico, Europe, and Canada. The even bigger and better *Dream* and *Fantasy* make the popular three-, four-, and seven-night sailings to the Bahamas and Disney's own island, Castaway Cay. With this fleet at its disposal, Disney has a wide variety of itineraries and ports of call. Check out all the offerings at ⊕ *www. disneycruise.com*.

No matter where you sail, the key thing about the Disney cruises is that the activities and the attitude are decidedly geared toward families. There are no casinos on board, entertainment is wholesome, drinking and carousing are de-emphasized, shore excursions tend toward kid-friendly pursuits like snorkeling and dolphin swims, and there are excellent (in fact, award-winning) child-care centers. Disney cruises are perfect for the family that needs a bit of everything in the course of a vacation: time for the adults to relax alone and time with everyone together. Families whose kids vary in age are especially sold on the cruises. Because there are so many kids on board and the age categories in the youth programs are tight, it's likely that your 3-year-old and 13-year-old will each have found a friend by the end of the first day. Let's face it—nothing beats a vacation where everyone is happy.

Cruising with Disney

Pre- and Post-Cruise Packages

Many Disney visitors combine a stay at Walt Disney World with a three-, four-, or five-day cruise. To call this a "package" is a bit of a misnomer, as Disney allows families to customize their vacation totally. In other words, you treat the Orlando segment as an add-on before or after your cruise, choosing any resort you like and staying as long as you decide. It's a good way to get the best of both worlds.

Although it's possible to reverse the order, most families like touring first and cruising last. That way the relaxing cruise segment follows the more exhausting theme-park segment of the week.

You're met at the Orlando airport and escorted directly to your resort, where you can find all the documentation you need for the week. After the theme-park segment of the trip is over, you're transported by a special Disney Cruise Line (DCL) bus to the ship, which waits in Port Canaveral harbor, approximately an hour from Orlando.

Disney does everything possible to make the transition seamless; the same charging privileges established in Orlando are extended to your onboard account. Your bags are picked up from your hotel room and transferred directly to your room on the ship. In short, the logistics of checking in and checking out, arranging transportation, and lugging baggage are all handled for you.

Families leaving from California or Europe on their cruises also have hotel options, which are detailed on the website.

Approximate Costs

Calculating the exact cost of your cruise depends on several factors: the time of year, the size of your family, the itinerary, and the level of cabin or stateroom you choose. It's probably a little too late to do anything about the size of your family, but the other three factors are within your control.

Time of year has a huge impact on price. If you're going in the middle of summer, spring break, or Christmas week, you'll pay top dollar. If you're traveling during the off-season, say the third week of October, the rates will automatically drop about 30%. Most of the specials and discounts you'll find through AAA and independent websites like ⊕ *www.mousesavers.com* are for the off-season.

Lodging also affects the bottom line. All staterooms are nicely appointed, designed for families, and therefore 25% larger than standard cruise-ship cabins, so it's really just a matter of how much space you're willing to pay for.

And then there's the issue of itinerary. Obviously, it costs considerably more to cruise to Hawaii for 14 nights than it does to take a three-day run to the Bahamas.

Let's see how all this shakes out with some examples. For instance, a family of four taking the basic four-day Bahamas cruise on the *Dream* in July might pay $5,000–$6,000. If that makes you gulp, consider that the same trip in February comes in at about $3,000. The type of stateroom is also a factor. If you want a private veranda and full stateroom for your seven-day cruise to Alaska in July, the cost for a family of four is $8,000–$9,000. Swap to an inside stateroom, and the cost drops to $5,000–$6,000. The length of the cruise and distance covered is the other big variable. The 14-day cruise from Los Angeles to Hawaii in April will cost that same family of four about $10,000. (Note: These quoted prices do not include airfare. Adding it on is always an option, and the price rises accordingly, depending on where your flight originates.)

Get the picture? Costs can vary dramatically. To estimate the price of your cruise, start by going to 🌐 *www.disneycruise.com* and typing in the destination you wish to visit, the month you wish to travel, the preferred length of the cruise, and the number of people in your party. This will direct you to a page that shows all of your options, from highest to lowest. You can fine-tune from there, and once you have a ballpark price you can more intelligently comparison shop. The website is also a great source of information on ports of call, shore excursions, and the layout of staterooms.

■**TIP→ The ship is going to sail no matter how many people are aboard, so cruise lines offer significant discounts as the time of departure approaches and staterooms remain unbooked. Disney is no exception to this rule, but be aware that the cheaper stateroom levels sell out first, so discounts are more likely to be available on the unsold concierge-level (premium) staterooms. Last-minute travelers might not find lower prices, but they may get more bang for their buck.**

Extra Expenses

One of the beauties of cruising is that most of your expenses are included in your package price. Here's a list of what *isn't* included.

- Alcoholic beverages

- Arcade games

- Child care for children under three

- Medical services

- Merchandise bought on board or at ports of call

- Palo, the adults-only restaurant on all four ships, which charges a $25 per person cover; Remy, the even-more-upscale adults-only restaurant on the *Dream* and the *Fantasy,* has an upcharge of $75 per person.

- Parking fees, if you drive to the port you're sailing from

- Photography

- Ship-to-shore phone calls

- ✦ Shore excursions

- ✦ Spa treatments

- ✦ Tipping (Based on industry suggestions, this will be about $12–$15 per person per day. This cost, along with any other purchases made aboard the ship, can be added to your general bill, so don't worry about bringing a lot of cash.)

On the Ships

Cabins

The Disney Cruise Line website contains renderings of all the staterooms, from the basic inside stateroom designed for three to a two-bedroom suite that can sleep as many as seven. Most staterooms are in the deluxe ocean-view category, many of them with verandas, and most about 200–250 square feet. (Most of the cabins are outside staterooms, so if you're planning to save a few bucks by booking an inside stateroom, call early.)

"The general rule is, the longer you'll be on the ship, the more important the size of your stateroom is," reported a mom of three from Florida, who describes herself as a "grizzled cruise veteran." She added: "For a three-day cruise we're okay with being piled on top of each other, and we go for the cheapest option we can find. On these short runs, you're hardly ever in the cabin anyway. But if you're on a longer cruise that includes multiple days at sea, the size and comfort of your stateroom matters a lot more."

One other innovation to note: The *Dream* and the *Fantasy* alleviate cabin fever by putting "virtual portholes" in the inside staterooms. High-definition cameras placed on the exterior of the ship feed live video to your screen. Keep an eye out—sometimes a character pops by as well. These portholes have been such a hit that Disney reports quite a few families now prefer the inside cabins. "We booked late and were initially disappointed we didn't have a veranda," reported one mom. "But our 3- and 4-year-old were so entranced by the portholes that it didn't matter. They kept screaming out the name of whatever character was drifting by."

Dining

Disney makes onboard dining very special. For starters, you don't dine in the same restaurant every night. "We figured that a family on vacation wouldn't ordinarily eat at the same restaurant three nights in a row," said Amy Foley of the DCL. "So why would a family on a cruise ship want to eat in the same dining room every night?"

Instead, you experience "rotation dining," trying a different onboard restaurant each evening of your cruise. (Your server and tablemates rotate along with you.) There's one "formal" restaurant in the mix. On the *Magic,* there's Lumiere's, with a theme based on *Beauty and the Beast.* On the *Wonder,* your fine-dining option is Triton's, named for the Little Mermaid's father. On the *Dream* it's the Royal Palace, and on the *Fantasy* it's the Royal Court; both are home to Cinderella and her princess pals.

Other nights are more casual. On the *Magic* there's the Brazil-themed Carioca's, and on the *Wonder* there's Parrot Cay, where the mood and the food is Bahamian. On the *Dream* and the *Fantasy* there's the Enchanted Garden, inspired by the gardens of Versailles and featuring an environment that changes from day to night in the course of your meal.

But Animator's Palate—which is available on all ships—is the real showstopper, an interactive dining experience in which the restaurant transforms itself as you dine. The meal begins in a room that is utterly black and white, right down to the framed animation sketches on the wall and the servers' somber attire. With each course, more color is added to the artwork, the walls, the table settings, and the servers' costumes. By dessert the whole room is glowing.

On the *Dream* and the *Fantasy,* the restaurant has one more wonderful touch. Crush, the surfer-dude turtle from *Finding Nemo,* appears and interacts with diners, using the same type of technology found in the popular Turtle Talk with Crush attraction at Epcot. "Having Crush greet him by name and interact with him was the highlight of the whole cruise for my 4-year-old son," said one father. "When he found out about the restaurant rotation—in other words that we wouldn't be going back to Animator's Palate the next night—he was, excuse the expression, completely crushed."

On all four ships, adults have a fourth dining option, Palo, an Italian restaurant perched high atop the ship, offering a sweeping view of the ocean. Palo serves wonderful food and is so popular that if you want to book a table, you need to do so either before you leave home or immediately upon boarding the ship. There's a well-worth-it $25 surcharge for dinner or brunch. Excellent wine-tasting classes are held there as well.

On the *Dream* and the *Fantasy* you'll find a second adults-only option called Remy's, with an opulent setting and a French-inspired menu that's a nod to the film *Ratatouille.* Scott Hummel, the executive chef at Victoria & Albert's at the Grand Floridian, was one of the consulting chefs, and many of his dishes are on the menu; in other words, while a meal at Palo's is on par with California Grill, Cítricos, Flying Fish, or Jiko, Remy's takes it a step further, offering cuisine and service more like you'd find at Victoria & Albert's. Note that there's a $75 per person upcharge for dining at Remy's. If you go with the six-course tasting menu and add a wine pairing with each course, the price goes up an additional $99. It's certainly not a cheap night out, but it's a meal to remember, with many little surprise touches designed to elevate your experience. If you'd like the Remy's experience for a little less, consider the champagne brunch, which is offered for $50, $75 with champagne pairings.

When you book your cruise, you'll have to choose your meal times: either early or late. The main seating means you have dinner as early as 6, depending on the ship, and the second seating is often as late as 8:30. If you have young kids the early seating works best, although it does mean a crack-of-dawn breakfast time. But I've seen preschoolers literally fall asleep at the table at late seatings—active days bring about early bedtimes. Besides, if you want to sleep in, you can always skip the full breakfast and grab breakfast at the buffet.

In fact, if you're not into spending a lot of time in restaurants, the buffets are a good, fast option for both breakfast and lunch. A breakfast buffet is available daily on the pool level for families who want to get an early start. You can also find a casual buffet lunch daily, and, in case you don't want to take even a minute out of your fun, pizza, burgers, salad, sandwiches, and ice cream are served all afternoon out by the pools.

Making a Good Thing Better

Walt Disney once famously said "our goal is to take things that are wonderful and make them better," and thus Disney is continually looking for ways to improve its family cruises. The original ship, the *Magic,* underwent a major renovation in 2013, and the *Wonder* will follow suit in a few years.

The biggest change to the *Magic* is the addition of the Aqua-Dunk thrill ride, which was undoubtedly prompted by the popularity of the AquaDuck on the *Dream* and *Fantasy.* But while the AquaDuck is a coaster-style ride that flows all around the deck, the Dunk is just what its name implies—one dramatic drop. Riders enter a glass chute three stories in the air, and then the bottom drops out, sending them plunging through a huge loop extending over the side of the ship before they come to rest at the bottom.

The kiddie pool area is also freshened up, with the Mickey Pool slide being replaced with the zippy, curved, but still kid-friendly Twist'n'Spout. Donald's nephews Huey, Dewey, and Louie host a special "splash zone" with fountains and water play areas for the preschool set.

As for restaurants, the casual Parrot Cay has been rethemed as Carioca's, named after José Carioca of Three Caballeros fame. Animator's Palate has had a brush-up in technology, and the casual buffet eatery Cabanas now has food stations and a *Finding Nemo* theme.

The Oceaneer's Lab boasts a new multiplayer pirate game, while the Oceaneer Club offers four new themed play areas, ranging from Pixie Hollow to the Avengers. And parents get some new toys, too. The adults-only entertainment zone, After Hours, has three new bars: Fathoms, which has club and cabaret acts as well as a dance floor; O'Gill's Irish Pub; and the Keys Piano Bar.

Kids' Programs On Board

Flounder's Reef is the nursery on the *Wonder,* while on the *Dream,* the *Magic,* and the *Fantasy* you'll find the It's A Small World Nursery. No matter what it's called, the baby center has plenty of cribs, high chairs, swings, and changing tables, along with play areas for children between three months and three years of age. The nurseries don't have the extensive hours of the other children's programs (at least not every day), but are open

Is Bigger Better?

The *Dream* and the *Fantasy*, which cover the shorter Bahamian cruises, have some real bonus features. They're 40% larger than the *Magic* or *Wonder*, and Disney used that extra space for expanded entertainment areas. Innovations include the virtual portholes for inside cabins, art that comes "to life," a ship-wide detective game, and separate areas for teens and tweens. But the star of the bigger ships, hands down, is the AquaDuck, a full-fledged water coaster. The AquaDuck is essentially a 765-foot Plexiglas tube stretching high above the top deck. Jets propel you along, and the track features a "swing out" loop that (briefly) shoots you over the side of the ship. The ocean—if you dare to look—is 150 feet below. The height requirement is 48 inches, and two family members can ride together.

daily to give the parents of infants and toddlers time to relax together or play with their older kids. This is the only child-care option on the ship that charges a fee ($9 per hour); they are usually open from 9 am to 11 pm, but the hours can vary.

Disney's Oceaneer Club for kids ages three to seven occupies a huge play area complete with a re-creation of Captain Hook's pirate ship. The well-trained and upbeat counselors lead the kids in games and crafts. On the first evening aboard the ship counselors meet with the parents to explain the program and help the kids ease in.

Kids ages 8 to 11 hang out in the Oceaneer Lab, where they have their own crafts and games, such as learning how to make flubber, draw animation cels, or carve race cars from soap. There's also plenty of outdoor action, from games on the sports deck to water activities in the sports pool.

The activities at Oceaneer Club and Oceaneer Lab run throughout the day and night. Whenever you drop your kids off, a pager ensures you can be reached in case of an emergency. But the most likely "emergency" is that your kids are having so much fun they refuse to leave.

As you're probably already only too aware, the 11 to 13 "tween" years are tough, with these "neither here nor there" kids often nearly impossible to entertain. Not to worry. Disney breaks out this age group and gives them their own spaces. Edge, the appropriately named lounge for tweens, offers high-tech entertainment such as video karaoke and separate sporting events. It works well, because they're neither forced into kiddie activities nor given as much freedom as the teenagers.

Teens ages 13 to 17 have their own spaces: a private haven called Vibe. The spaces look like a combination coffeehouse–dorm room. Teens are pretty much given the run of the ship—counselors lead them in ship-wide scavenger hunts, video-game tournaments, and pool parties.

> **INSIDER'S SECRET**
>
> Young children, already overwhelmed by the size of the ship, often suffer separation anxiety the first time they're dropped off at one of the programs. Try to persuade them to join the activities the first evening, when everyone is new and fast friendships are made. The counselors are trained to look out for shy children and help them make a smooth transition into the group activities.

Onboard Entertainment

There are three pools on board: one with a pint-size tube slide for little kids; a second "sports pool" for games and the rowdier activities of older children; and a third "quiet pool" for adults, complete with large, elevated hot tubs. In addition, the ship has a sports deck, a full-service spa, an exercise room, and several shops. The *Dream* and the *Fantasy* have the AquaDuck water coaster. The *Magic* has the AquaDunk thrill ride.

The cornerstone of onboard entertainment is the 975-seat Walt Disney Theater, one of the most technologically advanced theaters at sea. Here DCL showcases Broadway-style shows, some of them new and some based on Disney classics. All the productions are great, but the finale show is the stunning *Believe,* which always seems to bring half the audience to tears.

A family lounge—Studio Sea on the *Magic* and the *Wonder* and Studio D on the *Dream* and the *Fantasy*—provides dance

INSIDER'S SECRET

More and more, large families are meeting up on cruises, where everyone can be together but still go off and do their own thing. Consider this report from a mother of three from Michigan: "My sisters and I have a family reunion at Disney World every other year. When we get all the kids and spouses together, there are 14 of us, with a wide range of ages. Last year for the first time we took the cruise and found that worked great. Those with babies could go back to their cabins whenever someone got cranky or tired, those with school-age kids could just keep going, and those with older kids could let them go to the pools and arcades on their own."

music, parties, and participatory game shows starring the audience. The Mickey Mania trivia game is a real blast. The Buena Vista Theater shows a variety of Disney movies daily, and, come nightfall, a jumbo screen allows you to watch movies outdoors on the deck, a good way to coax wound-up kids to calm down and give way to sleep.

Of course, the characters are sailing right along with you. They turn out for deck parties—including the welcome-aboard and farewell bashes—and also appear around the ship. Check your daily onboard newsletter, the *Personal Navigator,* for times and locations.

After the shows wind down, adults can congregate in the entertainment districts, dubbed After Hours on the *Magic* and Route 66 on the *Wonder*. Expect a cabaret–dance club, a sports pub, and a piano bar. The District is the expanded adult area on the *Dream* and the *Fantasy*. It has five clubs: a live-music venue, a dance club, a sports bar, an upscale champagne lounge, and the Skyline Bar, where the sun sets over a different city every 15 minutes with artwork, music, and globally themed drinks to match each new destination. What will these people think of next?

The Spa

The onboard spa offers a range of services, including some designed exclusively for couples. Just hanging out in the beautiful sauna and steam area is a great way to kill an afternoon. If you want to book a massage or facial, especially on a day when the ship is at sea, go immediately to the spa after boarding the ship to make an appointment. The best times get snatched up early. The *Dream,* the *Magic,* and the *Fantasy* also offer Chill, a separate spa area for tweens and teens.

> ### INSIDER'S SECRET
>
> One of the cruise highlights is the rollicking Pirates in the Caribbean deck party, where passengers dress like buccaneers. Smee and Captain Hook show up and try to cause trouble; but not to worry, Captain Mickey prevails, and a good time is had by all.

Off the Ships

Ports of Call

The three- and four-day cruises spend one day in Nassau, giving you a chance to shop, sightsee, or visit a casino. There are shore excursions designed for families (and kids of all ages are apt to enjoy a horse-drawn carriage ride), but, frankly, the Nassau stop exists mostly to placate the adults on board who miss the presence of a casino. If you do want to try your luck at the slots, or if your children are too young to take along comfortably on a shopping trip to the straw market, you can always leave them on board in the kids' programs.

The seven-day cruises offer family-friendly shore excursions at every stop, such as sailing lessons, snorkeling, and submarine trips. The Alaskan, Hawaiian, and longer Caribbean–Mexican cruises also offer shore excursions at every port of call, and the list of possibilities is staggering. A complete list of all shore excursions for every port of call can be found at ⊕ *www. disneycruise.com.*

Once you book your cruise, reserve shore excursions online. Reserving early guarantees you can get everything you want and saves you from having to stand in line at the shore-excursion desk on the first day of your cruise.

Castaway Cay

All the Caribbean and Bahamas cruises stop at Castaway Cay, Disney's own private island and a true little piece of paradise. You disembark at the pier (cutting out the time-consuming tendering process often required when a large ship stops at a small island) and stroll or take a shuttle to a beautiful beach. Once there you can hike, bike, play volleyball, take a Jet Ski ride, rent sailboats or sea kayaks, or simply sun yourself. Organized excursions for families include a stingray swim and snorkeling tours. Lunch is cooked right on the island, and there are small shops in case you find yourself in need of beach toys, towels, or sunscreen.

The children's programs go full force on the island, so after you've played a while as a family, you can drop the kids off and have a little adult time. Counselors lead youngsters on scavenger hunts, "whale excavations," and sand castle–building contests; older kids participate in boat races or bike trips around the island with the counselors; teens have their own beach Olympics and *Survivor*-style games.

Meanwhile, adults can escape to the separate mile-long quiet beach called Serenity Bay, where they can sip a piña colada or have an open-air massage in a private cabana.

Castaway Cay is so popular that some itineraries stop there twice. If you'd like a lot of beach time on your cruise, consider one of those sailings.

INSIDER'S SECRET

The older, smaller ships, the *Magic* and the *Wonder,* sail from a variety of ports of embarkation and explore more exotic ports of call. For details on upcoming voyages, visit ⊕ *www. disneycruise.com.*

CHAPTER 13

★ ★ ★

UNIVERSAL ORLANDO

With two full theme parks (Universal Studios Florida and Islands of Adventure), a dining and entertainment complex called CityWalk, and four on-site resort hotels, Universal Orlando is no longer content to be the park you visit on the last day of vacation, after the bulk of your time and money have gone to Disney. On the contrary, Universal is poised to be a destination, not an afterthought, aiming to keep guests on-site and entertained for multiday stays.

As you prepare a touring plan for Universal, make sure to choose the right rides and shows for your family. Although Universal offers attractions for every age, it's best known for its high-thrill rides. In general, the attractions here are far more intense than those at Disney, so it's important to know that the shows and rides you choose are age appropriate. A mother of one from Missouri agreed: "The first time we went to Universal Studios our daughter was 4, and there wasn't too much she could ride or enjoy at such a young age. The next time we went back she was 8, and she loved it. Kids have to be a bit older to really get into the Universal Studios style of ride."

On the other hand, if you have teenagers, you may want to spend more time at Universal than at Disney. Consider this report from a father of three: "My children love roller coasters (the wilder the better) and prefer Universal to Disney. So we do the opposite of most families, staying at Universal and driving over for a day at Disney."

Universal Orlando is off Interstate 4 at Exits 74B and 75A. Road signs to the complex are well marked. The Universal parks are about a 20-minute drive from Walt Disney World. For more information, visit ⊕ *www.universalorlando. com* or call ☎ *407/363-8000.*

> **HELPFUL HINT**
>
> Universal suffers some confusion regarding the names of its parks. The entire complex, consisting of two theme parks (Universal Studios Florida and Islands of Adventure), four hotels (Hard Rock, Portofino Bay, Royal Pacific, and Cabana Bay Beach Resort), and the CityWalk nightlife and entertainment district, is called Universal Orlando.

Should We Stay On-Site?

Whether you decide to stay at one of Universal Orlando's four on-site resorts—the Portofino Bay Hotel, the Hard Rock Hotel, the Royal Pacific Resort, and the mid-priced Cabana Bay Beach Resort—depends on how much you're willing to spend for certain conveniences and privileges extended only to on-site guests. The on-site luxury resorts are all impressive, with the ultimate in amenities, and price tags to match. Depending on the resort and the season, rates average $220–$350 a night. At Cabana Bay Beach Resort prices are considerably lower: $130–$200 a night for the standard rooms and $180–$260 for family suites.

There are plenty of resorts on International Drive and other roads that flank the park, but Universal draws high-spending visitors by offering lots of perks for on-site guests.

Advantages of Staying On-Site

By far the biggest advantage is that luxury resort guests can use the Express Pass system on an unlimited basis. Just show your resort ID—that is, your room key card—and you'll be admitted into the Express ticket line on any ride you choose at any time you choose. This virtually eliminates having to wait in line, and it's a huge, huge perk. Depending on when you're traveling, it's also a $40–$90 per person value—the cost of an Express Pass. (Note that guests of the Cabana Bay Beach Resort do *not* qualify for this perk.)

At present, all resort guests can enter the Wizarding World of Harry Potter: Diagon Alley section in Universal Orlando a full hour ahead of day guests. Since Diagon Alley is insanely crowded all day long, the chance to ride and explore ahead of the bulk of the theme-park guests is an immeasurable advantage. Be sure to check to make sure this perk is still in place when you book your room. (Note that Cabana Bay Beach Resort guests do qualify for this perk.)

Other Perks of Staying On-Site

- ✦ Priority seating in restaurants and advance reservations privileges.

- ✦ Complimentary water-taxi or bus transportation between your resort and the theme parks. (All three of the luxury on-site hotels are linked to the two theme parks and CityWalk by a series of scenic waterways. Cabana Bay guests take the buses, but they run frequently. It's an eight-minute ride.) Not only does the transportation system make it easier for you to return to your room for a midday break, but it also saves you the time, effort, and expense of driving to the theme parks.

- ✦ Complimentary package delivery of in-park purchases to guest rooms.

- ✦ Resort IDs that allow you to charge merchandise, food, and tickets to your hotel room.

- ✦ Complimentary transportation to SeaWorld and Aquatica.

- ✦ Access to seasonal packages and periodic specials that provide significant perks during the off-season, such as discounts on rooms, "kids eat free" deals, upgrades to suites, or complimentary breakfasts.

For full reviews of the on-site Universal hotels, see Chapter 2, Choosing a Hotel.

Ticket Options

Universal offers several ticket options. It's smart to purchase them online at ⊕ *www.universalorlando.com*; prices are $8 to $20 more if you buy them at the gate.

One-Day, One-Park Ticket

Admits holders to either Universal Studios or Islands of Adventure for one day.

✦ Adults and children over 9: $102.

✦ Children ages 3 to 9: $97.

One-Day, Two-Park Ticket

Admits holders to Universal Studios and Islands of Adventure for one day.

✦ Adults and children over 9: $147.

✦ Children ages 3 to 9: $142.

Two-Day, Two-Park Ticket

Admits holders to both Universal Studios and Islands of Adventure for two days.

✦ Adults and children over 9: $195.

✦ Children ages 3 to 9: $185.

Two-Day, One-Park-Per-Day Ticket

Admits holders to Universal Studios one day and Islands of Adventure the other.

✦ Adults and children over 9: $150.

✦ Children ages 3 to 9: $140.

Flex Ticket

Admits holders to Universal Studios, Islands of Adventure, Wet 'n Wild, Aquatica, and SeaWorld for 14 consecutive days.

✦ Adults and children over 9: $336.

✦ Children ages 3 to 9: $316.

■TIP➜ If you buy your Universal tickets online (⊕ www.universalorlando.com), the savings can be significant. Specials vary with the season, but there's nearly always a reward for buying early.

> **INSIDER'S SECRET**
>
> Next on the horizon at Universal is a water park, rumored to be called Volcano Bay. Construction is just beginning at this writing, so make sure to ask if it will be open when booking your vacation.

Dining Plans

The Universal Dining Plan allows guests to choose either a Quick Service or Table Service option. The Quick Service plan includes one quick-service meal, one snack, and one beverage for $19.99 for adults and $12.99 for kids three to nine. If you do the math, you'll find that you're basically getting the snack for free. Any drink can be chosen, including the gillywater or pumpkin juice in the Harry Potter sections. The Table Service option includes one full meal with entrée, drink, and desert, one quick-service meal with entrée and drink, one beverage, and one snack at $51.99 for adults and $17.99 for kids three to nine and can only be purchased as part of a vacation package. In essence, the Table Service plan requires you to eat three meals within the park in the course of a day for it to really make financial sense, so the Quick Service plan works far better for most families. With either plan, the add-on drink option of unlimited soft drinks for $12 a person can be a bargain, considering the price of theme-park beverages.

Express Pass

You can avoid waiting in lines with the Express Pass (once called the Express PLUS Pass). The price to upgrade a one-day ticket into an Express Pass ranges from $40 to $90, depending on the season, and upgrading a two-day ticket ranges from $35 to $65. While the goal is the same—giving guests ways to reduce the time they spend waiting in line—Universal runs its pass program a bit differently from the Disney FastPass+ system. At Disney the use of FastPass+ is free, but you can only get three a day. At Universal, an Express Pass is unlimited, meaning that you can use it on any ride at any time, but you pay a significant surcharge for the privilege. (Unless, that is, you're staying on-site. Guests of Universal luxury resorts get Express Pass benefits for free.)

The key thing about the Express Pass is that it's *not* accepted at either Harry Potter and the Forbidden Journey or Harry Potter and the Escape from Gringotts, the centerpiece rides that make up the Wizarding World of Harry Potter and by far the attractions for which you're most likely to need it. (Pteranodon Flyers at Islands of Adventure doesn't qualify for the pass either.) Bottom line on the Express Pass? If you're staying at a Universal resort and it's free, then great. Use it. If you're visiting on a holiday or peak time in the summer and the crowds are huge, consider it. But most of the time it's simply not worth the extra money.

Ride Reservations

To make things even more complicated, in addition to Express Pass, Universal also offers the Ride Reservation System. Guests must pick up an electronic device that allows them to hold a place in line—virtually. Here's how it works. If, say, at 11 am the Incredible Hulk has a 45-minute wait, you punch into the device that you'd like to be in line, then show up to board at 11:45. You can only do this for one ride at a time, but the device can be used to make reservations for up to six people.

Of course, it's not free. You must pay $30 per person for the privilege to reserve every ride in the park once, $40 per person for unlimited reservations. On top of that there's a $50 deposit for each device, and it can only be used at one park. But the biggest drawback of all is that, just like the Express Pass, the Ride Reservation System can't be used on either Harry Potter and the Forbidden Journey or Harry Potter and the Escape from Gringotts. Bottom line on the Ride Reservation System? Skip it. If you're going through this much hassle and still paying $30 per person, you may as well spend a bit more and get the Express Pass. But frankly, until the two Harry Potter rides are included, it's hard to make a case for buying either one.

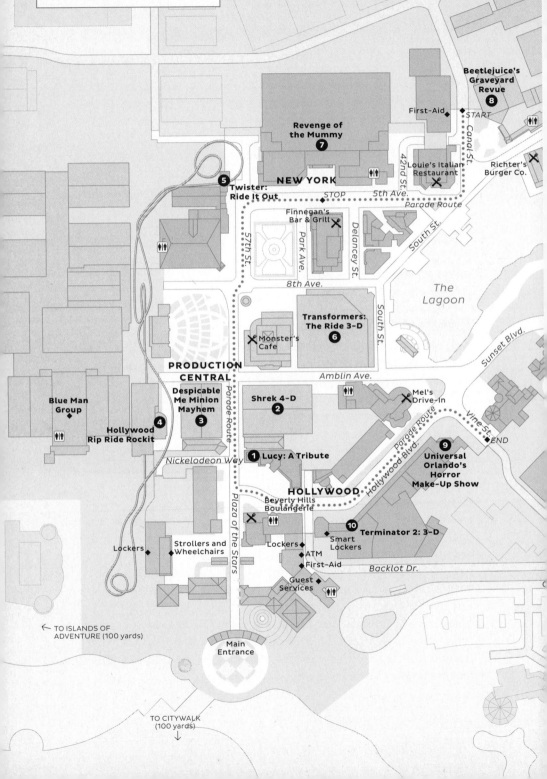

Universal Studios

Beetlejuice's
Graveyard
Revue
8

First-Aid

START

Richter's
Burger Co.

Revenge of
the Mummy
7

NEW YORK

Louie's Italian
Restaurant

42nd St.

Twister:
Ride It Out **5**

STOP

5th Ave.

Parade Route

Finnegan's
Bar & Grill

5th St.

Park Ave.

Delancey St.

South St.

The
Lagoon

8th Ave.

Transformers:
The Ride 3-D
6

**PRODUCTION
CENTRAL**

Monster's
Cafe

South St.

Sunset Blvd.

Amblin Ave.

Mel's
Drive-In

Blue Man
Group

Despicable
Me Minion
Mayhem
3

Shrek 4-D
2

Parade Route

Vine St.

END

Hollywood
Rip Ride Rockit **4**

Universal
Orlando's
Horror
Make-Up Show
9

Nickelodeon Way

Lucy: A Tribute **1**

HOLLYWOOD

Hollywood Blvd.

Lockers

Strollers and
Wheelchairs

Beverly Hills
Boulangerie

Terminator 2: 3-D
10

Lockers

Smart
Lockers

ATM

Backlot Dr.

First-Aid

Guest
Services

Plaza of the Stars

← TO ISLANDS OF
ADVENTURE (100 yards)

Main
Entrance

TO CITYWALK
(100 yards)
↓

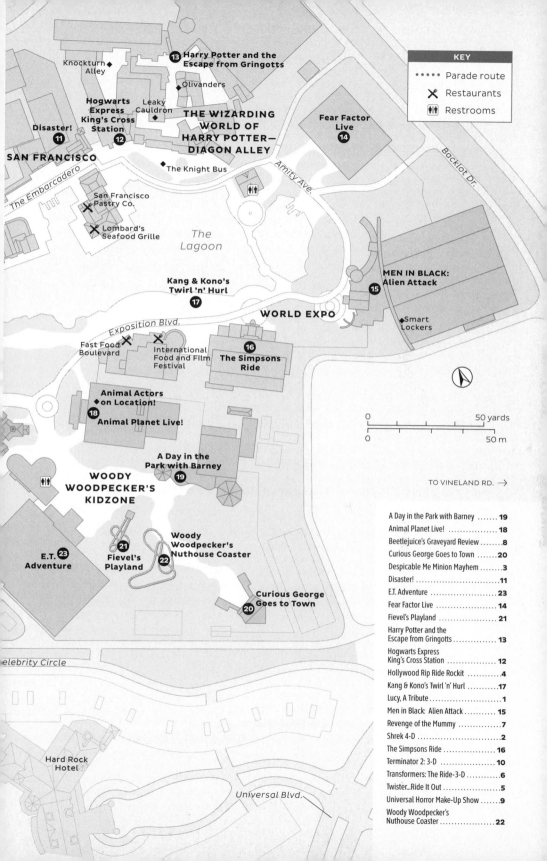

Knockturn Alley

13 Harry Potter and the Escape from Gringotts

Olivanders

Hogwarts Express King's Cross Station

Leaky Cauldron

THE WIZARDING WORLD OF HARRY POTTER— DIAGON ALLEY

Fear Factor Live **14**

Disaster! **11**

SAN FRANCISCO

12

The Knight Bus

KEY

••••• Parade route

✗ Restaurants

🚻 Restrooms

The Embarcadero

San Francisco Pastry Co.

✗ Lombard's Seafood Grille

The Lagoon

Amity Ave.

Backlot Dr.

MEN IN BLACK: Alien Attack

15

Smart Lockers

Kang & Kono's Twirl 'n' Hurl **17**

WORLD EXPO

Exposition Blvd.

Fast Food Boulevard

✗ International Food and Film Festival

The Simpsons Ride **16**

Animal Actors on Location!

18

Animal Planet Live!

A Day in the Park with Barney **19**

WOODY WOODPECKER'S KIDZONE

🚻

E.T. **23** Adventure

21 Fievel's Playland

22

Woody Woodpecker's Nuthouse Coaster

20 **Curious George Goes to Town**

Celebrity Circle

Hard Rock Hotel

Universal Blvd.

| 0 | | 50 yards |
| 0 | | 50 m |

TO VINELAND RD. →

Universal Studios Florida Touring Tips

Universal Studios is all about the movies—and especially about blockbuster thrill movies, which translates into blockbuster thrill rides, which are often more appropriate for teens and preteens than families with younger kids. In other words, strap in and hold on. This ain't Disney.

Universal Studios has recently undergone a multistep renovation aimed at keeping things fresh. Oldies like *Jaws, King Kong,* and *Earthquake,* which most kids don't remember at all, were pulled out to make way for attractions like the Diagon Alley section of the Wizarding World of Harry Potter. You'll still find tributes to *Shrek, Men in Black, The Simpsons, The Mummy,* and *Transformers.* The kiddie section is a bit of an afterthought, and even most of the shows are loud and high-tech, clearly aimed at appealing to older kids who aren't scared of anything—including going deaf.

Universal has created the Universal Orlando Resort app, which is much like the My Disney Experience app at Disney World. Use it to keep tabs on wait times and look up showtimes, but be aware that although the app claims to update every 30 minutes, some guests have reported a discrepancy in the wait times posted.

Tips for Your First Hour at Universal Studios

You're generally allowed through the main turnstiles and partway down Plaza of the Stars and Rodeo Drive about 20 minutes before the official opening time.

✦ The parking garage is in New Jersey (at least it seems that way), so arrive at least 30 minutes before the main gate opens. Parking costs $17 per car, $25 if you opt for the closer, preferred parking.

✦ Go down Rodeo Drive as far as you're allowed.

✦ In terms of rides, repeat after us: Harry Potter First. Got that? Say it again. Harry Potter first.

✦ After you've experienced the new Diagon Alley area, if your kids are older, visit Transformers: The Ride-3D or Revenge of the Mummy. Those with younger kids should backtrack to the entrance and visit the Despicable Me and Shrek attractions.

INSIDER'S SECRET

When the Wizarding World of Harry Potter: Hogsmeade opened next door at Universal Orlando's sister park, Islands of Adventure, it was so insanely popular that guests were standing in line to just get into the section. In response, Universal planned a Harry Potter section for Universal Studios as well, figuring that if guests were that gaga over the chance to meet Harry and the gang at Hogsmeade, they'd love to see the London scenes from the book re-created as well. The entire vision—the newer Diagon Alley section in Universal Studios and the original Hogsmeade section in Islands of Adventure, as well as the Hogswart Express train that runs between them—is now collectively called The Wizarding World of Harry Potter.

+ Families who haven't had breakfast may have time for a pastry at the Beverly Hills Boulangerie before the ropes drop.

+ Strollers are $15 a day for a single, $25 for a double. Wheelchair rental is $12, and Electric Convenience Vehicles (ECVs) are $50; both require a refundable $50 deposit. Lockers are available for $8–$10 a day.

+ In the off-season, some attractions open at 9, some at 10, and some (mainly the shows) start even later. Adjust your touring plan to take in the rides as they open. Times are all marked on your touring map.

Planning Your Time

+ Visit the major attractions—Harry Potter and the Escape from Gringotts, Revenge of the Mummy, Transformers, Men in Black, The Simpsons, Twister, Shrek, E.T. Adventure, Disaster!, and Hollywood Rip Ride Rockit—in the morning or in the evening. Take in the theater-style attractions in the afternoon.

+ If you miss one of the major continuously loading attractions in the morning, hold off on it until two hours before the park closes. Midday waits of up to 60 minutes are common at popular attractions, but the crowds ease off during the dinner hour.

✦ Most of the kiddie attractions—Woody Woodpecker's Nuthouse Coaster, A Day in the Park with Barney, Curious George Goes to Town, Fievel's Playland, E.T. Adventure, and Animal Planet Live!—are in the same general area of the park. This means that you can park the strollers once and then walk from attraction to attraction.

✦ The theaters that hold the Universal Horror Make-Up Show and Terminator 2: 3-D are high capacity, so even if the lines look discouraging, odds are you'll still be seated. Consult your entertainment schedule or check the board.

✦ Headed to The Simpsons, Rip Ride Rockit, Men in Black, or another intense attraction? Universal employees will help families traveling with a baby or toddler do a Baby Swap.

Afternoon Breaks

If you plan to see Universal Studios in one day, it's unlikely you'll have time for an afternoon break, but numerous theater-style attractions offer plenty of chances to rest up and let small kids nap. A lot of shows open around noon and begin a second performance around 2 pm. Ride in the morning and then catch a midday show, have lunch, and see a second show.

Parades

Universal's Superstar Parade, featuring characters from Nickelodeon, *Despicable Me,* and other Universal shows and movies, currently runs at 3 pm most days. If your kids are under eight, make time for this interactive parade. Numerous smaller performances happen throughout the day as well, themed to whatever movie is currently hot. Check your map for showtimes.

Height Restrictions in Universal Studios

Several rides at Universal have height restrictions. Here are the specifics:

✦ Harry Potter and the Escape from Gringotts   40 inches

- Men in Black — 42 inches
- Revenge of the Mummy — 48 inches
- Rip Ride Rockit — 51–79 inches
- The Simpsons — 40 inches
- Transformers: The Ride-3D — 40 inches
- Woody Woodpecker's Nuthouse Coaster — 46 inches

In addition, kids under 48 inches tall must ride with an adult companion on Transformers: The Ride-3D.

The Scare Factor at Universal Studios

Some of the shows and tours are family-oriented and fine for everyone, but several of the big-name attractions are too frightening for preschoolers. The motion-simulation rides may induce queasiness, and rides and shows are generally very loud. The volume level at Twister, Transformers, and Terminator can practically jolt the fillings from your teeth.

Universal seems to set its age rules based on how physically wild the motion of a ride is. Except for Revenge of the Mummy and Hollywood Rip Ride Rockit, none of the rides bounce you around too much. They're psychologically scary, however, and a few minutes inside Twister may lead to more bad dreams than the wildest of roller coasters. Indeed, Twister, Terminator 2: 3-D, Transformers, Beetlejuice's Graveyard Revue, and the Universal Horror Make-Up Show have parental-advisory ratings, indicating that they may be too violent, loud, or intense for younger children.

Because the rides are based on movies, how your child reacted to the movie is a good predictor of how well he or she will handle the ride. If *The Mummy* movie scared him, it's a safe bet he's not going to like the ride any better. Likewise, a movie that was relatively tame in the theater will probably yield a mild ride. Read the ride descriptions and scare-factor ratings to help you decide what's right for your child.

UNIVERSAL STUDIOS DON'T-MISS LIST

✦ Despicable Me Minion Mayhem

✦ Disaster!

✦ E.T. Adventure

✦ Harry Potter and the Escape from Gringotts

✦ Men in Black: Alien Attack

✦ Revenge of the Mummy

✦ Shrek 4-D

✦ The Simpsons Ride

✦ Transformers: The Ride-3D

Tips for Your Last Hour at Universal Studios

✦ Crowds thin at night, so it's a good time to revisit favorite attractions or drop by anything you missed earlier in the day.

✦ If you want to have dinner at CityWalk, leave Universal about an hour before the official closing time to avoid the rush of exiting guests. For more on CityWalk, Universal's dining and entertainment district, see Chapter 14.

Universal Studios Attractions

Check your entertainment schedule, and, if time permits, stop to watch some of the street entertainers who play around the park throughout the day. The Blues Brothers, featuring Jake and Elroy, play in the New York section and offer one of the liveliest shows in the park.

✳ Animal Planet Live!

This is an appealing show for all age groups, but younger kids will be especially drawn to the animal stars. Kid volunteers from the audience join the fast-paced and funny performance. Showtimes are printed on your map; because of the large size of the theater, this is a great choice for the most crowded times of the afternoon. Scare Factor➔ **It's not scary.**

☀ Beetlejuice's Graveyard Revue

This rock-and-rap show starring Dracula, the Wolfman, Frankenstein's monster, and his bride is primarily aimed at preteens and teens. Beetlejuice is the host, and he offsets the ghoulishness with plenty of goofy humor. The show plays several times in the afternoon, so getting in isn't hard; arrive about 15 minutes before showtime for good seats. Scare Factor→ **Younger kids won't be too frightened of the monsters themselves, but the extremely high volume of the music coupled with pyrotechnics might upset preschoolers. The parental advisory is largely due to some suggestive jokes and the convincing costuming of the characters.**

☀ Despicable Me Minion Mayhem

Gru, the world's most lovable villain, appears to have forgotten that it's the anniversary of the date he adopted his three daughters. But has he really? Needless to say, the story line is both cute and sweet, with plenty of surprises along the way, and the zippy 3-D show ends with an interactive dance party. It's a fun way for kids of all ages to work off a little steam and a great way to give them a laugh-based, not-very-scary introduction to the 3-D experience. Be warned that even on slow days this ride can draw despicable lines. Visit early. Scare Factor→ **Aiming more for laughter than screams, Despicable Me will be fine for kids six and over—those who have seen the movie will feel even better about it. Although the ride is somewhat jarring, it is located in a large open room that's relatively well lit. If you're still concerned, you can try the stationary seating first, and if the kids love it, go back for the whole enchilada.**

☀ Disaster!

The "musion" technology of the preshow, which transforms two-dimensional images into what appear to be three-dimensional images, is quite effective, creating a hologram of actor Christopher Walken interacting with a person on stage. Audience volunteers are pulled into the preshow action, which is a lot of fun. (Kim was recently chosen as the sweet, elderly grandma!) The ride itself puts you in the middle of a San Francisco subway car, where you become victims of an earthquake, complete with fires, broken water mains, and near misses with falling debris.

Quick Guide to Universal

Attraction	Height Requirement
Animal Planet Live!	None
Beetlejuice's Graveyard Revue	None
Curious George Goes to Town	None
A Day in the Park with Barney	None
Despicable Me Minion Mayhem	None
Disaster!	None
E.T. Adventure	Separate seating for kids under 40 inches
Fievel's Playland	None
Harry Potter and the Escape from Gringotts	40 inches
The Hogwart's Express	None
Hollywood Rip, Ride, Rockit	51 inches
Kang and Kodos' Twirl 'n' Hurl	None
Lucy, A Tribute	None
Men in Black: Alien Attack	42 inches
Revenge of the Mummy	48 inches
Shrek 4-D	None
The Simpsons Ride	40 inches
Terminator 2: 3-D	None
Transformers: The Ride-3D	40 inches*
Twister: Ride It Out	None
Universal Horror Make-Up Show	None
Woody Woodpecker's Nuthouse Coaster	36 inches

Scare Factor
0 = Unlikely to scare any child of any age.
! = Has dark or loud elements; might rattle some toddlers.
!! = A couple of gotcha! moments; should be fine for school-age kids.
!!! = You need to be pretty big and pretty brave to handle this ride.
* (below 48 inches with adult companion)

Studio Attractions

Speed of Line	Duration of Ride/Show	Scare Factor	Age Range
Fast	20 min.	0	All
Fast	25 min.	!	5 and up
n/a	n/a	0	All
Fast	15 min.	0	All
Moderate	15 min.	!	All
Moderate	20 min.	!	5 and up
Slow	15 min.	!	All
Moderate	n/a	0	All
Moderate	20 min.	!!	5 and up
Slow	7 min.	0	All
Moderate	7 min.	!!!	8 and up
Moderate	2 min.	0	All
Fast	n/a	0	All
Fast	25 min.	!!	7 and up
Moderate	15 min.	!!!	7 and up
Moderate	30 min.	!!	4 and up
Moderate	7 min.	!!	7 and up
Slow	25 min.	!!!	7 and up
Moderate	5 min.	!!	7 and up
Moderate	15 min.	!!	7 and up
Fast	20 min.	!!	7 and up
Moderate	2 min.	!	4 and up

During the ride your experiences are taped—because you're allegedly extras in a disaster movie—and played back to you in the form of a tongue-in-cheek (fake) movie trailer. Scare Factor→ **Disaster! is dramatic, but most kids aren't too frightened. The noise level may unnerve toddlers. Be aware that the show has a few adult innuendos that sail right over the heads of younger children but might be inappropriate for preteens.**

☀ Hollywood Rip Ride Rockit

Hollywood Rip Ride Rockit begins with a straight shot into the sky, sailing 17 stories up at speeds of up to 65 mph. The action never stops as you zoom over to the CityWalk lagoon and back, with six near-miss moments and a record-breaking loop.

The technology is pretty nifty, too. You get to choose your own music for the ride: LED boards in the queue area display song choices, or you can let the coaster's digital sound system choose for you. Scare Factor→ **With a height requirement of 51 inches (and a maximum of 79 inches), Hollywood Rip Ride Rockit is off-limits to many kids and too intense for most kids under eight, even if they're tall enough to ride. The coaster is really designed for the preteen and teen set.**

☀ Kang & Kodos' Twirl 'n' Hurl

Not nearly as foreboding as its name sounds, this ride is a good choice for younger kids that aren't up to The Simpsons Ride. Those pesky aliens Kang and Kodos are back to take over Springfield and are looking for helpful recruits. Families board spaceships and are off on a Dumbo-type attraction with the added bonus of trying to "blast" (really just fly by) some of Springfield's residents.

In fact, the entire Simpsons section of the park has recently been expanded to embody the town of Springfield. The biggest addition is a new food section featuring famous haunts from the show: Krusty Burger, The Frying Dutchman, Luigi's Pizza, Lard Lad's Donuts, and, of course, Homer's favorite hangout, Moe's Tavern. Scare Factor→ **It's not scary.**

☀ Lucy, A Tribute

Fans of *I Love Lucy* should take a few minutes to walk through this exhibit, which houses memorabilia from the famous TV show, including scale models of the Tropicana and the Ricardos' apartment, clothes and jewelry worn on the show, personal pictures and letters from Lucy and Desi's home life, and the numerous Emmys that Lucille Ball won through the years. **Scare Factor→ It's not scary but may prove uninteresting to kids.**

■**TIP→** Try not to let the kids stop to shop in the morning; not only should you keep moving between rides while Universal is relatively uncrowded, but each ride empties out through a shop that sells souvenirs related to that attraction. In other words, the shops encourage the ultimate in impulse buying, so hold off on purchases until late in the day when you've seen it all.

☀ Men in Black: Alien Attack

Remember the scene in *Men in Black* when Will Smith tries out for the force? Think you could do better?

The premise is that guests are rookie agents riding through the streets of New York and armed with laser guns called "alienators." As in Disney's Buzz Lightyear ride, you're supposed to shoot the aliens, but unlike in the Buzz ride, these aliens can strike back, sending your vehicle into an out-of-control spin.

As you shoot at the 120 animatronic aliens, the ride keeps track of your individual score and the collective score of the six people in your vehicle. You're not only fighting off aliens, but also competing against the team of rookies in the car beside you. Here's where it gets cute. Depending on how well you and your vehicle-mates shoot, there are alternate endings to the ride. Will you get a hero's welcome in Times Square or a loser's send-off?

Because you're actually in a video game, it makes sense that video-game rules apply—the more you play, the better you get. Can you spell addictive? Come early if you want to ride more than once.

Want to max your Men in Black score? Near the end of the ride (when you face the mega-alien in Times Square), you will hear Zed instructing you to push the red button on your control panel "now!" Whoever hits the button at this crucial point gets a whopping 100,000 bonus points. Take that, space aliens! **Scare Factor→ Most kids take the aliens in stride—especially if they've seen the movies and know what to expect. There's a fair amount of spinning in the cars, so motion sickness is a possibility, although the spinning is sporadic and not continuous, so few people have reported having a problem. There are lockers outside where you** can store purses and packages while you ride. Your child must be 42 inches tall to ride.

☀ Revenge of the Mummy

Revenge of the Mummy combines a high-speed roller coaster with robotics and pyrotechnic effects—no wonder it's billed as a "psychological thrill ride."

HELPFUL HINT

Shrek is often on hand for autographs and hugs as you exit Shrek 4-D. Check your entertainment schedule for the times he's due to appear.

As the story begins, you walk through shadowy Egyptian catacombs on a tour of the on-location set of the next Mummy movie. Once you're in the coaster, the ride's magnetic-propulsion launch system thrusts you forward, backward, and forward again as you dodge vengeful ghosts, mummies, and other monsters. In the final scene the ceiling above you catches on fire. Yowza! Scare Factor→ **Revenge of the Mummy scares the willies out of preschoolers and some school-age kids as well. Your child must be 48 inches tall to ride.**

☀ Shrek 4-D

In the preshow you learn that vile little Lord Farquaad has plans to destroy Shrek from the great beyond. (Note the clever digs at Disney in the preshow area.) As you enter the main theater, you'll be given 3-D glasses, but what makes this show different from the other 3-D attractions around town is that you're seated in special chairs that make the experience tactile as well as visual. What does that mean? You'll not only see and hear the action happening on the screen, you'll feel and smell some of it, too. (Mercifully, taste is the one sense not engaged in the show.) The adventures of Shrek and Donkey are predictably amusing as they rescue the hapless Fiona. Scare Factor→ **Although Lord Farquaad isn't exactly the most intimidating movie villain of all time, Shrek 4-D's special effects are convincing, and the whole show is very loud and dark, which may be too much for preschoolers. Kids age six and older should do fine.**

☀ The Simpsons Ride

The basic premise is that you and the Simpson family are inside Krusty the Clown's vision of an amusement park, and evil Sideshow Bob is, as usual, up to no good. You sit in a vehicle and watch the action on a giant screen—but since the vehicle in question is a motion simulator that pitches, leans, and rolls, and the special effects on the screen are at times overwhelming, this is a wilder experience than it sounds. The show is funny, hitting pretty hard on both Disney and SeaWorld, but also fairly gross; at one point you get put into Maggie's mouth as if you were a pacifier. Scare Factor→ **The first moments of the ride are by far the most jolting, and it takes a minute or two to get used to the sensations of motion-simulation technology. If you feel yourself getting queasy, look away from the screen, either at something within your car or at the other cars riding alongside you. In terms of the story line, what's there to say? Any kid who is used to the television series knows what to expect: It's a little sinister, a little screwy, more than a little tasteless, and pretty darn funny. Your child must be 40 inches tall to ride.**

☀ Terminator 2: 3-D

Universal's most high-tech action show combines 3-D effects, live action, and movie clips. The best special effect is the way the actors seem to emerge from the screen and then run back "into" the movie. The show is fast and dramatic, just like the film series it's based on, and the ending is explosive. Because of the size of the theater, Terminator 2: 3-D is relatively easy to get into and is best saved for the afternoon. Scare Factor→ **Although not as violent as the film series, Terminator 2: 3-D has some startling effects that may be too much for kids under seven. Again, it is extremely loud.**

☀ Transformers: The Ride-3D

The preshow, featuring Ironhide, Bumblebee, and, of course, Optimus Prime, explains to guests that the Decepticons have come to Earth looking for the AllSpark. Optimus Prime asks for your help and you are quickly loaded into an Autobot named Evac, who will help you evacuate the AllSpark. On your journey you'll battle Megatron and take a ride through the aptly named Vortex. This ride includes hairpin turns as well as an ascent to a second story.

As your car is moving along with the 3-D screens, motion sickness is possible, and the battle scenes do get a little rough. All in all, it's a terribly fun ride and has enough detail woven in that the story line stands up well during repeat visits. Scare Factor→ **Evac allows guests to sit side by side in rows of four, which can calm some nervous riders. Although the ride itself isn't overly intense, there are fog and water effects, as well as some seriously mean bad guys. Kids eight and older, especially those familiar with the movie, should be fine. The height restriction is 40 inches, and anyone who is under 48 inches must have adult supervision.**

☀ Twister ... Ride It Out

After a taped intro based on the film, you're led into the main show area. There, a five-story-high tornado is created right before your eyes. Along with accompanying fires and explosions, it swirls through the building while you watch from one of two platforms. You'll feel the wind, the rain, and the rumbles; and yes, the flying cow from the movie comes along for the ride. Scare Factor→ **Twister is extremely loud—at 110 decibels, twice the volume of a rock concert. Some families routinely bring earplugs to theme parks, but if you don't have them, try placing your hands over your kids' ears. The experience is too frightening for small children, but most kids six and up will be fine.**

☀ Universal Horror Make-Up Show

This show opens with a bang—or, more specifically, the startling effect of a man running on stage with a knife protruding from his chest. Everything that follows is fast-paced and funny, but a good deal edgier than anything you'd see at Disney. The actors illustrate special horror effects on stage including "cutting off" the arm of an (adult) audience volunteer, and you'll also see clips from *The Mummy*, *The Fly*, and *An American Werewolf in London*, which has an astounding man-to-beast transformation scene. Scare Factor→ **Although the movie clips and general gore level are too intense for preschoolers, most kids eight and over can stomach the Universal Horror Make-Up Show. Better than adults, frankly. The show has a parental-advisory rating because of the blood and a couple of risqué jokes. Nervous viewers will do best to sit toward the back.**

The Wizarding World of Harry Potter: Diagon Alley

Universal quickly realized that it had made a major mistake by inserting the original Wizarding World of Harry Potter into a small, landlocked section of Islands of Adventure. The popularity of the area meant that not only were the rides mobbed—which was to be expected—but that even the shops and eateries were constantly filled to capacity. But Universal has learned from this mistake and expanded the Harry Potter experience into the Universal Studios park.

Here you'll leave the Muggle streets of London to enter the magical Diagon Alley, which has a stunning level of detail. Be sure to save plenty of time to just walk around and soak in the experience. The new area contains a major ride, Harry Potter and the Escape from Gringotts; a major restaurant, The Leaky Cauldron; and an expanded shopping area. The Hogwarts Express conveniently runs between Platform 9¾ at King's Cross station in Universal Studios and Hogsmeade Station in Islands of Adventure (and thus requires a two-park ticket to ride). Universal has received a major boost from these dual Harry Potter lands and has raised ticket prices accordingly.

Universal built Diagon Alley with more breathing room, so the traffic jams and crowding of Hogsmeade don't seem to be quite as much of a problem here. There are also plenty of places in Diagon Alley to buy wizarding wands, without the long waits shoppers endure at Ollivander's Wand Shop over at Islands of Adventure. Prices are $35 for a wand and $45 for a special version programmed to interact with various exhibits throughout The Wizarding World of Harry Potter. (Just note that the experience of having your wand "pick you" is still unique to Ollivander's Wand Shop at Islands of Adventure. Whether it's worth it to wait up to an hour for the ceremony is up to you.)

Make sure to catch the street shows, whose times are marked on your theme-park map, especially Celestina Warbeck, who belts out tunes written just for Universal Studios. A troop of actors also presents The Tales of Beetle the Bard in puppet format.

And it's fun to stop by the money exchange, where a goblin converts your boring old muggle money (in units of $10 and $20) into wizard notes, which can be spent anywhere within Universal Orlando. And speaking of cash, that's all the food and drink carts within Diagon Alley accept, so if you want a quick snack of butterbeer or pumpkin juice, make sure you have some bills on hand.

☀ Harry Potter and the Escape from Gringotts

The entrance of Gringotts, the wizarding bank, is foreboding, with a dragon perched on top that periodically breathes fire. Upon entering the bank you will immediately encounter the goblins that run Gringotts, and the animatronics

INSIDER'S SECRET

Tired of the same old family picture? In Shutterbugs you can purchase 12 "photos" (which move like the newspaper photos in the Harry Potter movies) for $69.95. The pictures are actually short snippets of video embedded into scenes of the Diagon Alley area. It's a fun and unusual way to remember your visit.

effects are astounding. If you think they're making eye contact with you before looking away—you're right. Universal has developed a technology where the goblins sense and respond to human movement.

The premise of the preshow is pretty simple. You're at Gringotts to open an account and rent a vault. A holographic screen version of Bill Weasley materializes to help you, and then you board the actual attraction, sitting in rows of four. Your cart descends into the cavernous vaults—but surprise! Your mundane errand at the bank turns out to be anything but. You're attacked by Lord Voldemort and his crazed right-hand witch Bellatrix Lestrange. Harry and the gang, riding the dragon, dramatically come to your rescue by pulling your cart to the surface.

Like many new attractions boasting state-of-the-art technology, Harry Potter and the Escape from Gringotts can be a bit temperamental, and sometimes goes offline for 20 minutes or so. ("This happens all the time," muttered a Universal employee, obviously not trained to Disney cheerfulness standards, on our last visit when we made it to the front of line only to hear the dreaded "technical difficulties" announcement.) If you have this experience, stay put. Most of the time, they get issues resolved relatively quickly, and Universal does a good job of keeping guests informed. If the delay is expected to be a long one, they'll announce it, and you can move on to another attraction. Scare Factor→ **This is pri-**

marily a 3-D motion-simulator experience (much like Spider-Man and Transformers), although there are quite a few dips, twists, and spins along the way. Younger kids, who may not be up to the much more active Forbidden Journey at Islands of Adventure, will want to start with this attraction first. Your child must be 40 inches tall to ride.

☀ Hogwarts Express

Have you always wanted to take the train to Hogwarts? Well, here's your chance! Guests board a giant replica of the bright-red steam-engine train, which transports them from Diagon Alley (at Universal Studios) to Hogsmeade (at Islands of Adventure) and then back. The interior itself is delightfully authentic, right down to the stacks of baggage and the chatter of fellow passengers. Along the five-minute trip, you won't see dreary theme-park parking lots but, instead, scenes of the beautiful English countryside and quite a few of your favorite characters from the film series.

Be aware that because riding the Hogwarts Express will take you from one theme park to another, a multipark ticket is necessary to board. The return trip is a different experience, so make sure to take the journey both ways. Scare Factor→ It's not scary.

Woody Woodpecker's Kid Zone

All the attractions for very young children are in the same area of Universal. If you have preschoolers, hang an immediate right on Rodeo Drive after you enter the park and follow the signs to E.T. Adventure. This area of the park definitely needs a revamp, since most of the young visitors probably have no idea who E.T., Fievel, Woody Woodpecker, Barney, or Curious George are. So the area can seem a little dispirited in terms of theming, but the good news is that it is rarely crowded and does have lots of play areas where kids can blow off steam.

✳ Curious George Goes to Town

Perhaps a better name for this attraction would have been "Curious George Goes to the Car Wash." This large, interactive play area is a simulated city that includes climbing areas, ball pits, and lots of chances to get very, very wet. There are fountains in the center and water cannons up above; many parents let their kids wear bathing suits under their clothing so they can strip down and really get into the spirit of the place. If you're up for a maximum splash, a clanging bell over the Fire Department indicates when a big wave of water is under way. The impact is pretty impressive, and this may be the highlight of the park for young kids, but parents of preschoolers and toddlers, beware: The wave hits with enough force to knock small children off their feet.

It's a great way to cool off in summer, so save it for the warmest part of the afternoon. In chilly weather the water is shut off, and Curious George Goes to Town becomes a dry play area. Scare Factor➜ **It's not scary.**

✳ A Day in the Park with Barney

Designed to appeal to Universal's youngest guests, A Day in the Park with Barney is actually an enclosed, parklike setting with colorful, pop-art style flowers and trees. Barney appears several times a day in a song-and-dance show, and there's an interactive indoor play area for toddlers.

"The highlight of my 2-year-old daughter's day was the Barney show," a mother of two from Illinois wrote. "The kids sit so close to him and his friends, and the setting is beautiful. I loved watching my little girl sing along during the 'I Love You' song at the end." Scare Factor➜ **It's not scary.**

✳ E.T. Adventure

The ride begins with a brief preshow featuring Steven Spielberg and E.T. Next you move on to the queue area, which winds through the deep, dark woods—it even smells and sounds like a forest. (As a rule, Universal does a bang-up job of setting the mood in queue areas; E.T. is designed to make you feel small and childlike.)

After handing your "passports" to the attendant, you mount a fleet of bicycles; the lead bike in each group has E.T. in the front basket. You rise up and fly over the forest in a simple but effective simulation of the escape scene in the movie *E.T.* After narrowly

INSIDER'S SECRET

Universal is festively decorated for Christmas, and a special parade runs for the weeks around Mardi Gras. But Halloween Horror Nights, a time-honored tradition at Universal and very popular with Orlando locals, are the best. All the movie bad guys are out in full force, with plenty of special stage shows and "interactive experiences." Teenagers will love this ultimate spook house, but kids under seven definitely won't. If you have kids ages 7 to 11, just make sure to stay close to them. Separate tickets are required for this party and should be purchased in advance. While the Express Pass is rarely necessary during the day, seriously consider buying it for Halloween Horror Nights. The pass gets you into all those genuinely scary haunted houses, which regularly experience two hour (or longer) wait times. Visit ⊕ *www.universalorlando.com* for details.

missing being captured by the police, you manage to return E.T. to his home planet, which is populated by dozens of cuddly aliens.

There's a real possibility that the admittedly dated E.T. Adventure will soon be closing to make way for a new attraction. Check the website before you leave to make sure E.T. will be open while you are visiting. Scare Factor→ **It's only mildly scary.**

☀ Fievel's Playland

Fievel's Playland is filled with Wild West–style props, including a harmonica slide that plays notes as kids go down it, a giant talking cat named Tiger, canteens to squirt, cowboy hats to bounce in, spiderwebs to climb, and a separate ball pit and slide area for toddlers.

The centerpiece of the playground is a 200-foot water ride in which kids and parents are loaded into two-person rafts and swept through a "sewer." The ride is zippier than it looks, will get you soaking wet, and is so addictive that most kids clamor to get back on again immediately. Note that the water ride is closed on cold days.

Fievel's Playland often opens an hour or two after the general park opening. If you ride the big-deal rides and then show up at the playground at the opening time indicated on your map, you'll be able to try the water ride without much of a wait. Scare Factor→ **It's not scary.**

☀ Woody Woodpecker's Nuthouse Coaster

The Nuthouse Coaster is faster than you'd guess, and kids must be 36 inches tall to ride. Watch it make a couple of runs before you line up with your four-year-old. Scare Factor→ **It's a little fast but not really scary.**

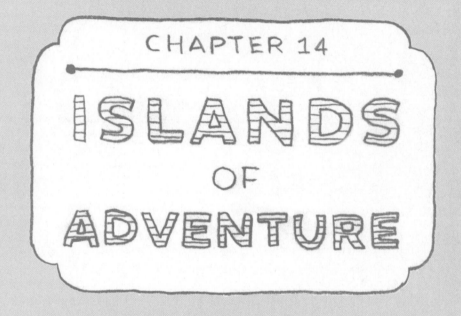

CHAPTER 14

ISLANDS

OF

ADVENTURE

We can sum up Islands of Adventure in two words: Harry Potter. There are plenty of other attractions, of course, many of them witty and wild, but it's the boy with the scar who keeps pulling in visitors. Even though the Wizarding World of Harry Potter has been open since 2010, it's still the most popular section of the park.

As the name implies, Islands of Adventure is themed around a variety of "islands" that are actually interconnected lands encircling a lagoon. Marvel Super Hero Island appeals to coaster warriors, Seuss Landing is for the younger set, Toon Lagoon is a watery playground for the whole family, and the other lands offer a mix of rides, restaurants, and shows. The Wizarding World of Harry Potter has proven so popular that an expansion has opened at Island of Adventure's sister park next door, Universal Studios.

The popularity of Harry Potter has made touring Islands of Adventure a sort of two-tiered experience. Most of the park is spread out nicely and easy to tour, with long waits a rarity, even for the thrill rides. But the Harry Potter section is always packed, even on a Tuesday morning in the off-season. Plan your time accordingly.

Islands of Adventure (IOA) is all about rides: full sensory-immersion 3-D experiences, state-of-the-art coasters, watery descents that'll leave you dripping, and kiddie rides so cleverly designed that even the most cynical adults totally get into the spirit. *For information on tickets and multiday passes, see Chapter 13, and note the financial advantages of buying online.* Check for any price changes by calling ☎ *407/363-8000* or visiting ⊕ *www.universalorlando.com.*

■**TIP➜ Are you a member of AAA? If so, you'll get a 10% price break on food and shopping throughout Islands of Adventure and Universal Studios. This discount can be quite a boon, especially in posh restaurants.**

■**TIP➜ Make sure to download the Universal Orlando Resort App to keep current on showtimes and wait times for attractions.**

Island of Adventure Touring Tips

Getting Around Islands of Adventure

The layout of Islands of Adventure is reminiscent of a big lollipop in which you enter through the stick—the Port of Entry, which has shops, restaurants, and service areas. Port of Entry ends at the lagoon, and around the water are clustered the six islands of the theme park: Marvel Super Hero Island, Toon Lagoon, Jurassic Park, the Wizarding World of Harry Potter, the Lost Continent, and Seuss Landing.

Because of IOA's essentially circular design, it's an easy park to tour. The sidewalks naturally lead you from one attraction to the next, with no crossroads or choices, and bridges connect the islands. The moods of the separate lands are quite distinct. As you walk into the mysterious and mythic Lost Continent, for example, you're greeted by the gentle tinkling of wind chimes, and you enter Jurassic Park through an enormous stone gate flanked by torches. Below your feet you'll see fossil prints in the sidewalk, and if you listen closely, you'll hear the rumbles and calls of dinos in the bushes.

We advise an early-morning lap of the park to ride the big-deal attractions; an afternoon lap to check out the shows, play areas, water rides, and minor attractions; then a final circle in early evening to ride anything you missed—or to revisit favorites. Sounds like a lot of walking, but in this user-friendly theme park touring is a snap.

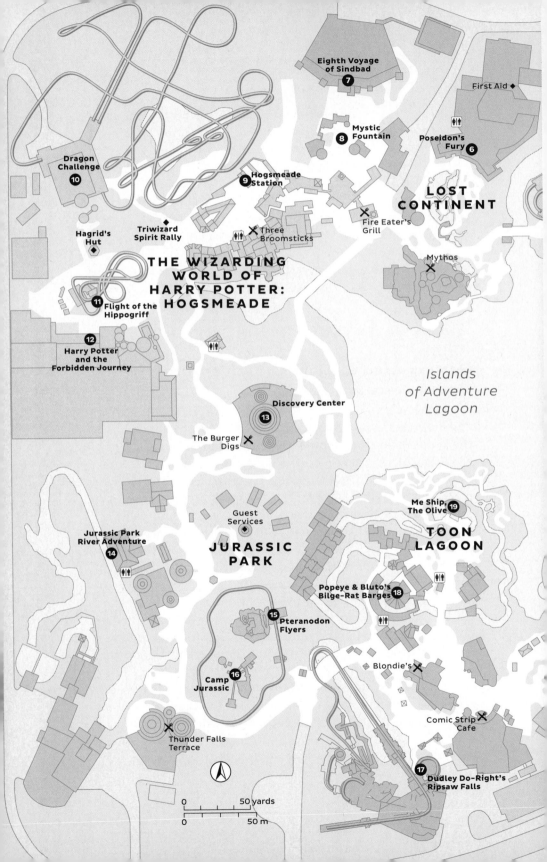

Eighth Voyage of Sindbad 7

Mystic Fountain 8

First Aid ◆

Poseidon's Fury 6

Dragon Challenge 10

Hogsmeade Station 9

LOST CONTINENT

Fire Eater's Grill ✕

Hagrid's Hut ◆

Triwizard Spirit Rally

Three Broomsticks ✕

Mythos ✕

THE WIZARDING WORLD OF HARRY POTTER: HOGSMEADE

Flight of the Hippogriff 11

Harry Potter and the Forbidden Journey 12

Islands of Adventure Lagoon

Discovery Center 13

The Burger Digs ✕

Me Ship, The Olive 19

Guest Services ◆

TOON LAGOON

Jurassic Park River Adventure 14

JURASSIC PARK

Popeye & Bluto's Bilge-Rat Barges 18

Pteranodon Flyers 15

Camp Jurassic 16

Blondie's ✕

Thunder Falls Terrace ✕

Comic Strip Cafe ✕

Dudley Do-Right's Ripsaw Falls 17

0   50 yards

0   50 m

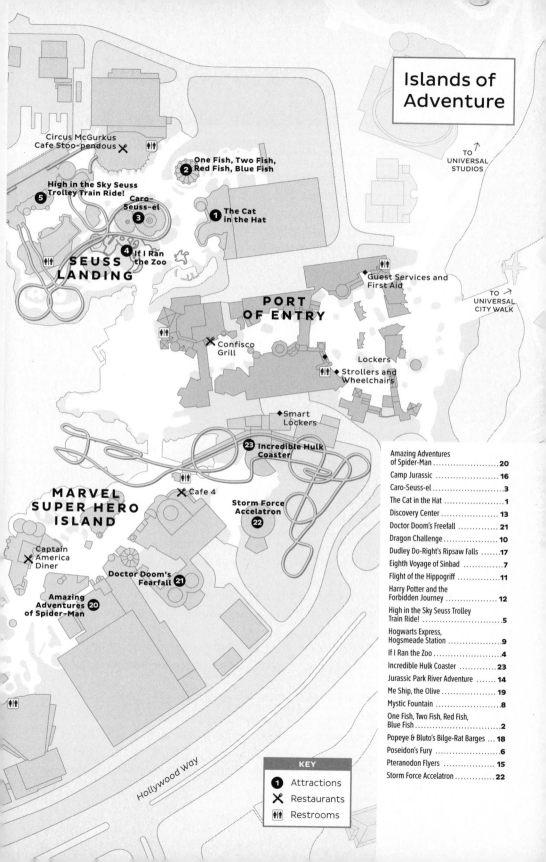

Islands of Adventure

TO
UNIVERSAL
STUDIOS

TO
UNIVERSAL
CITY WALK

Circus McGurkus
Cafe Stoo-pendous ✕ 🚻

One Fish, Two Fish,
❷ Red Fish, Blue Fish

High in the Sky Seuss
Trolley Train Ride!
❺

Caro-
Seuss-el
❸

❶ The Cat
in the Hat

❹ If I Ran
the Zoo

🚻 **SEUSS
LANDING**

Guest Services and
First Aid 🚻

**PORT
OF ENTRY**

🚻

✕ Confisco
Grill

Lockers

🚻 Strollers and
Wheelchairs

◆ Smart
Lockers

❷❸ Incredible Hulk
Coaster

🚻

✕ Cafe 4

**MARVEL
SUPER HERO
ISLAND**

Storm Force
Accelatron
❷❷

Captain
America ✕
Diner

Doctor Doom's
Fearfall ❷❶

Amazing
Adventures ❷⓪
of Spider-Man

🚻

Hollywood Way

KEY

❶ Attractions

✕ Restaurants

🚻 Restrooms

How Scary Is "Scary"? As Dr. Seuss Would Say, "Very!"

Ten of the 12 major attractions at Islands of Adventure have height restrictions—your first clue that this park is loaded with physically wild rides. Measure your kids before you leave home; there's no point in promising your kindergarten-age muggle a ride on Harry Potter and the Forbidden Journey if he's less than 48 inches tall. Here are the specific height restrictions:

- ✦ The Amazing Adventures of Spider-Man — 40 inches
- ✦ Doctor Doom's Fearfall — 52 inches
- ✦ Dragon Challenge — 54 inches
- ✦ Dudley Do-Right's Ripsaw Falls — 44 inches
- ✦ Flight of the Hippogriff — 36 inches
- ✦ Harry Potter and the Forbidden Journey — 48 inches
- ✦ The Incredible Hulk Coaster — 54 inches
- ✦ Jurassic Park River Adventure — 42 inches
- ✦ Popeye & Bluto's Bilge-Rat Barges — 42 inches
- ✦ Pteranodon Flyers — 36 inches

In addition, a couple of the shows are atmospherically scary; Poseidon's Fury and the Eighth Voyage of Sindbad have frightened some preschoolers.

The bottom line? Read the ride descriptions carefully before you board. If the ride is outside (and several IOA attractions are), watch it make a couple of cycles before you decide. And if someone in your family panics while in line, inform the attendant you'll need to do a Baby Swap (or husband swap, as the case may be).

Tips for Your First Hour at Islands of Adventure

Perhaps because most guests stay off-site and must rise, eat, drive, park, and undertake the substantial trek from the parking garage, Islands of Adventure is relatively empty in the morning (at least the islands that don't involve Harry Potter) and grows more crowded in the afternoon.

Arrive 30 minutes before the stated opening time, which is generally 9 am. Get your tickets and maps and take care of any business, such as locker or stroller rental.

> **HELPFUL HINT**
>
> Rides are most likely to be closed for maintenance in winter, especially the water rides. Check ⊕ *www. universalorlando.com* to see if any attractions are scheduled for refurbishment during your visit.

✦ Sometimes Port of Entry is open before the rest of the park. If so, browse the shops or have a quick breakfast at Croissant Moon Bakery.

✦ The tip board will tell you which rides are running. During the on-season, most rides will open immediately; on less crowded days the rides may come online section by section. Either way, Marvel Super Hero Island and Seuss Landing, the two islands adjoining Port of Entry, will be open; generally, the Wizarding World of Harry Potter will be as well.

✦ The Wizarding World of Harry Potter remains the hottest ticket in the park—not just the ride, but the shops as well. If that section is open, go there first. ∎**TIP→ Because guests at Universal Orlando resorts can now visit Diagon Alley for their bonus hour in the morning, Harry Potter and the Forbidden Journey isn't as quite as busy between 9 and 10 in the morning.**

✦ If you don't go to see Harry and your kids are old enough to enjoy intense rides, veer left to Marvel Super Hero Island. Ride the Incredible Hulk Coaster, the Amazing Adventures of Spider-Man, and Doctor Doom's Fearfall, in that order.

✦ If your kids are younger, veer right to Seuss Landing and start with One Fish, Two Fish and the Cat in the Hat.

Afternoon Tips

Families who'll be staying in the park all day need to build in afternoon rest stops to give everyone a chance to regroup. You basically have three options:

- **Restaurants.** Consider making lunch your big meal of the day. A sit-down meal, either at Confisco Grille, Mythos, or CityWalk, is a chance to get off your feet and relax.

- **Shows.** The Eighth Voyage of Sindbad will give you a chance to sit down in a theater for a while. The Jurassic Park Discovery Center, a museum-style attraction, is a quiet, calm, and cool place to catch your breath.

- **Play areas.** Sometimes kids just need to burn off their pent-up energy. If you suspect they need to climb, run, and play for a half hour, head for one of the three play areas.

Meeting the Characters

The times and places for character meetings are well marked on your map.

The superheroes, including Spider-Man, appear in Marvel Super Hero Island; cartoon characters show up in Toon Lagoon; and the Seuss characters can be found, logically, in Seuss Landing.

Sometimes kids are overwhelmed by the characters, especially the Masked Marvels who show up on Marvel Super Hero Island. If your child appears nervous, don't push her forward; let her watch other kids pose for pictures for a while and she may loosen up. Asking for an autograph is a great way to break the ice.

Port of Entry

As the name implies, Port of Entry is where you enter Islands of Adventure. It's a visually charming area, meant to resemble an exotic Middle Eastern seaport, and it's a great place for a group snapshot.

Many of the park services are in Port of Entry: Locker rentals ($8–$10), Guest Services (a.k.a Guest Relations), the Lost and Found, and an ATM are all here. You can rent a stroller ($15, $25 for a double), a wheelchair ($12), or an Electric Convenience Vehicle (ECV; $50).

In addition, there are shops and restaurants. The Universal Studios Islands of Adventure Trading Company is a store that's almost as big as its name, and, because it has merchandise from all five islands, it's a good place for wrap-up shopping on your way

Islands of Adventure Don't-Miss List

FOR KIDS 2 TO 6

✦ Caro-Seuss-el

✦ The Cat in the Hat

✦ Flight of the Hippogriff

✦ If I Ran the Zoo

✦ Me Ship, the Olive

✦ One Fish, Two Fish, Red Fish, Blue Fish

✦ Popeye & Bluto's Bilge-Rat Barges (for older kids)

FOR KIDS 7 TO 11

✦ The Amazing Adventures of Spider-Man

✦ Camp Jurassic

✦ The Cat in the Hat

✦ Dragon Challenge (older kids)

✦ Dudley Do-Right's Ripsaw Falls

✦ Harry Potter and the Forbidden Journey

✦ The Incredible Hulk Coaster (older kids)

✦ Jurassic Park River Adventure

✦ Popeye & Bluto's Bilge-Rat Barges

FOR KIDS 12 AND UP

✦ The Amazing Adventures of Spider-Man

✦ Doctor Doom's Fearfall

✦ Dragon Challenge

✦ Dudley Do-Right's Ripsaw Falls

✦ Harry Potter and the Forbidden Journey

✦ The Incredible Hulk Coaster

✦ Jurassic Park River Adventure

✦ Popeye & Bluto's Bilge-Rat Barges

out of the park. Note that the Trading Company has a good variety of Harry Potter merchandise and is infinitely less crowded than shops within that section of the park. You can even get a wand there, if you're willing to forego the full-throttle Ollivander's Wand Shop experience.

Food choices include the full-service Café La Bamba (with an adjacent bar) and the Croissant Moon Bakery, which offers bagels, pastries, and a variety of coffees—it's a great place for a quick breakfast as you enter the park. Later in the day sandwiches and desserts are added to the menu. The Arctic Express offers funnel cakes and ice cream, and the Cinnabon next door sells the same gooey treats you find in malls and airports. Some IOA restaurants close in the off-season, but Universal does a good job of estimating crowd flow, so there are always enough places open to serve everyone in the park.

Pause for a second as you near the end of Port of Entry. To your left is the tip board, which gives you information on the opening sequence of the rides, approximate wait times, and upcoming showtimes.

Marvel Super Hero Island

This is the island where superheroes fight bad guys, and you test your mettle on three high-thrill attractions. Most people are so busy dashing to the rides that they don't take the time to appreciate how well this section visually duplicates a comic-book world. Signs are intentionally generic as in "Store," "Arcade," or "Café," and the colors chosen give everything a flat, grainy appearance.

☀ The Amazing Adventures of Spider-Man
Spider-Man combines actual movement on a track, motion simulation, and 3-D effects. Unlike most 3-D shows, where you're sitting still and the action comes toward you, in Spider-Man you're moving from scene to scene through a comic-book story. It feels as if everything is really happening, especially the 400-foot simulated drop at the end, yet the actual ride movement is very mild. In other words, young kids or people who freak out on coasters can enjoy it. Spider-Man was revamped, with reanimation and

even higher definition. You can even see the stitching on Spidey's gloves, and the villains are closer and more real than ever.

The concept is that the Sinister Syndicate, made up of comic-book villains, has taken over New York City and stolen the Statue of Liberty. (Wonder why the bad guys never nab Seattle or Omaha?) The plucky young photojournalist Peter Parker, alias Spider-Man, is nowhere to be found, and the city is in a panic. J. Jonah Jameson, the bombastic newspaper editor, is "so desperate for the story that I might have to send a bunch of tourists out in the Scoop-Mobile." That's your cue.

As soon as you're loaded in you'll be stunned by the quality of the recently revamped effects, which make you feel as if Spider-Man is on the hood of your car and that bricks are flying toward your face. The ending of the ride, in which you're "thrown" off the top of a New York skyscraper and caught in Spider-Man's net, is the biggest thrill of all.

One mother of two from California wrote to us: "Spider-Man is a wonderful ride and my husband's favorite. The first time we rode it with our kids (ages 9 and 11), the younger one was terrified by the fact that the bad guys land on the hood of the car and it really feels like they're reaching out for you. But once she got off the ride and walked around a while, she wanted to try it again."

After you've braved the experience once and know that a happy ending is guaranteed, Spider-Man is an attraction that holds up through return trips. Pay attention to detail. For example, when Hobgoblin throws his fiery pumpkins at you, Spider-Man snares the first one in his web, but the second one goes awry and crashes through the wall and into the next scene. **Scare Factor→ Spider-Man has a 40-inch height requirement, which means quite a few preschoolers qualify to ride. The actual ride movement has plenty of spins and bumps, but the infamous "drop" at the end is totally simulated, making it far more fun than scary. The real issue is the villains. The Sinister Syndicate throws everything it has at you, and the characters often appear very abruptly. If the in-your-face bad guys are too much for your kids, tell them to shut their eyes.**

■TIP→ As you exit Spider-Man, you'll notice how Universal Orlando cleverly encourages souvenir shopping. While you're still excited about the ride, you exit through a shop full of Spider-

Quick Guide to Islands of

Attraction	Location	Height Requirement
Amazing Adventures of Spider-Man	Super Hero Island	40 inches
Camp Jurassic	Jurassic Park	None
Caro-Seuss-el	Seuss Landing	None
The Cat in the Hat	Seuss Landing	None
Discovery Center	Jurassic Park	None
Dr. Doom's Fearfall	Super Hero Island	52 inches
Dragon Challenge	Harry Potter	54 inches
Dudley Do-Right's Ripsaw Falls	Toon Lagoon	44 inches
The Eighth Voyage of Sindbad	Lost Continent	None
Flight of the Hippogriff	Harry Potter	36 inches
Harry Potter and the Forbidden Journey	Harry Potter	48 inches
High in the Sky Seuss Trolley Train Ride!	Seuss Landing	34 inches
The Hogwarts Express	Harry Potter	None
If I Ran the Zoo	Seuss Landing	None
Incredible Hulk Coaster	Super Hero Island	54 inches
Me Ship, the Olive	Toon Lagoon	None
One Fish, Two Fish, Red Fish, Blue Fish	Seuss Landing	None
Popeye & Bluto's Bilge-Rat Barges	Toon Lagoon	42 inches
Poseidon's Fury	Lost Continent	None
Pteranodon Flyers	Jurassic Park	36 inches
River Adventure	Jurassic Park	42 inches
Storm Force Accelatron	Super Hero Island	None

Scare Factor
0 = Unlikely to scare any child of any age.
! = Has dark or loud elements; might rattle some toddlers.
!! = A couple of gotcha! moments; should be fine for school-age kids.
!!! = You need to be pretty big and pretty brave to handle this ride.

Adventure Attractions

Speed of Line	Duration of Ride/Show	Scare Factor	Age Range
Moderate	15 min.	!!	7 and up
n/a	n/a	0	All
Slow	3 min.	0	All
Moderate	6 min.	0	All
n/a	n/a	0	All
Slow	2 min.	!!	7 and up
Moderate	7 min.	!!!	7 and up
Moderate	8 min.	!!	7 and up
n/a	25 min.	!!	8 and up
Slow	4 min.	!	All
Slow	25 min.	!!!	7 and up
Slow	8 min.	0	All
Slow	7 min.	0	All
n/a	n/a	0	All
Moderate	4 min.	!!!	8 and up
n/a	n/a	0	All
Slow	4 min.	0	All
Moderate	12 min.	!	4 and up
n/a	20 min.	!!	7 and up
Slow	80 sec.	!	4 and up
Slow	5 min.	!!	7 and up
Slow	3 min.	!!	All

Man merchandise. Remember this rule: No souvenir shopping until the afternoon, when you've tried out lots of rides and know what you really want.

☀ Doctor Doom's Fearfall

Dr. Victor von Doom is trying to defeat the Fantastic Four by sucking all the fear out of innocent citizens like you and using this collective fear to take over the world. (Logic isn't the strong point of these rides.) You're strapped into outdoor seats and shot 180 feet into the air. There's a bit of a yo-yo effect—you're raised and lowered several times—but the first five seconds of the ride are by far the scariest. Most riders report that once you're launched, you're fine. Scare Factor➔ **The height requirement is 52 inches for Doctor Doom's Fearfall, and whether your child should ride boils down to one question: How does she feel about heights? Most riders, including kids, think this ride is over too quickly to get truly scary. As they say, "The waiting is the hardest part."**

☀ The Incredible Hulk Coaster

This isn't your mother's roller coaster, on which you slowly crank up a hill getting ready for your first plunge. The Incredible Hulk Coaster is big, green, and mean—just like David Banner after he played around once too often with those gamma rays.

Those lockers at the Hulk entrance are there for a reason, and they're free to use. Store everything you can, because seven big flips can send car keys and sunglasses sailing.

The ride opens with a "cannon" shot from a 150-foot tube, zooming from 0 to 40 mph during the first two seconds of motion, then immediately flipping over to give riders the sensation of going weightless. You'll make seven different inversions during the course of your ride and twice disappear into a subterranean trench. Although the ride is wild, it's smooth, with very few jerky movements, and many coaster warriors swear that despite its intimidating appearance, Hulk is the most user-friendly coaster in the park.

There's a separate line for those who want to sit in the front row, which has the best views but the longest wait. The movement is slightly wilder in the back of the car. Note the word "slightly." Hulk is plenty intense no matter where you ride. Scare Factor➔ **The 54-inch height requirement eliminates many young** kids, and Hulk is a pretty heart-thumping experience—probably too intense for any child under 10. Watch it make a few laps before you decide to ride.

☀ Storm Force Accelatron

This simple spinning ride—the cups spin individually and the discs they're mounted on also move—is a cranked-up version of the Mad Tea Party at Disney World. It's a good way to entertain younger siblings while older kids tackle the nearby Hulk. Scare Factor→ **Storm Force Accelatron isn't scary, but the double spinning action makes some riders queasy.**

> **HELPFUL HINT**
>
> Long lines? Even without an Express Pass you can still cut your wait by using the single-rider line. If you've gone through an attraction like Spider-Man once as a family (and older kids want to ride again), direct them toward the fast-moving single-rider line. On a tight touring schedule? Spider-Man and Hulk are must-sees for thrill seekers, but skip Storm Force and Doctor Doom.

Toon Lagoon

Like Marvel Super Hero Island, Toon Lagoon is also devoted to comic-strip characters, but these are the stars of the Sunday funnies—such as Beetle Bailey, Betty Boop, Dagwood, and the kids of *Family Circus*. Young kids have no idea who any of these characters are, but the true focus of the island isn't the toon, it's the lagoon; the attractions here are designed to splash you silly.

Toon Lagoon is full of great photo ops. You can pose beneath the giant word bubbles, so that it appears you're saying, "It must be Sunday—we're in color!" or thinking, "I have the feeling people can read my thoughts!" The fountain on Comic Strip Lane is the hangout for every cartoon dog you can think of, and another fun place for a group snapshot.

☀ Dudley Do-Right's Ripsaw Falls

This log-flume ride, in which you're helping Dudley and Horse save the perpetually pitiful Nell from Snidely Whiplash, culminates in a breathtaking 75-foot drop. The ride facade is so enormous that it serves as a park icon, and hardly anyone can walk by without stopping to gawk. The actual fall is even more dramatic than it looks;

there's an explosion of light when the log enters the TNT shack at the bottom of the flume, followed by a second descent, in which you drop an additional 15 feet below the water level.

Needless to say, a descent of this magnitude isn't accomplished without a lot of splash. The water not only flies back in your face, but also sloshes into the log, puddling around your hips and feet. You'll enjoy the ride a lot more when you're ready to get wet—in other words, in the hottest part of the afternoon. Scare Factor→ **Kids ages seven and up name Dudley Do-Right as one of their favorite rides. The last drop is a definite squealer, so anyone with a fear of heights should think twice before getting in line. The height requirement is 44 inches.**

☀ Me Ship, the Olive

This is a compact play area designed like a ship, with slides, climbing webs, and buttons that make tooting and beeping noises. Swee' Pea's Playpen is a separate play area for toddlers.

By far the most enjoyable feature of Me Ship, the Olive, is the water guns that allow you to take aim at the occupants of Popeye & Bluto's Bilge-Rat Barges below. If you have a child too young to ride Popeye, take him aboard the Olive while you wait for the rest of the family to ride; he can seek revenge on his siblings as they pass. But watch out—the squirt guns can squirt back! Scare Factor→ **It's not scary.**

☀ Popeye & Bluto's Bilge-Rat Barges

If Dudley Do-Right is all about splashing, Popeye is about getting drenched straight through to your underwear. Parties of eight are loaded into circular rafts and sent on a wild and winding water journey. If through some miracle you manage to avoid the waves, the boat wash at the end of the ride spares no one. To add insult to injury, you're squirted with water guns by the kids aboard the nearby play area, Me Ship, the Olive.

For this reason, riding Popeye requires a bit of planning. Families in the know wear lightweight soccer-style shorts, don ponchos or plastic bags, or perhaps even bring a change of clothes. (If you were planning on buying a souvenir T-shirt anyway, hold off until after you ride, when fresh, dry clothes are bound to feel great.) Leave cameras and valuables inside the nearby lockers, and stow everything else that you can in the central pouch, including shoes and socks.

> ### INSIDER'S SECRET
>
> The three major water rides—Dudley Do-Right and Popeye in Toon Lagoon and the River Adventure in Jurassic Park—are fairly close together. Ride them all in a row, and you'll only have to dry off once. And consider wearing those drip-dry soccer-style shorts instead of denim. Otherwise you're facing an entire day of "wet butt."

Although there are some sizable dips and drops along the way, the fact that the whole family rides together in a circular raft somewhat dilutes the intensity, making this ride a good choice for kids who are not quite up to Dudley Do-Right's megadrop but still want to try a water ride. And because the rafts hold a fair number of people and load quickly, Popeye never seems to have daunting lines. All in all, it's a good choice for the afternoon. **Scare Factor→ Popeye & Bluto's Bilge-Rat Barges is one of the best big-deal rides for young kids, and parents with kids as young as age five report that they loved it. The height requirement is 42 inches. "Our 6-year-old daughter freaked out when she first saw Dudley Do-Right," wrote one father, "and that big drop does look pretty intimidating, even to an adult. But after she'd gone on the Popeye boat ride—three times—she was totally over her fear and willing to go on Dudley Do-Right."**

Jurassic Park

As you walk through the high stone entryway with its torches, note the distant rumbling of unseen beasts and look down at the fossilized leaves and footprints in the sidewalk before you. The Canadian pines around Dudley Do-Right's Ripsaw Falls have given way to lush tropical vegetation, and the merry beat of Toon Lagoon slows to an ominous jungle rhythm. Is there any doubt you've entered Jurassic Park?

☀ Camp Jurassic

Of the three play areas in Islands of Adventure, this is the best one for kids ages 6 to 10. The setting is a group of post-eruption volcanoes, with caves for hiding, and a multilevel, fairly rough terrain perfect for jumping, climbing, and exploring. There are slides, plenty of netting, and some take-no-prisoners water cannons. Because the Camp Jurassic play area is bigger and more spread out than Me Ship, the Olive in Toon Lagoon and If I Ran the Zoo in Seuss Landing, it's easy for kids to get lost. Unless you're sure they can find their way back to one of the benches where Mom and Dad sit waiting, you may need to go with them. The loud dino roars may scare some preschoolers. Scare Factor→ **It's not scary.**

☀ Discovery Center

The Discovery Center is like a small, very hip museum. Little kids can make dinosaur sounds while the older ones X-ray eggs and guess which species is inside. The Dino DNA sequencing profile lets you superimpose your face onto a dinosaur, or you can test your scientific knowledge against two other contestants in a game show called You Bet Jurassic.

The biggest kick is when a raptor hatches from an egg, a wonderful little treat in which an authentic-looking animatronics baby pecks his way through the shell. The kids in the crowd get to name it. Being in the Discovery Center for a birth is a bit of a hit-or-miss proposition, but a honking noise alerts you that one of the eggs is getting ready to crack.

The center is cool and relatively uncrowded, making it a good place to drop by in the afternoon, when everyone's energy is flagging. Scare Factor→ **It's not scary.**

☀ Jurassic Park River Adventure

The River Adventure starts out with a mild cruise through the habitats of gentle vegetarian dinosaurs. Hmm, do you think we'll stay on course? If you don't know the answer to that, you have to go back to Theme Park 101.

Sure enough, a playful dino bangs your boat, sending you drifting into a restricted zone, and once you're inside the dangerous containment area, your boat is pulled up a long ramp past vicious little raptors that leap around, spitting at you. When the

T-Rex at the top decides you'll make a good snack, you escape via an 85-foot plunge—and that's one long, fast, steep descent. **Scare Factor→ Eighty-five feet may sound like a T-Rex-size drop, especially in contrast to the 75-foot drop next door at Dudley, but because you're loaded into much larger boats, the River Adventure fall doesn't feel that intense. Most families report that they found this plunge less frightening than the one at Dudley Do-Right. There's some atmospheric scariness, however, in the form of some very real-looking dinos. It's key to let nervous youngsters know what to expect in advance—that is, you'll get pushed in with the raptors. If it's any consolation, this part of the ride is very short—less than two minutes from the beginning of the climb to the final plunge. Our surveys indicate that most kids seven and up love the ride. Your child must be 42 inches tall to ride.**

INSIDER'S SECRET

Pteranodon Flyers generally opens around 10 am. The tip board will give you exact times. If your kids are determined to ride, be at the entrance to Camp Jurassic as close to opening time as possible. Once Camp Jurassic is open, the line at Pteranodon Flyers can jump to a 20-minute wait within seconds. This attraction is not included in the Express Pass.

☀ Pteranodon Flyers

This aerial ride, in which children dangle beneath the wide wings of a gentle flying dinosaur, is the first thing you see when you enter Jurassic Park—and so most kids insist on making a bee-line there. It is indeed a pleasant 80-second flight around lushly landscaped Camp Jurassic, offering you great views of Islands of Adventure. The catch is that only three birds, each holding two riders, are on the track at a time. That adds up to lines that stretch all the way back to the Cretaceous period, even on days when the park isn't crowded. On busy days you can wait more than an hour, and there's no Express Pass.

In an effort to cut down on the line, Islands of Adventure has limited the ride to kids 36 to 56 inches tall, allowing one adult to ride with each child. In fact, the entrance signs almost try to talk you out of riding, telling you that there are height requirements on both sides of the ruler and the ride lasts only 80 seconds. People flock to it anyway. Try to talk the kids out of riding unless you're there on a quiet day when the wait is less than 20 minutes. Scare Factor→ **Pteranodon Flyers is fine for anyone who doesn't have a fear of heights, although there's a bit more swing to the pteranodons than you'd guess.**

> **HELPFUL HINT**
>
> Feeling queasy from too many coasters? A first-aid station where you can sit and recover is among the shops of Sindbad Village.

The Lost Continent

The Lost Continent is probably the most thematically complex island in the park, with two separate sections. The Arabic section is home to the Eighth Voyage of Sindbad and a jumble of tented, Middle Eastern shops in the marketplace known as Sindbad Village. There are fortune-tellers, and you can get your hair wrapped, your face painted, or your arm temporarily tattooed.

The second section of the Lost Continent is based on Atlantis. Here you can find the amazing-looking theater where Poseidon's Fury plays, and IOA's most elegant restaurant, Mythos.

☀ The Eighth Voyage of Sindbad

This stunt show usually plays four to six times daily in the early afternoon and evening. (Showtimes are listed on your map.) The 25-minute show has everything you'd expect—fights, falls, drops, daring escapes, and comedy in the form of an inept sidekick whose pratfalls are a lot more dangerous than they look. The theater is large, so you shouldn't have any trouble being seated as long as you show up 15 minutes before showtime. Sindbad is a good choice for afternoon, when you'll welcome the chance to sit down and rest for a while. Scare Factor→ **Sindbad is a loud performance with lots of pyrotechnics, including strobe lights and fog effects. In fact, there's so much fire on stage that those in the first three rows of the audience will feel the heat on their skin. If your kids are easily frightened and sensitive to loud noises, sit farther back.**

☀ The Mystic Fountain

As you enter the theater where Sindbad plays, pause for a minute at the fountain in the courtyard. At various times throughout the day—including the periods just before and after a show—the mysterious spirit trapped within the Fountain of Knowledge will talk to you. The result is pretty funny, as the spirit loves riddles, jokes, and questions and will gently tease any kids willing to step forward and enter the game. Encourage the kids to ask a question and be prepared for lots of punk attitude, as well as an occasional blast of water. Scare Factor→ **It's not scary.**

> ### HELPFUL HINT
>
> Need a little adult time? A glass of wine? A civilized menu? Decadent chocolate desserts? Just across from Poseidon's Fury is Mythos, a great place for a leisurely meal.

☀ Poseidon's Fury

This 20-minute walk-through show takes place in one of the most impressive buildings in the whole theme park, a crumbling castle from the lost underwater city ruled by the water god Poseidon. The story line is established in the long, dark (and somewhat scary-for-kids) queue area, where we learn that we're on an archaeological dig at the ancient temple of Poseidon. But there's trouble—the power keeps flickering on and off, a professor is missing, and the sleep of an evil priest has been disturbed. He wants to find a powerful trident, and it's up to you, as the new archaeological team, to find the trident and restore it to its rightful owner, Poseidon.

You stand during the whole presentation of Poseidon's Fury, so young kids in the back won't see much (this may be a blessing—see the scare factor). If you want a good view of the action, be sure to be among the first in your tour group to exit every room so that you can be in the front row in the next room.

You move from room to room, and there are some great special effects along the way. At one point you walk through a swirling tunnel of water. The final scene is a battle between fire and water, with plenty of splashing and pyrotechnics. Scare Factor→ **Poseidon's Fury is a walk-through show, not a ride, but the special effects are intense and the noise level is very high in places. Once you enter the castle, you're literally a captive audience;**

there are a couple of exit points along the way if children become frightened, but for most of the show you're in a series of
darkened rooms. If your children are nervous, stand near the
back, especially in the final room where the battle reaches its
peak; viewers in the front will feel the fire-and-water effects
more intensely than those in the rear.

The Wizarding World of Harry Potter: Hogsmeade

When the Wizarding World of Harry Potter debuted in 2010, it
was one of the most hotly anticipated theme-park attractions
ever. It's actually home to three rides. The Dragon Challenge is a
spiffed-up revamp of the megacoaster Dueling Dragons, while
the Flight of the Hippogriff is a new and improved version of the
Flying Unicorn. The big news is the centerpiece attraction, Harry
Potter and the Forbidden Journey.

Hogsmeade Village, the dining and shopping section of the
Wizarding World, offers great photo ops and fun experiences—
such as the chance to mail a postcard home from the official
Hogsmeade Post Office and some mystical wand-shopping at
Ollivanders. The shops offer replicas of almost everything mentioned in the books, including some rather alarmingly named can-
dies at Honeydukes. Street entertainment includes the Frog Choir,
a group of Hogwarts students accompanied by their large, croak-
ing, and quite comical frogs, and the Triwizard Spirit Rally, a pro-
cessional designed to rev up the already-revved-up crowd.

Wand-shopping at Ollivanders is one of the most popular experiences in the Wizarding World, so much so that you almost always find long lines of people waiting to get into the shop. The
ceremony in which your wand "chooses" you is a large part of the
appeal for most kids, but if you just want a wand without the fuss,
there's a separate, rarely crowded wand kiosk near the entrance
to the Forbidden Journey, and you can also buy wands at the Islands of Adventure Trading Company at Port of Entry.

Guests are so enamored of the wand, jelly-bean, and robe
shopping that Hogsmeade Village can become extremely
crowded. Don't imagine you can browse the shops whenever

you're ready to drop some cash. There are lines to get into the shops and sometimes even lines to get out, especially at Olli-vanders, where the wand-choosing ceremony takes a little time. Young wizards don't like to be rushed.

The restaurant Three Broomsticks, which is a terrific setting in its own right, could probably serve anything and still be packed. The menu includes tasty barbecue, shepherd's pie, and fish-and-chips as well as the über-popular butterbeer and pumpkin juice. The nonalcoholic butterbeer is extremely sweet, almost like melted butterscotch, and geared toward kids' palates. The pumpkin juice tastes a lot like cider and is quite good. Both are also available at kiosks outside the restaurant.

Hogsmeade Village was designed to emulate the narrow winding streets, nooks, and alleys of the Harry Potter film series, and the fact that they've done a good job also means that traffic bottlenecks are the norm all day long. It's best to embrace the fact that you'll be moving slowly and use the time to savor all the wonderful details of this magical and painstakingly re-created world.

☀ Dragon Challenge

This double roller coaster is one of the wildest rides in the park, running at speeds of up to 60 mph. Two suspension-style coasters (that is, they hang beneath the track for maximum side-to-side swinging action) operate at once, coming within inches of each other at certain points. For the ultimate thrill seekers, riders in the outside seats are most aware of how close these close calls really are and riders in the front seats get the best view of the impending danger. Scare Factor→ **Dragon Challenge is a very intense coaster with a height requirement of 54 inches. Coaster warriors love it, but it's too much for most kids under 10. The swinging action of the cars makes it a rougher ride than the Hulk, for example, and it's not a good choice for anyone prone to motion sickness. Watch it make a few runs before you decide.**

☀ The Flight of the Hippogriff

This is a fun little coaster for the younger set and zippier than you'd guess, with some sharp dips and turns. Young Harry Potter fans who aren't up to the Dragon Challenge will enjoy the ride, which is a good "first coaster" experience. The really cool part is that you zoom beside a perfect replica of Hagrid's Hut. Scare Factor→ **The**

Flight of the Hippogriff is fast enough to elicit a few squeals, but most kids love it. Your child must be 36 inches to ride.

☀ Harry Potter and the Forbidden Journey

This attraction, which lies deep within Hogwarts Castle, is the heart and soul of the Wizarding World. The queue is wonderful—which is good news, considering you might be in it for quite a while. You'll meet the four founders of Hogwarts, in the form of framed portraits that come to life and converse with each other. Dumbledore greets you in his office, you pass the famed Sorting Hat, and you ultimately wind up in the Defense Against the Dark Arts classroom. Harry, Ron, and Hermione—played by the movie actors, naturally—persuade you that going off with them to a Quidditch match is far more fun than staying behind for a boring history lecture. One wave of Hermione's wand, and your bench becomes capable of flight.

Your first clue to the intensity of the attraction is that your enchanted school bench comes equipped with harness restraints. Indeed, Harry Potter and the Forbidden Journey is a big-deal ride in both a physical sense, with lots of pitching and jerking action, and a psychological sense, as various villains from the books show up and try to divert your flight. The spider section is especially scary for kids, and let's just say that the Whomping Willow ain't kidding around. When Harry shows up to rescue you and you do finally make it back to Hogwarts, you experience the real feeling of flight. The story line is a bit confusing—it pretty much throws random experiences from the series at you with no real regard for a logical sequence—but it all ends on a happy note, with the students of Hogwarts cheering your successful return.

This is a 360-degree wraparound experience, combining live action, robotic technology, and filmmaking tricks that make you feel as if you're actually flying from scene to scene. Make no mistake—Harry Potter and the Forbidden Journey is Island of Adventure's signature ride, representing its best technology to date. The entire experience, including the interactive queue, takes close to an hour. Note that this ride has a minimum height requirement (48 inches) *and* maximum height and weight limits (6 feet, 3 inches; 250 pounds). Scare Factor→ **The 48-inch height requirement on Harry Potter and the Forbidden Journey means that many kids ages five to eight will be able to ride. That said, there are reasons** this journey is forbidden. Older kids love it, and young fans of the book will probably be determined to ride. Just prepare everyone: The bench sometimes feels as if it's flipping over backward, and much of the journey is dark and scary, with dragons and spiders coming from all angles. Note, too, that the attraction has an exit for those who want to go through the queue and see the characters but aren't up to taking on the actual ride.

☀ Hogwarts Express: Hogsmeade Station

The Hogwarts Express train has moved from being a mere prop to Island of Adventure's newest ride. A railway between Universal Studios and Islands of Adventure links The Wizarding World of Harry Potter—Hogsmeade to a new section of Universal Studios, The Wizarding World of Harry Potter—Diagon Alley, which highlights the King's Cross and London sections of the books. The train ride itself is a kick, with screens showing simulated scenes of your journey, and Diagon Alley has its own shops, restaurants, and a new (milder) themed ride. Note that since you're moving from Islands of Adventure to Universal Studios during the ride, you will need a two-park ticket. (Also, it's a different experience in each direction, so you may want to ride this train back, too.) Scare Factor→ **It's not scary.**

Seuss Landing

You'll find nothing but pastel colors and curved lines—even the trees are bent!—on this dreamlike island, where everything looks like it popped out of a Dr. Seuss book. Almost everyone stops in their tracks at the sight of the amazing Caro-Seuss-el and the bright flying beasties of One Fish, Two Fish. But take your time strolling through—some of the best visual treats aren't so obvious.

☀ Caro-Seuss-el

The 54 mounts of this ultimate merry-go-round are all lifted directly from the stories of Dr. Seuss. While the up-and-down and round-and-round motion is familiar to any kid who has ever been on a carousel, the real kick is that you can make the beasties blink, flick their tails, and turn their heads. Snapping the kids aboard the colorful Caro-Seuss-el is one of the best photo ops in the whole park. Scare Factor→ **It's not scary.**

☀ The Cat in the Hat

This is a kiddie ride that's not just for the kiddies. A surprising number of kids age 7 to 15 ranked Cat in the Hat as one of their favorites.

You board adorable couch-style cars to ride through 18 scenes taken straight from the well-loved book. The basic plot: Mom leaves, and the Cat in the Hat shows up with those well-known literary rowdies, Thing 1 and Thing 2. All sorts of mayhem results, sometimes enough to send your couch spinning wildly, and through it all the poor goldfish frantically tries to maintain order. The Cat in the Hat is like Spider-Man for the younger set. A lot goes on in a short time frame, and if you ride a second time you'll notice even more clever details. The effects are so funny that all riders, no matter what their age, exit with a grin on their face. Scare Factor→ **Expect some bumping and a few fast, tight spins of the car. Cat in the Hat is designed to appeal to any age, however, and most kids love it.**

> **HELPFUL HINT**
>
> Preschoolers will enjoy the Cat in the Hat ride, as well as the other Seuss Landing attractions, much more if they're familiar with the Dr. Seuss books. Read them on the trip to Orlando.

☀ High in the Sky Seuss Trolley Train Ride!

Once purely decorative, the little cars that circle Seuss Landing were eventually put into motion and are now part of a slow, gentle trolley ride overlooking the attractions and at one point going through the Circus McGurkus Café Stoopendous. The 34-inch height restriction is more due to the construction of the cars than the intensity of the ride; shorter kids might be tempted to stand up just to be able to see out. It's a cute way to get an aerial view of Seuss Landing, but due to the fact there are relatively few cars and they move slowly, the Seuss Trolley can draw surprisingly long lines for such a simple ride. Scare Factor→ **It's not scary.**

☀ If I Ran the Zoo

IOA's third interactive play area was designed with preschoolers in mind, although older kids enjoy it, too. You can jump, climb, and squirt, as well as play tic-tac-toe with a Gak. Trap your friends in a cage of water or wait for the scraggly foot Mulligatawny to sneeze—there's a silly surprise around every corner. A small water area gives younger kids a chance to cool off and splash around on a hot day.

The emphasis on the big-deal rides makes many families automatically assume that Islands of Adventure is only for older kids. But the three play areas and the attention to detail in all of Seuss Landing show that Islands of Adventure has plenty to offer younger siblings as well. Scare Factor→ **It's not scary.**

☀ Oh The Stories You'll Hear

This is a simple little show aimed toward the preschool set that runs several times a day beside One Fish, Two Fish. It's primarily a meet-and-greet for the Dr. Seuss characters. Scare Factor→ **It's not scary.**

☀ One Fish, Two Fish, Red Fish, Blue Fish

One Fish, Two Fish is a circular thrill ride designed for young kids. Each fish has a joystick that controls the height of his flight, and throughout the ride you're given instructions such as "Red Fish fly high." If you opt to follow the instructions, that is, go "with the book," you stay dry. But if you disobey and go "against the book," one of the "bad fish" will spit on you. The idea is that this teaches kids to follow directions—I suspect it really shows them how much fun it can be to rebel—but either way it's a terrific ride, and in the finale everyone aboard gets a spritz.

One Fish, Two Fish can draw long lines in the afternoon. Come in the morning if you can. Scare Factor→ **One Fish, Two Fish is fine for any age. The joystick lets you keep it low for kids who dislike heights. Everyone flies high at the end of the ride for a few seconds, but by that time nervous kids have been aboard long enough to get used to the idea. The two-fish cars are big enough to let family members ride together.**

CityWalk

CityWalk is the dining, shopping, and entertainment complex that links Universal Studios with Islands of Adventure. A lively destination in its own right, CityWalk also provides more dining options than what's in the parks. If you'd like a break from touring, exit the park and head for lunch at CityWalk.

Restaurants include the Bubba Gump Shrimp Co., the Hard Rock Cafe, Jimmy Buffet's Margaritaville, the NASCAR Sports Grille, NBA City, Pastamore, and Emeril's. The first six are geared toward families, while the more elegant Emeril's is a great choice for a parents' night out.

Speaking of parents'-night-out options, CityWalk has shows and concerts every night, including a Blue Man Group production and live shows at the Hard Rock Cafe. There is also a wide selection of bars, clubs, and dance venues, including Antojitos, Bob Marley's, Pat O'Brian's, Red Coconut Lounge, and Rising Star—truly a little something for everyone. And just wandering around sampling all the clubs can make for a fun adult evening.

Index

My Magic Kingdom Itinerary

_____

_____

_____

_____

_____

_____

_____

_____

_____

_____

_____

_____

_____

_____

_____

_____

_____

_____

_____

_____

_____

My Epcot Itinerary

_____

_____

_____

_____

_____

_____

_____

_____

_____

_____

_____

_____

_____

_____

_____

_____

_____

_____

_____

_____

_____

My Hollywood Studios Itinerary

_____

_____

_____

_____

_____

_____

_____

_____

_____

_____

_____

_____

_____

_____

_____

_____

_____

_____

_____

_____

_____

_____

My Animal Kingdom Itinerary

_____

_____

_____

_____

_____

_____

_____

_____

_____

_____

_____

_____

_____

_____

_____

_____

_____

_____

_____

My Universal Studios Itinerary

My Islands of Adventure Itinerary

_____

_____

_____

_____

_____

_____

_____

_____

_____

_____

_____

_____

_____

_____

_____

_____

_____

_____

_____

_____

_____

Notes

Notes

Notes

Notes

Notes

Notes

Write to Us

We love to hear from families about their trips to Walt Disney World, Universal Orlando, and SeaWorld. Stories and feedback from families like yours help shape this book. If you'd like to share your travel experiences with us, please take a few minutes to respond to any or all of the questions below. We might quote your responses in the next edition. You can either fill out this survey online at www.fodors.com/disneysurvey, email us at kwwiley@fodors.com or write to me at Fodor's, 1745 Broadway, New York, NY 10019. Thanks for your time!

— Kim and Leigh

1. When did you last visit Walt Disney World and/or Universal Orlando? How long did you stay?

   _____

   _____

2. What are the ages of your children?

   _____

   _____

3. Did your family travel alone or with friends and extended family? How many people were in your party?

   _____

   _____

4. Where did you stay? Were you pleased with the hotel? Did you feel it offered a fair level of services and amenities for the price?

   _____

   _____

5. Which park did your family most enjoy? (For questions 6–12, if there's a split of opinion among family members, please put the age of the respondent beside the choice.)

_____

_____

6. What was your family's favorite attraction in the Magic Kingdom?

_____

_____

7. What was your family's favorite attraction at Epcot?

_____

_____

8. What was your family's favorite attraction at Disney's Hollywood Studios?

_____

_____

9. What was your family's favorite attraction at the Animal Kingdom?

_____

_____

10. Did you visit Universal Orlando? If so, what was your family's favorite attraction at Universal Studios? At Islands of Adventure?

_____

_____

_____

11. Did you visit SeaWorld or Discovery Cove? If so, what was your family's favorite attraction?

_____

_____

12. Were there any attractions that proved to be too frightening or too intense for your child? If so, please describe the situation.

_____

_____

13. Did you take part in any character meals? If so, did you enjoy it?

_____

_____

_____

14. Did you purchase a dining plan? If so, did you think it offered good value?

_____

_____

15. Besides character meals, did you have any other memorable dining experiences?

_____

_____

_____

16. Did you visit either of the Walt Disney World water parks? If so, which one and how did you like it?

_____

_____

17. Did you visit Downtown Disney or CityWalk? If so, which shops, restaurants, and attractions were your favorites?

_____

_____

18. Do you have a "never again" story—something about traveling around Walt Disney World or Universal Orlando that you learned the hard way?

_____

_____

_____

_____

19. Do you have a "best of all" story or experience that stands out as the highlight of your trip?

_____

_____

_____

_____

20. What advice would you give to other families traveling to Walt Disney World or Universal Orlando?

_____

_____

_____

_____